D1531319

Writing
Southern
Politics

★★★★★★★★★★★★★★★★★★★★★★★

Writing Southern Politics

*Contemporary Interpretations
and Future Directions*

Edited by

Robert P. Steed
Laurence W. Moreland

★★★★★★★★★★★★★★★★★★★★★★★

THE UNIVERSITY PRESS OF KENTUCKY

Publication of this volume was made possible in part by
a grant from the National Endowment for the Humanities.

Copyright © 2006 by The University Press of Kentucky

Scholarly publisher for the Commonwealth,
serving Bellarmine University, Berea College, Centre
College of Kentucky, Eastern Kentucky University,
The Filson Historical Society, Georgetown College,
Kentucky Historical Society, Kentucky State University,
Morehead State University, Murray State University,
Northern Kentucky University, Transylvania University,
University of Kentucky, University of Louisville,
and Western Kentucky University.
All rights reserved.

Editorial and Sales Offices: The University Press of Kentucky
663 South Limestone Street, Lexington, Kentucky 40508-4008
www.kentuckypress.com

10 09 08 07 06   5 4 3 2 1

Library of Congress Cataloging-in-Publication Data

Writing Southern politics : essays on the post-World War II literature of Southern
politics / edited by Robert P. Steed and Laurence W. Moreland.
    p. cm.
  Includes bibliographical references and index.
  ISBN-13: 978-0-8131-2382-0 (alk. paper)
  ISBN-10: 0-8131-2382-8 (alk. paper)
  1. Political science—Southern States—History. 2. Southern States—Politics and
government—1951-   I. Steed, Robert P. II. Moreland, Laurence W.
  JA84.U5W74 2006
  324.0975'09045—dc22   2005034686

This book is printed on acid-free recycled paper meeting
the requirements of the American National Standard
for Permanence in Paper for Printed Library Materials.

Manufactured in the United States of America.

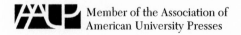

Member of the Association of
American University Presses

Contents

Foreword
    Jack Bass   vii

Acknowledgments   xiii

Introduction. The Literature of Southern Politics
    Robert P. Steed and Laurence W. Moreland   1

1. Southern Political Party Development since World War II
    Charles Prysby   11

2. Who Wants to Party? Activists and Changing Southern Politics
    John J. McGlennon   41

3. Unfinished Business: Writing the Civil Rights Movement
    Richard K. Scher   65

4. Race and Southern Politics: The Special Case of Congressional Districting
    Richard L. Engstrom   91

5. Writing about Women in Southern Politics
    Penny M. Miller and Lee R. Remington   119

6. Reflections on Scholarship in Religion and Southern Politics
    Ted G. Jelen   141

7. Population Shifts Change a Region's Politics: The Old South Morphs into the New
    Susan A. MacManus with the assistance of Brittany L. Penberthy and Thomas A. Watson   167

8. Issues, Ideology, and Political Opinions in the South
    Patrick R. Cotter, Stephen D. Shaffer, and David A. Breaux   189

9. Presidential Elections and the South
    Harold W. Stanley   219

10. Congress and the South
    Stanley P. Berard   241

11. Southern Governors and Legislatures
    *Branwell DuBose Kapeluck, Robert P. Steed, and
    Laurence W. Moreland*   269

Conclusion. Looking Back and Looking Forward:
    A Research Agenda for Southern Politics
        John A. Clark   291

Contributors   303

Index   305

Foreword

Jack Bass

The subject of southern politics has been my lifelong professional interest, beginning when I was a print reporter and continuing when I was a scholar and a college professor. Consequently, I am pleased to be associated with a volume that inventories and reviews the scholarly literature that has addressed the profound political changes that have characterized the American South since World War II.

When Walter DeVries and I spent two years based at Duke University bringing out *The Transformation of Southern Politics* in 1976, we—like virtually all others who have focused on the subject before and since—followed the trails blazed by V. O. Key. We made no pretense of emulating Key's unique insights, but did follow the methodology he used in *Southern Politics in State and Nation*. With support from the Ford and Rockefeller foundations and keeping our ears alert for what Key called "the telling anecdote," we traveled two weeks in each of the eleven states of the Confederacy, taping interviews with more than 360 people. They included politicians at all levels, political reporters, party officials, scholars, and labor leaders, almost all of them open and candid.

We sought to capture the changes that followed the crumbling of what Key saw as four props of the old order: disfranchisement of blacks, the one-party system, malapportionment in state legislatures, and Jim Crow segregation laws. Key perceived the emerging trends but wrote, "They only create conditions favorable to change." We met the men and women who, in Key's words, were "disposed to take advantage of the opportunity to accelerate the inevitable." A few displayed special qualities that alerted us to watch them in the future.

In Atlanta in 1974 we spent a half hour riding in a highway patrol car with Jimmy Carter from the capitol to the governor's mansion. He sat beside the driver, leaning to talk to us in the backseat. Jody Powell had set up the interview in the car, telling us, "This way you'll get his undivided attention." Carter's disciplined, first-rate mind, his focus, and his intense interest in searching for new solutions to old problems especially impressed DeVries, who combined academic credentials and broad experience inside political campaigns. Walt, who seldom commented after an interview, said quietly, "This guy could go all the way."

Two bright, young, and obscure college professors heading for defeat as congressional candidates that fall caught our attention. Determination and ambition marked both Newt Gingrich and Bill Clinton. Clinton narrowly lost to a Republican incumbent in northwest Arkansas after defeating six other candidates in a Democratic primary. Sitting in a cabin in the Ozark Mountains, he told us, "I happen to believe that the way that I can best sell myself, and the way that I can get the best organization going, is by having a better grasp of the issues than the people I'm running against, knowing more about it and being able to pose constructive alternatives."

In words that would echo eighteen years later in his winning 1992 presidential campaign, he continued, "I think the main thing is to take the tides that are flowing now and the skills that I can bring and the issues that I want to speak on, which the people respond to—and run with it just as damn hard as I can. I'm saying that my presentation of the issues is something that the average voter just distills into his general perception of me as a person. I do it because I think it's the responsible thing to do and because it's the only way I know to sell myself."

He told us of spending four hours with the somewhat disgraced former governor Orval Faubus, soaking up his "encyclopedic" knowledge of local politics, such as whom to see at whichever crossroads and being sure not to mention the guy half a mile down the road because they hate each other. The second Mrs. Faubus sat quietly through it all and then asked the twenty-seven-year-old law professor, "What do you think of the Communist conspiracy that's taking over the country?" When we asked his response, Clinton said, "I told her I was against it." I left believing that some day this guy would be president. He already projected the charisma, energy, and intellect—and now the political instinct—that would lead him to the White House.

Gingrich, armed with a doctorate in history from Tulane, viewed the Republican leadership in Georgia as "a disaster." Having campaigned among voters, he observed with prescient insight, "There's a psychological constituency out there very angry at what's going on in Washington." He also was fiercely determined to build a Republican party in Georgia and the region based on "organizational strength, long-range strategy, and patience."

Almost as an aside, he remarked, "Probably one of the beauties of open elective politics is that if you work hard enough it doesn't matter what people think—you may win." After losing that year and again two years later, Gingrich got elected in 1978. Although the lone Republican congressman from Georgia in 1990, he took a leadership role in launching the strategy that in 1994 moved the Republican Party to a position of dominance in the South and a majority in the House of Representatives, which elected him Speaker in 1995.

The 1994 election reflected the full beginning of political realignment in the South. Republicans emerged with a 6–5 edge among the governors, 13–9 in the Senate, and 64–61 in the House. In newly reapportioned congressional districts after the 1990 census, southern Republicans gained nine new U.S. House seats in 1992 and sixteen more in 1994. All twenty-five came from districts that, according to the 1994 *Almanac of American Politics*, had voted 60 percent or more for George H. W. Bush in the 1988 presidential elections.

As federal judicial interpretation of the Voting Rights Act evolved, two groups—blacks and Republicans—made gains in the South that resulted from single-member, majority-black legislative and congressional districts. The changes, however, undermined moderate and progressive white Democrats who got elected by biracial coalitions. Black congressional representation from the South jumped from three in 1990 to seventeen in 1992. Although blacks retained all of those seats in 1994, they found twenty-five fewer moderate and progressive white Democrats from the South with whom to form an effective coalition on policy issues.

Another major boost to Republican strength had developed from the political activism of white fundamentalists and evangelicals, spurred in 1976 by support for Jimmy Carter in his campaign for president as a born-again Christian. After Carter's director of internal revenue denied tax exemptions to segregated "Christian" private schools in the South, however, Republican operatives developed wedge "moral" issues that made the "Christian coalition" and its allies a solid component of party success, one that cared little about economic issues.

In the Republican sweep of 2004, George W. Bush painted the region a solid bright red, receiving a higher percentage of the vote in every southern state than his national average, ranging from 62.5 percent in Alabama to 50.7 percent in Florida. His coattails proved sufficiently long to sweep five U.S. Senate seats in the South left open by retiring Democrats, catapulting Republicans from their 13–9 lead in the Senate to an 18–4 dominance. Republicans held a 7–4 edge among governors.

In 2004 Edison/Mitofsky exit polls showed 24 percent of voters in the South considered "moral values," much of their concern centered on opposition to legalized abortion and the perceived threat of gay marriage, as the most important issue in the presidential election. Among that group, 89 percent voted for President Bush.

Below the Senate level and in state races, however, political independents were more receptive to Democrats, and traditional political issues played a larger role that suggested the genuine two-party competition foreseen by Key, with the parties battling over public policy. In North Carolina, the only southern state that elects its governor in a presidential year, voters in 2004 reelected Governor Mike Easley, who had won legislative support for increased taxes to strengthen public schools and higher education. It marked the fourth time in a row in which a Democrat won. The North Carolina vote for George W. Bush, however, marked the ninth time the state went Republican in the last ten presidential elections; the GOP in 2004 also picked up a U.S. Senate seat. But in the state legislature, Democrats won seats in both houses, regaining control of the house of representatives and strengthening control in the senate. The state remained intensely competitive.

In contrast, Georgia Republicans not only picked up a second Senate seat after winning the governor's office in 2002 for the first time since Reconstruction, but made big gains in the state legislature, picking up twenty-four house seats (including three party switches after the election) to gain a decisive majority and adding four seats to their majority in the senate. But even in Georgia, a Democrat defeated an incumbent Republican congressman.[1]

On a different issue, Key wrote in his opening to *Southern Politics in State and Nation,* "Whatever phase of the southern political process one seeks to understand, sooner or later the trail of inquiry leads to the Negro." In the 1960s that trail led to the Republican "southern strategy" launched by Barry Goldwater, who before his 1964 presidential campaign told southern Republican leaders meeting in Atlanta, "We're not going to get the Negro vote as a bloc in 1964 and 1968, so we ought to go hunting where the ducks are," adding his belief that school deseg-regation should be the responsibility of the states. Goldwater's Senate vote against the transforming 1964 Civil Rights Act—combined with the Dixiecrat presidential candidate Strom Thurmond's switch to the Re-publican Party—attracted white Democrats who felt betrayed by their party on the race issue.

In an interview with the Republican White House strategist Lee Atwater of South Carolina, Alexander Lamis asked whether President Reagan made a racist appeal by cutting back the food stamp program and Legal Services. (In 2005 President Bush opened his second term with a budget that called for less spending for forty-eight education pro-grams, food stamps, and Medicaid and ending the Community Food and Nutrition Program.) As Lamis reported in *Southern Politics in the 1990s,* Atwater's response remains instructive:

> You start out in 1954 by saying "Nigger, nigger, nigger." By 1968 you can't say "nigger"—that hurts you. Backfires. So you say stuff like forced busing, states' rights, and all that stuff. You're getting so abstract now you're talking about cutting taxes, and all these things you're talking about are totally economic things and a by-product of them is blacks get hurt worse than whites. And sub-consciously maybe that is part of it. I'm not saying that. But I'm saying that if it is getting that abstract, and that coded, that we are doing away with the racial problem one way or the other. You follow me—because obviously sitting around saying, "we want to cut this," is much more abstract than even the busing thing *and* a hell of a lot more abstract than "Nigger, nigger."

Republican growth in the region, however, steadily developed also on the basis of political organization, economic issues responsive to the region's rapidly expanding suburban, white middle class, and northern migrants who brought their Republican allegiance with them. The South appears to be settling into a region of national Republicans, statewide ticket-splitters, and challenging local Democrats.

As Key predicted, despite all the changes since his book was pub-lished in 1949, the South remains distinctive, and books about the re-gion's politics continue to be written. Just as The Citadel Symposium on Southern Politics, a biennial gathering of scholars of the region's politics, has provided a continuing source of stimulation and ferment for nearly three decades, this book provides readers a useful and unique scholarly guide to the full literature spawned by Key. The contributors are all accomplished students of southern politics, and their work published in this volume will itself become a part of the important literature that documents and analyzes political change in the South.

Note

1. Election data for 2004 drawn from *SouthNow* (January 2005), published by the Program on Southern Politics, Media and Public Life, University of North Carolina at Chapel Hill.

Acknowledgments

We very much appreciate the support, encouragement, and assistance of many people in the development and completion of this book. Foremost, we are indebted to our contributors for their commitment to the project and for their hard work in writing informative chapters in accordance with challenging guidelines. They should be duly credited with producing the heart of this book. All are fine scholars, but they are also our good friends, and we have enjoyed our association with them in this effort.

We are also indebted to the dozens of other southern politics scholars who have participated in the biennial Citadel Symposium on Southern Politics since its inception in 1978. All of them have contributed to our understanding of southern politics through their research presentations and related observations and commentary. As the citations in this volume affirm, many of them have contributed significantly to the literature on southern politics discussed in this book. We are also proud to regard them as our friends.

The Citadel Foundation has financed our work over the years with generous grants for the symposia and for a variety of related research and publication projects, and we gratefully acknowledge that support. We are also appreciative of the encouragement and support of The Citadel administration, which has helped to develop an academic environment conducive to scholarly work. We especially appreciate the support of Major General John S. Grinalds (USMC, ret.), president of The Citadel, Dr. Harrison S. Carter, recent past provost of The Citadel, and Dr. Donald A. Steven, present provost of The Citadel.

Stephen M. Wrinn, director of the University Press of Kentucky, has been particularly important to the completion of this work. His enthusiasm for and encouragement of the project have been instrumental to its publication. We thank him for his patience, good humor, and efficiency. We also appreciate the friendly professional support provided by the staff at the University Press of Kentucky. Steve Wrinn's assistant, Anne Dean Watkins, and editing supervisor Nichole Lainhart have been especially helpful in guiding us through the publication process. All who participated in the production process eased our work in countless ways.

Finally, a personal note from Bob to Angelyn to say thanks for patiently supporting a career-long effort to understand southern politics and to share with others his passion for the topic. It is an acknowledgment long overdue.

Introduction

The Literature of Southern Politics

Robert P. Steed and Laurence W. Moreland

IN HIS LANDMARK 1949 BOOK, *Southern Politics in State and Nation*, V. O. Key Jr. wrote: "Of books about the South there is no end. Nor will there be so long as the South remains the region with the most distinctive character and tradition" (Key 1949, ix). Written virtually on the eve of a period of sweeping social, economic, and political change in the region, Key's work served as a launching pad for a host of other research and helped to give impetus to even more books about the South.

Scholarly interest in southern politics, already high at midcentury, as the passage from Key suggests, increased even more in subsequent decades. For one thing, the South's distinctiveness begged to be examined—the unusual, the weird, the extraordinary generally arouse more interest than the usual and mundane—and there were plenty of researchers willing to heed the call. Much of the early research, and some of the later, was focused on detailing regional distinctiveness and examining areas of change and continuity (see, for example, Havard 1972; Bartley and Graham 1975; Steed, Moreland, and Baker 1990).

Additionally, as the South changed dramatically in the postwar years, it became a laboratory that offered an unparalleled opportunity to examine a culture and its political system in transition. Examples abound, but two should illustrate the point sufficiently: scholars of political parties jumped at the rare chance to do research on a system in the process of transforming itself from a one-party system to a two-party system (see, for example, Lamis 1984; Hadley and Bowman 1995; Steed, Clark, Bowman, and Hadley 1998); similarly, policy specialists found an opportunity to follow the dismantling of an entire social and legal system as the

South's Jim Crow system of racial segregation came under increasingly vigorous attack in the 1950s and 1960s (examples include Moreland, Steed, and Baker 1987; Davidson and Grofman 1994). This line of research even occasionally delved into the field of comparative politics, inasmuch as the South offered a domestic example of political and economic development that could be compared with developing societies in other parts of the world.

A third large area of research focused on the South's role in national politics. Scholars were particularly interested in examining how southern political change affected the national political system. In this vein, for example, research on southern party transformation has been related to the emergence of a Republican majority in Congress in the past decade (Kuzenski, Moreland, and Steed 2001; Black and Black 2002, for example) and to the key developments in presidential voting in recent years (such as Black and Black 1992).

A final category of research includes those many studies that range across two or more of the areas identified above. For example, Earl and Merle Black's monumental work *Politics and Society in the South* (1987) addressed social, economic, and political change in the South as they relate to internal politics (the changing southern party system is but one example) and as they affect the connections between the South and the national political system. This line of research often incorporated multiple avenues of investigation addressing such topics as the connections among changing race relations in the South, regional patterns of voting and representation, and national patterns of party and electoral change (examples include Edsall and Edsall 1991; Black and Black 2002).

While Key's work justifiably stands as the cornerstone of this impressive body of literature, considerable credit is also due a host of other scholars who recognized good stories when they saw them and proceeded to define southern politics as an identifiable subfield within the larger discipline of political science. During the 1950s and 1960s Key's two research associates, Alexander Heard and Donald Strong, expanded Key's work through a series of books, articles, and data compilations focused on the southern states (see, for example, Heard 1952; Strong 1955; Strong 1960; Heard and Strong 1970). The partisan and social (especially racial) ferment of the period created a context for further election analyses, such as Bernard Cosman's study of the 1964 election, *Five States for Goldwater* (1966), and for more expansive efforts to understand the increasingly complex interplay between race and southern politics, which was exemplified by Donald R. Matthews and James W. Prothro's *Negroes and the New Southern Politics* (1966). As an aside, not only was this latter work substantively significant, but the research project underlying it also served as a training ground for a group of graduate research associates such as R. Lewis Bowman, G. Robert Boynton, Charles Cnudde, William J. Crotty Jr., Jack Fleer, and Donald M. Freeman, who went on to distinguished careers and produced some of the important work on southern politics over the next decades.

In the early to mid-1970s three major works solidified the status of southern politics as a legitimate research and teaching focus. In a sense they were the culmination of the expanding research of the previous twenty years. At the same time they provided a foundation for and encouraged much of the southern politics research over the following three decades. The first to appear (in 1972) was *The Changing Politics of the South,* a collection of essays edited by William C. Havard. While the main thrust of the book was a series of state-by-state analyses of political change in the region, it also included expansive introductory, concluding, and bibliographical essays by Havard, which served to set the post–World War II changes in southern politics in a broader social, cultural, and historical context.

The second book was *Southern Politics and the Second Reconstruction,* written by Numan V. Bartley and Hugh D. Graham in 1975, and the third was *The Transformation of Southern Politics,* published the following year by Jack Bass and Walter DeVries. Bartley and Graham focused on party and electoral change in the region and placed this transformation in the broader historical framework of national party systems change. They paid special attention to the impact of changing race relations in the South on party and electoral dynamics and, like Havard, concluded with a strong bibliographical essay that placed post–World War II research in the larger bodies of literature on southern history and national party development. Indeed, the bibliographical essays in both *The Changing Politics of the South* and *Southern Politics and the Second Reconstruction* demonstrated the depth and breadth of the research being done in the field by the mid-1970s and provided valuable guidance to students and scholars interested in joining the effort.

In *The Transformation of Southern Politics* Bass and DeVries focused not only on regionwide political changes during the period 1945–1975 but also on social, economic, and demographic changes. Migration patterns, economic modernization, the rise of southern Republicanism

together with a national "southern strategy," and the increasing participation of African Americans in the political process (as the black population moved "from object to participant") were all cited as helping to
illuminate a changing southern politics. Notably, too, Bass and DeVries
were among the first to pay attention to the declining regional differences between the South and the rest of the nation, a topic that has attracted significant attention in the literature since 1975 as well. All these
topics were addressed regionwide but also on a state-by-state basis, an
analysis that constituted most of the book. The volume also included an
extensive set of appendixes that provided useful data (presented in maps
and tables) on changing demographic and political patterns in the eleven
states of the Confederacy.

The line of research extending from Key through Bass and DeVries
provided both foundation and momentum for a new generation of students and scholars emerging in the 1970s and early 1980s. Some of the
early work of scholars who would become distinguished in the field appeared in this period: examples include Harold W. Stanley (*Senate vs.
Governor, Alabama 1971: Referents for Opposition in a One-Party Legislature*, 1975), Earl Black (*Southern Governors and Civil Rights: Racial
Segregation as a Campaign Issue in the Second Reconstruction*, 1976),
Merle Black (*Perspectives on the American South*, coedited with John
Shelton Reed, 1981), and Alexander P. Lamis (*The Two-Party South*,
1984), to mention a few. Moreover, work by historians such as Bartley
and Graham, mentioned above, and sociologists such as John Shelton
Reed (*The Enduring South: Subcultural Persistence in Mass Society*,
1972) increasingly provided a cross-disciplinary context for understanding southern politics.

As the decade of the 1970s drew to a close, research on southern
politics had grown enough to encourage the development of a conference devoted exclusively to the presentation and discussion of work on
the topic. The first Citadel Symposium on Southern Politics was held in
Charleston, South Carolina, in February 1978, and the series has continued on a biennial schedule to the present. Over the twenty-eight years
of its existence, the symposium has served as a forum for the presentation of well over eight hundred scholarly papers that address virtually
every aspect of southern politics—race, elections, party development,
interest group activity, gender, religion, the regional role in national
politics (presidential and congressional elections and politics), policy,
regional distinctiveness, population movement, historical context, and

regional research methodology. In the process almost everyone conducting southern politics research has participated, many on a regular basis, and in many instances the symposium has facilitated discussions that resulted in valuable collaborative projects, many of which eventually led to important publications. A significant number of the papers originally presented at the symposium over the years were subsequently published, thereby becoming a part of the expanding literature on the politics of the South. Many of these were included as chapters in the series of books edited by the conference directors—*Party Politics in the South* (Steed, Moreland, and Baker 1980), *Contemporary Southern Political Attitudes and Behavior: Studies and Essays* (Moreland, Baker, and Steed 1982), *Religion and Politics in the South: Mass and Elite Perspectives* (Baker, Steed, and Moreland 1983), *Blacks in Southern Politics* (Moreland, Steed, and Baker 1987), *The Disappearing South? Studies in Regional Change and Continuity* (Steed, Moreland, and Baker 1990), *Southern Parties and Elections: Studies in Regional Political Change* (Steed, Moreland, and Baker 1997), and *Eye of the Storm: The South and Congress in an Era of Change* (Kuzenski, Moreland, and Steed 2001). Others were published as articles in a series of special issues of the *American Review of Politics* in 1998, 2000, 2002, and 2004.

The main point here is that by 1978, and continuing largely unabated to the present, southern politics research flourished sufficiently to sustain such a conference. Indeed, the longevity of the symposium (coupled with the continuing presence of southern politics panels on the programs of the annual meetings of the Southern Political Science Association during the same period) is testimony to the range and scope of such research. It also helps to explain the breadth of the southern politics literature.

This literature continued to grow during the 1980s and to the present. Wide-ranging work, such as the important books by Earl and Merle Black (1987, 1992, and 2002), Robert H. Swansbrough and David M. Brodsky (1988), Charles S. Bullock III and Mark J. Rozell (1998), Richard K. Scher (1998), Alexander P. Lamis (1999), and David Lublin (2004), and more narrowly focused work by such scholars as Nicol C. Rae (1994), James M. Glaser (1996), Joseph A. Aistrup (1996), David Lublin (1997), and Chandler Davidson and Bernard Grofman (1997) added further richness and depth. Additionally, there are other useful publications, such as the biweekly *Southern Political Report* (edited by Hastings Wyman), which provides continuing coverage and interpretation of the contemporary politics of the South. In short, Key's observation about the expansiveness of published work on southern politics is more appropriate now than when it was made over half a century ago.

Of course, a major problem with any broad overview such as this is that it only scratches the surface in its description of how the body of literature developed. Many important contributions and contributors are omitted for the sake of concision and brevity. Still, the general outline should be helpful in establishing the central thesis that southern politics research is important and that, as a reflection of this importance, the past half century has witnessed continued and expanded attention to the topic.

In sum, for a variety of reasons and in many ways, the literature on southern politics has grown significantly since the publication of *Southern Politics in State and Nation.* It has addressed a wide range of important topics, and it has connected in many ways to other elements of political science. For those interested in southern politics, serious students and scholars as well as more casual observers, this literature is a rich source of information. As is true of any vast literature, however, the very volume of sources constitutes an obstacle to understanding. It would be useful, therefore, to have review essays available to help organize and relate this large array of past research.

Building on the skillful summary of southern politics since V. O. Key's 1949 work by Jack Bass in his foreword to this volume, we should add a brief word on the significance of the southern politics literature. More substantial changes have taken place in the South in demographic, social, and, above all, political terms in the past half century than in any other region. The dramatic shift of the South from a region dominated by Democrats to one dominated by Republicans, together with relatively stable political patterns elsewhere around the nation, has resulted in near parity—nationwide—between the two parties. That, together with the increasing ideological homogeneity of both activists and officeholders at the highest levels within each party, has resulted in presidential elections now notable for their closeness, their unpredictability, and their intense, relentless partisanship. As we suggested at the outset, then, the literature on southern politics has become crucial for those seeking to understand where we are and how we got here, both in terms of the regional politics of the South and in terms of the national politics of the country.

The purpose of this book is to provide a set of essays devoted to reviewing the key literature in the various topical areas of southern politics. It was inspired by the highly acclaimed *Writing the Civil War,* edited by James M. McPherson and William J. Cooper Jr., which has provided welcome guidance for understanding the vast literature on the Civil War. We asked some of the leading southern politics scholars to develop these essays with a view toward identifying key works, major themes, main conclusions, points for debate, continuing knowledge gaps, and future research questions or directions in their topical areas. Our guidelines for the essays were relatively broad and thus allowed for variation in organization and approach. Moreover, inasmuch as the literature in some areas (for example, civil rights, public opinion and political behavior, party development) is considerably larger than in other areas (such as population movement and governors and state legislatures), the essays vary in their breadth and depth of coverage. All, however, address important topics.

In some topical areas there is overlap. For example, the chapters on the civil rights movement and southern politics and on race and southern politics obviously cross paths on occasion. We have sought to reduce such overlap, usually by having the authors make cross-references where appropriate, but there are instances where some chapters of necessity address common works.

These essays are not intended to be comprehensive bibliographical reviews in the traditional sense, and they make no claim to include or address all that has been published in each topical area. Indeed, they tend to focus primarily on book-length works as opposed to journal articles (although some chapters, such as that on Congress by Stanley Berard, do include a number of key articles), and even then some books may be mentioned only briefly or omitted altogether. In each area the authors made judgments as to which of the published works should be included to outline the basic research questions, themes, directions, debates, and issues related to the topic.

The first two chapters deal with party development in the South. This has been one of the most important and far-reaching features of regional political change and, consequently, one of the most intensely researched. Charles Prysby and John J. McGlennon separately examine the research on party organizations and activism and the connections between the party system and the larger regional political system in chapters 1 and 2.

The parallel changes in the South's system of race relations are similarly important and have also been heavily examined. Like concern with party change, interest in the civil rights movement and the transformed role of race in the region has generated a large and rich literature, and this is the focus of the next two chapters, by Richard K. Scher and Richard L. Engstrom. Inasmuch as race, in one way or another, permeates the southern politics literature, it is addressed in various ways in practically every chapter in the book. Engstrom's chapter, however, focuses more narrowly on the literature of race and representation in relation to congressional districting in the South, a topic of considerable interest and importance in contemporary southern (and national) politics.

In addition to race, such issues as gender, religion, and in-migration and other forms of regional population movement have played significant roles in southern politics over the past half century. The efforts to sort out the impact of these variables on the southern electorate and within the southern political system are the focus of chapter 5, by Penny M. Miller and Lee R. Remington; chapter 6, by Ted G. Jelen; and chapter 7, by Susan A. MacManus. Closely connected to the research in these areas is interest in the nature of southern public opinion, which has generated a body of literature that is reviewed in chapter 8 by Patrick R. Cotter, Stephen D. Shaffer, and David A. Breaux.

Finally, chapter 9, by Harold W. Stanley; chapter 10, by Stanley P. Berard; and chapter 11, by Branwell DuBose Kapeluck, Robert P. Steed, and Laurence W. Moreland, explore the literature on the connections between the South and key political institutions—the presidency (mainly in the context of the electoral process), Congress, and governors and state legislatures.

The goal is to produce a book that will be valuable to those seeking a basic understanding of southern politics as well as to those advanced students and scholars doing research in southern politics. We are confident the book will serve to synthesize previous research, summarize the current state of knowledge, and help frame future research on southern politics.

References

Aistrup, Joseph A. 1996. *The Southern Strategy Revisited: Republican Top-Down Advancement in the South.* Lexington: University Press of Kentucky.
Baker, Tod A., Robert P. Steed, and Laurence W. Moreland, eds. 1983. *Religion and Politics in the South: Mass and Elite Perspectives.* New York: Praeger.
Bartley, Numan V., and Hugh D. Graham. 1975. *Southern Politics and the Second Reconstruction.* Baltimore: Johns Hopkins University Press.
Bass, Jack, and Walter DeVries. 1976. *The Transformation of Southern Poli-*

tics: Social Change and Political Consequence since 1945. New York: Basic Books.

Black, Earl. 1976. *Southern Governors and Civil Rights: Racial Segregation as a Campaign Issue in the Second Reconstruction*. Cambridge: Harvard University Press.

Black, Earl, and Merle Black. 1987. *Politics and Society in the South*. Cambridge: Harvard University Press.

———. 1992. *The Vital South: How Presidents Are Elected*. Cambridge: Harvard University Press.

———. 2002. *The Rise of Southern Republicans*. Cambridge: Harvard University Press.

Black, Merle, and John Shelton Reed, eds. 1981. *Perspectives on the American South*. London: Gordon and Breach.

Bullock, Charles S., III, and Mark J. Rozell, eds. 1998. *The New Politics of the Old South*. Lanham, Md.: Rowman and Littlefield.

Cosman, Bernard. 1966. *Five States for Goldwater: Continuity and Change in Southern Presidential Voting Patterns*. Tuscaloosa: University of Alabama Press.

Davidson, Chandler, and Bernard Grofman, eds. 1994. *Quiet Revolution in the South: The Impact of the Voting Rights Act, 1965–1990*. Princeton: Princeton University Press.

Edsall, Thomas B., and Mary D. Edsall. 1991. *Chain Reaction: The Impact of Race, Rights, and Taxes on American Politics*. New York: W. W. Norton.

Glaser, James M. 1996. *Race, Campaign Politics, and the Realignment in the South*. New Haven: Yale University Press.

Hadley, Charles D., and Lewis Bowman, eds. 1995. *Southern State Party Organizations and Activists*. Westport, Conn.: Praeger.

Havard, William C., ed. 1972. *The Changing Politics of the South*. Baton Rouge: Louisiana State University Press.

Heard, Alexander. 1952. *A Two-Party South?* Chapel Hill: University of North Carolina Press.

Heard, Alexander, and Donald S. Strong. 1970 (1950). *Southern Primaries and Elections, 1920–1949*. Freeport, N.Y.: Books for Libraries Press.

Key, V. O., Jr. 1949. *Southern Politics in State and Nation*. New York: Knopf.

Kuzenski, John C., Laurence W. Moreland, and Robert P. Steed, eds. 2001. *Eye of the Storm: The South and Congress in an Era of Change*. Westport, Conn.: Praeger.

Lamis, Alexander P. 1984. *The Two-Party South*. New York: Oxford University Press.

———, ed. 1999. *Southern Politics in the 1990s*. Baton Rouge: Louisiana State University Press.

Lublin, David. 1997. *The Paradox of Representation: Racial Gerrymandering and Minority Interests in Congress*. Princeton: Princeton University Press.

———. 2004. *The Republican South: Democratization and Partisan Change*. Princeton: Princeton University Press.

Matthews, Donald R., and James W. Prothro. 1966. *Negroes and the New Southern Politics*. New York: Harcourt, Brace and World.

McPherson, James M., and William J. Cooper Jr., eds. 1998. *Writing the Civil War*. Columbia: University of South Carolina Press.

Moreland, Laurence W., Tod A. Baker, and Robert P. Steed, eds. 1982. *Contemporary Southern Political Attitudes and Behavior: Studies and Essays*. New York: Praeger.

Moreland, Laurence W., Robert P. Steed, and Tod A. Baker, eds. 1987. *Blacks in Southern Politics*. New York: Praeger.

Rae, Nicol C. 1994. *Southern Democrats*. New York: Oxford University Press.

Reed, John Shelton. 1972. *The Enduring South: Subcultural Persistence in Mass Society*. Chapel Hill: University of North Carolina Press.

Scher, Richard K. 1998. *Politics in the New South: Republicanism, Race, and Leadership in the Twentieth Century*. Armonk, N.Y.: M. E. Sharpe.

Stanley, Harold W. 1975. *Senate vs. Governor, Alabama 1971: Referents for Opposition in a One-Party Legislature*. Tuscaloosa: University of Alabama Press.

Steed, Robert P., John A. Clark, Lewis Bowman, and Charles D. Hadley, eds. 1998. *Party Organization and Activism in the American South*. Tuscaloosa: University of Alabama Press.

Steed, Robert P., Laurence W. Moreland, and Tod A. Baker, eds. 1980. *Party Politics in the South*. New York: Praeger.

———, eds. 1990. *The Disappearing South? Studies in Regional Change and Continuity*. Tuscaloosa: University of Alabama Press.

———, eds. 1997. *Southern Parties and Elections: Studies in Regional Political Change*. Tuscaloosa: University of Alabama Press.

Strong, Donald S. 1955. *The 1952 Presidential Election in the South*. Tuscaloosa: University of Alabama Bureau of Public Administration.

———. 1960. *Urban Republicanism in the South*. Tuscaloosa: University of Alabama Bureau of Public Administration.

Swansbrough, Robert H., and David M. Brodsky, eds. 1988. *The South's New Politics: Realignment and Dealignment*. Columbia: University of South Carolina Press.

★ **Chapter 1** ★

Southern Political Party Development since World War II

Charles Prysby

A SUBSTANTIAL PARTISAN REALIGNMENT occurred during the last half of the twentieth century in the American South. Although this was a gradual realignment, marked by uneven and sometimes even contradictory changes, the cumulative result was the transformation of the old, one-party South into a new, two-party South. The growth of a two-party South is discussed in many books and journal articles, a collective body of literature that makes the South the most studied region within the United States by far.

The focus of this study is on one particular aspect of this transformation, the development of the political party system in the South. The emphasis on the development of the *party system* indicates that the concern here is with more than just the growth of two-party competition, although competition certainly is an important aspect of a party system. The term *political party system* refers to a variety of aspects of the parties, their relationships to each other, and their relationships with the electorate. The concept of the development of a party system is widely used in the literature on comparative political parties. The term *party system development* appears far less frequently in the literature on contemporary American political parties, although the concept is used by those who discuss the historical emergence of parties in this country (Aldrich 1995; Chambers and Burnham 1975; Ladd 1970). But even the literature on contemporary American political parties is replete with discussions of changes in the party system. Those interested in electoral patterns refer to critical re-

11

alignments, secular realignments, and even dealignment of the electorate (Burnham 1970; Petrocik 1981; Sundquist 1983; Wattenberg 1994).
Those who focus on party organizations have examined the decline of parties, the renewal of parties, and the adaptation of parties to changed circumstances (Broder 1971; Coleman 1996a; Crotty 1984; Green and Farmer
2003; Green and Shea 1999; Kayden and Mahe 1985; Maisel 1998; Pomper
1980; Price 1984; Schlesinger 1985; White 2001). Thus, change in or development of the party system is a common concern of scholars.

This study considers the development of the southern political party
system in the post–World War II era. It does so by examining and evalu-
ating the analyses and conclusions of scholars who have written on this
topic over the past half century. To create a useful theoretical framework
for a systematic review of this literature, I draw upon several different
sources. From the literature on American political parties, I particularly
rely on the writings on responsible political parties, on party decline or
renewal, and on party organizational strength, three overlapping but separate bodies of literature. From the literature on American electoral behavior, I particularly use the literature on realignment. From the field of
comparative politics, I draw from the literature on political party development, particularly in the European context. My use of these writings
is selective. Some key elements in their theoretical frameworks, such as
party system fragmentation, are not very relevant to an examination of
party system development in the South. I have used these writings to the
extent that their theoretical concepts seem applicable to recent developments in the southern political party system.

Political Party System Development

Political party system development can be analyzed along three dimensions: competition between the parties, party system cleavages, and party
organizational strength. Each dimension is elaborated below, with an attempt to identify specific criteria that can be used to assess the nature of
party system development. After elaborating the theoretical framework,
I examine the development of the southern political party system along
these three dimensions.

Party Competition

Political parties are essential for democracy, and competition between
the parties is an important aspect of a political party system in a democ-

racy. By offering alternative officeholders to the voters, parties provide a mechanism through which voters are able to influence government and hold leaders responsible. Without sufficient competition between the parties, the voters lack credible alternatives and thus are less able to influence government. Moreover, a lack of competition is likely to mean that the parties are not structuring policy alternatives for voters. When one party dominates, as happened in the first half of the twentieth century in the South, the situation may not be much different from a no-party system, although this depends on the character of the dominant party (Key 1949, 299; Sartori 1976, 82–88).

Competition between political parties can be judged or measured from two basic perspectives. First, we can consider the division of the popular vote (David 1972). The closer the popular vote is to an even division, the more competitive the election is. A pattern of highly competitive elections indicates that the party system is highly competitive. Closeness of the vote does not provide a complete measure of competition, however. A situation where one party consistently wins 52 percent of the vote for statewide offices would result in one partys continually controlling those offices despite the narrowness of the vote margin, a situation that we might hesitate to classify as highly competitive. Hence, we should also consider control of elected offices: a highly competitive party system is one in which both parties regularly win office. Moreover, alternation in control of the chief bodies of government—the chief executive and the legislature in the American states—can be considered a particularly important aspect of control of office (Ranney 1965; Schlesinger 1955). For legislatures, we should consider both control of the legislature and the partisan division of seats. Even if one party retains control of a legislature for an extended period, there is a difference in control with a bare majority of the seats and control with two-thirds of the seats, for example.

It also is important to judge both aspects of competition—the popular vote division and party control of elected office—across different office levels. Competition can be much greater for some offices than for others. Any analysis of party competition in the contemporary South that looks only at the top of the ticket will obtain quite a different picture from one that looks farther down the ballot. The evenness of competition levels across office levels is not a minor or unimportant point. Where there is a fairly even level of competition across offices, it will be easier for parties to present a clearer and more coherent image to the voters. Where a party is competitive for offices at the top of the ticket but uncompetitive farther down, the party has not penetrated deeply into society.

Party System Cleavages

If political parties in a democracy are supposed to offer alternatives to the voters, then party differences are clearly an important aspect of the party system. The literature on comparative political parties emphasizes the development of clear and stable cleavages between the parties in a system, so that the parties represent different political viewpoints. For example, many of the observers of party politics in the new democracies of eastern and central Europe are concerned about parties that lack a clear programmatic identity (Bielasiak 2002; Evans and Whitefield 1993; Kitschelt, Mansfeldova, Markowski, and Toka 1999, 224; Miller, Erb, Reisinger, and Hesli 2000; Pridham and Lewis 1996). A party system composed of parties without much of an ideological or programmatic identity is likely to be one that does not adequately link voters to elites and one that does not structure the electoral choices for voters in a meaningful way.

Similar concerns have been voiced by scholars of American political parties. Most notably, those who desire a more responsible party system in the United States emphasize the need for more programmatic parties (American Political Science Association 1950; Broder 1971, 189–212; Sabato and Larson 2002, 164–66; Schattschneider 1942, 206–10). This argument has generated some controversy. Some scholars have been critical of the responsible party argument, especially its expression in the 1950 report of the American Political Science Association's Committee on Political Parties. These critics argue that the institutional structure of the American political system makes strong party government impossible and perhaps even undesirable (Herrnson 1992; Kirkpatrick 1971; Ranney 1951; White 1992). A more qualified position on this issue, however, one that argues simply that American political parties could or should be *more* responsible and programmatic than they were in 1950 (which, after all, was the title of the report), is a position that seems to have much more support among students of American political parties (Coleman 2003; David 1992; Green and Herrnson 2002; Pomper 1971; Price 1984, 109–11; White 2001; White and Mileur 2002). Furthermore, there is a large literature on party renewal in this country that argues that though parties are weaker in some ways than they were decades ago, they also are stronger in some important ways, and most of this literature either implicitly or explicitly suggests that party renewal is a desirable development, that the United States is better off with stronger parties, and that one aspect of stronger parties is greater party clarity and cohesiveness on major issues of public policy (Cohen, Fleisher, and Kantor 2001; Green and Farmer 2003; Green and Shea 1999; Kayden and Mahe 1985; Maisel 1998; Pomper 1980, 2001).

Party system cleavages may be analyzed from another perspective, one that emphasizes the substantive basis of the cleavages that divide the parties. The question here is not how clearly or sharply the parties are divided, but what policy issues or social divisions divide them. This perspective is central to much of the literature on comparative party system development in Europe, which places great emphasis on how cleavages develop and are reflected in the party system (Bielasiak 2002; Evans and Whitefield 1993; Kitschelt 1992; Kitschelt et al. 1999, 262–306; Lewis 2000, 123–49; Lipset and Rokkan 1967; Olson 1998; Walker 1996). In American politics the literature on electoral realignments similarly emphasizes the development or emergence of party cleavages. Realignments are generally defined as durable alterations in the fundamental partisan attachments of the electorate, and this usually means that the social and issue bases of partisan attachments are substantially altered (Burnham 1970, 6–7; Key 1955, 1959; Petrocik 1981, 15–16; Sundquist 1983, 298–321). The result after a realignment is not simply an alteration in the level of strength of each party; the cleavage lines in the party system are also shifted or redrawn.

Party system cleavages also may be judged in terms of the extent to which elite cleavages reflect social and ideological divisions in the population (Bielasiak 2002; Kitschelt 1992; Lipset and Rokkan 1967; Pomper and Weiner 2002; Pridham and Lewis 1996; Weisberg 2002). Important divisions within the population should be reflected by divisions between the candidates and the activists of the parties. We can judge not only whether there is congruity between mass and elite cleavages but also the extent to which elites and masses are similarly positioned on major dimensions of public policy. A common expectation is that elites will be more polarized than voters, but the degree to which this is the case varies considerably (Jackson, Brown, and Bositis 1982; Jackson and Clayton 1996; McClosky, Hoffman, and O'Hara 1960). Differences in elite and mass positioning on major policy dimensions are less important than the degree of congruence of the substantive basis of elite and mass cleavages, but the former can be important when a party is perceived by many as too extreme.

Party Organizational Strength

Parties have an organizational presence both in and out of government. In the American system the party in government has dominated, especially at the state and national levels. Even the strong local organizations that were once present in many American cities have atrophied. The situation in a number of European countries is quite different, as we find parties with strong external organizations, sometimes with a substantial mass base. These external organizations sometimes rival the party in government in power, rather than being clearly subservient to it. But even in the American setting, the strength of party organizations has been a topic of great interest. At the very least, strong party organizations are better able to help party candidates in their election efforts (Aldrich 1995, 48–50; Crotty 1986; Herrnson 1988, 84–111; Hopkins 1986). Moreover, many scholars have found that over the past two or three decades American parties have greatly improved their service role, particularly at the national level (Bibby 1998; Coleman 1996b; Herrnson 1988, 30–46; Longley 1980).

Party organizational strength can be assessed in terms of resources and activities. Important resources are money and people (Cotter, Gibson, Bibby, and Huckshorn 1984, 16–18; Gibson, Cotter, Bibby, and Huckshorn 1983, 1985; Gibson, Frendreis, and Vertz 1989). Activities can be divided into election activities and organizational maintenance activities. Important election activities include recruiting candidates, providing resources and assistance to candidates, and working to get out the vote (Frendreis, Gibson, and Vertz 1990; Hogan 2003). Organizational maintenance activities include ongoing public relations efforts, communication and party-building activities between elections, and fund-raising efforts (Huckshorn, Gibson, Cotter, and Bibby 1986). Thus, a strong party organization is not active just during election campaigns. It engages in a continuous range of activities, all of which may be viewed as at least indirectly improving the party's fortunes in future elections.

These three dimensions of a party system—competition, cleavages, and organizational strength—are interrelated. Increased competition encourages increased organizational strength, just as improved organizational strength is likely to affect competition. Many other potential relationships between these party system aspects could be identified. It also is true, however, that changes in one dimension can be accompanied by what might seem to be contradictory changes in other dimensions. Competition can increase even while differences between the parties decline, for example. It is for this reason that the different dimensions need to be outlined and examined separately to obtain a complete picture of the development of the contemporary southern political party system. The remainder of this chapter engages in that examination; it relies on the findings of existing studies of southern political behavior.

Party Competition

Despite his unflattering description of the Solid South, Key saw trends that could transform the political character of the region (1949, 664–75). Alexander Heard, who assisted Key in the research for *Southern Politics in State and Nation,* was even more optimistic about the emergence of a two-party South. He argued that in the long run southern conservatives would be happy neither in the Democratic Party nor in a third party and thus would turn to the Republicans (Heard 1952, 247–49). The possibility of substantial political change in the South became the dominant concern of subsequent scholarship.

Themes of the Literature of the 1960s and 1970s

Speculation about realignment in the South advanced when Republican presidential candidates carried several southern states in 1952, 1956, and 1960. Interpretations of this success varied, however. For example, Converse (1963) focused on the limited change in the party identification of southerners, which led him to see little prospect for the South's becoming a reliably Republican region in presidential voting. Strong (1963), however, disagreed with Converse's analysis, arguing that recent voting patterns indicated the emergence of a more durable Republicanism in the South, not just deviations due to short-term forces associated with particular presidential elections, such as Eisenhower's personal appeal or Kennedy's Catholicism. Although scholars differed on the likely amount and speed of fundamental change in the South, there was widespread agreement in the earlier literature that Republican growth would be primarily among upper- and middle-income voters in urban areas, especially in the rim South. These voters would be motivated more by economic than racial issues, and over time they would be likely to vote much like northern urban middle-class voters.

The civil rights revolution of the mid-1960s and the accompanying relative lack of southern support for Democratic presidential candidates in 1964 and 1968 stimulated more scholarly interest in the possibility of fundamental change in the partisan character of the region. Phillips put forth probably the most optimistic scenario for Republican growth; he saw the region as part of an emerging Republican majority (1969, 286–89). Others made more qualified predictions but nevertheless felt that substantial change was likely to occur. Cosman's analysis of the 1964 Goldwater vote in the South concluded that it was not just a temporary deviation in voting but instead would likely have a lasting impact (1966, 119–32). Bartley and Graham felt that by the 1970s two-party politics had emerged not just at the presidential level but at other levels as well (1975, 184–200). Studies that investigated southern political change through a state-by-state approach also found considerable Republican growth across the region, although the details and nature of the growth varied among the states (Bass and DeVries 1976; Havard 1972).

Disagreements over the extent and durability of Republican gains depended in part on interpretations of data on party identification. For example, Beck (1977) argued that little realignment had occurred in the region through 1972, as Republican identification had increased only somewhat since 1952. The biggest gains were in the proportion of southerners calling themselves Independents, which led Beck to conclude that dealignment was a more accurate description of the change that had taken place in the region. Gatlin (1975) concurred with the dealignment characterization, arguing that the South was not becoming part of a new Republican majority. On the other hand, Schreiber (1971) viewed the growth of Independents in the South as greatly benefiting Republicans, as these new Independents tended to be conservative; moreover, their new independence might well be a stepping-stone to Republican identification. Wolfinger and Arseneau (1978) more carefully examined Independents, distinguishing between partisan leaners and pure Independents. They concluded that many of the Independents claimed to lean toward the Republicans and that these leaners were almost as reliably Republican in their voting as Republican identifiers. Democratic leaners, by contrast, were much less loyal in their vote. Thus, the growth of Independents greatly benefited Republican candidates.

The literature of the 1970s emphasized that Republican voting was much stronger at the top of the ticket than it was farther down the ballot. While Republicans were doing well in presidential elections and in prominent statewide elections, Democrats continued to elect most of the congressmen from the region and to dominate most state legislatures. Disparities in Republican success at different office levels were greater when the focus was on offices won than when it was on the percentage of the vote. For example, Republicans captured 37 percent of the southern U.S. House vote in 1976, but they won only one-fourth of the southern congressional seats. These patterns indicate one reason why studies sometimes differed in their assessment of Republican success. A focus on presidential, gubernatorial, and U.S. Senate elections produced a more favorable picture of Republican success in the 1970s than did a focus on lower-level offices. An emphasis on offices won rather than share of the vote, especially if the focus was on lower-level offices, yielded a less favorable portrait of Republican strength. Moreover, because change in voting was more dramatic than change in partisanship, scholars whose analyses focused primarily on voting patterns rather than on party identification were more likely to see substantial permanent shifts in those patterns (Bartley and Graham 1975; Bass and DeVries 1976, 23–40; Ladd and Hadley 1978, 129–77; Phillips 1969, 187–289).

A common theme in this literature was the relative contributions of conversion, generational change, and migration to the growth of Republicanism. Migration was identified as an early contributor to partisan change in the South. Those moving to the region were heavily Republican, while those departing were heavily Democratic, which resulted in a substantial net gain for the Republicans. Converse (1963) estimated the contribution of migration to Republican growth in the 1950s to be very large. Beck (1977) and Wolfinger and Arseneau (1978) concurred with this assessment on the basis of their analysis of data through 1972. Campbell (1977), however, came to a different conclusion, arguing that migration made only a modest contribution to the growth of Republicanism. Furthermore, Campbell found that conversion—the change in partisanship among individuals—was a dominant source of change among white natives, whereas Beck concluded that generational replacement was more important than conversion, as did Wolfinger and Arseneau. All agreed, however, that the mobilization of blacks into the electorate and the development of very strong Democratic loyalties among this group following the civil rights revolution of the mid-1960s were very important to the Democrats' ability to remain competitive.

Another theme in the literature of this period was the substantial geographical unevenness in the Republican vote. While some states had become quite competitive, others remained more strongly Democratic, except perhaps in presidential voting. Within states, similar geographical unevenness appeared. Some of the commonly analyzed geographical distinctions were the rim versus the deep South, urban versus rural areas, and areas with a high concentration of blacks versus those with a small black population. Analyses that employed a state-by-state approach often added other geographical factors that were peculiar to one or two states, such as the mountain areas of Tennessee and North Carolina, the suburban areas of northern Virginia, the Catholic areas of Louisiana, or south Florida. The emphasis on these geographical differences in partisan strength indicated that scholars viewed the South as diverse and complex and that an understanding of southern politics required an appreciation of this diversity and complexity.

Themes of the Literature from the 1980s to the Present

Following the 1980 presidential election and the subsequent gains made by Republicans in the South, scholars began to shift their assessments of southern realignment. The emergence of a competitive two-party South now appeared to be a certainty, not just a possibility. Lamis (1984) surveyed change in the region by examining each state individually and concluded that a two-party South had been firmly established. Another state-by-state analysis came to similar conclusions (Swansbrough and Brodsky 1988). The comprehensive examination of southern political change by Black and Black (1987, 213–56) emphasized both shifts in party identification and the conservative advantage in public opinion, both of which contributed to Republican success at the polls. Stanley (1988) concluded that change in the South reflected realignment more than dealignment, although some of the latter existed. Wattenberg (1991) also concluded that a secular realignment had occurred. His analysis, which focused on party identification and combined Independent leaners with partisans, found substantial growth in Republican identification during the 1980s, to the point that Republicans had a significant advantage in party identification among white southerners by 1988.

By the 1990s some scholars saw the Republicans as the new majority party in the region. Black and Black argued that the South had become reliably Republican in presidential elections (1992, 3–28). Others, perhaps because they wrote after Clinton's success in the South, were somewhat less definite about the South's being solidly Republican but nevertheless felt that Republicans started with a sizable advantage in presidential races (Bullock and Rozell 2003a; Scher 1997, 113–17; Stanley 2002). Similar assessments were extended to congressional races. The extensive study of change in southern congressional elections by Black and Black found that by the end of the twentieth century Republicans had established an advantage in congressional races, although the authors argued that the South was too diverse to allow the Republicans to become dominant (2002, 364–68). Bullock and Rozell (2003a), Knuckey (2000), Prysby (2000), and Shafer and Johnston (2001) concluded that Republican presidential success was now paralleled by similar success in southern congressional elections. Republican strength also was clear in gubernatorial elections (Lamis 1999a; Scher 1997, 133). Democrats retained an advantage in state legislative elections across the region, however, a fact that reflects the top-down nature of Republican growth (Bullock and Rozell 2003a; Lamis 1999a; Lublin 2004, 46–53; Scher 1997, 141–43; Shaffer, Pierce, and Kohnke 2000).

The top-down nature of Republican advancement in the South was most thoroughly studied by Aistrup (1996), but it was examined by others as well (Aldrich 2000; Bullock 1988; Glaser 1996, 7–16). Several reasons for the earlier emergence of Republican presidential voting have been discussed in the literature. Democratic candidates for sub-presidential offices were often more conservative than the Democratic presidential candidate, from whom they often distanced themselves (Black and Black 2002, 171–73; Glaser 1996, 186; Knuckey 2000; Rae 1994, 73–79). Democrats also benefited greatly from the simple fact that they controlled so many elected offices, which meant that the Democratic candidate in any given election frequently was either an incumbent or an individual who had held prior elected office, while Republican candidates often were neither (Aistrup 1996, 184; Black and Black 2002, 155–59; Bullock 1988; Glaser 1996, 181–82; Martorano, Anderson, and Hamm 2000; Stanley 2002). Republicans also found it easier to recruit a few high-quality candidates for highly visible statewide offices than to recruit a stable of candidates for lower-level offices, such as state legislator, which accounts for their earlier success in prominent statewide races, such as for governor or U.S. senator (Aistrup 1996, 183–210; Bullock 1988; Lublin 2004, 79–80; Martorano, Anderson, and Hamm 2000). The top-down nature of Republican growth was both an outgrowth of the structural situation that Republicans confronted and a consequence of a deliberate party strategy that sought to use party resources in the most efficient manner (Aistrup 1996, 69–70).

Assessing Party Competition

Drawing upon the criteria for assessing competition discussed previously and on the findings of the studies reviewed above, we can attempt a systematic and comprehensive assessment of the level of political party competition in the contemporary South. As I discussed earlier, the division of the vote is one indicator of party competition; the closer the overall vote is to a 50–50 split, the more competitive the system. From this standpoint the South is now competitive—but not highly so—for the more prominent offices. Recent gains by Republicans have eliminated the gap between presidential and congressional voting and produced a Republican advantage across several offices. A good way of examining the vote division is to consider results pooled over a four-year election cycle, a method that evens out some of the random fluctuations that occur from year to year and also includes one gubernatorial and at least one senatorial election for each state in each cycle. In the last two four-year election cycles, 1996–99 and 2000–2003, southern voters were as likely to cast a Republican vote for governor, U.S. representative, or U.S. senator as they were to cast a vote for Dole or Bush in the presidential races (Prysby 2004). In state legislative elections, however, voters remained more inclined to vote Democratic.

By the start of the twenty-first century, the two-party vote division was competitive across a range of offices, which was not the case two decades before. The Republican share of the vote in presidential, congressional, and gubernatorial elections during the late 1990s and early 2000s hovered around 55 percent, which still represented a reasonably competitive party system, albeit one with a Republican advantage. Also, many scholars found that the Democratic advantage in state legislative elections was steadily eroding, a process that has been making these elections more competitive (Anderson 1997; Lublin 2004, 46–53; Lublin and Voss 2000; Shaffer, Pierce, and Kohnke 2000). One can see in the trends of the past decade the possibility of the Democrats becoming a more clearly minority party in the future, but such a development is far from certain.

It is equally important to examine control of office to determine competition. Using this measure yields a picture of greater competition than does looking at vote percentages alone. Although Democrats have averaged only around 45 percent of the vote in recent senatorial and gubernatorial elections, there has been enough variability in the vote division over time and across states to produce a number of Democratic victories. Democrats won one-third of the Senate elections held from 1996 to 2002 and 40 percent of the gubernatorial elections held from 1996 to 2003. Moreover, Democrats won at least one of these prominent statewide offices in every state save Texas during the years 1996–2003. Democrats also have been able to win over 40 percent of the U.S. House seats in the region in recent years. Farther down the ballot, Democrats have been more successful. At the beginning of 2001 they constituted about 60 percent of the state legislators in the region. Republicans controlled both houses of the state legislature in only two states, and in two others they controlled one house, while Democrats controlled both state legislative houses in seven of the eleven southern states.

It also is desirable to examine alternation of control of office in order to determine party competition. To examine this we can focus on two prominent statewide offices, governor and U.S. senator. Change in control of these offices occurred only in a small minority of elections in earlier decades but more frequently in later years. Over one-half of the gubernatorial elections held after 1991 were elections in which the office changed party hands. Every state except Georgia has had at least three changes in party control of the governorship (Democrat to Republican to Democrat to Republican) during the post–World War II era, and eight states have had two changes in party control of the governorship since 1989. U.S. Senate elections have displayed less change in party control, perhaps because of the greater importance of incumbency. Nevertheless, of the sixteen senate elections held in 2000 and 2002, four involved a change of party control (two each way). All this suggests that there is sufficient volatility in the vote to allow either party to win prominent statewide offices, at least when conditions are favorable. Control of the state legislature has changed party hands much less frequently, but this in part reflects the fact that Republicans have only recently become highly competitive in state legislative elections in many states. It is very likely that there will be more alternation in control of state legislative houses in the next decade.

Overall, the conclusions of scholars that the contemporary South is a competitive region seem supported by the data reported in a variety of studies. Despite the widespread concern with competition and the willingness of scholars to provide summary evaluations of competition, however, there are significant shortcomings in the treatment of party competition in the existing literature. Most notable is the lack of an attempt to measure party competition systematically and comprehensively. One exception is Lamis (1999a), who employed the index developed by David (1972). The David index has its limitations, as it uses only the vote division and covers only three offices. As I have suggested here, a good measure of party competition should include both the division of the popular vote and control of offices, and it should encompass a range of offices. Clearly, there is room in future research on southern political parties for more systematic and comprehensive attempts to measure levels of party competition. Better measures of party competition should allow us more precisely to identify changes in competition over time and differences in competition among states in the region.

Party System Cleavages

Realignment in the South has done more than alter the competitive balance between the two parties. It has greatly altered the substantive sources of party cleavages, in terms of both the social base of each party's support and the programmatic distinctions between the parties. This development has been extensively analyzed in the literature, and we have a clear picture of how party system cleavages have been altered. These aspects of party cleavages may be viewed from the perspective of the party in the electorate, the party in government, and the party organizational activists.

Party in the Electorate

At the time that Key (1949) wrote his masterpiece on southern politics, the differences between the two parties in the South were difficult to determine, even though partisan differences at the national level were clearly present. Voting was not significantly based on major social divisions in the population. Some racial differences in voting existed, but blacks were largely excluded from voting in the late 1940s. Class and religious differences in voting were extremely weak. There were some clear regional voting patterns—for example, areas of Republican strength in the mountain areas of Virginia, North Carolina, and Tennessee—but these regional patterns often reflected nineteenth-century conflicts rather than contemporary divisions over public policy.

A half century later the situation is much different. The social bases of party cleavages now are much more sharply defined. Race, religion, and socioeconomic status all help to distinguish Democratic voters from Republican ones. More important, partisans divide over a number of areas, including race-related, social, and economic and social welfare issues. Though the two parties are still diverse, a necessary feature if they wish to capture a majority of the vote, they are more cohesive and distinct than they were before.

We can start by examining changes in how social factors are tied to partisan choice. First of all, race has emerged as the most important social factor affecting voting (Black and Black 1992, 217–37; 2002, 244–49; Glaser 1996, 16–23; Lamis 1984, 31–39; Shafer and Johnston 2001; Wattenberg 1991). Democrats now routinely win around 90 percent of the black vote, while Republicans usually capture a majority of the white vote. Furthermore, blacks now constitute about one-fifth of the southern electorate, so their electoral significance is far greater than it was a half century ago. The sharp racial division between the parties appeared after the civil rights revolution of the 1960s, although southern whites took longer to shift their voting patterns for lower-level offices than they did for those at the top of the ticket. It is beyond the scope of this chapter to discuss the complicated story behind the emergence of these racial divisions, but that topic is discussed in a number of studies (Black and Black 1987; Glaser 1996; Scher 1997) and in other chapters in this volume.

In addition to race, religion has become an important factor in voting behavior, as religious and evangelical voters have disproportionately supported Republicans. This cleavage did not clearly emerge until the 1980s, and the dynamics of this conflict are too complicated to recount in this study. Chapter 6 in this volume provides a more thorough discussion of this topic. The important points that need to be made here are that this religious cleavage involves both religious affiliation and religiosity and that it is limited to white voters. Republicans do better among white evangelical Protestants than among white mainstream Protestants (a similar split does not hold for blacks) and better among whites who are more religious than among those who are less religious (Baker 1990; Baker, Steed, and Moreland 1998; Green 2002; Green, Kellstedt, Smidt, and Guth 2003).

Finally, socioeconomic status has become a basis for partisan choice. Even among whites, those who are poorer are more likely to vote Democratic (Black and Black 2002, 244–66; Nadeau and Stanley 1993; Petrocik 1987; Wattenberg 1991). When blacks and whites are considered together, the relationship between socioeconomic status and partisan choice strengthens. These class cleavages in voting emerged in the 1950s in presidential voting (Bartley and Graham 1975, 86–92). During the 1960s this relationship disappeared and even sometimes reversed itself, as lower-class whites sometimes provided more support for Republicans than did higher-class whites, a fact that can be explained by the greater conservatism of lower-class whites on race-related and social issues (Bartley and Graham 1975, 111–35). In recent decades, however, the class cleavage has reverted to the pattern that has more generally characterized the party system nationally since the New Deal (Black and Black 2002, 244–66; Nadeau and Stanley 1993; Petrocik 1987; Wattenberg 1991). The emergence of class cleavages in the southern electorate can be attributed to several developments, especially economic development (urbanization and industrialization) and declining racial conflict (Black and Black 1987; Nadeau and Stanley 1993).

The clear presence of racial, religious, and class cleavages in voting behavior means that the major social divisions of the population are reflected in the party system. There are other social divisions, such as gender, that influence partisan choice, but the factors that divide the southern population the most, socially and politically, are race, religion, and class. If it is desirable to have major societal divisions reflected in party cleavages, a position supported by a number of scholars of comparative political parties, then this development in the southern party system is a positive one.

Ideological cleavages also have emerged. Republicans identify themselves as conservatives much more than do Democrats (Black and Black 1987, 249–56; 1992, 220–34; Carmines and Stanley 1990; Cowden 2001; Knuckey 2001). This new alignment of ideology and partisanship developed partly through conversion and partly through replacement (Carmines and Stanley 1990; Wattenberg 1991). Many conservative white voters ceased to identify themselves as Democrats, becoming either Independents or Republicans, a process of conversion that sometimes operated slowly. Younger voters entering the electorate in the post–civil rights era generally had less firmly established party loyalties and were more likely to align along class lines than the older members of the electorate whom they were replacing. Even when older, conservative white Democrats retained their party identification, they became unreliable Democratic voters (Black and Black 2002, 243). Migration also may have contributed to the emergence of class cleavages, as northern upper-class migrants to the South tended to be Republicans. Furthermore, the ideological differences between Democratic and Republican voters now involve the full range of policy issues—economic and social welfare issues, race-related issues, social issues, and even foreign policy and defense issues (Knuckey 2001; Lublin 2004, 172–216). The breakup of the Solid South may have been precipitated by civil rights issues, but the current party cleavages go far beyond that one dimension. In many ways southern and northern party cleavages have converged, so that we have more truly national cleavages than in the past (Cowden 2001; Petrocik 1987; Prysby 1989).

Party in Government

Party differences at the elite level also were blurred in the Solid South. The Democratic Party may have been the party of white supremacy, but Republicans at that time hardly championed civil rights. There were some notable populists among southern Democrats, and some among mountain Republicans as well, but for the most part the Democrats and Republicans supported business interests equally well. The lack of pronounced policy differences between Democratic and Republican candidates and officeholders was a major reason that the southern electorate was not divided by clear ideological or policy cleavages at that time.

A half century after the demise of the Solid South, clear policy differences now exist between Democratic and Republican officeholders and candidates. We can most easily see these differences among members of Congress, as we have considerable data on their voting behavior in Congress. A number of studies have analyzed the changes in congressional voting patterns, and they all have found that southern Democratic members of Congress have moved closer to northern Democrats, creating a large gap between themselves and southern Republican members (Berard 2001, 111–20; Lublin 2004, 184–89; Whitby and Gilliam 1991; Wink and Hayes 2001). These changes resulted in part from the replacement of conservative southern Democrats by more liberal Democrats, but they also were due to southern congressional Democrats altering their voting patterns, shifts that can be attributed to changes in the composition of their districts (Berard 2001, 143–74; Whitby and Gilliam 1991). More detail on these changes can be found in chapter 10 of this volume.

Systematic data on ideological and policy differences in state government elections, such as for governor or for the state legislature, are more difficult to obtain. Discussions of contemporary politics in individual southern states, however, suggest that clearer differences between Democratic and Republican candidates are appearing at that level as well (Bullock and Rozell 2003b; Lamis 1999b). Unfortunately, discussions of this topic are often based on less systematic analyses. Much could be done to improve our understanding of party differences at the state government level. For example, it would be useful to learn how Democratic and Republican gubernatorial candidates differ on the issues that they stress in campaigns or on the policies that they pursue when in office. Similarly, we have a great deal to learn about the ideological differences of Democratic and Republican state legislators, a topic that should become more important as state legislative elections become more competitive.

Party Organizational Activists

Two surveys of county-level party activists conducted in 1991 and 2001 provide ample information on the ideological and issue orientations of those who are involved in the party organization (Clark and Prysby 2003, 2004; Hadley and Bowman 1995, 1998; Steed, Clark, Bowman, and Hadley 1998). The key points for our purposes can be briefly summarized. First, in 1991 there already were substantial differences between Democratic and Republican activists (Brodsky and Cotter 1998; McGlennon 1998; Steed 1998). Republicans were clearly conservative; over 80 percent identified themselves as such. Democrats were fairly diverse; about 35 percent called themselves liberal, about 35 percent moderate, and about 30 percent conservative. Ten years later the differences had grown considerably (Cotter and Fisher 2004). Our most recent data show that nearly all Republican activists now claim to be conservative, and over one-half say that they are very conservative. Fewer than one-fifth of the Democratic activists call themselves conservative, and over 40 percent classify themselves as liberal. While Democratic activists still have somewhat mixed orientations in contrast to the clearly conservative orientation of Republicans, there is a very deep ideological gap between the two groups. These overall ideological differences are nicely reflected in differences on domestic issue positions. In the 2001 survey Democratic and Republican activists disagreed sharply on a wide range of issues (Cotter and Fisher 2004).

Summary of Party System Cleavages

The southern party system now has clear cleavages between the parties. The two parties are more ideologically distinct and more ideologically cohesive than they were several decades ago. Democrats are more liberal and Republicans are more conservative, regardless of whether we are talking about voters, politicians, or party activists, although it is likely that the party activists are the most ideologically divided and the voters the least divided. Further, important social cleavages in the electorate—race, religion, and class—are now reflected in party differences, also a change from earlier decades. Party cleavages in the South are now fairly similar to those in the North, which was not the case decades ago.

Party Organizational Strength

A third feature of a political party system involves the strength and nature of the party organizations. This aspect of the southern political party system has been studied much less than the growth of competition or the development of party cleavages, but enough work has been done to provide us with some evidence of the changes that have occurred in the party organizations. As I discussed earlier, we can assess party organizational strength by examining resources (money and people) and activities (electoral and organizational maintenance). Furthermore, we should look at both the state party organizations and the grassroots organizations at the county level, as there can be enormous differences in organizational development between these two levels.

Before the development of a competitive two-party South, neither party had a strong state party organization. The Republicans were too weak to support a strong organization, and the Democrats were too dominant to need one, not to mention that a strong state party organization could even be seen as threatening in the factionalized Democratic Party. In the 1970s and 1980s stronger state party organizations began to emerge; Republicans were often first, but Democrats were usually quick to respond to the growing Republican threat. The development of state party organizations varied considerably from one state to another; discussions of state party organizational development in individual states are in Appleton and Ward (1997), Clark and Prysby (2003), and Hadley and Bowman (1995). Unfortunately, the treatment of this topic varies considerably among these books, partly because it was not their primary focus. From what has been reported, it appears that in most states both parties have established a permanent state headquarters, with a permanent staff and a sizable budget. Moreover, the state parties provide services to candidates, including assistance with fund-raising, campaign training, and voter mobilization efforts.

Some systematic evidence on the strength of state party organizations is provided by Aldrich (2000), who reports the results of his national survey of state party chairs. His data show that both parties are significantly better organized now than they were two decades ago. Moreover, the southern state party organizations compare favorably to those in other regions. Republicans seem better organized than Democrats in the South, although that could be a result of the fact that Aldrich's survey received responses from all eleven southern Democratic state party chairs but from only five Republican chairs. Another discussion of the development of state party organizations is provided by Aistrup (1996), who examined data collected by Cotter and his colleagues (1984). His analysis is useful for understanding earlier development of state party organizations, but it does not include the critical decades of the 1980s and 1990s. Aistrup also examined the development of county party organizations, and he concluded that though Republicans emphasized the building of county organizations in the 1950s, the emphasis shifted to state organizations in the late 1960s. It was not until the 1980s that attention was again turned to developing grassroots organizations (Aistrup 1996, 71–85).

The best data that we have on local political party organizations in the South come from the surveys of grassroots party activists cited above. These studies are discussed in more detail in chapter 2 in this volume, so the relevant points will be briefly summarized here. The 1991 survey found substantial activity at the county level. County chairs and other members of the county executive committee both rated many activities as important parts of their job and reported activities in these areas (Brodsky and Brodsky 1998; Clark, Lockerbie, and Wielhouwer 1998; Feigert and Todd 1998). These included both campaign activities (for example, registering and mobilizing voters, distributing campaign materials) and organizational maintenance activities (such as having regular meetings, raising money). Since comparable surveys were not conducted before 1991, it is difficult to judge how much a change from earlier periods the 1991 figures represent, but the estimate is that the increase was considerable. The increase seems particularly significant for Republicans, as they reported somewhat higher levels of activity than did Democratic activists (Brodsky and Brodsky 1998; Clark, Lockerbie, and Wielhouwer 1998; Feigert and Todd 1998). Moreover, Democrats generally had relatively stronger grassroots organizations than Republicans in earlier decades, if for no other reason than that Republican organizations were extremely weak in many areas, so the current level of Democratic grassroots organizational activity undoubtedly represents less of an increase than we find among Republicans. The 2001 data indicate that the local parties not only remain reasonably active but have increased their activity levels somewhat (Hogan 2004). These data also indicate that Republicans remain more active, although the differences are not that great and Democrats narrowed the gap during the 1990s (Bruce and Clark 2004; Hogan 2004).

Although the work that has been done on southern political party organizations is notable, many questions have not been fully answered. More information on organizational activity at both the state and local levels would help to fill in the gaps in our knowledge. Also, more study of how party organizations interact with candidates and elected officials would advance our understanding of the role played by contemporary parties. The relative lack of work on these aspects of the southern party system, especially when compared with what has been done on party competition and party system cleavages, undoubtedly reflects the greater difficulty of obtaining appropriate data. It also may be that in an era of candidate-centered elections, party organizations appear less worthy of study. Yet the work that has been done indicates that this is a fruitful area for further research. Moreover, such research will contribute to our understanding of American political parties generally, not just to our knowledge of southern politics.

Conclusion

In the last half of the twentieth century a new party system emerged in the South. We currently have not just a competitive two-party system, but also a party system in which party cleavages are much more clearly drawn along major social divisions, including race, religion, and social class. Furthermore, the parties are now more ideologically distinct, in terms of both the orientations of their supporters in the electorate and the orientations of party elites and officeholders. These social and ideological cleavages, which reinforce each other, make the southern party system similar to the party system in the rest of the nation.

Growing party competition has been accompanied by stronger state party organizations. Republican Party organizations improved the most and in most places improved first. But Democrats generally were quick to respond, building up their own state party organizations. Thus, candidates now are able to rely on their party's greater campaign support than in the past, although campaigns still remain highly centered on the candidates. Party organizations also display life between elections, a sign of organizational institutionalization.

In sum, the southern political party system is far closer to the responsible party model than it was a half century ago. Of course, this is in large part because of the extraordinary weakness of the party system at that time. Still, scholars who feel that democracy requires strong political parties will find much to applaud in the developments that have taken place in the region, as well as much to study in the new South.

Note: I gratefully acknowledge the research assistance of two University of North Carolina–Greensboro students, Michelle Anifant and Jon Rogowski, and the advice and comments of Bill Crowther, a faculty colleague at the University of North Carolina–Greensboro.

References

Aistrup, Joseph A. 1996. *The Southern Strategy Revisited: Republican Top-Down Advancement in the South.* Lexington: University Press of Kentucky.

Aldrich, John H. 1995. *Why Parties? The Origin and Transformation of Party Politics in America.* Chicago: University of Chicago Press.

———. 2000. "Southern Parties in State and Nation." *Journal of Politics* 62: 643–70.

American Political Science Association. Committee on Political Parties, 1950. *Toward a More Responsible Two-Party System. A Report of the Committee on Political Parties of the American Political Science Association.* New York: Rinehart.

Anderson, R. Bruce. 1997. "Electoral Competition and Southern State Legislatures." In *Southern Political Parties and Elections: Studies in Regional Political Change,* ed. Robert P. Steed, Laurence W. Moreland, and Tod A. Baker. Tuscaloosa: University of Alabama Press.

Appleton, Andrew M., and Daniel S. Ward, eds. 1997. *State Party Profiles.* Washington, D.C.: Congressional Quarterly Press.

Baker, Tod A. 1990. "The Emergence of the Religious Right and the Development of the Two-Party System in the South." In *Political Parties in the Southern States: Party Activists in Partisan Coalitions,* ed. Tod A. Baker, Charles D. Hadley, Robert P. Steed, and Laurence W. Moreland. New York: Praeger.

Baker, Tod A., Robert P. Steed, and Laurence W. Moreland. 1998. "Culture Wars and Religion in the South: The Changing Character of the Party Struggle." In *Party Activists in Southern Politics: Mirrors and Makers of Change*, ed. Charles D. Hadley and Lewis Bowman. Knoxville: University of Tennessee Press.

Bartley, Numan V., and Hugh D. Graham. 1975. *Southern Politics and the Second Reconstruction*. Baltimore: Johns Hopkins University Press.

Bass, Jack, and Walter DeVries. 1976. *The Transformation of Southern Politics: Social Change and Political Consequence since 1945*. New York: Basic Books.

Beck, Paul Allen. 1977. "Partisan Dealignment in the Postwar South." *American Political Science Review* 71: 477–96.

Berard, Stanley P. 2001. *Southern Democrats in the U.S. House of Representatives*. Norman: University of Oklahoma Press.

Bibby, John F. 1998. "Party Organizations, 1946–1996." In *Partisan Approaches to Postwar American Politics*, ed. Byron Shafer. New York: Chatham House.

Bielasiak, Jack. 2002. "The Institutionalization of Electoral and Party Systems in Postcommunist States." *Comparative Politics* 34: 189–210.

Black, Earl, and Merle Black. 1987. *Politics and Society in the South*. Cambridge: Harvard University Press.

———. 1992. *The Vital South: How Presidents Are Elected*. Cambridge: Harvard University Press.

———. 2002. *The Rise of Southern Republicans*. Cambridge: Harvard University Press.

Broder, David. 1971. *The Party's Over.* New York: Harper and Row.

Brodsky, David, and Simeon Brodsky. 1998. "Communication Patterns." In *Party Organization and Activism in the American South*, ed. Robert P. Steed, John A. Clark, Lewis Bowman, and Charles D. Hadley. Tuscaloosa: University of Alabama Press.

Brodsky, David M., and Patrick R. Cotter. 1998. "Political Issues and Political Parties." In *Party Activists in Southern Politics: Mirrors and Makers of Change*, ed. Charles D. Hadley and Lewis Bowman. Knoxville: University of Tennessee Press.

Bruce, John M., and John A. Clark. 2004. "Organizational Activity and Communication: More Vibrant Southern Grassroots Organizations?" In *Southern Political Party Activists: Patterns of Conflict and Change, 1991–2001*, ed. John A. Clark and Charles Prysby. Lexington: University Press of Kentucky.

Bullock, Charles S., III. 1988. "Regional Realignment from an Officeholding Perspective." *Journal of Politics* 50: 553–74.

Bullock, Charles S., III, and Mark J. Rozell. 2003a, 2nd ed. "Introduction to Southern Politics in the Twenty-first Century." *The New Politics of the Old South: An Introduction to Southern Politics*, ed. Charles S. Bullock III and Mark J. Rozell. Lanham, Md.: Rowman and Littlefield.

———, eds. 2003b, 2nd ed. *The New Politics of the Old South: An Introduction to Southern Politics*. Lanham, Md.: Rowman and Littlefield.

Burnham, Walter. 1970. *Critical Elections and the Mainsprings of American Politics.* New York: W. W. Norton.

Campbell, Bruce A. 1977. "Change in the Southern Electorate." *American Journal of Political Science* 21: 37–64.

Carmines, Edward G., and Harold W. Stanley. 1990. "Ideological Realignment in the Contemporary South: Where Have All the Conservatives Gone?" In *The Disappearing South? Studies in Regional Change and Continuity,* ed. Robert P. Steed, Laurence W. Moreland, and Tod. A. Baker. Tuscaloosa: University of Alabama Press.

Chambers, William Nisbet, and Walter Dean Burnham, eds. 1975, 2nd ed. *American Party Systems: Political Stages of Development.* New York: Oxford University Press.

Clark, John A., Brad Lockerbie, and Peter W. Wielhouwer. 1998. "Campaign Activities." In *Party Organization and Activism in the American South,* ed. Robert P. Steed, John A. Clark, Lewis Bowman, and Charles D. Hadley. Tuscaloosa: University of Alabama Press.

Clark, John, and Charles Prysby, eds. 2003. "Southern Grassroots Party Activists." Special issue, *American Review of Politics.*

————, eds. 2004. *Southern Political Party Activists: Patterns of Conflict and Change, 1991–2001.* Lexington: University Press of Kentucky.

Cohen, Jeffrey E., Richard Fleisher, and Paul Kantor, eds. 2001. *American Political Parties: Decline or Resurgence?* Washington, D.C.: Congressional Quarterly Press.

Coleman, John J. 1996a. *Party Decline in America.* Princeton: Princeton University Press.

————. 1996b, 2nd ed. "Resurgent or Just Busy? Party Organization in Contemporary America." In *The State of the Parties: The Changing Role of Contemporary American Parties,* ed. John C. Green and Daniel M. Shea. Lanham, Md.: Rowman and Littlefield.

————. 2003, 4th ed. "Responsible, Functional, or Both? American Political Parties and the APSA Report after Fifty Years." In *The State of the Parties: The Changing Role of American Contemporary Parties,* ed. John C. Green and Rick Farmer. Lanham, Md.: Rowman and Littlefield.

Converse, Philip E. 1963. "On the Possibility of Major Political Realignment in the South." In *Change in the Contemporary South,* ed. Allan P. Sindler. Durham, N.C.: Duke University Press.

Cosman, Bernard. 1966. *Five States for Goldwater: Continuity and Change in Southern Presidential Voting Patterns.* Tuscaloosa: University of Alabama Press.

Cotter, Cornelius P., James L. Gibson, John F. Bibby, and Robert J. Huckshorn, eds. 1984. *Party Organizations in American Politics.* New York: Praeger.

Cotter, Patrick R., and Samuel H. Fisher III. 2004. "A Growing Divide: Issue Opinions of Southern Party Activists." In *Southern Political Party Activists: Patterns of Conflict and Change, 1991–2001,* ed. John A. Clark and Charles Prysby. Lexington: University Press of Kentucky.

Cowden, Jonathan A. 2001. "Southernization of the Nation and Nationalization of the South: Racial Conservatism, Social Welfare, and White Partisans in the United States, 1956–92." *British Journal of Political Science* 31: 277–302.

Crotty, William J. 1984, 2nd ed. *American Parties in Decline*. Boston: Little, Brown.

———. 1986. "Local Parties in Chicago: The Machine in Transition." In *Political Parties in Local Areas*, ed. William J. Crotty. Knoxville: University of Tennessee Press.

David, Paul T. 1972. *Party Strength in the United States, 1872–1970*. Charlottesville: University of Virginia Press.

———. 1992. "The APSA Committee on Political Parties." *Perspectives on Political Science* 21: 70–79.

Evans, Geoffrey, and Stephan Whitefield. 1993. "Identifying the Bases of Party Competition in East Europe." *British Journal of Political Science* 23: 521–48.

Feigert, Frank B., and John R. Todd. 1998. "Party Maintenance Activities." In *Party Organization and Activism in the American South*, ed. Robert P. Steed, John A. Clark, Lewis Bowman, and Charles D. Hadley. Tuscaloosa: University of Alabama Press.

Frendreis, John P., James L. Gibson, and Laura L. Vertz. 1990. "The Electoral Relevance of Local Party Organizations." *American Political Science Review* 84: 225–35.

Gatlin, Douglas S. 1975. "Party Identification, Status, and Race in the South: 1952–1972." *Public Opinion Quarterly* 39: 39–51.

Gibson, James L., Cornelius P. Cotter, John F. Bibby, and Robert J. Huckshorn. 1983. "Assessing Party Organizational Strength." *American Journal of Political Science* 27: 193–222.

———. 1985. "Whither the Local Parties? A Cross-Sectional and Longitudinal Analysis of the Strength of Party Organizations." *American Journal of Political Science* 29: 139–60.

Gibson, James L., John P. Frendreis, and Laura L. Vertz. 1989. "Party Dynamics in the 1980s: Change in County Party Organizational Strength, 1980–1984." *American Journal of Political Science* 33: 67–90.

Glaser, James M. 1996. *Race, Campaign Politics, and the Realignment in the South*. New Haven: Yale University Press.

Green, John C. 2002. "Believers for Bush, Godly for Gore: Religion and the 2000 Election in the South." In *The 2000 Presidential Election in the South: Partisanship and Southern Party Systems in the 21st Century*, ed. Robert P. Steed and Laurence W. Moreland. Westport, Conn.: Praeger.

Green, John C., and Rick Farmer, eds. 2003, 4th ed. *The State of the Parties: The Changing Role of Contemporary American Parties*. Lanham, Md.: Rowman and Littlefield.

Green, John C., and Paul S. Herrnson. 2002. "Party Development in the Twentieth Century: Laying the Foundations for Responsible Party Government." In *Responsible Partnership? The Evolution of American Political Parties since 1950*, ed. John C. Green and Paul S. Herrnson. Lawrence: University Press of Kansas.

Green, John C., Lyman A. Kellstedt, Corwin E. Smidt, and James L. Guth. 2003, 2nd ed. "The Soul of the South: Religion and Southern Politics at the Millennium." In *The New Politics of the Old South: An Introduction to*

Southern Politics, ed. Charles S. Bullock III and Mark J. Rozell. Lanham, Md.: Rowman and Littlefield.

Green, John C., and Daniel M. Shea, eds. 1999, 3rd ed. *The State of the Parties: The Changing Role of Contemporary American Parties*. Lanham, Md.: Rowman and Littlefield.

Hadley, Charles D., and Lewis Bowman, eds. 1995. *Southern State Party Organizations and Activists*. Westport, Conn.: Praeger.

———, eds. 1998. *Party Activists in Southern Politics: Mirrors and Makers of Change*. Knoxville: University of Tennessee Press.

Havard, William C., ed. 1972. *The Changing Politics of the South*. Baton Rouge: Louisiana State University Press.

Heard, Alexander. 1952. *A Two-Party South?* Chapel Hill: University of North Carolina Press.

Herrnson, Paul S. 1988. *Party Campaigning in the 1980s*. Cambridge: Harvard University Press.

———. 1992. "Why the United States Does Not Have Responsible Parties." *Perspectives in Political Science* 21: 91–99.

Hogan, Robert E. 2003. "Candidate Perceptions of Political Party Campaign Activity in State Legislative Elections." *State Politics and Policy Quarterly* 2: 66–85.

———. 2004. "Party Activists in Election Campaigns." In *Southern Political Party Activists: Patterns of Conflict and Change, 1991–2001*, ed. John A. Clark and Charles L. Prysby. Lexington: University Press of Kentucky.

Hopkins, Anne H. 1986. "Campaign Activities and Local Party Organization in Nashville." In *Political Parties in Local Areas*, ed. William J. Crotty. Knoxville: University of Tennessee Press.

Huckshorn, Robert J., James L. Gibson, Cornelius P. Cotter, and John F. Bibby. 1986. "Party Integration and Party Organizational Strength." *Journal of Politics* 48: 976–91.

Jackson, John S., III, Barbara L. Brown, and David Bositis. 1982. "Herbert McClosky and Friends Revisited: 1980 Democratic and Republican Party Elites Compared to the Mass Public." *American Politics Quarterly* 10: 158–80.

Jackson, John S., III, and Nancy L. Clayton. 1996, 2nd ed. "Leaders and Followers: Major Party Elites, Identifiers, and Issues, 1980–92." In *The State of the Parties: The Changing Role of Contemporary American Parties*, ed. John C. Green and Daniel M. Shea. Lanham, Md.: Rowman and Littlefield.

Kayden, Xandra, and Eddie Mahe Jr. 1985. *The Party Goes On*. New York: Basic Books.

Key, V. O., Jr. 1949. *Southern Politics in State and Nation*. New York: Knopf.

———. 1955. "A Theory of Critical Elections." *Journal of Politics* 17: 3–18.

———. 1959. "Secular Realignment and the Party System." *Journal of Politics* 21: 198–210.

Kirkpatrick, Jeane J. 1971. "Toward a More Responsible Two-Party System: Political Science, Policy Science, or Pseudo-Science?" *American Political Science Review* 65: 965–90.

Kitschelt, Herbert. 1992. "The Formation of Party Systems in East Central Europe." *Politics and Society* 20: 7–50.

Kitschelt, Herbert, Zdenka Mansfeldova, Radoslaw Markowski, and Gabor Toka. 1999. *Post-Communist Party Systems: Competition, Representation, and Inter-Party Cooperation.* Cambridge: Cambridge University Press.

Knuckey, Jonathan. 2000. "Explaining Republican Success in Southern U.S. House Elections in the 1990s." *American Review of Politics* 21: 179–200.

———. 2001. "Ideological Realignment and Partisan Change in the American South, 1972–1996." *Politics and Policy* 29: 337–60.

Ladd, Everett Carll, Jr. 1970. *American Political Parties: Social Change and Political Response.* New York: W. W. Norton.

Ladd, Everett Carll, Jr., and Charles D. Hadley. 1978, 2nd ed. *Transformations of the American Party System.* New York: W. W. Norton.

Lamis, Alexander P. 1984. *The Two-Party South.* New York: Oxford University Press.

———. 1999a. "Southern Politics in the 1990s." In *Southern Politics in the 1990s,* ed. Alexander P. Lamis. Baton Rouge: Louisiana State University Press.

———, ed. 1999b. *Southern Politics in the 1990s.* Baton Rouge: Louisiana State University Press.

Lewis, Paul G. 2000. *Political Parties in Post-Communist Eastern Europe.* London: Routledge.

Lipset, Seymour M., and Stein Rokkan. 1967. "Cleavage Structures, Party Systems, and Voter Alignments: An Introduction." In *Party Systems and Voter Alignments,* ed. Seymour M. Lipset and Stein Rokkan. New York: Free Press.

Longley, Charles H. 1980. "National Party Renewal." In *Party Renewal in America: Theory and Practice,* ed. Gerald M. Pomper. New York: Praeger.

Lublin, David. 2004. *The Republican South: Democratization and Partisan Change.* Princeton: Princeton University Press.

Lublin, David, and D. Stephen Voss. 2000. "Racial Redistricting and Realignment in Southern State Legislatures." *American Journal of Political Science* 44: 792–810.

Maisel, L. Sandy, ed. 1998, 3rd ed. *The Parties Respond.* Boulder, Colo.: Westview Press.

Martorano, Nancy, R. Bruce Anderson, and Keith E. Hamm. 2000. "A Transforming South: Exploring Patterns of State House Seat Contestation." *American Review of Politics* 21: 201–23.

McClosky, Herbert, Paul J. Hoffman, and Rosemary O'Hara. 1960. "Issue Conflict and Consensus among Party Leaders and Followers." *American Political Science Review* 54: 406–29.

McGlennon, John J. 1998. "Ideology and the Southern Party Activist: Poles Apart or Reflecting the Polls?" In *Party Activists in Southern Politics: Mirrors and Makers of Change,* ed. Charles D. Hadley and Lewis Bowman. Knoxville: University of Tennessee Press.

Miller, Arthur H., Gwyn Erb, William M. Reisinger, and Vicki L. Hesli. 2000. "Emerging Party Systems in Post-Soviet Societies: Fact or Fiction?" *Journal of Politics* 62: 455–90.

Nadeau, Richard, and Harold W. Stanley. 1993. "Class Polarization in Partisanship among Native Southern Whites, 1952–90." *American Journal of Politi-
cal Science* 37: 900–919.
Olson, David M. 1998. "Party Formation and Party System Consolidation in the
New Democracies of Central Europe." *Political Studies* 46: 432–64.
Petrocik, John R. 1981. *Party Coalitions: Realignment and the Decline of the
New Deal Party System.* Chicago: University of Chicago Press.
———. 1987. "Realignment: New Party Coalitions and the Nationalization of
the South." *Journal of Politics* 49: 347–75.
Phillips, Kevin P. 1969. *The Emerging Republican Majority.* New Rochelle,
N.Y.: Arlington House.
Pomper, Gerald M. 1971. "Toward a More Responsible Two-Party System?
What? Again?" *Journal of Politics* 33: 916–40.
———, ed. 1980. *Party Renewal in America: Theory and Practice.* New York:
Praeger.
———. 2001. "Party Responsibility and the Future of American Democracy."
In *American Political Parties: Decline or Resurgence?* ed. Jeffrey E. Co-
hen, Richard Fleisher, and Paul Kantor. Washington, D.C.: Congressional
Quarterly Press.
Pomper, Gerald M., and Marc D. Weiner. 2002. "Toward a More Respon-
sible Two-Party Voter: The Evolving Bases of Partisanship." In *Responsible Partnership? The Evolution of American Political Parties since 1950,*
ed. John C. Green and Paul S. Herrnson. Lawrence: University Press of
Kansas.
Price, David E. 1984. *Bringing Back the Parties.* Washington, D.C.: Congressional Quarterly Press.
Pridham, Geoffrey, and Paul G. Lewis. 1996. "Introduction: Stabilizing Fragile Democracies and Party System Development." In *Stabilizing Fragile
Democracies: Comparing New Party Systems in Southern and Eastern Europe,* ed. Geoffrey Pridham and Paul G. Lewis. London: Routledge.
Prysby, Charles L. 1989. "The Structure of Southern Electoral Behavior."
American Politics Quarterly 17: 163–80.
———. 2000. "Southern Congressional Elections in the 1990s: The Dynamics
of Change." *American Review of Politics* 21: 155–78.
———. 2004. "Southern Political Party Development since World War II." Pa-
per presented at The Citadel Symposium on Southern Politics, Charleston,
S.C.
Rae, Nicol C. 1994. *Southern Democrats.* New York: Oxford University Press.
Ranney, Austin. 1951. "Toward a More Responsible Two-Party System: A Com-
mentary." *American Political Science Review* 45: 488–99.
———. 1965. "Parties in State Politics." In *Politics in the American States,* ed.
Herbert Jacob and Kenneth Vines. Boston: Little, Brown.
Sabato, Larry J., and Bruce Larson. 2002, 2nd ed. *The Party's Just Begun: Shap-
ing Political Parties for America's Future.* New York: Longman.
Sartori, Giovanni. 1976. *Parties and Party Systems: A Framework for Analysis.*
New York: Cambridge University Press.
Schattschneider, E. E. 1942. *Party Government.* New York: Rinehart.

Scher, Richard K. 1997, 2nd ed. *Politics in the New South*. Armonk, N.Y.: M. E. Sharpe.

Schlesinger, Joseph A. 1955. "A Two-Dimensional Scheme for Classifying the States According to Degree of Inter-Party Competition." *American Political Science Review* 49: 1120–28.

———. 1985. "The New American Political Party." *American Political Science Review* 79: 1152–69.

Schreiber, E. M. 1971. "'Where the Ducks Are': Southern Strategy versus Fourth Party." *Public Opinion Quarterly* 35: 157–67.

Shafer, Byron E., and Richard D. Johnston. 2001. "The Transformation of Southern Politics Revisited: The House of Representatives as a Window." *British Journal of Political Science* 31: 601–25.

Shaffer, Stephen D., Stacie Berry Pierce, and Steven A. Kohnke. 2000. "Party Realignment in the South: A Multi-Level Analysis." *American Review of Politics* 21: 129–54.

Stanley, Harold W. 1988. "Southern Partisan Changes: Dealignment, Realignment or Both?" *Journal of Politics* 50: 65–88.

———. 2002. "The South in the 2000 Elections." In *The 2000 Presidential Election in the South: Partisanship and Southern Party Systems in the 21st Century*, ed. Robert P. Steed and Laurence W. Moreland. Westport, Conn.: Praeger.

Steed, Robert P. 1998. "Parties, Ideology, and Issues: The Structuring of Political Conflict." In *Party Organization and Activism in the American South*, ed. Robert P. Steed, John A. Clark, Lewis Bowman, and Charles D. Hadley. Tuscaloosa: University of Alabama Press.

Steed, Robert P., John A. Clark, Lewis Bowman, and Charles D. Hadley, eds. 1998. *Party Organization and Activism in the American South*. Tuscaloosa: University of Alabama Press.

Strong, Donald S. 1963. "Durable Republicanism in the South." In *Change in the Contemporary South*, ed. Allan P. Sindler. Durham, N.C.: Duke University Press.

Sundquist, James L. 1983, rev. ed. *Dynamics of the Party System*. Washington, D.C.: Brookings Institution Press.

Swansbrough, Robert H., and David M. Brodsky, eds. 1988. *The South's New Politics: Realignment and Dealignment*. Columbia: University of South Carolina Press.

Walker, Michael. 1996. "Party Inheritances and Party Identities." In *Stabilizing Fragile Democracies: Comparing New Party Systems in Southern and Eastern Europe*, ed. Geoffrey Pridham and Paul G. Lewis. London: Routledge.

Wattenberg, Martin P. 1991. "The Building of a Republican Regional Base in the South: The Elephant Crosses the Mason-Dixon Line." *Political Opinion Quarterly* 55: 424–32.

———. 1994. *The Decline of American Political Parties, 1952–1992*. Cambridge: Harvard University Press.

Weisberg, Herbert F. 2002. "The Party in the Electorate as a Basis for More Responsible Parties." In *Responsible Partnership? The Evolution of Ameri-*

can Political Parties since 1950, ed. John C. Green and Paul S. Herrnson. Lawrence: University Press of Kansas.

Whitby, Kenny J., and Franklin D. Gilliam Jr. 1991. "A Longitudinal Analysis of Competing Explanations for the Transformation of Southern Congressional Politics." *Journal of Politics* 53: 504–18.

White, John Kenneth. 1992. "Responsible Party Government in America." *Perspectives on Political Science* 21: 80–90.

———. 2001. "Reviving the Political Parties: What Must Be Done?" In *The Politics of Ideas*, ed. John Kenneth White and John C. Green. Albany: State University of New York Press.

White, John Kenneth, and Jerome E. Mileur. 2002. "In the Spirit of Their Times: 'Toward a More Responsible Two-Party System' and Party Politics." In *Responsible Partnership? The Evolution of American Political Parties since 1950*, ed. John C. Green and Paul S. Herrnson. Lawrence: University Press of Kansas.

Wink, Kenneth A., and Allison L. Hayes. 2001. "Racial Redistricting and Ideological Polarization in Southern U.S. House Delegations." *Politics and Policy* 29: 361–84.

Wolfinger, Raymond, and Robert E. Arseneau. 1978. "Partisan Change in the South, 1952–1976." In *Political Parties: Development and Decay*, ed. Louis Maisel and Joseph Cooper. Beverly Hills: Sage.

★ **Chapter 2** ★

Who Wants to Party?

Activists and Changing Southern Politics

John J. McGlennon

IN MUCH OF THE LITERATURE on political parties in the twentieth-century United States, references to the role of activists generally came with a qualifier: "except in the South." Studies of southern politics devoted little attention to the organizational workers' efforts in party building and maintenance because there was little evidence of such activity. The growing body of research on party activists focused on places where competition was alive, which effectively precluded the states of the Confederacy until the 1960s at the earliest.

Early summaries of political party research treated the role of the party activist lightly. Although V. O. Key focused attention on party activists in his text *Politics, Parties and Pressure Groups* (1958), he acknowledged the lack of understanding about them. As he described them, activists are "the 'pros,' the 'politicians,' the amateur politicians—those who devote time and effort to the business of politics. How many such persons there are can only be guessed; they surely do not measure more than three or four million in an electorate of more than 100,000,000" (Key 1958, 345).

Even at that point there was a growing body of research focused on the street-level workers of political parties. Harold Gosnell (1937) had been a pioneer, surveying Chicago party committeemen to discern differences in background, education, and economic status and finding the party faithful to be of a lower socioeconomic class. His respondents reported their wide range of activities in maintaining an electoral "machine," from distributing food baskets to resolving domestic problems to fixing tickets and taxes to attending weddings and wakes.

Much of the effort to understand the role of the party activist took the individual city or a small sample of cities as the unit of analysis. For example, works by Bowman and Boynton (1964, 1966a, 1966b), Conway and Feigert (1968), Eldersveld (1964), Hirschfield, Swanson, and Blank (1962), and Ippolito (1969) used urban and suburban precinct activists to illuminate the characteristics of the party core, and Althoff and Patterson (1966) presented similar data on rural party workers. Their efforts variously produced evidence about the recruitment of party workers, their attitudes on issues and ideology, their motivations, and their long-term objectives.

James Q. Wilson's 1962 study of party activists in New York and Los Angeles in the 1950s documented the emergence of a new breed of party activists, attracted not by jobs or the promise of organizational favors but by ideology and issues, by candidates and causes. These "amateurs" were contrasted to the "professionals." Explanations for involvement in party politics for nonmaterial benefit were important in understanding the continued recruitment of workers to parties that were increasingly unable to guarantee jobs attractive enough to compel intense activity.

Studies of these organizations were conducted in areas where competition was a given: both parties had active cohorts of supporters working to produce dependable groups of voters. The one-party characteristics of the southern states made party organization seem less than an afterthought.

Key's 1949 study of the southern states devoted chapters to party organization and activity, although it mostly described their absence. In one memorable selection he recounted newspaper headlines that reported citizens' complete lack of interest in serving as party workers. Despite the dominance of the Democrats in the Old South, party committee slots went unfilled and organizations were moribund. Key noted that there was little purpose in organizing and mobilizing support for general elections, and so people interested in working in politics satisfied their impulse in candidate-centered or factional contests within the Democratic primaries and runoffs.

With no party organization to recruit new members and no campaigns to use their efforts, party activists were not a topic of interest in the study of southern politics before the 1960s. Though occasional references can be found in them, those studies were primarily focused on party roles in the few areas where party competition managed to remain, or where presidential politics provided attractive patronage possibilities.

Of course, it would be incorrect to assume that party organization thrived in communities outside the South in some uniform fashion. Key reported significant gaps in party organization nationally and noted that in many instances parties fill their organizational holes only in the midst of important election contests (1958, 375). Still, the South of the mid-twentieth century stands out for its lack of party structure.

Early Southern Research

The stirrings of southern party competition in presidential and statewide contests that began in the 1950s and 1960s created an environment in which party organization slowly took hold. Especially in fast-growing metropolitan areas, where migrants from other states (or regions) brought their electoral experience and party affiliation with them, we began to see the emergence of party activity.

An early effort to investigate the role of activists in party organizational development was William Crotty's survey of North Carolina county chairmen (1968). His analysis of a 1962–63 survey was presented as an effort to provide a base on which other studies across the country could build, but it also took into account the specific implications of party activism in a system just beginning to show the uneven development of organization in a predominantly Democratic state. Crotty provided a detailed analysis of the activities of county chairs, comparing interparty differences as well as intraparty distinctions based on the level of strength the party had in a county. This study was remarkable both for its effort at theory building and for its acknowledgment of the limitations of a single-state study. Crotty set out a number of propositions for further study and noted in particular the relationship between party electoral strength and organizational activity.

This attention to a political system in transition was significant as an effort to distinguish between the established organizations found in mature party-competitive areas and the newly emerging competition of the South. Although party fortunes in presidential politics were beginning to reverse, the extent to which this would carry down to lower-level offices was not at all clear.

The 1960s and 1970s were decades of upheaval in party organizations of the southern states. As the Solid South of presidential politics gave way to division, the region attracted far more attention from national parties. Deep South states such as Georgia, Alabama, South Carolina, and Mississippi went from Democratic to Republican to Independent in the three successive national elections of 1960, 1964, and 1968. Peripheral states such as Virginia, North Carolina, Tennessee, and Florida went from Republican to Democratic and back again in those same three contests.

As the electoral patterns were changing, so were the party affiliations of elected officials and activists. Some public officials switched parties, almost entirely from Democrats to Republicans, while a smaller number declared themselves unaffiliated with any party. Some Democrats were defeated or replaced by Republicans in areas that had previously been uncompetitive. Party activists likewise adapted to the new terrain, as some switched along with voters and elected officials, others withdrew from active involvement, and some stayed on with an organization now required to comply with a need for more activity without the guarantee of reward.

Especially in the context of party transformation in the South, then, there appeared some early efforts to explore change through the lens of party activists. For example, Charles Wiggins examined data from a national survey of state party chairs to test some of Key's hypotheses about southern party distinctiveness, finding in the process that activists at this level of party organizational structure differed little from region to region. He speculated that this reflected "the fact that southern electoral politics is becoming more competitive and more like national politics" (Wiggins 1973, 492). Similarly, a survey of county chairs in South Carolina and North Carolina found evidence that, in sharp contrast to the period of Key's research, the parties in those two states were beginning to structure issue discussion and political conflict (Baker and Steed 1974).

Still, these types of studies were rare and were typically limited to relatively small groups of party activists, often in narrowly defined geographic areas. They were important mainly because they rose out of party and political ferment that would create heightened interest conducive to further study of party activists in the region.

Surveying the Activists

The upheaval provided an opportunity to open another avenue of research on party activists, one that reflected the need for reexamination of the motivations of the party worker. The decision of Virginia Democrats to utilize a caucus and convention system for their 1978 senatorial nomination provided an unusual opportunity. Nominations for election in Virginia allowed parties considerable latitude. Under state law a political party had the right to designate whether a nomination for a state or local office would be carried out in a primary election or a party caucus or convention, except where an incumbent might insist on a primary.

Democrats in Virginia, like those in other states, had gone through several election cycles confronted with a divisive primary contest between conservative and liberal factions, only to lose to Republicans able to run from the left or the right depending on which faction won the primary. Opting out of the primary, Democrats elected grassroots activists to serve as convention delegates to nominate their candidate for an open U.S. Senate seat. Republicans, meanwhile, used their traditional convention method again, although in this case they managed to draw nearly eighty-five hundred delegates, who were attracted by the strong ideological appeal of Richard Obenshain, the deeply rooted party support for the GOP's first elected governor, Linwood Holton, and the celebrity of one candidate's spouse (John Warner's wife at the time was Elizabeth Taylor).

Surveying a sample of delegates to these two conventions presented the opportunity to examine the new composition of one transitional state's party activist cadre and to simultaneously explore the factors most important to them in selecting a candidate for office. The survey, with a follow-up mail questionnaire conducted after the general election, provided both insight into the changing party dynamics and the impetus to do a more broadly based examination of the role of the activists in the selection of party candidates.

This Virginia study (Abramowitz, McGlennon, and Rapoport 1981) examined activists who were empowered to nominate candidates for office and probed the relative importance of issue and ideological proximity versus electability, among other things. The success of this survey led to the development of a more comprehensive project.

The nominating convention delegates were not necessarily part of the ongoing organizational structure of the two parties in Virginia. In fact, significant numbers of both party convention delegates had not been members of their local committees before the convention. But these types of activists were about to become very important to both national parties as a source of recruitment to the organization and as decision makers in the most important decision made by a national party organization: who will represent it on the presidential ballot.

Though not specifically focused on the South, a follow-up project targeted several southern states. Under a National Science Foundation grant, the Workshop on Comparative State Party Activists identified a number of states using the caucus and convention method to select presidential nominating convention delegates. Political scientists in eleven states, including Virginia, Mississippi, South Carolina, and Texas, conducted surveys among state convention delegates. These surveys were analyzed on both a national and state-by-state basis, and they provided more insight into the questions of how party activism was changing and what motivations, incentives, and preferences guided their actions and choices.

The Citadel Symposium on Southern Politics played an important role in the development of this project, as several of the participants were recruited from among the organizers and presenters at the first two symposia, which were organized by Robert Steed, Laurence Moreland, and Tod Baker. Project participants collected more than seventeen thousand surveys during the 1980 nominating process and produced a number of papers and articles, as well as an edited volume on party activists (Rapoport, Abramowitz, and McGlennon 1986).

Among the work most relevant to the study of southern party activists were chapters on the variability among state party activists (Abramowitz, McGlennon, and Rapoport 1986a), the impact of migration on party activism (Moreland, Steed, and Baker 1986), issue and ideological factionalism (Brudney and McDonald 1986), and permeability of parties and party switching (Kweit and Kweit 1986). The state-to-state variations helped to document the degree to which party activists in the southern states were already moving toward much greater consistency with nonsouthern party members. Despite the long history of southern exceptionalism, the average ideological positioning of Democrats regardless of state was more liberal than that of their Republican counterparts, and Republicans across the board were more conservative than even the most conservative southern Democratic party activists.

The issue examination of the parties revealed the regional distinctions that can be found among the parties, as there was much more factional division in Democratic southern state parties and more consistency within the southern GOP than was found in their northern counterparts. Even with the ideological distinctions between the GOP and Democrats in all states, the southern Democrats in particular still retained a sizable number of conservatives with issue stances at some variance from their fellow party members.

With the influx of nonsoutherners to southern states, the increased activity of African Americans, and the reactivation of religiously oriented activism, the issue of party permeability took on special significance in the South. The delegate surveys allowed for the examination of both the degree to which such infusion had occurred and the effects that it was having on the states.

The replication of this study in six southern states in 1984, under the direction of Robert Steed, Laurence Moreland, and Tod Baker, offered an opportunity to monitor activism, especially with the reorientation of politics in southern states caused by the Reagan presidency and the Democratic candidacy of the Reverend Jesse Jackson. A major contribution of the book resulting from this study (Baker, Hadley, Steed, and Moreland 1990) was the identification of the constituencies of the presidential nominating conventions in the southern states. Here we see the differences between black and white delegates (Hadley and Stanley 1990; Steed 1990) and between women and men both within and across party lines (Darcy, Clark, and Hadley 1990), and we see evidence of the tendency of younger voters to support more nontraditional candidates and causes (Shaffer 1990).

While study of the delegates to presidential nomination conventions provided a valuable insight into the nature of political activists in the South and elsewhere, these party officials were of a specific type. They were in many cases drawn to political activism by a particular candidate or issue, unlike those who had historically staffed party positions on a more permanent basis. Party convention delegates have a short official tenure. While they may become part of the party's official organization and certainly are added to party mailing lists, they have no formal obligations or position beyond the state nominating convention. The conventions, however, also serve the purpose of recruiting new members to the organization. The surveys of both 1980 and 1984 allowed for the comparison of those who had been part of the organization before their election as delegates and those who were new to the process or only occasional participants. In fact, the differing paths followed by party activists after the conventions became yet another topic for consideration.

The focus on presidential-level activists, those who were elected by their local party caucuses to attend state conventions and select delegates to the national presidential nominating conventions, appropriately reflected the growing importance of presidential-level politics in the state parties. The growth of party competition in the South paralleled the increasingly candidate-centered politics of the late twentieth century. As party organizations began their early formation in some places and experienced widespread realignment in others, the driving forces were often presidential campaigns.

Presidential politics also raised another issue, at least in the initial stages of renewed party activist research: were there in fact dual-party systems, one focused on national candidates and issues, and the other a state party system in which the parties confronted a different landscape in races for state and local office? The attachment of party elites to their own parties was much more in question, especially for Democrats but also for Republicans who worked for GOP presidential candidates but returned to still-dominant Democratic Party organizations when it came time to back candidates for state legislature or county supervisor. This idea of dual-party systems was highlighted by Malcolm Jewell, who raised the concept in time to allow researchers to watch it recede as parties completed their realignments, though not before we were able to see how the parties differed in their "split" personalities (Clark and Lockerbie 1998).

Presidential activism and realignment ultimately permeated competition at all levels, and the Republican success in national contests eventually resulted in active and effective state and local Republican organizations. This focus led to a shift of attention away from presidential activists back to the local-level activists so prominently featured in nonsouthern research of earlier times.

Once again, The Citadel Symposium provided the venue for stimulating a collaborative effort to add to our understanding of party systems. Lewis Bowman, William Hulbary, and Anne Kelley presented research at the symposium on their survey of Florida party committee members, which they conducted again two years later. With the encouragement of the symposium's organizers, Robert Steed, Laurence Moreland, and Tod Baker, who conducted a parallel study in South Carolina, a core group of scholars led by Charles Hadley and Lewis Bowman devised a plan to conduct mail surveys of county chairs and precinct committee members in all eleven states of the South. The Southern Grassroots Party Activists Project ultimately produced a data set from 10,458 party activists in 1991. This sample differed from the presidential nominating activists in that it represented a group whose current involvement in party affairs was not driven by national candidates and issues, even if many of them were drawn into the party organization through the presidential contest.

This study provided the opportunity for some of the most extensive examination of party elites, not only in the South but in the nation as a whole. Ultimately, the project resulted in three edited volumes and an extensive number of conference papers, all illuminating important aspects of party organization and the role of activists. One volume (Hadley and Bowman 1995) focused on the individual states and their parties, providing the contextual information to understand better the changes occurring in the states and how parties were adapting to the new electoral environment of the South. The other volumes (Hadley and Bowman 1998; Steed, Clark, Bowman, and Hadley 1998) examined the incentives and motivations for activism and the changing nature of party work in the South.

These three volumes provided a rich pool of findings about a party system that was in the midst of significant transformation. But there was little doubt that the changes were not over and that the transitional nature of the parties deserved further investigation. That opportunity was fulfilled when Charles Prysby and John Clark organized the second Southern Grassroots Party Activists Project in 2001, with many of the original survey teams reprising their roles as participants in the decade-later follow-up. The result was an addition to the original data set that allowed comparison of party activists and organizations over a critical ten-year period during which the GOP became the dominant party in statewide and federal elections and made significant gains in state legislative elections (including gaining control of a number of legislative chambers).

At this point the 2001 data have resulted in the publication of a two-issue series in the *American Review of Politics* that analyzes change in party activism across the states and an edited volume looking more comprehensively at the transformation of party activism in the South between 1991 and 2001 (Clark and Prysby 2004). More exploration of the data is continuing, with a particular effort to identify the questions yet to be investigated and new directions for research that has provided enormous information on southern activism but that has as yet been unmatched by research in other regions.

Other recent efforts to analyze party activism have focused on the impact within each party; Nicol Rae (1994) and Joseph Aistrup (1996) addressed Democrats and Republicans respectively. Rae gave particular attention to the efforts of southern Democratic activists to maintain a moderate identity. They hoped to distinguish the regional party from a national image of Democrats that had limited appeal to southern whites while they worked to moderate the national party itself. In particular, Rae showed how the Democratic Leadership Council was created as a centrist faction with the goal of providing a counterweight to labor, civil rights, and women's rights activists; it paralleled the earlier if less successful Ripon Society in the GOP.

Aistrup documented the extension of Republican organization and party strength below the presidential level in the South. He devoted considerable attention to the party-building activities of the 1950s and 1960s and the switch in emphasis to candidate-centered activities after the 1964 election. He also demonstrated the considerable degree to which Republican Party organization had been constructed over the course of the preceding fifty years and how it contributed to the ability of the GOP to emerge as a competitive force in the region's sub-presidential politics.

Other studies of party organization began to incorporate rather than exclude the South for purposes of analysis, and they often still found differences, which now appeared to be more of degree than of kind. The study by Huckshorn, Gibson, Cotter, and Bibby of county party organizations conducted in 1979, for instance, found southern parties less well organized than their nonsouthern counterparts but making significant strides toward the base of what was admittedly a weak party structure across the nation (Huckshorn et al. 1986).

The rich and growing collections of data on southern party activists have allowed for the examination of the individuals who populate party committees and conventions as well as the impact they have on the organizations, electoral process, and partisan balance in the South. The data are important not only for better understanding the American South, but also for affording the opportunity to study the implications of a party system in transition.

Party Activists

The collections of surveys conducted over the past twenty-five years have provided enormous help in understanding who the party activists are and how they are evolving. They have illuminated the degree to which those motivated to participate in a particular year are younger and more frequently from minority groups (especially among Democrats) than are the members of local party committees, those whose commitment to party extends beyond a particular election or candidate.

Like the activists described by Wilson, Ippolito, and Crotty, party activists are demographically distinctive (Hadley and Bowman 1995; Hulbary and Bowman 1998). Committee members are older, richer, and better educated than their average electorates, unlike the party machine worker of Gosnell's Chicago. Women and men are both well represented in the conventions and party organizations of the South and have been for decades now, but there has been little change in the racial composition of party committees and conventions. Democrats have a significant number of African American delegates and committee members, while Republicans do not (Abramowitz et al. 1986a; Barth 2004; Bowman, Hulbary, and Kelley 1990; Clawson and Clark 1998; Hadley and Stanley 1990, 1998; Hulbary, Kelley, and Bowman 1998; Steed, Moreland, and Baker 1995).

Party activists reflect a wide range of religious preferences, but the partisan split proves illustrative of the broader society: evangelicals and adherents of the "religious right" are much more prominent in the GOP, whereas Jews, other non-Christians, and nonbelievers are more likely to find a place in the Democratic committees and conventions (Baker, Steed, and Moreland 1998). Though the interparty differences declined between 1991 and 2001, the broad pattern remains (Clark 2004).

The vitality of party committees has been very much in question, and the evidence from the two surveys of local committee members demonstrates that the grass roots of the party structures are very mature indeed. Among both Republicans and Democrats, the average age of committee members increased over the course of the decade (Shaffer and Breaux 1998).

The research on activists has demonstrated that interest in activity is found among a wide range of southern voters who are perhaps not representative of the full demographic diversity of the region but who include a range of racial, religious, and occupational groups. When well-educated and affluent southerners are motivated by a candidate or cause, they propel themselves into party decision-making positions, especially in the presidential nominating process. They seem to have less interest in the ongoing functions of the parties, however, and have left the party committees to a smaller group of consistently involved, older activists (Brudney and McDonald 1986; Hauss and Maisel 1986; Kweit and Kweit 1986).

Ideologies and Issue Stances

The undeniable conclusion that has been produced by the four major studies of presidential and party activists is that the southern party leaders are losing their distinctiveness in ideology and partisanship. Throughout the course of more than two decades, the responses given by political activists reveal increasing consistency within parties (Cotter and Fisher 2004; McGlennon 1998a; Moreland 1990; Rapoport et al. 1986; Steed 1998; Stone and Abramowitz 1986). Southern Democrats now make little distinction between their national and state party affiliations. Southern Republicans share ideological and issue positioning with nonsouthern members of the GOP.

The data collected provide clear evidence of realignment and declining distinctiveness. There is still a clear effort among southern Democratic candidates to present themselves as more "centrist," but a recently released *National Journal* rating of U.S. senators demonstrated the degree to which party membership has become as consistent at the elite level as at the grassroots level. Although earlier, similar studies often found southern Democrats far more conservative than their party colleagues and even than several Republicans, the latest (2003) numbers showed only two Democrats with liberalism scores lower than even one Republican, and one of these was from Nebraska. The other, Senator Zell Miller of Georgia, was a lame duck not seeking reelection in 2004, having savaged his party as unrepresentative of the South in a 2003 book (and at the 2004 Republican national convention).

While it is still evident from public statements that Democratic candidates have to tailor their appeal to the broad electorate, their party base looks increasingly like that found in most other states. Republican activists now appear to be in the vanguard of conservative opinion in the GOP, having left northeastern moderates such as Olympia Snowe and Susan Collins of Maine, Arlen Specter of Pennsylvania, and Lincoln Chafee of Rhode Island as an increasingly isolated faction.

These ideological patterns are also felt among grassroots activists who have become increasingly consistent within each party, and while Democrats still tend toward slightly greater ideological diversity, they are predominantly liberal. Republicans have moved inexorably toward the right, according to the studies.

Issue positions among the party activists demonstrate similar movements and provide further evidence of the realignment of the parties. Recognizing that some issues do not provide a sharp contrast of party distinction, party activists now support very different policies in a number of areas, which translates into the need for party candidates to bring their own positions into line with activists'.

Incentives and Motivations

With only a small percentage of Americans choosing to involve themselves in the party system as delegates and committee members, the question of motivation inevitably arises. Gosnell's machine activists had strong personal motivation: jobs and financial rewards. Wilson's "amateur" activists were stimulated by party, candidate, or issue. Eventually, research focused on three main forces for political activism: material, solidary, and purposive incentives. The first was the jobs and tangible rewards of patronage; the second was the satisfaction from associating with kindred spirits in enjoyable activities; the third was the pursuit of general policy goals to be accomplished by party effort (Wilson 1962).

Since the beginning of research on southern activists, the last two have been the more powerful explanations. In the absence of widespread urban patronage machines and with the ineffectiveness of party organizations in providing control over public office, ambitious politicians or office seekers may have operated outside the party organization, building or populating personal followings. The research on party activists had shown that as party organization has developed in the South, its members' motivations have been to support party or candidate or issue (Abramowitz et al. 1986b).

Stephen Shaffer and David Breaux (1998) noted in the 1990s a distinction to be drawn between the parties: Democrats tended to rely more on solidary incentives, whereas Republicans were more likely to be drawn into activity by purposive incentives. This would be consistent with the shifting political environment in which Republicans were increasingly becoming an ideologically unified party with greater success in accomplishing their policy objectives. Democrats, on the other hand, focused more strongly on the maintenance of party and social contacts and friendships. The 2001 data on local activists reinforced this conclusion inasmuch as they demonstrated essentially the same patterns as were seen a decade earlier (see Newman, Shaffer, and Breaux 2004).

Other research focused on the activist studies has shown that ambitious party activists, those who hope to use their activism to advance themselves politically, follow different recruitment patterns, have more contact with elected officials and party leaders, and push the party to perform its historic electoral functions more effectively (Steed, Moreland, and Baker 1998).

Pragmatism and Purism

As the 2001 Southern Grassroots Party Activists Project demonstrated, both parties continued to move toward ideological polarization, with the plurality of Republicans describing themselves as "very conservative" and only a handful of Democratic conservatives remaining. As Charles Prysby (2004) reported, however, this does not necessarily translate into a more "purist" orientation of party activists.

Considerable attention has been devoted to the distinction to be drawn between "purist" party activists (those who place a premium on candidates' and parties' standing for principles regardless of electoral consequences) and "pragmatists" (who are inclined to temper their party's preferences for the sake of winning elections). The studies of southern activists showed considerable shifting over time and illustrated the importance of context (Stone and Abramowitz, 1986).

The picture of Republican activists that emerges is of a more "purist" group that has become more ideologically uniform over time. But the GOP activists were actually becoming slightly more pragmatic, apparently in concert with their greater success in winning office and recognizing the need to maintain broader voter appeal. Prysby (2004) also reported that Democrats showed some increase in purism, but that it came not from an ideological basis but rather from generational replacement. He speculated that this reflects, at least in part, the movement of the Democratic Party in the South toward greater ideological homogeneity as younger activists with more liberal orientations replace older, more moderate to conservative activists.

The research on party activists lays out a picture of a system in which a minority party is energized by a more unified, consistent candidate and is driven by issues, with activists motivated by purposive goals that they expect their party and candidates to share. A once-dominant party finds itself increasingly relying on personal relationships, establishing a defense of the party as "different" from its national counterpart, and losing the ability to deliver either material or purposive rewards.

With the benefit of the most recent research, we see the dynamic aspects of the party system and its impact on the activists, as Republicans seek to protect their gains in winning elections by taking more pragmatic stances and Democrats move toward expecting their party and candidates to stand for policies and positions consistent with most activists. One can imagine that the basis for recruitment to party committees may reflect these changes, as Democrats increasingly draw from people looking for policy outcomes different from those offered by the Republicans, and as the GOP tries to hold together its recently successful coalition as policy choices start to pull it apart.

One important set of findings that emerged from the early research on presidential activists and that has continued to find validation in the activist studies is the challenge to the concept that ideologically polarized parties are more purist and less concerned about electability. As several studies have documented, the perception that a candidate is more likely to win an election trumps ideological proximity for many activists. Though they may see one candidate as being a better reflection of their own issue preferences and ideology, many activists are willing to support another, more electable candidate.

There is no certainty that activists will accurately discern electability (nor that elites will do any better: witness Howard Dean), but the research on southern activists has made it clear that party activists take this factor into account, and it is often decisive.

Groups and Factions among Party Activists

An important source of recruitment to party activism can be found in numerous interest groups and factions that seek to influence elections and public policy. The role of interest groups has attracted its share of attention in the study of southern activists, especially in terms of the role of religious activists in the Republican Party. Similarly, the role of Jesse Jackson in drawing new African American activism to the Democratic Party during his presidential campaigns has drawn considerable interest. In the former case, the documentation of increasing activity within the GOP corresponds to a sharp decline in division over issues of importance to religious interests. As for the delegates drawn into activism by the Jackson candidacy, there was considerable attention paid to the distinctions between them and African Americans who supported other candidates (most notably Walter Mondale in 1984), and the degree to which they might change the Democratic Party or the party might change them (Baker, Steed, and Moreland 1991; Bernick and Prysby 1987; Francis and Benedict 1986; McGlennon 1987; Steed and McGlennon 1990). In both parties there is evidence of potential for fracturing along these fault lines, and this fact represents a continuing challenge to the party organizations seeking unity in an increasingly competitive electoral environment.

Factionalism in party organizations has been an ongoing concern of southern politics, but in recent years it has shifted to a consideration of how that factionalism displays itself among the activists and how it affects party organizations (McGlennon 1998a; McGlennon 2004). Both parties' activists continue to see division within their parties, but the basis for the schisms seems to be changing. Regional and urban-rural divisions are replacing ideological and candidate-based splits, but they seem still to be a cause for worry to the parties, even if there is little indication that they are creating particularly worrisome effects (Baker 1990).

Organizational Activism

All organizations depend ultimately on what those in the organization do to move the organization toward its goals. Parties are no different. If parties are to be viable participants in the political process, those working in the party organizations must perform a variety of activities both to maintain the party organizationally and to promote its electoral efficiency. Because parties do not monopolize the political stage, they are in an ongoing competition with interest groups, the media, candidates' personal organizations, and other political actors and organizations for influence in the political process. In this context the work of their activists is very important.

The data on southern party activists show a relatively high level of commitment to doing the work of the party. Frank Feigert and John Todd (1998) found high levels of party maintenance activism (participating in party meetings and related business, county party organizational work) among these local party officials. Similarly, John Clark, Brad Lockerbie, and Peter Wielhouwer (1998) found a relatively high level of campaign activity among these officials in the early 1990s, a marked improvement over that found in studies of southern party activism in the early 1980s (Cotter, Gibson, Bibby, and Huckshorn 1984; Mayhew 1986). This commitment to doing the party's campaign and election work continued through the decade to the turn of the century and actually increased, especially among Democrats (Hogan 2004).

The analyses not only demonstrated high activity performance in general, but also delved into examinations of variables related to differing types and levels of activities. For example, party position clearly makes a difference in how active a party official is in both maintenance and campaign work, with county chairs consistently outdistancing precinct officials pretty much across the board (Clark, Lockerbie, and Wielhouwer 1998; Feigert and Todd 1998; Hogan 2004). Clark and his colleagues also found a degree of specialization among these activists: county chairs concentrated more than precinct officers on managerial activities, and precinct officers focused more on labor-intensive campaign activities. There was also evidence in all these analyses that such variables as gender, age, income, education, purism or pragmatism, level of party attachment, and ideology had some association with levels of activity among these local party officials.

Taking a somewhat different approach, John McGlennon (1993) looked at the activity data on a state-by-state basis and found that though levels vary, the more active party organizations tend to be located in the same states and the less active party organizations tend to be located in the same states, which suggests that party activity involves a sort of reciprocal response. McGlennon also found little evidence of any clear relationship between party activity levels and evaluations of party organizational strength; although this is modestly surprising, it suggests that a relatively high level of activity performance has become institutionalized in the southern party system, even in those instances where the parties' organizations are less vigorous.

Finally, Robert Steed (1996) examined the data in the context of Samuel Eldersveld's classic analyses of local party leaders in Wayne County, Michigan (Eldersveld 1964). Like Eldersveld three decades earlier, Steed found that those activists who communicate more frequently with other party officials, whose ideological orientations are most congruent with their party's ideological center of gravity, and who have ambitions for a political career are more active than their fellow activists. A key observation here is that an understanding of contemporary southern party activism is closely connected to understanding nonsouthern party activism in the 1950s and 1960s, a further reflection of how the southern party system has changed dramatically over the past thirty to forty years as it has moved more toward the partisan organizational patterns found nationally.

Future Direction for Research on Activism

The evidence accumulated from tens of thousands of surveys of party activists over the past few decades provides rich detail on the fundamental state and dynamic character of political parties in the region and the nation. As we have learned more about the characteristics and attitudes of activists in an increasingly competitive region, we have also seen that the door is open to understand better the relationship between activism and political environment.

With significant data available for an examination of the region as a whole, we have also seen the value of closer examination of the contextual variations from state to state. This suggests that party activist research can be profitably pursued at both the regional and the subregional levels. The transitions that are evident in southern parties give us an opportunity to explore how parties adapt to changing circumstances. Will the Democratic Party emerge with a consistent image and message for southern voters and attract activists who wish to advance this message and its party? Will the Republicans face tension within their organization as it achieves greater levels of success, only to find that it may not be able to satisfy all the activists who fueled its rise?

On the subregional level we have more opportunity to explore the variations already evident between states with long-standing party competitiveness and those where parties have only recently become competitive, between states with stgronger party organizations and those with weaker party organizations, and between states whose activists are more unified and those whose activists are less unified. If regional and urban-rural conflicts seem to be emerging, perhaps we can better identify the sources of such factionalism and its possible repercussions. How do differences among party activists compare to party status in the general electorate?

Research on party activism in the South over the past several decades has shown the changing nature of the political activists. It has challenged the hypothesis that party organizations are withering. Party organization has shown itself to be vibrant, adaptive, and politically important, and the South's emergence as a two-party region has given scholars a great opportunity to test their understanding of the party system.

References

Abbott, David W., and Edward T. Rogowsky, eds. 1971. *Political Parties: Leadership, Organization, Linkage.* Chicago: Rand McNally.

Abramowitz, Alan I., John J. McGlennon, and Ronald B. Rapoport, eds. 1981. *Party Activists in Virginia: A Study of Delegates to the 1978 Senatorial Nominating Conventions.* Charlottesville: Institute of Government, University of Virginia.

Abramowitz, Alan I., John J. McGlennon, and Ronald B. Rapoport. 1986a. "An Analysis of State Party Activists." In *The Life of the Parties: Activists in*

Presidential Politics, ed. Ronald B. Rapoport, Alan I. Abramowitz, and John J. McGlennon. Lexington: University Press of Kentucky.

———. 1986b. "Incentives for Activism." In *The Life of the Parties: Activists in Presidential Politics*, ed. Ronald B. Rapoport, Alan I. Abramowitz, and John J. McGlennon. Lexington: University Press of Kentucky.

Aistrup, Joseph A. 1996. *The Southern Strategy Revisited: Republican Top-Down Advancement in the South*. Lexington: University Press of Kentucky.

Althoff, Phillip, and Samuel C. Patterson. 1966. "Political Activism in a Rural County." *Midwest Journal of Political Science* 10: 39–51.

Baker, Tod A. 1990. "The Impact of Urbanization on Party Coalitions." In *Political Parties in the Southern States: Party Activists in Partisan Coalitions*, ed. Tod A. Baker, Charles D. Hadley, Robert P. Steed, and Laurence W. Moreland. Westport, Conn.: Praeger.

Baker, Tod A., Charles D. Hadley, Robert P. Steed, and Laurence W. Moreland, eds. 1990. *Political Parties in the Southern States: Party Activists in Partisan Coalitions*. Westport, Conn.: Praeger.

Baker, Tod A., and Robert P. Steed. 1974. "Southern Political Elites and Social Change: An Exploratory Study." In *Politics '74: Trends in Southern Politics*, ed. Tinsley E. Yarbrough. Greenville, N.C.: East Carolina University.

Baker, Tod. A., Robert P. Steed, and Laurence W. Moreland. 1991. "Preachers and Politics: Jesse Jackson, Pat Robertson, and the 1988 Presidential Nomination Campaign in South Carolina." In *The Bible and the Ballot Box: Religion and Politics in the 1988 Election*, ed. James L. Guth and John C. Green. Boulder, Colo.: Westview Press.

———. 1998. "Culture Wars and Religion in the South: The Changing Character of the Party Struggle." In *Party Activists in Southern Politics: Mirrors and Makers of Change*, ed. Charles D. Hadley and Lewis Bowman. Knoxville: University of Tennessee Press.

Barth, Jay. 2004. "The Continuing Role of Race in Southern Party Organizations." In *Southern Political Party Activists: Patterns of Conflict and Change, 1991–2001*, ed. John A. Clark and Charles L. Prysby. Lexington: University Press of Kentucky.

Bernick, E. Lee, and Charles L. Prysby. 1987. "Reactions to the Jackson Candidacy among Southern Black Political Activists." In *Blacks in Southern Politics*, ed. Laurence W. Moreland, Tod A. Baker, and Robert P. Steed. Westport, Conn.: Praeger.

Bowman, Lewis, and G. R. Boynton. 1964. "Coalition as Party in a One-Party Southern Area: A Theoretical and Case Analysis." *Midwest Journal of Political Science* 8: 277–97.

———. 1966a. "Activities and Goal Orientations of Grassroots Party Officials." *Journal of Politics* 28: 121–43.

———. 1966b. "Recruitment Patterns among Local Party Officials: A Model and Some Preliminary Findings in Selected Locales." *American Political Science Review* 60: 667–76.

Bowman, Lewis, William E. Hulbary, and Anne E. Kelley. 1990. "Party Sorting at the Grassroots: Stable Partisans and Party Changers among Florida's Precinct Officials." In *The Disappearing South? Studies in Regional Change and Continuity*, ed. Robert P. Steed, Laurence W. Moreland, and Tod A. Baker. Tuscaloosa: University of Alabama Press.

Brudney, Jeffrey L., and Jeanne G. McDonald. 1986. "Issue Constellations in 1980." In *The Life of the Parties: Activists in Presidential Politics*, ed. Ronald B. Rapoport, Alan I. Abramowitz, and John J. McGlennon. Lexington: University Press of Kentucky.

Clark, John A. 2004. "Religion: Culture Wars in the New South." In *Southern Political Party Activists: Patterns of Conflict and Change, 1991–2001*, ed. John A. Clark and Charles L. Prysby. Lexington: University Press of Kentucky.

Clark, John A., and Brad Lockerbie. 1998. "Split-Partisan Identification." In *Party Activists in Southern Politics: Mirrors and Makers of Change*, ed. Charles D. Hadley and Lewis Bowman. Knoxville: University of Tennessee Press.

Clark, John A., Brad Lockerbie, and Peter W. Wielhouwer. 1998. "Campaign Activities." In *Party Organization and Activism in the American South*, ed. Robert P. Steed, John A. Clark, Lewis Bowman, and Charles D. Hadley. Tuscaloosa: University of Alabama Press.

Clark, John A., and Charles L. Prysby, eds. 2004. *Southern Political Party Activists: Patterns of Conflict and Change, 1991–2001*. Lexington: University Press of Kentucky.

Clawson, Rosalee A., and John A. Clark. 1998. "Party Activists as Agents of Change: Women, Blacks, and Political Parties in the South." In *Party Organization and Activism in the American South*, ed. Robert P. Steed, John A. Clark, Lewis Bowman, and Charles D. Hadley. Tuscaloosa: University of Alabama Press.

Conway, M. Margaret, and Frank B. Feigert. 1968. "Motivation, Incentive Systems and the Political Party Organization." *American Political Science Review* 62: 1159–73.

Cotter, Cornelius P., James L. Gibson, John F. Bibby, and Robert J. Huckshorn. 1984. *Party Organizations in American Politics*. New York: Praeger.

Cotter, Patrick R., and Samuel H. Fisher III. 2004. "A Growing Divide: Issue Opinions of Southern Party Activists." In *Southern Political Party Activists: Patterns of Conflict and Change, 1991–2001*, ed. John A. Clark and Charles L. Prysby. Lexington: University Press of Kentucky.

Crotty, William J., ed. 1968. *Approaches to the Study of Party Organization*. Boston: Allyn and Bacon.

Darcy, Robert, Janet M. Clark, and Charles D. Hadley. 1990. "The Changing Roles of Women in Southern State Party Politics." In *Political Parties in the Southern States: Party Activists in Partisan Coalitions*, ed. Tod A. Baker, Charles D. Hadley, Robert P. Steed, and Laurence W. Moreland. Westport, Conn.: Praeger.

Eldersveld, Samuel J. 1964. *Political Parties: A Behavioral Analysis*. Chicago: Rand McNally.

———. 1982. *Political Parties in American Society*. New York: Basic Books.

Feigert, Frank B., and John R. Todd. 1998. "Party Maintenance Activities." In *Party Organization and Activism in the American South*, ed. Robert P.

Steed, John A. Clark, Lewis Bowman, and Charles D. Hadley. Tuscaloosa: University of Alabama Press.

Francis, John G., and Robert C. Benedict. 1986. "Issue Group Activists at the Conventions." In *The Life of the Parties: Activists in Presidential Politics*, ed. Ronald B. Rapoport, Alan I. Abramowitz, and John J. McGlennon. Lexington: University Press of Kentucky.

Gitelson, Alan R., M. Margaret Conway, and Frank B. Feigert. 1984. *American Political Parties: Stability and Change*. Boston: Houghton Mifflin.

Gosnell, Harold F. 1937. *Machine Politics: Chicago Style*. Chicago: University of Chicago Press.

Hadley, Charles D., and Lewis Bowman, eds. 1995. *Southern State Party Organizations and Activists*. Westport, Conn.: Praeger.

———, eds. 1998. *Party Activists in Southern Politics: Mirrors and Makers of Change*. Knoxville: University of Tennessee Press.

Hadley, Charles D., and Harold W. Stanley. 1990. "Blacks, the Biracial Coalition and Political Change." In *Political Parties in the Southern States: Party Activists in Partisan Coalitions*, ed. Tod A. Baker, Charles D. Hadley, Robert P. Steed, and Laurence W. Moreland. Westport, Conn.: Praeger.

———, eds. 1998. "Race and the Democratic Biracial Coalition." In *Party Activists in Southern Politics: Mirrors and Makers of Change*, ed. Charles D. Hadley and Lewis Bowman. Knoxville: University of Tennessee Press.

Hauss, Charles S., and L. Sandy Maisel. 1986. "Extremist Delegates: Myth and Reality." In *The Life of the Parties: Activists in Presidential Politics*, ed. Ronald B. Rapoport, Alan I. Abramowitz, and John J. McGlennon. Lexington: University Press of Kentucky.

Hirschfield, Robert, Bert E. Swanson, and Blanche Blank. 1962. "A Profile of Political Activists in Manhattan." *Western Political Quarterly* 15: 489–506.

Hogan, Robert E. 2004. "Party Activists in Election Campaigns." In *Southern Political Party Activists: Patterns of Conflict and Change, 1991–2001*, ed. John A. Clark and Charles L. Prysby. Lexington: University Press of Kentucky.

Huckshorn, Robert J., James L. Gibson, Cornelius P. Cotter, and John E. Bibby. 1986. "Party Integration and Party Organizational Strength." *Journal of Politics* 48: 976–91.

Hulbary, William F., and Lewis Bowman. 1998. "Recruiting Activists." In *Party Organization and Activism in the American South*, ed. Robert P. Steed, John A. Clark, Lewis Bowman, and Charles D. Hadley. Tuscaloosa: University of Alabama Press.

Hulbary, William F., Anne E. Kelley, and Lewis Bowman. 1998. "Gender Differences in Careers and Policy Preferences." In *Party Activists in Southern Politics: Mirrors and Makers of Change*, ed. Charles D. Hadley and Lewis Bowman. Knoxville: University of Tennessee Press.

Ippolito, Dennis S. 1969. "Political Perspectives of Suburban Party Leaders." *Social Science Quarterly* 49: 800–815.

Key, V. O., Jr. 1949. *Southern Politics in State and Nation*. New York: Knopf.

———. 1958, 4th ed. *Politics, Parties and Pressure Groups*. New York: Thomas Y. Crowell.

Kweit, Robert W., and Mary Grisez Kweit. 1986. "The Permeability of Parties." In *The Life of the Parties: Activists in Presidential Politics*, ed. Ronald B. Rapoport, Alan I. Abramowitz, and John J. McGlennon. Lexington: University Press of Kentucky.

Ladd, Everett Carll, Jr., and Charles D. Hadley. 1978, 2nd ed. *Transformations of the American Party System*. New York: W. W. Norton.

Mayhew, David R. 1986. *Placing Parties in American Politics*. Princeton: Princeton University Press.

McGlennon, John J. 1987. "The Jackson Campaign in Virginia: Precinct and State-Level Activists." In *Blacks in Southern Politics*, ed. Laurence W. Moreland, Tod A. Baker, and Robert P. Steed. Westport, Conn.: Praeger.

———. 1993. "Party Activity and Party Success: Southern Precinct Leaders and the Evaluation of Party Strength." Paper presented at the annual meeting of the American Political Science Association, Washington, D.C.

———. 1998a. "Factions in the Politics of the New South." In *Party Organization and Activism in the American South*, ed. Robert P. Steed, John A. Clark, Lewis Bowman, and Charles D. Hadley. Tuscaloosa: University of Alabama Press.

———. 1998b. "Ideology and the Southern Party Activist: Poles Apart or Reflecting the Poles?" In *Party Activists in Southern Politics: Mirrors and Makers of Change*, ed. Charles D. Hadley and Lewis Bowman. Knoxville: University of Tennessee Press.

———. 2004. "Factionalism Transformation in the Two-Party South: It's Getting Harder to Pick a Fight." In *Southern Political Party Activists: Patterns of Conflict and Change, 1991–2001*, ed. John A. Clark and Charles L. Prysby. Lexington: University Press of Kentucky.

Miller, Zell. 2003. *A National Party No More: The Conscience of a Conservative Democrat*. Atlanta: Stroud and Hall.

Moreland, Laurence W. 1990. "The Ideological and Issue Bases of Southern Parties." In *Political Parties in the Southern States: Party Activists in Partisan Coalitions*, ed. Tod A. Baker, Charles D. Hadley, Robert P. Steed, and Laurence W. Moreland. Westport, Conn.: Praeger.

Moreland, Laurence W., Robert P. Steed, and Tod A. Baker. 1986. "Migration and Activist Politics." In *The Life of the Parties: Activists in Presidential Politics*, ed. Ronald B. Rapoport, Alan I. Abramowitz, and John J. McGlennon. Lexington: University Press of Kentucky.

———, eds. 1987a. *Blacks in Southern Politics*. Westport, Conn.: Praeger.

———. 1987b. "Black Party Activists: A Profile." In *Blacks in Southern Politics*, ed. Laurence W. Moreland, Robert P. Steed, and Tod A. Baker. Westport, Conn.: Praeger.

Newman, James, Steven D. Shaffer, and David A. Breaux. 2004. "Motives for Involvement among Grassroots Party Activists in the Modern South." In *Southern Political Party Activists: Patterns of Conflict and Change, 1991–2001*, ed. John A. Clark and Charles L. Prysby. Lexington: University Press of Kentucky.

Paulson, Darryl, ed. 1975. *Contemporary Southern Politics*. Washington, D.C.: College and University Press.
Prysby, Charles. 1998. "Purist versus Pragmatist Orientations." In *Party Organization and Activism in the American South*, ed. Robert P. Steed, John A. Clark, Lewis Bowman, and Charles D. Hadley. Tuscaloosa: University of Alabama Press.
———. 2004. "Purist versus Pragmatist Orientations among Southern Political Party Activists." In *Southern Political Party Activists: Patterns of Conflict and Change, 1991–2001*, ed. John A. Clark and Charles L. Prysby. Lexington: University Press of Kentucky.
Rae, Nicol C. 1994. *Southern Democrats*. New York: Oxford University Press.
Rapoport, Ronald B., Alan I. Abramowitz, and John J. McGlennon, eds. 1986. *The Life of the Parties: Activists in Presidential Politics*. Lexington: University Press of Kentucky.
Rhodes, Terrel L. 2000. *Republicans in the South: Voting for the State House, Voting for the White House*. Westport, Conn.: Praeger.
Shaffer, Stephen D. 1990. "Southern State Party Convention Delegates: The Role of Age." In *Political Parties in the Southern States: Party Activists in Partisan Coalitions*, ed. Tod A. Baker, Charles D. Hadley, Robert P. Steed, and Laurence W. Moreland. Westport, Conn.: Praeger.
Shaffer, Stephen D., and David A. Breaux. 1998a. "Activists' Incentives." In *Party Organization and Activism in the American South*, ed. Robert P. Steed, John A. Clark, Lewis Bowman, and Charles D. Hadley. Tuscaloosa: University of Alabama Press.
———. 1998b. "Clashing Generations: Youthful Purists Challenge Pragmatic Professionals." In *Party Activists in Southern Politics: Mirrors and Makers of Change*, ed. Charles D. Hadley and Lewis Bowman. Knoxville: University of Tennessee Press.
Steed, Robert P. 1990. "Civil Rights Activists: Contributions to Party Transformation." In *Political Parties in the Southern States: Party Activists in Partisan Coalitions*, ed. Tod A. Baker, Charles D. Hadley, Robert P. Steed, and Laurence W. Moreland. Westport, Conn.: Praeger.
———. 1998. "Parties, Ideology and Issues: The Structuring of Political Conflict." In *Party Organization and Activism in the American South*, ed. Robert P. Steed, John A. Clark, Lewis Bowman, and Charles D. Hadley. Tuscaloosa: University of Alabama Press.
Steed, Robert P., John A. Clark, Lewis Bowman, and Charles Hadley, eds. 1998. *Party Organization and Activism in the American South*. Tuscaloosa: University of Alabama Press.
Steed, Robert P., and John J. McGlennon. 1990. "A 1988 Postscript: Continuing Coalitional Diversity." In *Political Parties in the Southern States: Party Activists in Partisan Coalitions*, ed. Tod A. Baker, Charles D. Hadley, Robert P. Steed, and Laurence W. Moreland. Westport, Conn.: Praeger.
Steed, Robert P., Laurence W. Moreland, and Tod A. Baker, eds. 1980. *Party Politics in the South*. Westport, Conn.: Praeger.

———. 1995. "Party Sorting at the Local Level in South Carolina." *National Political Science Review* 5: 181–96.

———. 1996. "Influences on Party Organizational Activity: Lessons from the Southern Grassroots Party Activists Project." Paper presented at the annual meeting of the Southern Political Science Association, Atlanta.

———. 1998. "Ambition and Local Party Activists." In *Party Organization and Activism in the American South,* ed. Robert P. Steed, John A. Clark, Lewis Bowman, and Charles D. Hadley. Tuscaloosa: University of Alabama Press.

Stone, Walter, and Alan I. Abramowitz. 1986. "Ideology, Electability and Candidate Choice." In *The Life of the Parties: Activists in Presidential Politics,* ed. Ronald B. Rapoport, Alan I. Abramowitz, and John J. McGlennon. Lexington: University Press of Kentucky.

Wiggins, Charles W. 1973. "Are Southern Party Leaders Really Different?" *Journal of Politics* 35: 487–92.

Wilson, James Q. 1962. *The Amateur Democrat: Club Politics in Three Cities.* Chicago: University of Chicago Press.

★ **Chapter 3** ★

Unfinished Business

Writing the Civil Rights Movement

Richard K. Scher

IN THE INTRODUCTION TO their volume *Writing the Civil War,* the editors liken the task of understanding the scholarship on that calamity to a group of blind persons examining an elephant, with each reporting on what the beast supposedly looks like (McPherson and Cooper 1998). Using their metaphor for examining the writings on the American civil rights movement holds, except that it understates the difficulty. Perhaps a better metaphor is that of H. G. Wells's time machine: ambitious, imaginative, magnificent in scope, and doomed to failure.

The Civil War at least was a finite moment in time, lasting from 1861 to 1865. Scholarship on the war can of course include materials and analyses of events and historical currents leading up to the onset of hostilities. Likewise, it is possible to examine the impact of the Civil War on what came later, both in the South and elsewhere.

But the difficulty of examining the civil rights movement in the South, or in the United States, is that there is no agreement on when it started, when it ended, or if indeed it is over. Did it begin with *Brown v. Board of Education* in 1954? With the 1943 race riots in Detroit? With *Plessy v. Ferguson* in 1896? With the passage of the Thirteenth, Fourteenth, and Fifteenth amendments to the U.S. Constitution following the Civil War? With the Emancipation Proclamation? With the slave revolts of the eighteenth and nineteenth centuries? Did it end with the passage of the Voting Rights Act in 1965? With the assassination of Dr. Martin Luther King Jr. in 1968? With the collapse of the Black Panther movement? Is not the onset of the women's and feminist movement in the U.S. in the 1970s and 1980s part and parcel of the civil rights movement? What about the emergence of gay rights issues in the 1980s and 1990s? Some might argue that these last two are national, not strictly southern, in scope. So what? Do they not also have southern manifestations? And are they not part of the spirit of the southern phase of the civil rights movement in which African Americans sought their civil rights? The fiasco of the Florida presidential election in 2000, in which it is well documented that more than 120,000 African Americans were not allowed to vote or had their votes discarded: is this not evidence that the civil rights movement as envisioned by Dr. King, and so many others, is still very much alive and very much needed?

These important questions scarcely scratch the surface of identifying just what the civil rights movement was. Was it only about access to public accommodations and voting rights, important as these are? Was it about school desegregation? Was it solely about African Americans? Was (or is) it just about the South? In the end anyone who wants to understand the civil rights movement, even just in the South, or even the writings about the civil rights movement in the South, has to make some decisions that draw boundaries and limitations around the topic, decisions that unfortunately are inevitably arbitrary. This chapter fearlessly makes some; it is to be hoped that readers will find that they are at least acceptable, perhaps even reasonable.

The chapter is divided into two parts. First, the following series of questions is posed about the civil rights movement, which will allow at least some of the major literatures on subthemes and topics within these larger questions to be considered.

What was the origin of the movement?
What moved the movement?
What were the dynamics of the movement?
What were some of the outcomes of the movement?

Within these broad questions the chapter examines some of the critical themes with which the literature deals; the chapter thus engages the writings in scholarly debate on major issues of the civil rights movement.

The second part of the chapter seeks to place the scholarship on the civil rights movement into a theoretical context. We shall inquire about the major theoretical frameworks that most of the literature employs and ask about the possible limitations of interpretation these frameworks elicit. And finally we shall ask if using other theoretical frameworks might create a new and rich set of literatures that can illuminate questions not yet asked that are important and can help us grasp the meaning of this truly monumental period in southern, and American, life.

No claim is made that the selection of literatures discussed in this chapter is comprehensive. After all, a search of Google for "U.S. civil rights movement" lists nearly two million items; the online Library of Congress catalogue stops at ten thousand. Undoubtedly even these lists are not exhaustive. It is to be hoped, however, that the literatures considered here are at least illustrative of major works available on this topic and in places may rise to the level of representative selections.

Beginning the Movement

There is uncertainty as to when the civil rights movement began in the South. Why is it difficult to fix its origin temporally, if not geographically?

One obvious answer to this question is that it depends on how one conceives of the civil rights movement and what its goals were. Nonetheless, even if we assume a broad conception of what the civil rights movement consisted of—that is, at its most basic level it dealt with overthrowing the yoke of Jim Crow laws and other forms of discrimination in the South—the problem of fixing its origins in time does not go away.

A common interpretation suggests that the movement started, at least in its active phase, with the *Brown v. Board of Education* decision in 1954. Two standard works on the origins of the civil rights movement lead us to this conclusion. John Egerton in his massive *Speak Now against the Day* wrote about the generation before the civil rights movement in the South (Egerton 1994). He stopped his account in 1954, with the *Brown* decision. Similarly, Aldon D. Morris wrote in *The Origins of the Civil Rights Movement* that he confined his study to "the crucial first ten years of the modern movement, 1953–1963" (Morris 1984, vi).

And yet neither of these authors claimed that nothing of significance happened earlier. Like Egerton, Doug McAdam moved the clock back to the thirties in his *Political Process and the Development of Black Insurgency, 1930–1970* (McAdam 1982). Morris himself pointed to the creation of the National Association for the Advancement of Colored People in 1909–10 "specifically to fight for equal rights for black Americans" (Morris 1984, 12). Indeed, it is not stretching the point to suggest that the real impetus, not just for the origin of the NAACP but for the whole civil rights movement to come, was *Plessy v. Ferguson* in 1896.

While it would be wrong to say that without this case there would have been no civil rights movement, it is also true that the seventy-five years— at least—following *Plessy* were aimed at dismantling that decision, the Jim Crow laws it sanctioned, and the cultural values and practices it both reflected and strengthened. It is precisely the effort to accomplish these purposes that constitutes that phase of southern and American political life we call the civil rights movement.

Indeed, if one is looking for a starting point of the active civil rights movement, the 1940s makes as much sense as any other period, even conceding that 1954 onward saw most of the active phase. World War II of course was raging during the first half of the decade; the impact of that horrific episode in world history on American blacks, who fought fascism and racism abroad while serving in the segregated American armed forces, was profound.

But in addition two major events that propelled civil rights activity occurred in the early 1940s. One of these was the Supreme Court's decision in *Smith v. Allwright* (1944). Steven F. Lawson in *Black Ballots* argued that *Smith* was the first critical step toward securing black voting rights in the South, as it opened the door to black participation in previously all-white Democratic primaries (Lawson 1976). The other was the publication of Gunnar Myrdal's *An American Dilemma* (1944). Originally commissioned in 1938, the book concluded that southern discrimination against blacks would eventually be resolved by application of the principles of the Constitution, which seems excessively optimistic, even naïve. On the other hand, his position that it would be possible to overcome Jim Crow in the South was undoubtedly an impetus to awakening black political consciousness and activism.

Indeed, Myrdal's optimistic outlook was actually undermined the year before his book was published by the destructive 1943 race riots in Detroit; if nothing else, the event told southern blacks, and the nation as a whole, that racial prejudice and discrimination were alive and well throughout the nation. But within a few years it became clear to African Americans that expansion of opportunities and active pursuit of civil rights might indeed be possible. In 1948 President Harry S Truman issued an executive order desegregating the armed forces and called for extension of the Fair Employment Practices Commission. At the same time Truman's Committee on Civil Rights produced a report that, as I. A. Newby noted in *The South: A History*, "offered a bold challenge to segregation and disenfranchisement" (Newby 1978, 480). The report was endorsed by no less a figure than Frank P. Graham, then president of the University of North Carolina at Chapel Hill and later a U. S. senator from that state, as well as a host of other prominent progressive southerners. And the Korean War in the early 1950s provided the first opportunity for whites and blacks to experience desegregated living and working, if only through the military. As Newby concluded, "The experience was thus an important step toward breaking down racial barriers in the larger society" (ibid.).

These works suggest that the origins of the civil rights movement can be traced to at least ten years before *Brown*. Indeed, some analysts—including Egerton and McAdam—argue that the roots of the early civil rights activity of the 1940s can be traced to the Depression of the 1930s. Perhaps the most telling evidence comes from the eminent historian George Brown Tindall, in his *The Emergence of the New South 1913–1945* (1967). He noted that students of black life in the South during the 1930s observed "a process of acculturation to middle-class standards, a stimulus from outside influences in remote communities, and undercurrents of defiance among people who could no longer 'ignorantly accept their "place" as once they could'" (Tindall 1967, 573). He concluded that "few Negroes had yet entered the paths of upward mobility that millions of Southern whites traveled during the early decades of the twentieth century. . . . But underneath the stagnant surface of Negro life new forces stirred, new directions emerged, new expectations quickened" (ibid.).

Tindall believed that Myrdal was right: "The age of segregation 'was only a temporary balancing of forces which was just on the verge of being broken'" (ibid., 574). If this were true, historical inevitability would have characterized the process by which southern blacks achieved their civil rights. The civil rights movement would have occurred as a natural course, energized and guided by historical forces that no one—not even troglodytic white southern politicians—could resist.

In fact of course no such thing happened. There was nothing inevitable about the origins of the civil rights movement. Too much blood was spilled, too many lives broken, too much hostility and hatred expressed to make such a view tenable. Such a view mocks and trivializes the efforts and sacrifices—including the ultimate sacrifice—that so many southern blacks made in pursuit of their civil rights. It also ignores the enormous and powerful structural features of southern politics and society—firmly in place since the late nineteenth century—that existed for the sole purpose of keeping southern blacks in their place.

On the other hand, in some sense Tindall was right, just as McAdam and Egerton and a host of other observers were. To misquote Eldridge Cleaver, the first shifting of gears in the universe that resulted in the active phase of the civil rights movement did not occur when Mrs. Rosa Parks sat down on a Montgomery bus because her feet hurt. It occurred some two decades earlier, as southern blacks became impatient and decided they were not going to take it any more. As the post–World War II era began, it was obvious that southern blacks were becoming energized and eager to pursue their civil rights. Momentum toward that end increased as the decade closed and extended through Korea into the early 1950s.

Moving the Movement

The second question with which this chapter is concerned has to do with the active phase of the civil rights movement, roughly the period 1954–65. It can perhaps best be posed as, What moved the movement? Why did it go forward, gain momentum, become front-page news by the end of the 1950s, and even become a national obsession by the mid-1960s—to be eventually replaced on the front burner only by the catastrophe of Vietnam?

The literature on this phase of the civil rights movement constitutes an immense chunk of the available materials on this subject. Putting one's arms around it is simply impossible. It is possible, however, to simplify, even deconstruct, the question in an attempt to determine what was going on during this period. So doing allows us to redirect it into the following: How important were indigenous factors within the movement, and within the South, in moving it forward? How important were external factors? What was the relative importance and balance between the two in determining what happened? (These are issues that Sid Tarrow, the eminent scholar of social movements, poses as crucial to understanding how social movements begin and acquire a life of their own—matters to which we will return later in this chapter.) These questions essentially frame much of the literature on the active phase of the civil rights movement, and it is to them that we now turn.

Moving the movement forward required a minimum of two prerequisites. The first of these was the development of political consciousness among southern blacks. By now it is a truism to observe the extraordinary physical and political isolation in which southern blacks lived following Reconstruction. Not only did they live in a separate social world from whites; they were physically, socially, politically, even spiritually separated from one another as well. Part of this was a result of the extraordinary ruralism of the South at the end of the nineteenth century. Even in towns and cities blacks lived on the periphery, and in many instances of course they were forbidden by Jim Crow laws from residing in town, or even being present in town after dark. The lack of urban concentration in the South prevented blacks from readily communicating with one another. The "critical population mass" necessary to develop a sense of community, of commonality of purpose, of mutual identification and support that culminate in the creation of political consciousness was lacking. Even basic communication technologies such as newspapers and telephones, which might have fostered a greater sense of political identity and consciousness, scarcely existed for southern blacks in the first third of the twentieth century, as President Franklin D. Roosevelt's National Emergency Council reported in 1938 and as was documented further by the southern regionalists Howard Odum (1936) and Rupert Vance (1946) at the University of North Carolina at Chapel Hill.

But of course it was not just the physical and emotional and political separation of blacks from one another that prevented the development of a sense of commonality and political consciousness. The very existence of Jim Crow discrimination served to keep blacks apart, to keep them from communicating, to keep them from becoming a community. White southern elites—social and political—as well as outside observers such as V. O. Key were acutely aware of the threat that southern blacks who were politically conscious and mobilized posed for those in power. Thus, every possible means had to be employed to keep them isolated, separate, vulnerable, and dependent on whites. These white southern elites understood that a united, focused southern black community would constitute a powerful weapon against the Jim Crow culture they so desperately sought to maintain and protect.

Contemporary observers of southern blacks were deeply sensible of their lack of political consciousness. W. E. B. Du Bois, in particular, noted in any number of his writings that until blacks came together in a common assault on Jim Crow, little progress was likely to be made. At the same time he noted the powerful way in which white politicians, and the white community generally, worked to keep blacks isolated from one another, unable to form coalitions and organizations designed to attack segregation. A. Philip Randolph was a union organizer and political activist, not an intellectual like Du Bois. But his attempt to organize a protest march against American participation in World War I was as much an effort to raise the political consciousness of southern blacks as to hold an antiwar rally. His depiction of U.S. participation in the war as "a mockery, a rape of decency and a travesty on common justice [as long as] lynching, Jim Crow, segregation and discrimination in the armed forces and out [continued]" (quoted in Scher 1997, 169) was a call to arms to blacks throughout the nation to realize that they had an obligation to fight discrimination at home before they could do so in Europe. In a more scholarly vein, the eminent historian John Hope Franklin (1989; Franklin and Moss, 2000) in a variety of writings examined the awakening of black political consciousness in the South as a precondition for a full-fledged attack on Jim Crow.

Whether the major impetus for the rise of black political consciousness came from within the southern black community or from forces outside it—World War I, for example, which virtually every writer on its development notes as a key element—is not really the concern of Du Bois, Randolph, or the others. Mostly they were concerned that it happened at all. In this regard, there seems little doubt that forces inside and outside the South aided its growth. Black migration out of the South, for example, actually aided the growth of political consciousness; as southern blacks sought a better life elsewhere, they sent word or even traveled back to tell family and neighbors that though segregation existed in the North and Midwest, it lacked the virulence of the southern variety and potentially could be attacked. Southern urbanization, which was under way early in the twentieth century and mushroomed after World War I, did provide critical population masses in the form of neighborhoods, churches, and other social institutions (including schools), which, while rigidly segregated, allowed blacks to communicate, to establish mutual support systems, and to think in terms of commonalties.

Too much should not be made of this. Even as the 1930s waned and war clouds gathered on the horizon, the South remained rigidly segregated. Southern blacks continued to remain fragmented, discontinuous, out of contact with any other but relatively proximate black neighborhoods. Jim Crow laws, and the larger culture they represented, acted as a practical check against any existing black desires to think in terms of commonalties or collectivities; the idea of collective action may well have been hatched during the 1930s, but as a practical matter there was little to show for it.

It took decades for southern blacks to begin to overcome the cleavages that characterized black social life during the first third of the twentieth century. It was for this reason that Randolph could rightly observe, as he sought to mobilize blacks for an antiwar protest march on Washington in 1941, like the one he had planned in 1917, that "nobody expects 10,000 Negroes to get together and march anywhere for anything at any time. . . . They are supposed to be just scared and unorganizable. Is this true? I contend it is not" (quoted in Scher 1997, 163).

What Randolph was actually noting in issuing this broadside was that political consciousness had begun to develop among southern blacks. His claim was clearly credible: both President and Mrs. Roosevelt (herself a strong advocate of civil rights for blacks) called on Randolph not to hold the march because of the outbreak of hostilities in Europe. They were joined in this appeal by a number of black leaders. Had Randolph's claim not been credible, they would not have gone to the trouble.

Randolph's pronouncement points to the second precondition for moving the civil rights movement forward: political mobilization. Developing political consciousness was a necessary but insufficient prerequisite for the movement: it had to be activated, in the sense that blacks had to find a way to channel their newfound political consciousness into focused, productive political activity. They had, then, to get out of their homes and churches and barber shops and into community-based groups and organizations that could spark and spearhead the attack on Jim Crow.

How did this happen? There is general agreement among scholars of this phase of the civil rights movement that it occurred through the development of organizations and leadership. Beyond this, however, there is little agreement. Did local, indigenous organizations provide most of the support—physical and emotional—for everyday citizens to risk their lives in the assault on discrimination? Or were the highly visible "Big Four" nationally based civil rights organizations—NAACP, Congress of Racial Equality (CORE), Southern Christian Leadership Conference (SCLC), and Student Nonviolent Coordinating Committee (SNCC)—ultimately more important in eliminating Jim Crow? The same questions can be asked about leadership: what was the relative contribution of local, often invisible clergy and others in confronting Jim Crow versus that of the very public national civil rights leaders, the most prominent of whom was Dr. Martin Luther King Jr.? The answer to these questions depends on where one looks and what one reads.

There were of course a variety of indigenous, sometimes neighborhood-based urban black organizations that played significant roles during the active phase of the civil rights movement. Some of them, such as voter leagues and "improvement" associations, actually predated World War II; others were established, even during the movement, on an ad hoc basis.

But there is general agreement that the most important of the indigenous, locally based civil rights organizations were urban black churches. The literature on these institutions is itself enormous. Whether one views the role of the urban black church through the scholarship of Samuel Hill (1984, 1999)—especially in his monumental *Encyclopedia of Southern Religion*—or through the detailed analysis of it in the early chapters of Taylor Branch's equally monumental *Parting the Waters* (1988) or through the eyes of participants as archived in such diverse works as Aldon D. Morris's *The Origins of the Civil Rights Movement* (1984), Harvard Sitkoff's *The Struggle for Black Equality* (1981), Thomas Brooks's *Walls Come Tumbling Down* (1974), or especially Howell Raines's *My Soul Is Rested* (1977), the conclusion is the same: the urban black church was the sine qua non for the active civil rights movement to move forward.

Reasons for this are well known. The black church provided institutional support and succor beyond the spiritual for its congregants. It offered material assistance, a place to meet in relative safety, ready-made communications networks, and a sense of commonality. Urban black ministers, especially those who were well educated, were usually regarded as legitimate (or at least acceptable) leaders in the eyes of white elites. They also had a degree of economic and social independence from the white community, as their paychecks came from their congregations, not whites. But what was most crucial in the urban black church was that the distinction between the secular and spiritual worlds became blurred. Sermons were expected to deal with issues of the day, including civil rights. The church was used as a base for community planning and action. As any number of observers and participants have noted, during civil rights rallies held frequently in black churches it was often difficult to tell what was going on—a prayer service or a planning session for some civil rights activity. Hymns, prayers, hallelujahs, hosannas, inspirational singing, and a spirit of religiosity pervaded the secular, even mundane, business of planning a street demonstration or sit-in. The emotional style and eloquence by which clergy rallied the troops for one more day, one more effort, were exactly the same by which they sought to inspire their congregants in their sermons on Sunday morning. One inevitably reaches the conclusion that the spirit of the civil rights movement was exactly parallel to, and even overlapped with, the most fervent Sunday morning church services led by urban black ministers in full fig. Even the nonministerial leaders of the civil rights movement copied the clergy's rhetorical and hortatory appeals for their speeches and challenges; it is likely that it was from the urban black church and its clergy that secular civil rights leaders learned to mobilize their forces.

But what of the national organizations, NAACP, CORE, SCLC, and SNCC? What was their contribution to moving the movement? It is precisely on this point that viewing the movement through the lenses of the literature on the Big Four both illuminates and distorts the reality of what happened. The scholarship on each of them is substantial. Such works as David Garrow's *Bearing the Cross* (1986), Meier and Rudwick's *CORE* (1973), and Howard Zinn's *SNCC* (1964) give extraordinary insight into the founding, purposes, success, and failures of these organizations.

The difficulty is that by viewing the civil rights movement solely through the lens of these organizations, one sees only a part of the picture, albeit a very significant one. The civil rights movement was much more than NAACP, CORE, SCLC, and SNCC considered either individually or collectively. There is no argument that these organizations were not essential to the development, momentum, and success of the movement. Each in its own way contributed immensely to it: the NAACP through its legal battles beginning in the early twentieth century designed to undermine Jim Crow, the early activism of CORE and its role in developing strategies and techniques of nonviolence, the energy and high-profile style of SCLC, and the determination and outright bravery of SNCC, especially during Freedom Summer in Mississippi, 1964. We must recognize that these organizations provided a national spotlight on and publicity for the movement (no one was better at this than King), some resources (mostly time, manpower, and intelligence rather than money), and a conduit to the White House, Congress, editorial boards of major national newspapers, and other centers of power. These contributions were anything but trivial.

Yet, after reading the literature on these organizations, one is left with the feeling that their reputations depended as much on the commitment and goodwill and energy of their local branches (each was a kind of federated organization that relied heavily on its local subsidiaries) as on the charismatic leadership of people such as Roy Wilkins, James Farmer, James Forman, John Lewis, and especially Dr. Martin Luther King Jr. The SCLC is a case in point; it is well recognized in any number of writings about its role in the civil rights movement that the SCLC's—and King's—participation in local activities could occur only at the behest of its local chapters or related organizations. To a greater or lesser degree this was also true of the NAACP and CORE. Probably only SNCC, especially when it "adopted" voting rights in Mississippi as its mission, had a free hand to come and go as it chose and to conduct its activism in its own way.

These considerations also apply to the role of leadership in moving the movement forward. While Wilkins, Farmer, King, and a few other nationally recognized figures secured all the publicity (for better or worse, but certainly inaccurately, King was identified in the public mind as the very personification of the movement), local leadership, especially the clergy, had to provide the organization, manpower, and other resources (often including bail money for arrested demonstrators) to make anything happen. There is no doubt that the appearance of King or Hosea Williams or Roy Wilkins or James Forman or any of a host of other luminaries at a neighborhood church provided immense energy and stimulus for local citizens to take the risks needed to demonstrate. And if King or one of the others joined them in a demonstration, the spillover effect in the form of enthusiasm and renewed commitment would last for weeks or months.

But in a sense this was exactly the problem. The literature on civil rights organizations and leadership acknowledges that King and local leaders, including clergy, often clashed. King's stormy relationship with the Reverend Fred Shuttlesworth, the fire-breathing activist from Birmingham, is very well known. King was often criticized for "cherry picking" those sites of activity where he could secure a good deal of publicity for himself. He was further criticized for blowing into town, taking over the civil rights activity regardless of what plans had been previously laid or demonstrations engaged in, spending a few days in the spotlight, and then suddenly disappearing, leaving local civil rights leaders somehow to fill the void.

What this suggests is that leadership in the civil rights movement, while seemingly top-down, was in fact much more bottom-up. The national and international attention that King and others drew (he was, after all, awarded the Nobel Peace Prize in 1964) was essential for molding public opinion to a position of sympathy for the civil rights movement, at least outside the South. And the important role he and others played in Washington, New York, Chicago, and other major urban centers, with the media and in academic circles, should never be minimized. Yet King's success depended first and last on what happened at the local level, before he showed up on the scene as well as after he left (especially if he made one of his well-documented sudden departures). If a prescriptive note can be made at this point, it is that the literature on leadership in the civil rights movement needs to look much longer and harder at the local level than it generally has.

There is an additional point about King's leadership that abounds in the literature about him and that needs a brief word here: the type of leadership he demonstrated over time. It is particularly the way it developed and changed during the period 1955–65 and beyond that has caught the attention of scholarly and other writers. Writings on the Montgomery bus boycott in 1955–56 invariably note King's political naïveté, his moral and religious fervor, and his firm belief that nonviolent demonstration could and would overcome Jim Crow. But those on the later campaigns in Birmingham, St. Augustine, and Selma note that he changed into a hard-boiled, media-conscious, politically savvy architect of movement activity. Did he in fact abandon his early moral principles and belief in the efficacy of nonviolence? Was he not in fact willing to use nonviolence to provoke a violent response, as Garrow (1978), Colburn (1985), and others have noted? King was severely criticized—by whites and blacks—for his "children's campaign" in Birmingham during the spring of 1963 because he deliberately placed children in harm's way to show the nation and world how deeply Jim Crow was entrenched in the social and political fabric of that city and the South generally. Does this not mean that by engaging in the children's campaign, King so sullied the moral cloak in which he continually wrapped himself that it no longer had credibility?

The question is an important one, but it suggests a superficial understanding of what King's leadership was at the beginning of his civil rights career and what it became. As Branch (1988) and others have noted, King did not take the Dexter Avenue Baptist Church pulpit in Montgomery with the idea of promoting civil rights in that city, or anywhere else. He was hired to be the spiritual leader of that church, and he felt an obligation to fill that position. But King came to understand his obligation to the black community of Montgomery when E. D. Nixon and others decided he was the right one to lead a campaign against Jim Crow there.

Similarly, his evolution into political realism came as a matter of experience. There were too many setbacks, too many defeats (Albany, Georgia, being only one of the more public ones), and too many hurdles to overcome to perpetuate a belief that his and the movement's moral rectitude could defeat the moral turpitude of Jim Crow. As Garrow, Colburn, and other writers show, King may very well have wanted to conduct his version of the civil rights movement through the force of rhetoric and the power of moral suasion. The problem, as he learned, was that these did not work against dynamite and billy clubs and police dogs and bullets and the other forms of political terror and bodily harm being waged against him and other movement participants.

In the end, as Branch points out, King's leadership did become far more political than it was when he began. But—and this is the crucial point—he never lost sight of the moral principles by which he led. He never abandoned the moral high ground he seized in 1955, and it stood him in good stead through all the difficulties and discomforts and personal dangers into which he put himself and his followers. King remained a moral leader to the end—a "pillar of fire," as Branch (1988, 922) describes him at the conclusion of his book—but he evolved into a shrewd political realist as well. It was the melding of these two disparate, even contradictory styles of leadership that made King the remarkable and effective leader that he was.

Movement Dynamics

The period 1954–65 was a time, as many observers have noted, when southern blacks were very much "in motion." The activity was not limited to the South, although of course that was its focus. Dr. Martin Luther King Jr., among other leaders, spent considerable time outside the South on speaking tours to publicize the movement, build public support for it, and most especially raise money for it.

To make a gross generalization, writings on this period of the civil rights movement fall into three categories: (1) detailed case studies of singular moments or campaigns—for example, Watters and Cleghorn's *Climbing Jacob's Ladder* (1967), Richard Kluger's *Simple Justice* (1975), David Colburn's *Racial Change and Community Crisis* (1985), William Chafe's *Civilities and Civil Rights* (1981), and Elizabeth Huckaby's *Crisis at Central High* (1980); (2) interpretive studies that reflect on the meaning and significance of events, such as Mark Stern's *Calculating Visions* (1992), Numan Bartley's *The Rise of Massive Resistance* (1969), Bartley and Graham's *Southern Politics and the Second Reconstruction* (1975), and Jacoway and Colburn's *Southern Businessmen and Civil*

Rights (1982); and (3) eyewitness and participants' accounts of particular events, of which there are too many to mention, although Howell Raines's *My Soul Is Rested* (1977) and Florence Mars's *Witness in Philadelphia* (1977) are examples of the best of this genre.

Relatively few of the writings on movement dynamics were prepared by social scientists; most were by historians, journalists, or people involved at ground level. As a body, this literature provides an extraordinarily rich insight into the story of the civil rights movement. Perhaps the most valuable and revealing contribution they make concerns the bravery and courage of individual members of the southern black community as they put themselves in harm's way in pursuit of their civil rights. Economically and socially vulnerable and potentially the target of physical violence, ordinary black citizens nonetheless took extraordinary risks as they sought to secure their rights and gain access to the promise of American life.

In spite of the different foci of the writings, especially the accounts of on-the-scene movement activity in which local details differed considerably, a powerful common theme emerges from all this literature: the firm entrenchment of Jim Crow in the social fabric and political culture of the South and the extraordinary amount of effort—and bloodshed—required to loosen it. This statement is almost as true in border states as in recalcitrant deep South ones. In this regard the Huckaby and Chafe books are most revealing, although in truth their observations are replicated in numerous other places, perhaps most notably by Bartley. Bartley's important further point that moderate white voices in the South were squelched during the period of massive resistance by extremists is powerfully underscored by Florence Mars: she herself was a target—and nearly a victim—of the extremist forces controlling the political agenda.

Both Little Rock and Greensboro looked, on the surface, to be "moderate" southern cities where desegregation of schools and other types of public accommodation could occur without violence, at least the level of violence that came to be associated with deep South civil rights activity. Yet both locations—and there are others—witnessed violent tragedies, and civil rights "success" could at best be regarded as partial, at least in the short term. Writings on why this sad scenario was played out over and over again throughout the South repeatedly point to the same causes:

white elites who refused to recognize that the community had a "race problem" and declined to discuss racial issues with the black community at virtually any point;

white elites who refused to recognize the legitimacy of black voices and concerns, or of the black community's chosen leaders;

white extremists who could control the political agenda by polarizing attitudes and creating an "us against them" mentality, which prevented the rise of voices of moderation, compromise, and understanding;

cities' inexperience, both in the public and private sectors, in dealing with racial issues and especially confrontations, which often led to situations spiraling out of control;

white uncertainty about how to respond to black demands, except to dig in and circle the wagons;

prodding and encouragement by state officials, including governors, aimed at strengthening the resolve of local white citizens and officials not to give in to black demands.

The list could be expanded, of course, and different authors can and do add specifics relevant to particular circumstances. But in the end, writings on the active phase of the movement, including those on the urban border South, reach similar conclusions: white leaders, and perhaps white citizens generally, held on to their Jim Crow beliefs and practices with extraordinary tenacity, gave in as little as possible to black protesters, and spent immense amounts of energy and creativity seeking to avoid any appearance of complying with black demands. The active phase of the civil rights movement was a time when the irresistible force met the immovable object. In a sense, the real wonder of the active phase of the civil rights movement was not that progress was so slow, but that there was any progress at all.

Outcomes of the Movement

This chapter does not investigate the large empirical literature, much of it written by political scientists, on the outcomes of the civil rights movement. Other scholars have been given that charge. However, there is a small but important micro-literature that takes a much more personal look at the results of the civil rights movement than social scientists are inclined to pursue. At the top of this list are Chet Fuller's *I Hear Them*

Calling My Name (1981) and Carol Stack's *Call to Home* (1996). Fuller, writing in the early 1980s, traveled throughout the South talking to ordinary, mostly poor blacks. His goal was to find that elusive "New South." He finds that for too many people, the New South looks distressingly like the Old South, at least in terms of the struggle poor blacks have to endure daily. Carol Stack, who returned to the South some fifteen years after Fuller wrote, finds a place different from Fuller's. While the struggle for those blacks who returned from the urban North to find their roots in the rural parts of the region was no less acute than what they endured in the North, or what Fuller's people had experienced, it was nonetheless a struggle they willingly undertook as they sought to find a sense of community, and identity, in the places their grandparents and great-grandparents had left decades earlier. Did the civil rights movement in any way influence their desire and willingness to shoulder these hardships? Stack is ambiguous on this point, but it is also clear that if the civil rights movement had not occurred, and met with some measure of success (in the sense that at least some things had changed), blacks could not have taken the remarkable step of returning to their roots in the South.

This same sense of ambiguity about the outcomes of the civil rights movement is portrayed most effectively and movingly in Melissa Fay Greene's *Praying for Sheetrock* (1991). Set in rural McIntosh County in southeastern Georgia, the book recounts how the civil rights movement there allowed blacks to achieve a measure of political power that a generation earlier had not been possible; it also relieved them of the burden of a sometimes condescending (at best), sometimes hostile (more often) white sheriff. On the other hand, it is not clear from Greene's account how far black political power has actually extended—given the amount of resistance from whites and the amount of infighting among blacks. Nor is it clear that the quality of life in what was then one of the nation's poorest counties has improved very much for the local black population. Perhaps Chester Devillers, retired African American mayor pro tem in Darien, summed up matters best when he said, "There are still too many bigots and racists among both black and white. It has gotten better, but we still haven't arrived. We have a long way to go" (Greene 1991, 334).

Yet in the end Fuller, Stack, and Greene point to a conclusion to which not enough attention has been paid, even by them: the nature of the civil rights revolution. That it was a revolution in every sense of the word is beyond dispute. The civil rights movement attacked—not always successfully, but always directly—the very cultural foundation of southern society. It had as its goal the destruction of Jim Crow laws, values, traditions, and mores. It sought to change attitudes of both blacks and whites on the nature of race, and how people from different races can and must live together. It sought to replace old beliefs and attitudes and practices with something completely new in the South, the idea that "all men are created equal."

That the movement was not successful in reaching this goal is not the point. The mayor is right, there is still a long way to go. What is more important is that the civil rights movement represented a revolution of a very unusual kind, at least in America and perhaps the West generally. It was a conservative, not a radical, revolution. It sought to gain for southern blacks the promise of American life, not to undermine it. Its purpose was to secure rights provided and guaranteed by the U.S. Constitution to all Americans, not to rewrite or overthrow that Constitution. Thus, ultimately the outcome of the civil rights revolution was that it underscored and reinforced the goals and values of the unique American experiment in democracy and did not seek to destroy them. By so doing, it reaffirmed that those goals and values apply to all Americans, white and black, southern and northern. By moving these considerations onto the front burner of American political life, and for searing them into the conscience of the American political community, the civil rights movement has to be considered a remarkable success, even as the struggle continues in pursuit of its fundamental goals.

Whither the Writings?

What about the writings on the civil rights movement? Seen in toto, or at least in partial toto, can we make any judgments about what they tell us about the movement, its place in American politics, and the contribution it has made to American democracy? Do we know more about the nature of race in American politics, and perhaps in America generally, as a result of the enormous quantity of literature available about the movement and the herculean efforts needed to produce it?

On the one hand, the richness of the literature cannot be gainsaid; indeed, it must be admired. There is an immense wealth of material available about the movement, including what happened, where, by whom, and to some extent why. Future scholars reexamining the civil rights movement will be deeply indebted to the extant literature for source material, documents, firsthand accounts, and interpretations of what it was all about. And yet there is something unsatisfying about writings on the civil rights movement. While any reaction of this sort is necessarily personal and even idiosyncratic, in fact two specific points and a more general one can be made in support of it.

The first is the paucity of literature dealing with the role of women in the civil rights movement. This is surprising. There were any number of women who emerged as key figures and leaders of the movement in different parts of the South: such figures as Rosa Parks, Jo Ann Robinson, and Fannie Lou Hamer come to mind as among the more famous and prominent, but there were many, many others. Yet the writings on the civil rights movement are nearly silent on their contribution. (For a discussion of what work has been done with regard to women in the civil rights movement, see chapter 5 in this volume.) So much of the writing on the leadership of the movement focuses on black males, especially the clergy. This is not to minimize the contribution black males—clergy and otherwise—made to the movement. It is to suggest that the nearly exclusive focus on them misses the major role that women played.

To be sure, in recent years some writings about the role of black women in the civil rights movement have appeared. One thinks for example of Lani Guinier's *Lift Every Voice* (1998) or the edited volume *Sisters in the Struggle* (Collier-Thomas and Franklin 2001). There are also a number of works on individual women who figured prominently in local struggles, many of which look suspiciously like reworkings of Ph.D. dissertations. These all are valuable. But there are too few of them, and particularly too few that seek to interpret and understand the role of women in the context of the larger civil rights movement.

More generally, to anticipate a point to be made shortly, why is there no, or very little, literature about the civil rights movement written from a feminist theory perspective? There are after all important and powerful works on international relations (among other topics in political science) written from a feminist perspective. Why not the civil rights movement as well?

Second, a political scientist examining the literature on the civil rights movement cannot help being struck by the fact that so little of it has actually been produced by colleagues in the field. Overwhelmingly, the literature has been written by historians, sociologists, journalists, general writers, and on-the-scene autobiographers or chroniclers. With the exception of empirical literature on the outcomes of the civil rights movement and some analyses of how specific institutions were involved in the movement—such as Ruth Morgan's examination of the use of executive orders as a mechanism for presidential policy development (1970)—political scientists have contributed very little to the literature. Even here, however, many of the analyses of institutional involvement were produced by journalists, such as Victor Navasky, who recounted the epic struggles in the 1960s between the U.S. Department of Justice, Attorney General Robert Kennedy, and President John F. Kennedy on the one hand, and recalcitrant and unrelenting southern governors such as Ross Barnett on the other (*Kennedy Justice*, 1972). The work of Jack Bass (who for most of his distinguished career has worked as a journalist) has been particularly prominent, including his account of the role of the judges of the U.S. Court of Appeals for the Fifth Circuit in implementing the *Brown* decision (*Unlikely Heroes*, 1981) and his biography of Frank M. Johnson, a pivotal U.S. District Court judge of Alabama (*Taming the Storm: The Life and Times of Judge Frank M. Johnson and the South's Fight over Civil Rights*, 1993). Not so incidentally, Bass's other work relating to the civil rights movement is also notable, especially his account of one of the tragedies of the civil rights era detailed in *The Orangeburg Massacre* (Bass and Nelson 1970) and his biography of one of the legends, for good or ill, of southern politics, *Ol' Strom: An Unauthorized Biography of Strom Thurmond* (Bass and Thompson 1998).

Why the contribution of political scientists is so small is a matter of speculation, but it is very much a matter of concern. Do political scientists not have anything to say about, much less contribute to the literature on, civil rights? More generally, as Rogers M. Smith has recently noted (so pointedly that his essay constitutes an indictment of the professional literature), political scientists studiously avoid dealing with questions of race except as some sort of independent, exogenous variable to be included in their regression equations (Smith 2004). The reason, according to Smith, is that most political scientists fail to see the connection between political institutions and structures—including constitutions and laws—and our definitions and perceptions of race. They have, rather, accepted the idea that "race" is defined by culture, or biology, or the U.S. Bureau of the Census, or other social institutions outside the purview of most political science research. In effect, Smith is saying that political scientists have not looked in their own backyards for race because there was no need to; it was in somebody else's backyard.

Exploring the implications of Smith's provocative and insightful essay is beyond the scope of this chapter. And yet my conclusion bears witness to Smith's point: there just is not much literature about the civil rights movement written by political scientists. Smith may well help us understand why. Toni Morrison is also correct and insightful when she says that all of us are so programmed to think about race in particular ways that it requires a superhuman effort to think about it in ways other than preprogrammed ones (Morrison and Lacour, 1997). Sadly, at least as far as the civil rights movement is concerned, many political scientists—well socialized into the ways of knowing in the discipline and, as human beings, into particular cultural views of race—probably never even consider asking scholarly questions about what our discipline could bring to bear in understanding the civil rights movement.

This raises a final, more general point about writings on the civil rights movement. From both theoretical and normative standpoints, the range of the writings is disturbingly narrow. Surely this range can and should be expanded.

It is of interest that the vast majority of writings—historical, sociological (with a few major exceptions), journalistic, and especially the few political science materials available—are prepared from a pluralistic, democratic elitist perspective. That is, they view political activity primarily from the standpoint of contending elites, who may be influenced by mass public opinion and behavior (such as voting or revolutions) but who rise and maintain themselves above them. From a democratic elitist perspective, the question of the civil rights movement becomes how governing elites come to recognize a wannabe group or movement, convey legitimacy, and offer a seat at the table. According to this way of viewing political activity, the civil rights movement then becomes the process by which southern blacks sought admission to the elite democratic table through persistent and ever-stronger demonstrations.

Likewise, most of the writings are written from a fairly standard normative reflection of American democratic theory, if only implicitly. That is, they accept the idea that disenfranchising and otherwise discriminating against southern blacks was counter and injurious to values and goals of American democracy. Removing the barriers against voting, giving access to public accommodations, and reducing other forms of discrimination are good in and of themselves, but they also improve and strengthen American democracy.

There is nothing wrong with any of this; they are all standard, mainstream views of American politics and democracy. But when we view the literature against other possibilities and lines of inquiry, the conclusion is inescapable that it is incomplete and excessively and unnecessarily narrow. Broader theoretical and normative perspectives would enrich the literature and illuminate still further the importance of the civil rights movement in American politics.

Several possibilities come to mind. Earlier I mentioned that an examination of the civil rights movement from a feminist perspective would be entirely appropriate. The line of inquiry would be enriched especially if it were carried out from a black feminist theoretical perspective. It is particularly important to point out that a feminist examination of the civil rights movement would not simply illuminate the role of women. It would enhance and deepen our understanding of the attitudes and behaviors of male participants, the Jim Crow political institutions the movement attacked, and the larger set of cultural forces that gave rise to social conditions that required that a civil rights movement even begin and persist in the American South.

Another possible theoretical avenue would be to utilize the literature on social movements and apply it to the civil rights movement. In some respects this route has already been explored, albeit in a preliminary way. The sociologists Doug McAdam (1982, 1988; McAdam, Tarrow, and Tilley 2001) and Aldon Morris (1984; Morris and Mueller 1992), the political scientist Sidney Tarrow (1998), and the geographer Bobby Wilson (2000), among others, have sought to use both the theory and empirical literature on social movements as a means of illuminating aspects of the civil rights movement. What would such an approach look like if pursued systematically? As Tarrow writes, it would ask "how ordinary people take advantage of the incentives created by shifting opportunities and constraints; how they combine conventional and challenging repertoires of action; [and] how they transform social networks and cultural frameworks into action, and with what outcomes" (Tarrow 1998, 2).

It is precisely this line of research that McAdam, Morris, and Wilson pursue in their works. Wilson in fact extends the analysis of social movements to include postmodern interpretations, by which he means that a full understanding of what occurred during the civil rights movement must combine not only a focus on movement organization and activity, but a careful analysis of time and space (what political scientists call "environmental" or exogenous factors) and their impact on the movement as well. It is not clear from Wilson's approach what makes it uniquely post-modern rather than an extension of the extant social movement literature. But the point may not be important. What is important is that Wilson, McAdam, Morris, Tarrow, Giugni (1999), and others have pioneered an approach to examining the beginnings, dynamics, and outcomes of the civil rights movement using (and expanding) a well-established theoretical foundation with considerable profit. Further work is essential, work in which political scientists can and must engage. And it needs to be combined with comparative empirical analyses of social movements elsewhere to enhance our understanding, as Tarrow notes, of "contentious politics that are based on underlying social networks and resonant collective action frames, and which develop the capacity to maintain sustained challenges against powerful opponents" (Tarrow 1998, 2). This is also a task that political scientists could undertake.

These considerations point to another potentially fruitful avenue of research on the civil rights movement: Marxist perspectives. Much, but not all, of the literature on social movements has a base in Marxist theory, or perspectives close to it. In truth, some work of a Marxist sort has been carried out on the civil rights movement. One thinks of the early work by Harold Cruse, George Breitman, and Clifton DeBerry (1972). More recent studies by Sethard Fisher (1992), Eugene Wolfenstein (1993), Manning Marable (1984, 1993, 1995), and Bobby Wilson (2000), among others, suggest the fecundity of Marxist interpretations of civil rights activity. It must be pointed out that much of the available Marxist literature concerns the interplay among the rise of black nationalism, black power, and black separatism in the context of the larger black struggle in America, and it is not limited to the civil rights movement per se; this is especially true of Marable's work as well as that of authors such as Henry Lewis Gates and bell hooks (who has also pioneered investigations of civil rights activity from a black feminist perspective).

Some might argue that because of the themes that the Marxist and near-Marxist literature develops, its relevance to the active phase of the civil rights movement—which was aimed at breaking down barriers of discrimination and giving blacks access to the promise of American life—is dubious. In fact, the opposite is true. It is precisely because, as McAdam, Wilson, Gates, Morrison, hooks, and others have shown, the movement was also aimed at enhancing a sense of self-identity in the African American community and promoting the growth of political consciousness that a Marxist perspective on what happened in the movement—from its origins to the present—is both desirable and essential.

In the end we must return to a point mentioned a few pages earlier. Regardless of what theoretical and normative perspectives are used, political scientists need to enter the study of the civil rights movement, and of race generally, more vigorously than they have. Race is not simply an independent variable that political scientists can manipulate to suit the needs of sophisticated, au courant statistical models they choose to employ in their research. Race is a fundamental element in American politics in exactly the same way V. O. Key saw it as fundamental to southern politics more than fifty years ago. If political scientists have as one of their goals the illumination of the American political system, then their full, systematic attention to its place and importance in that system, both during the civil rights movement and in other ways, is long, long overdue.

In short, there is a good deal of professional writing to be done about the civil rights movement. It is no exaggeration to say that, just like the pursuit of civil rights itself, a lot of unfinished business remains in the literature to which political scientists must attend.

References

Bartley, Numan. 1969. *The Rise of Massive Resistance: Race and Politics in the South during the 1950s.* Baton Rouge: Louisiana State University Press.

Bartley, Numan, and Hugh D. Graham. 1975. *Southern Politics and the Second Reconstruction.* Baltimore: Johns Hopkins University Press.

Bass, Jack. 1981. *Unlikely Heroes: The Dramatic Story of the Southern Judges of the Fifth Circuit Who Translated the Supreme Court's* Brown *Decision into a Revolution for Equality.* New York: Simon and Schuster.

———. 1993. *Taming the Storm: The Life and Times of Judge Frank M. Johnson and the South's Fight over Civil Rights.* New York: Doubleday.

Bass, Jack, and Jack Nelson. 1970. *The Orangeburg Massacre.* New York: World.

Bass, Jack, and Marilyn W. Thompson. 1998. *Ol' Strom: An Unauthorized Biography of Strom Thurmond.* Atlanta: Longstreet.

Branch, Taylor. 1988. *Parting the Waters: America in the King Years, 1954–63.* New York: Simon and Schuster.

Brooks, Thomas R. 1974. *Walls Come Tumbling Down: A History of the Civil Rights Movement, 1940–1970.* Englewood Cliffs, N.J.: Prentice-Hall.

Chafe, William H. 1981. *Civilities and Civil Rights: Greensboro, North Carolina, and the Black Struggle for Freedom.* New York: Oxford University Press.

Colburn, David R. 1985. *Racial Change and Community Crisis: St. Augustine, Florida, 1877–1980.* New York: Columbia University Press.

Collier-Thomas, Bettye, and V. P. Franklin, eds. 2001. *Sisters in the Struggle:*

African American Women in the Civil Rights–Black Power Movement. New York: New York University Press.

Cruse, Harold, George Breitman, and Clifton DeBerry. 1972. *Marxism and the Negro Struggle*. Atlanta: Pathfinder Press.

Egerton, John. 1994. *Speak Now against the Day: The Generation before the Civil Rights Movement in the South*. New York: Alfred A. Knopf.

Fisher, Sethard. 1992, 2nd ed. *From Margin to Mainstream: The Social Progress of Black Americans*. Lanham, Md.: Rowman and Littlefield.

Franklin, John Hope. 1989. *Race and History: Selected Essays 1938–1988*. Baton Rouge: Louisiana State University Press.

Franklin, John Hope, and Alfred A. Moss Jr. 2000, 8th ed. *From Slavery to Freedom: A History of African Americans*. Boston: McGraw-Hill.

———. 2000, 8th ed. *From Slavery to Freedom*. Boston: McGraw-Hill.

Fuller, Chet. 1981. *I Hear Them Calling My Name: A Journey through the New South*. Boston: Houghton Mifflin.

Garrow, David J. 1978. *Protest at Selma: Martin Luther King, Jr., and the Voting Rights Act of 1965*. New Haven: Yale University Press.

———. 1986. *Bearing the Cross*. New York: William Morrow.

Giugni, Marco, Doug McAdam, and Charles Tilley, eds. 1999. *How Social Movements Matter*. Minneapolis: University of Minnesota Press.

Greene, Melissa Fay. 1991. *Praying for Sheetrock: A Work of Nonfiction*. Reading, Mass.: Addison-Wesley.

Guinier, Lani. 1998. *Lift Every Voice: Turning a Civil Rights Setback into a Strong New Vision of Social Justice*. New York: Simon and Schuster.

Hill, Samuel S., ed. 1984. *Encyclopedia of Religion in the South*. Macon, Ga.: Mercer University Press.

———. 1999. *Southern Churches in Crisis Revisited*. Tuscaloosa: University of Alabama Press.

Huckaby, Elizabeth. 1980. *Crisis at Central High, Little Rock, 1957–58*. Baton Rouge: Louisiana State University Press.

Jacoway, Elizabeth, and David R. Colburn, eds. 1982. *Southern Businessmen and Desegregation*. Baton Rouge: Louisiana State University Press.

Kluger, Richard. 1975. *Simple Justice: The History of Brown v. Board of Education and Black America's Struggle for Equality*. New York: Knopf.

Lawson, Steven F. 1976. *Black Ballots: Voting Rights in the South, 1944–1969*. New York: Columbia University Press.

Marable, Manning. 1984. *Race, Reform and Rebellion: The Second Reconstruction in Black America, 1945–1982*. Jackson: University Press of Mississippi.

———. 1993. *Blackwater: Historical Studies in Race, Class Consciousness, and Revolution*. Niwot, Colo.: University Press of Colorado.

———. 1995. *Beyond Black and White: Transforming African-American Politics*. New York: Verso.

Mars, Florence. 1977. *Witness in Philadelphia*. Baton Rouge: Louisiana State University Press.

McAdam, Doug. 1982. *Political Process and the Development of Black Insurgency, 1930–1970*. Chicago: University of Chicago Press.

————. 1988. *Freedom Summer*. New York: Oxford University Press.

McAdam, Doug, Sidney Tarrow, and Charles Tilley. 2001. *Dynamics of Contention*. New York: Cambridge University Press.

McPherson, James M., and William J. Cooper Jr., eds. 1998. *Writing the Civil War: The Quest to Understand*. Columbia: University of South Carolina Press.

Meier, August, and Elliott Rudwick. 1973. *CORE: A Study in the Civil Rights Movement, 1942–1968*. New York: Oxford University Press.

Morgan, Ruth P. 1970. *The President and Civil Rights: Policy-Making by Executive Order*. New York: St. Martin's Press.

Morris, Aldon D. 1984. *The Origins of the Civil Rights Movement: Black Communities Organizing for Change*. New York: Free Press.

Morris, Aldon D., and Carol McClurg Mueller, eds. 1992. *Frontiers in Social Movement Theory*. New Haven: Yale University Press.

Morrison, Toni, and Claudia Brodsky Lacour, eds. 1997. *Birth of a Nation'Hood: Gaze, Script, and Spectacle in the O. J. Simpson Case*. New York: Pantheon. (See especially Morrison's introduction.)

Myrdal, Gunnar. 1944. *An American Dilemma*. New York: Harper and Brothers.

Navasky, Victor S. 1972. *Kennedy Justice*. New York: Atheneum.

Newby, I. A. 1978. *The South: A History*. New York: Holt, Rinehart and Winston.

Odum, Howard W. 1936. *Southern Regions of the United States*. Chapel Hill: University of North Carolina Press.

Raines, Howell. 1977. *My Soul Is Rested: Movement Days in the Deep South Remembered*. New York: Putnam.

Scher, Richard. 1997, 2nd ed. *Politics in the New South: Republicanism, Race, and Leadership in the Twentieth Century*. Armonk, N.Y.: M. E Sharpe.

Sitkoff, Harvard. 1981. *The Struggle for Black Equality, 1954–1980*. New York: Hill and Wang.

Smith, Rogers M. 2004. "The Puzzling Place of Race in American Political Science." *PS: Political Science and Politics* 37: 41–45.

Stack, Carol. 1996. *Call to Home: African Americans Reclaim the Rural South*. New York: Basic Books.

Stern, Mark. 1992. *Calculating Visions: Kennedy, Johnson, and Civil Rights*. New Brunswick: Rutgers University Press.

Tarrow, Sidney. 1998, 2nd ed. *Power in Movement, Social Movements and Contentious Politics*. New York: Cambridge University Press.

Tindall, George Brown. 1967. *The Emergence of the New South, 1913–1945*. Baton Rouge: Louisiana State University Press.

Vance, Rupert B. 1946. *All These People: The Nation's Human Resources in the South*. Chapel Hill: University of North Carolina Press.

Watters, Pat, and Reese Cleghorn. 1967. *Climbing Jacob's Ladder: The Arrical of Negroes in Southern Politics*. New York: Harcourt, Brace and World.

Wilson, Bobby M. 2000. *America's Johannesburg: Industrialization and Racial Transformation in Birmingham*. Lanham, Md.: Rowman and Littlefield.

Wolfenstein, Eugene Victor. 1993. *Victims of Democracy: Malcolm X and the Black Revolution*. New York: Guilford Press.

Zinn, Howard. 1964. *SNCC, the New Abolitionists*. Boston: Beacon Press.

★ **Chapter 4** ★

Race and Southern Politics

The Special Case
of Congressional Districting

Richard L. Engstrom

AS V. O. KEY NOTED at the outset of his monumental work on southern
politics, "In its grand outlines the politics of the South revolves around
the position of the Negro. It is at times interpreted as a politics of cotton,
as a politics of free trade, as a politics of agrarian poverty, or as a politics
of planter or plutocrat. Although such interpretations have a superficial
validity, in the last analysis, the major peculiarities of southern politics
go back to the Negro. Whatever phase of the southern political process
one seeks to understand, sooner or later the trail of inquiry leads to the
Negro" (Key 1949, 5). Changes since the publication of *Southern Politics
in State and Nation* have altered much of the South's political landscape,
and the race issue has taken a different form and direction as a result.
It is generally safe to say, however, that the vast majority of research on
southern politics over the past half century has addressed the issue of
race to some extent and on some level. Herein lies the main challenge to
anyone writing about the literature on race and southern politics.

First, as Richard Scher laments in his chapter on the civil rights
movement and southern politics, the literature is simply too huge and
scattered over too many topical areas to be reduced to the space of one
chapter in one book. Race is addressed at length by most of the standard
works on the evolution of southern politics during the post–World War
II period, all of which have been included extensively in discussions in
the other chapters: Havard (1972), Bartley and Graham (1975), Bass
and DeVries (1976), Lamis (1984, 1999), Black and Black (1987, 1992,

2002), Swansbrough and Brodsky (1988), Aistrup (1994), Scher (1997), Bullock and Rozell (1998), and Lublin (2004), to name a few. Additionally, there is a large literature more narrowly focused on specific elements of race and southern politics (see, for example, Matthews and Prothro 1966; Moreland, Steed, and Baker 1987; Glaser 1996; Fenno 2000; Streb 2002). Within the electoral arena, the Praeger series on presidential elections in the South from 1984 through 2000 (Steed, Moreland, and Baker 1985; Moreland, Steed, and Baker 1991; Steed, Moreland, and Baker 1994; Moreland and Steed 1997; Steed and Moreland 2002) documented the continuing importance of race as a variable in analyzing campaign strategy and voting patterns in the region. This very partial listing does not even address those works such as Thomas and Mary Edsall's *Chain Reaction* (1991), which examined southern politics and race (and the related issues of taxes and welfare) in the post-Key period within the context of national political patterns. In short, the massive literature is beyond the scope of one essay.

Second, inasmuch as the race issue extends into almost every area of southern politics, much of the key work is addressed to some degree in other chapters in this book; reviewing those works again here would be repetitious. This chapter focuses on the literature of one significant contemporary component of race and southern politics, the issue of racial redistricting (and, by extension, the issue of electoral consequences and governmental representation). This topic illustrates the continuing importance—even centrality—of race in current southern politics, and it addresses one of the key outcomes of the civil rights struggle that has been given a great deal of attention by political scientists.

Race, Voting, and Congressional Districting

A striking change in the racial politics of the South occurred in the post-1990 round of redistricting. The concept of racial redistricting took on a new meaning. Instead of referring to the past practice of designing districts to impede the election of African Americans, it is now used to refer to efforts to design districts to facilitate their election. Any recent study that has "racial redistricting" or a similar expression in its title no doubt deals with these affirmative efforts to include African Americans in legislative bodies, rather than exclude them.

This form of racial redistricting, like the previous one, occurs across the United States, but the attention it receives tends to be focused primarily on the South.[1] This is not surprising, given the intense role race has played in the region in the past and still plays today. As Earl and Merle Black quickly inform the readers of *The Rise of Southern Republicans,* race has been and continues to be "the central political cleavage" in the region (2002, 4). One manifestation of this cleavage is racial divisions in voting. These divisions have tended to be pronounced when voters are presented with a choice between African American and white candidates. African Americans demonstrate in their voting behavior a distinct preference to be represented by people from within their own group, as do whites. The efforts to facilitate the election of African Americans therefore has focused on creating districts in which African Americans can be expected to constitute a comfortable majority of the voters.

The resulting "majority-African-American" districts have been the subject of considerable scholarly attention. Studies focusing on such districts, especially in the South, have proliferated. One set of scholars recently observed, quite accurately, that "the literature on racial redistricting is large, contested, and evolving rapidly" (Smith, Kedrowski, and Ellis 2004, 797). Much of this work entails normative and legal concerns raised by these districts. When it comes to their partisan consequences, there is no debate about whether these districts have increased the descriptive representation of African Americans, for they surely have. And the African Americans elected in these districts are invariably Democrats, which is the party of preference for African Americans across the country (see Frymer 1999). The studies focus, instead, on what are called their perverse effects, consequences that raise questions about the extent to which such districts benefit African Americans. The critical fact stimulating these concerns has been the growth in the number of Republicans elected to legislative bodies along with the African American Democrats, and the relationship between the two phenomena.

African Americans in the South, like those across the United States, are predominantly Democratic in their partisan identifications and voting behavior (Black and Black 2002; Lublin 2004, 134–71). They are said to feel "completely unwelcome" in the Republican Party (Lublin 2004, 145). Changes in the partisan preferences of whites in the region, however, have favored Republicans, which has resulted in a change in the southern party system from one of Democratic dominance to one that is two-party competitive. In this competitive context, "the racial divide remains the most important partisan cleavage" (Black and Black 2002,

244). With party and race so entwined in the South, the partisan impact
of additional majority-African-American districts has been a major issue
in redistricting.

The perverse effect, at least from the African American perspective, is an increase in the election of Republicans due to the election of
African Americans. This is attributed to the so-called packing of African
American voters into black districts, which leaves the adjacent districts
with higher percentages of whites. These "bleached" districts are viewed
as especially hospitable to Republican candidates. As Byron Shafer and
Richard Johnston have observed, "It has become commonplace to note
that the process of creating these [majority-African-American districts
in the South] is also a process of advantaging Republican candidates
overall" (2001, 616–17). (Indeed, many believe, not surprisingly, that
when Republicans supported new majority-minority districts, they fully
intended this consequence.) The increase in Republican legislators is
said in turn to produce another consequence, which is the decline in
legislative support for the policy preferences of African Americans. A
conservative Republican who does not include African Americans in his
or her "reelection constituency" (which "contains all voters who support or might support the member"; Fenno 2003, 7) is not expected to
be sensitive to African American concerns, so if the Republicans' gains
in legislative seats exceed those of African Americans, an increase in
the descriptive representation of African Americans may well be at the
expense of their substantive representation (see especially Lublin 1997;
also Cameron, Epstein, and O'Halloran 1996). It is even common to
hear that the spillover effect of the new African American districts in
the South was a major cause of the Republicans' gaining control of the
U.S. House of Representatives in 2004 (see, for example, Swain 1995,
227, 232; McKee 2002, 123), something few African Americans would
consider to be beneficial to them (as only about 10 percent of African
Americans in the South cast their votes for Republican House candidates; see Black and Black 2002, 370–71); it is also common to hear that
these districts continue to impede the electoral success of the Democratic Party in the South (see, for example, the comments of Thomas
Schaller in Walsh 2005, 25).

This review of the literature addressing these partisan consequences
will focus exclusively on studies concerning the U.S. House of Representatives, which constitute almost all the studies concerning this linkage (for an exception, which deals with state legislatures in the South,

see Lublin and Voss 2000b). This concentration of attention on the U.S. House is no doubt driven by the deep partisan division within that body, a division that can be affected by the way House districts are drawn, especially in the South, where the growth of the Republican Party has been the greatest. Indeed, the southern focus of this literature is reinforced by the fact that all but one of the thirteen new majority-African-American U.S. House districts created following the 1990 census were established in southern states. Incidentally, the exception was the Fourth District in Maryland. As David Lublin noted, "In the North, large numbers of white Democrats live in close proximity to blacks, so racial redistricting does not usually make surrounding districts more likely to elect Republicans" (1997, 97).

A careful reading of the studies examining the relationship between the election of African Americans and Republicans reveals that this linkage tends to be exaggerated. The Republicans gained nine southern seats overall in the House in 1992, the same number of seats that southern states gained in the new apportionment based on the 1990 census. In 1994 the Republicans gained another sixteen overall, which resulted in the southern delegation to the House being, like the House itself, majority Republican (64 of 125). The extent to which these Republican gains can be "blamed" on the new African American districts is limited, however. Even authors who argue forcefully for the empirical presence of this linkage present specific findings that reveal a more modest impact (Lublin 1997; Lublin and Voss 2000a; Hill and Rae 2000; McKee 2002).

Voting Rights Districts

One might wish to attribute the change in districting practices to the recognition by white state legislators and other whites participating in the redistricting process of the benefits of more inclusive legislative bodies. But this would conflict with reality. Legal requirements, based primarily on the Voting Rights Act (VRA), were perceived to mandate an "if you can, you must" approach to the new lines. This statute—and its enforcement—was widely interpreted during the post-1990 redistricting to mean that if new majority-African-American districts could be drawn, they must be included in the plan adopted. Section 2 of the VRA, as amended in 1982, prohibits the dilution of African American voting strength through electoral arrangements, including district lines. And

Section 5, the coverage of which is geographically targeted primarily at the South, was viewed as precluding the implementation of districting arrangements that did the same (covered by Section 5 are Alabama, Georgia, Louisiana, Mississippi, South Carolina, Texas, and Virginia, and specified counties in Florida and North Carolina). Whereas Section 2 placed the burden of challenging what were viewed as dilutive districting arrangements on plaintiffs in federal courts, Section 5 blocked implementation of any districting plan in a covered jurisdiction unless the jurisdiction demonstrated to the Department of Justice or a three-judge federal district court in Washington, D.C., that there was no racially discriminatory purpose or effect in the design or the expected consequences of the new districts. The Justice Department was widely viewed at this time as requiring that all possible majority-minority districts be included in a plan as a condition for Section 5 "preclearance" (see, for example, Bullock 1995b; Hill 1995, 385–86). When districts were redrawn, therefore, white legislators and others involved in the process did so with a "legal club" over their heads (Bullock 1995a, 22).[2]

Districts established in response to these legal provisions are frequently referred to as voting rights districts. Redistricting plans in place for the 1992 U.S. House elections in the South, as noted above, contained twelve new majority-African-American districts (see table 4.1). African Americans in the South tend to live in geographical concentrations, but these concentrations themselves are dispersed across each state. Districts that would include a sufficient number of African Americans to constitute a majority, along with the other political considerations that infect redistricting, usually required boundaries that were more contorted than those of previous districts, which themselves were far from models of compactness. The shapes of these voting rights districts attracted considerable attention, stimulating names for them such as the "mark of Zorro district" for Louisiana's Fourth, the "I-85 district" for North Carolina's Twelfth, and the "Sherman's march district" for Georgia's Eleventh (Hill 1995, 386; see also Engstrom 2001, 4).

The immediate purpose of these districts was to provide African Americans with opportunities to elect representatives of their choice. On this criterion they worked superbly, as an African American Democrat was elected in each. The number of African Americans in the southern congressional delegation therefore increased from five to seventeen in one election (with the election of an African American in Maryland's new Fourth District as well, there was an overall increase of African

Table 4.1: The New Majority-African-American Districts			
State	District Number	African American % of Total Population	African American % of Voting Age Population
Alabama	7	67.5	63.5
Florida	3	55.0	50.6
	17	58.4	54.0
	23	51.6	45.7
Georgia	2	56.6	52.3
	11	64.1	60.4
Louisiana	4	66.4	62.6
North Carolina	1	57.3	53.4
	12	56.6	53.3
South Carolina	6	62.2	58.3
Texas	30	50.0	47.1
Virginia	3	64.1	61.2

Source: Engstrom 1995.
Note: The Florida Twenty-third and Texas Thirtieth were not majority-African-American in voting age population (VAP) but were considered to be majority-minority districts because of the Hispanic VAP within them. Three new majority-Hispanic districts were also created, two in Texas and one in Florida. These districts are not usually included in the studies dealing with the unintended partisan consequences of redistricting and therefore are not addressed in this chapter.

Americans in the House from twenty-five to thirty-eight). These were the first African Americans to be elected to the U.S. House in the twentieth century in five of these states (Alabama, Florida, North Carolina, South Carolina, and Virginia). These districts were in place for both the 1992 and 1994 U.S. House elections, except in Louisiana, where the new majority-African-American district was extensively redrawn in a way that lowered the African American percentage of the voting age population within it from 62.6 to 54.5 percent (see Engstrom and Kirksey 1998, 255–63).

The Perverse Partisan Effects Thesis

Reading the literature concerning majority-African-American districts gives one the impression that a positive relationship between African American districts and Republican districts is virtually axiomatic. It is as if the creation of African American districts automatically results in an increase in Republican districts. While the relationship is certainly plausible and has intuitive appeal, there is nothing inevitable about it (see Shotts 2001). It depends, of course, on geographical residential patterns, but also, and perhaps more important, on the discretion those in control of the redistricting process have in where they place the lines. Even when residential patterns might lead one to expect the linkage, "it is sometimes possible by creative cartography to create new black Democratic districts while holding constant (or even increasing) the total number of districts held by Democrats of either race" (Brace, Grofman, and Handley 1987, 183).

Some of the post-1990 congressional redistricting plans adopted in the South themselves offer evidence of this. Louisiana was the only southern state to lose a U.S. House seat in the new apportionment. The state already had one majority-African-American district, the Second, created in 1983 after a federal court invalidated its prior plan for splitting the African American vote in New Orleans in violation of Section 2 of the VRA (see Engstrom 1986). The creation of a second majority-African-American district in 1992, the Fourth, came at the expense of the Republicans, not the Democrats. Before redistricting, the state's House delegation was split evenly, four Democrats and four Republicans. The new apportionment meant one party would have to lose at least one seat (see Engstrom, Halpin, Hill, and Caridas-Butterworth 1994, 117–20).

From the many possible arrangements that contained two majority-African-American districts in Louisiana, the state chose one that paired two Republican incumbents in a district adjacent to the new voting rights district. The result was that the Democrats retained four seats and the Republicans dropped to three. It could have been worse for the Republicans. The state senate at one point adopted another plan with two majority-African-American districts that placed three Republican incumbents in one district. The four-to-three partisan split was repeated in 1994 when a vastly different yet still majority-African-American Fourth District was used (Engstrom 1995, 24, 46).[3]

Virginia was another state in which a new majority-African-American district resulted in the Republicans' losing a seat. An additional seat was allocated to Virginia as a result of reapportionment. The voting rights district, the Third, was created out of two previously Republican districts and therefore, unlike the case in Louisiana, was not just a loss for Republicans but a gain for the Democrats as well (see Lublin 1997, 110, 123; Lublin and Voss 2000a, 429, 431, 433; on Virginia's congressional redistricting, see Hagens 1998, 328–29, 332, 336).

David Lublin has identified post-1990 congressional redistricting plans in four southern states as pro-Democratic gerrymanders. The plans in all these states created new majority-African-American districts. These states included Texas and North Carolina as well as Louisiana and Virginia (Lublin 1997, 109–10). Many others agree that these plans were pro-Democratic arrangements. The Texas plan has been described by Donald Beachler, for example, as "an excellent example of simultaneous racial and partisan gerrymandering" (1998, 6). It was even selected by Michael Barone and Grant Ujifusa for the facetious Phil Burton Award, named for a California Democrat famous for being the architect of a pro-Democratic gerrymander of California congressional districts following the 1980 census (1993, 1209). No Democratic incumbent in a district adjacent to a new majority-African-American district lost his seat under the Texas plan. When the state's Republicans in 2003 pushed through a second post-2000 redistricting of the House districts in that state, they argued that the plan used in 2002, a federal court's revision of the 1991 plan, was a continuation of this gerrymander (see Gaddie 2004).

The North Carolina congressional plan adopted in 1992 was said to be a "stroke of political genius"; it left all the Democratic incumbents with "a good chance of winning reelection" despite its containing two new majority-African-American districts (Gronke and Wilson 1999, 161, 169). The plan reportedly made Republicans "apoplectic" (Sellers, Canon, and Schousen 1998, 280). It was itself the subject of a partisan gerrymandering case in which Republicans complained that its primary purpose was "to further the interests of white Democratic Congressmen in avoiding competitive elections." A federal district court held, however, that this was not grounds for invalidation (Engstrom 1995, 46). The plan worked as Democrats had intended in 1992: all six of the Democratic incumbents were reelected, as were two African American Democrats, the result being an overall increase of one Democrat (Engstrom 1995, 46; Lublin and Voss 2000a, 432). When the Republican vote expanded in 1994 in North Carolina, however, four of the six white Democratic incumbents were defeated (Engstrom 1995, 46).[4]

Assessing the Partisan Effects of the New Districts

The congressional elections of the 1990s, especially those in 1992 and 1994, took a serious toll on the Democratic Party in the South. The Republicans' overall gain of nine seats in 1992, and another sixteen in 1994, resulted in their having a majority of the southern members of the House for the first time since Reconstruction. These elections have been said to constitute, for the Democrats, a "debacle," an "implosion," an "electoral disaster," a "political 'earthquake,'" and a "sudden electoral flashpoint" (Bullock 1995b, 33; Hill and Rae 2000, 6, 9; Knuckey 2001, 258; McKee 2002, 126). But how much of this debacle can be attributed to another phenomenon: the election of twelve African American Democrats from new majority-African-American districts? How many of these twenty-five seats gained by Republicans can be attributed to the packing of African Americans, the most reliable supporters of the Democratic Party, into these twelve districts?

It hardly needs to be said, of course, that "not *all* Republican gains in the South were related to racial redistricting" (Hill 1995, 400). Many Republican victories occurred in areas not affected, at least directly, by the new black districts. The Republican surge in electoral support was far from limited geographically to areas around these districts. It may be, as one author has stated, "difficult, if not impossible, to determine how many seats underwent partisan change because of race conscious redistricting" (Beachler 1995, 76; see also Bullock 1995b, 35). But a careful examination of the published studies that address this question points to a surprising consensus among the authors—far fewer seats than might be thought. Research designs employed in pursuing the answer to this question vary from a "commonsense head count," which requires authors to "dirty their hands" with the particular details of the different election contests (Lublin and Voss 2000a, 428), to the more sophisticated statistical analyses in which numerous U.S. House elections serve as the units of analysis and patterns across these elections are examined. Despite these differences, when one focuses on the results for southern districts in these studies the conclusions vary little.

In assessing the partisan consequences of the new voting rights districts, it is important to keep the question clear. The question is not how much better the Democrats might have done if the states had not felt compelled to adopt new majority-African-American districts. There is little doubt, if any, that the new districts could have been more favorable to the Democrats "had African-American voters in the South been treated as 'sandbags' and optimally deployed to protect Democratic beachheads from the Republican tide" (Grofman and Handley 1998, 62). The magnitude of the benefit, however, might well be debated (ibid., 59). The question, rather, is how many of the Republican gains are attributable to the twelve new black districts. These questions are sometimes confused, and districts that Republicans retained but Democrats might have won had more African Americans been included in them are counted as losses along with those that the Democrats actually lost to the Republicans (see, for example, Bullock 1995b, 35; Lublin and Voss 2000a, 430–31).

It is common for the studies of racial redistricting in the South to include all eleven states of the Confederacy in the analysis. It is important, therefore, in counting how many Republican gains can be attributed to new African American districts to exclude the Republican gains in the three southern states—Arkansas, Mississippi, and Tennessee—that did not adopt a new majority-African-American district following the 1990 census. The Republicans picked up one seat in Arkansas in 1992 and two each in Mississippi and Tennessee in 1994. This means the maximum number of Republican gains due to the new districts, at least theoretically, is twenty rather than twenty-five.

As I noted earlier, some if not most of the Republican gains in the southern states that did adopt new African American districts were not due to these new districts. The perverse partisan effects thesis, if taken literally, concerns districts *adjacent to* these majority-African-American districts that were bleached as a consequence of them.[5] The number of Republican gains in the South in these types of districts is what is at issue and about which there seems to be more consensus than debate.

The 1992 election was held under a new apportionment of congressional seats based on the 1990 census. This reapportionment awarded ten new seats to five southern states: Florida gained four, Texas gained three, and Georgia, North Carolina, and Virginia each gained one. This complicates partisan effects analyses because the new African American districts may be viewed as the new seats (and, therefore, at least theoretically, they did not cost any incumbents their seats in some of these states) and because drastic changes in district lines can cause problems deciding which new districts are to be matched with which old ones. In Florida and Texas the number of new seats exceeded the number of new African American districts, and in Virginia these numbers were equal. It can be difficult to determine whether Republican gains resulted from new seats or new voting rights districts, or a combination of the two, in these states. Indeed, African American districts could be a gain for the Democrats while costing Republicans a proportional, but not an absolute, decline in seats in these states. In Georgia and North Carolina, in contrast, the number of new majority-African-American districts exceeded the number of new seats, as was the case in Louisiana as well. These differences do not, however, clearly separate the states that Lublin says gerrymandered in favor of the Democrats from those that did not.

Given the amount of attention that the new majority-African-American districts generated, and the popularity of the perverse partisan effects thesis among commentators, we may be surprised at how few analysts have placed a number on how many times Republicans replaced Democrats because of them. Many studies note the rise in the number of both African American Democrats and Republicans being elected and attribute this to the perverse relationship without identifying any specific instances of the two being connected. The most extreme example is Carol Swain's claim that "since the race-conscious redistricting of the 1990s, the loss of *no fewer than 17* Democratic seats can be directly attributable to the creation of majority-black districts in the South" (1995, 227, emphasis added). These districts are not identified, and no evidence is offered to substantiate the claim. This tendency may be a reflection of the fact that "it is difficult to determine what share of the explanation for GOP success is uniquely attributable to redistricting" (Bullock 1995b, 35).

The 1992 Elections

The most widely cited study of the 1992 congressional elections focusing on the perverse effects thesis is Kevin Hill's examination of the eight southern states that adopted new majority-African-American districts (1995).[6] On the basis of both an examination of the racial changes in districts and their election outcomes and a multivariate analysis that included variables reflecting the racial composition of the districts, Hill concluded that four of the nine seats gained by the Republicans were attributable to bleaching that resulted from the newly created majority-African-American districts. These were identified by Hill as the Alabama Sixth District, adjacent to the new majority-African-American Seventh District, and the Georgia First, Third, and Fourth districts, which were adjacent to one or both of the new majority-African-American districts, the Second and Twelfth, in that state (1995, 388, 391, 397). None of these districts, it should be noted, is a part of a plan that Lublin identified as a pro-Democratic gerrymander.

These districts were the ones Lublin identified as the southern districts Republicans gained because of majority-African-American districts in 1992. Although he ultimately concluded that racial redistricting accounted for "five to six" Democratic losses, he included in this number the failure of Democrats to pick up a Republican seat in Alabama and another one in Florida, which he found only "minimally" linked to racial redistricting (1997, 111–12). Lublin and Stephen Voss revisited this issue in another article and identified seven districts they considered to be Democratic losses, the same four as Hill identified and three districts in which the Democrats failed to pick up Republican seats, including the one that Lublin previously found to be only minimally related to racial redistricting (Lublin and Voss 2000a, 430–31). Seth McKee likewise has concluded that the Sixth Alabama and First, Third, and Fourth Georgia are the districts Republicans gained in 1992 due to the bleaching of districts adjacent to new majority-African-American districts (2002, 133–34),[7] and Charles Bullock also appears to have reached the same conclusion, assuming his reference to a district in Mississippi is meant to be the Alabama Sixth District (1995b, 35).

Donald W. Beachler identified only two districts as Republican gains due to the new voting rights districts. These were the Alabama Sixth and Georgia Third (1995, 74–77). It is not clear why Georgia's First was not included, but as for Georgia's Fourth, he stated in another article that the district had a "racial balance that was not substantially altered by redistricting" and reported a change in its African American percentage from 13 percent in 1988 to 12 percent in 1992 (1998, 10). This may be a comparison of the 1980 census figure with the 1990 figure, which would thereby miss the growth in the African American population over the decade.

There is a clear consensus about the number of Republican gains attributable to the new voting rights districts in 1992. The number is four, and the districts were the Alabama Sixth and the Georgia First, Third, and Fourth. It must also be remembered, however, that the Republicans lost seats in Louisiana and Virginia because of the creation of new African American districts. And the elections of new African American Democrats in some states no doubt constituted Democratic gains in 1992. The reapportionment of the U.S. House across the states resulted in five southern states' gaining ten seats, and all these states created at least one new majority-African-American district. North Carolina, for example, has been identified as a state in which one of the new minority districts constituted a Democratic gain in a new seat (Lublin and Voss

2000a, 432). The new majority-African-American districts created in the South following the 1990 census were certainly not as devastating, at least through the 1992 elections, as many have thought.

The 1994 Elections

The 1994 congressional elections used the same districts in seven of the states that adopted new majority-African-American districts. Louisiana was the only state to revise its districts between the elections, adopting a new version of its majority-African-American Fourth District (see Engstrom and Kirksey 1998, 253–60). The twelve new African American members of the House from the South were all reelected, as were the five previously elected to that body.[8] There was no additional growth in the African American representation from the region. There were, however, more Republicans elected. The 1994 elections were more beneficial to the Republicans than those in 1992: they gained sixteen additional seats to add to the nine gained in 1992.

Given the larger gain by the Republicans, and their new majority status within the region's congressional delegation (as well as the House itself), one might be surprised that few studies have addressed the extent to which these additional gains could be attributed to the voting rights districts. Only districts in North Carolina have been identified as districts in the South that were won by Republicans in 1994 as a consequence of bleaching resulting from the creation of the majority-African-American districts. Lublin identified the Second and Third districts in North Carolina as lost by the Democrats for this reason (1997, 114). He and Voss later added the North Carolina Fourth to the list of losses (Lublin and Voss 2000a, 431, 433). The Fourth District, however, was not bleached. It actually gained a percentage point in African American population in the post-1990 plan (ibid., 431). Donald Beachler, in a study examining only Texas, Georgia, and North Carolina, concurred with the identification of North Carolina's Second and Third districts, but not the Fourth, noting that it had not undergone a significant change in its racial composition (1998, 12). The Democratic incumbent in the Fourth District won reelection in 1992 with over 64 percent of the vote but lost by less than a percentage point in 1994. In 1996 he won the seat back with just under 55 percent of the vote. It seems as if only two of the sixteen Republican gains in 1994 are attributable to the spillover effects from the new majority-minority districts. Added to the four gains in 1992, this results in a total of only six districts that are consistent with the perverse effects thesis, far fewer than the seventeen or more claimed by Swain.[9]

It may be that focusing on bleached districts adjacent to majority-African-American districts is too narrow an approach to test properly the perverse effects notion. As a Louisiana congressman stated in regard to creating a new majority-African-American district in that state, "How you shape it shapes all the others" (quoted in Engstrom and Kirksey 1998, 243). The more distant a district is from an African American district, however, the more likely it is that factors other than race play the dominant role in its design. But the domino effect that districting cartographers are so familiar with might necessitate a broader search.

Bernard Grofman and Lisa Handley undertook such a study. Rather than focusing on adjacent districts, they conducted a statistical analysis to estimate how the overall distribution of changes in the racial composition of districts affected the probability of Democrats' being elected, regardless of the location of the districts. Their method allowed them to disaggregate the estimated effects attributed to the racial composition of districts from the effects due to changes in voting behavior. They employed data for the U.S. House districts in all eleven states of the South, so districts in Arkansas, Tennessee, and Mississippi, where Republicans gained five seats despite there being no new majority-African-American districts, have an impact on the outcomes. When they compared the changes in 1994 to the situation in 1990, they concluded that "as few as 2 to 5" of the seats lost by the Democrats in 1994 can be attributed to changes in the racial composition of districts (1998, 53, 56–57). A separate analysis comparing the changes in 1992 with the situation in 1990 resulted in an estimate that places the range of Democratic losses due to racial redistricting at "a little under 4 seats" to 6 (ibid., 58n15). It is unclear how much overlap there may be in the results for the two elections, but they, like the more focused analyses, certainly offer no support for assertions like Swain's that the number is seventeen or more.

Likewise, Kevin Hill and Nicol Rae created multivariate models to predict the percentage of the vote won by Democratic candidates in the 1992 and 1994 House elections. These models included the African American percentages in all the districts in the South (again including Arkansas, Tennessee, and Mississippi) for 1992 and 1994. When the 1990 figures were substituted in order to estimate "what would have happened without race-based redistricting," they concluded that in 1992 the Democrats would have retained Georgia's First and Third districts (but not the Fourth and not Alabama's Sixth), and in 1994 Georgia's Third and Eighth and North Carolina's Second and Third (Hill and Rae 2000, 16). Again, discarding the adjacency requirement and looking at all the districts, regardless of where they were located, the number of seats won by Republicans because of the racial differences is well below seventeen.[10]

If the large number of Republican gains is not attributable to the districts themselves, then what does account for them? In the words of Grofman and Handley, "Almost all of the Democratic congressional loss in the South from 1990 to 1994 can be attributed to one simple fact: namely, Republican candidates made substantial vote gains in virtually all districts" (1998, 67). Few will argue with this conclusion. Indeed, this is the obvious (and now standard) explanation for the partisan seat changes in the South. As Jonathan Knuckey has noted, "Any search for an explanation of southern Republican congressional gains in the 1990s requires a focus on the dramatic change in the vote choice of white southerners" (2001, 259). Beachler likewise writes, "Clearly the major source of the Democrats' problems in southern House elections is the growing percentage of southern whites who vote Republican" (1995, 78; see also Lublin 1997, 112; Engstrom's comments on Georgia and North Carolina in 1995, 46). In another article Beachler presented exit poll data indicating that white southerners' support for Democratic candidates in U.S. House elections dropped from 50 percent in 1990 to 47 percent in 1992 and then to 35 percent in 1994 (2000, 359). John R. Petrocik and Scott Desposato have added, in their analysis of the changes in districts, that the direct effect of majority-African-American redistricting was trivial; it was, rather, the indirect effect of Democratic incumbents' taking on many voters who had not previously been in their districts and with whom they would not have the normal incumbency advantage. They maintain that Democratic-friendly redistricting in the South would have given the advantage to the Democrats had it not been for the pro-Republican electoral tide (1998, 630). This GOP surge, they concluded, was "*the* critical factor" in the Democratic loses (ibid., 616). Against the Republican tide, spreading African American voters around to preserve Democratic districts would be "little more than a finger in the dike" (Squire 1995, 231; see also Beachler 1995, 79; Knuckey 2001, 259).[11]

The new majority-African-American districts in the South have been alleged to be accountable for far more than they deserve. This has extended into assertions that they were responsible for the Republicans' gaining control of the U.S. House after the 1994 elections. Swain stated in 1995, for example, that had the Democrats held the seventeen or more districts in the South that she asserts they lost due to the new majority-African-American districts, "the Democrats would still control the House" (1995, 232). Based on the counts focused on adjacent districts, the number of districts won by the Republicans for this reason is not close to enough to have caused the change in party control. And even the statistical analyses that ignore the adjacency requirement do not agree. The study coming closest to this view is that by Hill and Rae. On the basis of their counterfactual models, which also indicated that far fewer than seventeen districts went to the Republicans by 1994 because of racial redistricting, they concluded that Republican control of the House came two years earlier than it would have without the racial changes in the districts. According to them, "It would have happened anyway," even if there been no race-based redistricting (2000, 17–18). Grofman and Handley, however, concluded on the basis of their analyses that "given the scope of the Republican 1994 tidal wave, even had no new black majority seats been drawn in the 1990s districting round, the Republicans would still have gained control of the House" by 1994 (1998, 62), a conclusion with which Lublin and Voss agree (2000a, 433).

The creation of twelve new majority-African-American districts in the South following the 1990 census did benefit the Republicans, but the studies of these districts that examine the perverse partisan effects thesis concluded that this benefit was not nearly as great, or as consequential, as many commentators have assumed.

The Post-1994 Round of Redistricting

The new voting rights districts were controversial. Some people objected to enhancing the opportunities of minority voters to elect representatives of their choice by manipulating the electoral system in this way. The districts were viewed by many whites as the product of an affirmative action policy. Objections were also made to their shapes, which in many instances were bizarre. And objections were made to their perceived partisan consequences. The expected simultaneous advantages they provided Republicans were viewed, of course, as a negative by many Democrats.

The districts were also judicially challenged. Some whites took their objections to them to court, where they were very successful. The Supreme Court put these districts in serious jeopardy when, in 1993 in *Shaw v. Reno* (509 U.S. 630), it held that such districts could constitute violations of the equal protection clause of the Fourteenth Amendment (on the *Shaw* litigation, see Yarbrough 2002). This five-to-four decision held that, if race was the "predominant factor" in the creation of a district, the district was to be considered a "racial gerrymander." This was a district-specific notion of a gerrymander that was not based on the votes of any group, racial or partisan, being diluted by district lines. If a district was found to be a racial gerrymander, then it had to be reviewed by a court under the "strict scrutiny" standard for assessing compliance with the equal protection clause. Compliance under this standard requires that a state show that the application of the racial criterion was "narrowly tailored" to achieve a "compelling governmental interest" (*Shaw* at 658). Though the precise meaning of these words is not clear, this elevated test is popularly referred to as "strict in theory, fatal in fact."

Under the *Shaw* precedent, several of the new majority-African-American districts were invalidated. These included Louisiana's Fourth, Georgia's Second and Eleventh, North Carolina's Twelfth, Florida's Third, Texas's Thirtieth, and Virginia's Third. Revised districts were in place for the 1996 elections in Florida, Georgia, Texas, and Louisiana, and for the 1998 elections in North Carolina and Virginia. African Americans sought reelection in all these districts except Louisiana's Fourth.[12] Only the new Virginia district was above 50 percent in total African American population (53.6), while the African American percentages of the total populations in the others ranged from 35.6 to 47.0 percent. Yet all the incumbents in these districts who sought reelection were successful. This was taken by some critics of these districts as further evidence that the voting rights districts had been unnecessarily packed with African Americans (Bullock and Dunn 1999; see also Bullock and Dunn 2003).[13] Less attention was placed, however, on the fact that at the same time that African American incumbents were being reelected, so were the Republicans who had benefited from the bleaching of their previous districts. (North Carolina's Second District had already reverted to the Democrats in 1996, before the change in that state's districts.) African Americans were more broadly dispersed among districts, some of which were now "unbleached," yet no Democrats replaced Republicans in these districts.

Although incumbency advantages may have had a role in this result, this may also be attributed to the Republican surge. White flight to the Republican Party has resulted in fewer whites participating in Democratic primaries, which has permitted African American candidates to win the Democratic nomination in districts where African Americans are in the minority. The Democratic nomination may stimulate enough crossover support from white Democrats that, when combined with typically solid African American support, it is sufficient for victory (see Voss and Lublin 2001, 171–72). But the election of African Americans, especially in open seats, can be placed at risk by shaving these districts, while the tradeoff—more white Democrats being elected from the other white districts—may not occur, given the Republican dominance of the white electorate.

Finally, one of the voting rights districts, at least in its reincarnated form, was still the subject of U.S. Supreme Court attention a year after the 2000 census was taken. On April 18, 2001, the Court handed down its last redistricting decision, *Easley v. Cromartie* (532 U.S. 234), before the post-2000 round of redistricting began. At issue was the Twelfth District in North Carolina, which had been adopted by that state in 1997 but never used in an election because it was twice found to be an unconstitutional "racial gerrymander" by federal courts in North Carolina. This was the fourth time that the role that race played in the post-1990 congressional redistricting in North Carolina was before the Supreme Court (of which *Shaw* was the first); ironically, even if the district was approved, it was not to be used in the 2002 election because it was based on the 1990 census. This version of the Twelfth District was 47 percent African American in voting age population.

The issue was whether race had predominated in the creation and adoption of the district, or whether the district's makeup was the product of partisan politics. The issue clearly illustrates the entwined nature of race and partisan politics in the South. Plaintiffs claimed that the predominant purpose was race, while the state maintained it was designed to be a safe Democratic district and was part of a statewide plan intended to maintain the partisan balance in the state's congressional delegation at that time. Noting the high correlation between race and party in North Carolina, the majority of the Court concluded it could not determine which motive prevailed and, given that the burden of persuasion was on the plaintiffs, upheld the plan.

Conclusion

The adoption of the voting rights districts in the post-1990 round of congressional redistricting constituted, according to Lublin, "the greatest upheaval in congressional district boundaries" since the adoption of the one-person-one-vote rule (1997, 6). These districts were controversial and contested, and court-ordered revisions in them necessitated a round of "re-redistricting" in six southern states. The feature of these districts that created the most attention, after their shapes, was their widely assumed partisan effects. They have been viewed as the cause of numerous southern Democratic members of Congress's (as many as seventeen or more, as we have seen) losing their seats and of making it possible for the Republicans to gain control of the House in 1994.

The perverse effects thesis held that the spillover effect of creating these districts was the bleaching of adjacent districts, making these districts favorable to Republican candidates. African American districts, it was said, beget Republican districts. This thesis was certainly plausible, and it was popular and continues to be so. Yet the actual impact of these voting rights districts was not as perverse as widely proclaimed. Serious analyses demonstrate that the Republican Party would have controlled the House by 1995, or at latest by 1997, even without its southern gains, impressive as they were.

The voting rights districts did accomplish their immediate purpose, to enhance the descriptive representation of African Americans in the U.S. House. And many analysts continue to believe that there are numerous benefits to descriptive representation, to having African Americans representing and working for African American constituents in Congress (see especially Canon 1999; Tate 2003; Fenno 2003). The question of whether this has come at the expense of their substantive representation is a contentious one and will certainly remain so as long as the evidence for less substantive representation relies exclusively on roll call votes in Congress (see especially Canon 1999, 30–31, 149–51, 172–77).

No additional majority-African-American congressional districts were created in the South, or anywhere in the country, following the 2000 census. Racial residential patterns would have made creating more very difficult, especially in light of *Shaw*, its progeny (see, for example, *Miller v. Johnson*, 515 U.S. 900 [1995]) and other Supreme Court decisions that made it more difficult to deny Section 5 preclearance to redistricting plans (*Reno v. Bossier Parish School Board*, 520 U.S. 471 [1997] and 528 U.S. 320 [2000]). African Americans, however, continued to be elected in 2002 and 2004 elections in the eleven districts that can be traced back to the post-1990 voting rights districts.

In examining the issue of political representation and its partisan effects, we are reminded once again of the importance of race in post–World War II southern politics. Throughout this period, even as the de jure Jim Crow system was attacked and largely dismantled and African Americans were allowed more fully into the political process, the issue continued to have both emotional and practical components.

The emotions associated with the South's racial history have surfaced in numerous ways and have been intertwined with such issues as the design of Georgia's state flag, the public presence of monuments to Confederate soldiers, and the economic boycott promoted by the NAACP in South Carolina over the proper placement of the Confederate battle flag on the state capitol grounds. Indeed, a recent book, *Confederate Symbols in the Contemporary South,* edited by J. Michael Martinez, William D. Richardson, and Ron McNinch-Su (2000), demonstrated the continuing emotional racial undercurrent of politics in the region.

Ultimately, to scholars of southern politics, the race issue is important because it has a host of political consequences. Who gets to participate in the decision-making process, and how and to what end, is at the heart of southern (and all) politics. The large literature on the related questions of districting and representation addresses this principle vividly.

Notes

1. Unless otherwise specified, in this chapter the South comprises the eleven states of the Confederacy: Alabama, Arkansas, Florida, Georgia, Louisiana, Mississippi, North Carolina, South Carolina, Tennessee, Texas, and Virginia.

2. For more on these provisions of the VRA, see Engstrom 1988. Party reactions to this "club" no doubt differed between Democrats and Republicans in some settings. Depending on the state and the residential patterns therein, Republicans could expect to gain seats as a result of concentrating African American voters in majority-African-American districts. Indeed, in some states, Republicans did support African American demands for such districts. When courts handled redistricting issues, Republicans in some states placed the maximum number of majority-minority districts in their plans as part of an effort to win their preferred districts in the rest of the state.

3. The Republicans did gain two seats following that election, however, when white Democrats Billy Tauzin and Jimmy Hayes switched their party af-

filiation to Republican in 1995. Tauzin's party switch could not have had much to do with electoral security, however, given that he was unopposed for reelection in 1992 and won with 76.2 percent of the vote in 1994. Hayes was reelected in 1992 with 73.0 percent of the vote, but in 1994 (when he faced a former Republican congressman) he won with only 53.0 percent. It was not until the 1996 election, when the new voting rights district was dismantled completely and Louisiana was back to only one majority-African-American district, that the Republican Party, with Tauzin now running as a Republican incumbent, won a majority of the seats on election day (Engstrom and Kirksey 1998).

4. A study projecting the partisan strength of the new congressional districts adopted after the 1990 census provides additional evidence of Democratic incumbents' being protected in these gerrymandered states. Projecting partisan strength on the basis of the 1988 and 1990 House elections and the 1988 presidential election, it predicts partisan gains when all incumbents are running for reelection and when all the seats are open. These predictions, with and without incumbents running, were +6 Democrats versus +2 Republicans in Texas, +3 Democrats versus +1 Republican in Virginia, and +1 Republican versus +2 Republicans in North Carolina. (Louisiana was not included in the study.) For the four states not identified as gerrymandered by Lublin, these numbers are no change versus +2 Republicans in Alabama and South Carolina, +2 Republicans versus +1 Republican in Georgia, and +7 Republicans versus +2 Republicans in Florida (Swain, Borrelli, and Reed 1998, 954–55).

5. The perverse partisan effects thesis is typically expressed as concerning the districts that are "adjacent to," "surrounding," "bordering," or "neighboring" a new majority-African-American district (see, e.g., Bullock 1995a, 22, and 1995b, 33; Overby and Cosgrove 1996, 541; Knuckey 2001, 258; Black and Black 2002, 197; McKee 2002, 124, 131, 137).

6. A study of the 1992 elections by Richard Niemi and Alan Abramowitz concluded that "Republicans did better, in the sense of gaining seats relative to votes, in states *not* required to obtain Justice Department approval" (1995, 814). This study does not provide a test of the perverse effects thesis, however, or a South versus non-South comparison. It does not concern the linkage between the majority-African-American districts and the election of Republicans, and it compares states covered even partially by Section 5 of the VRA (which include Arizona, California, and New York), as well as most of the southern states, with those that are not so covered, which include Arkansas and Tennessee.

7. It should be noted that one of these districts, the Georgia Fourth, does not appear to have been seriously bleached in McKee's table 6 (2002, 134). This district is listed as having an African American voting age population (VAP) of 11.0 percent in 1990, and one of 10.8 percent in 1992, a loss of only 0.2 percentage points. Hill, however, lists this district as having a total population that was 25 percent African American in 1990, which declined to 12 percent in 1992 (1995, 388). Lublin reports (1997, 111) the same figures as Hill. This discrepancy is due to McKee's reporting the *1980* VAP for this district (as reported in Barone and Ujifusa 1989, 304) and Hill's and Lublin's reporting the *1990* figure for total population (as reported in Barone and Ujifusa 1991, 311). The African

American presence in the district no doubt increased substantially between the 1980 and the 1990 censuses. The 2002 version of the district is reported to be, based on the 1990 census, 12 percent African American in total population and 11 percent in VAP (Barone and Ujifusa 1993, 341), which indicates a substantial bleaching of the district. In Lublin's latest work, however, he states that attributing the loss of the Fourth District to racial redistricting may be "dubious," given that "the black population declined by slightly more than 1 percent" (2004, 106).

8. Eva Clayton won a special election to fill a vacancy in North Carolina's First District on November 2, 1992, the same day she won the identical district in the regular general election. She is not identified here as a previous member.

9. In his latest book Lublin included a table reporting that the Democrats "lost" ten districts through 1994 because of racial redistricting (2004, 109), but four of them concern the failure to pick up Republican seats due to the drop in African American population in them. Six districts were Democratic seats lost to Republicans. Given the states in which these losses occurred, they were, no doubt, Alabama Sixth; Georgia First, Third, and Fourth; and North Carolina Second and Third.

10. Another study that disregarded whether districts were adjacent to majority-African-American districts and that included all eleven southern states in the analysis reported counterintuitive findings about the 1994 elections. The votes for white Democratic southern incumbents who had been reelected in 1992 varied with the change in the African American percentages in their districts, but not in a positive way, as expected, but rather in a negative way. The more the African American percentage of their district declined, compared to their 1990 districts, the more their vote increased (Overby and Brown 2002, with suggested explanations at 345, 347; see also Petrocik and Desposato 1998, 624).

11. In 1995 the Republicans gained five additional seats as a result of party switching. In addition to the two Louisianans, Tauzin and Hayes (see note 3 above), one Democrat each from Georgia, Texas, and Mississippi changed parties. These were Nathan Deal, Greg Laughlin, and Mike Parker, respectively. Deal was elected in 1992 with 59.2 percent of the votes and reelected in 1994 with 57.9 percent, Laughlin was reelected in 1992 with 68.1 percent and again in 1994 with 55.6 percent, and Parker was reelected in 1992 with 67.3 percent and in 1994 with 68.5 percent.

12. The incumbent in the Louisiana Fourth District, Cleo Fields, was reelected in 1994 in a revised district that was reduced from 62.6 percent African American in VAP to 54.5 percent. The second revision, before the 1996 election, dismantled the voting rights district and placed Fields in a new Sixth District that was only 29.4 percent African American in VAP, and which also contained a second incumbent, a white Republican. Fields, not surprisingly, chose not to seek reelection in this district (see Engstrom and Kirksey, 1998).

13. A study of the 1992 U.S. House elections by Charles Cameron, David Epstein, and Sharyn O'Halloran (1996) is frequently cited as supporting the idea that majority-African-American districts were not needed to elect African

Americans to the House in the South (presumably defined as the eleven states of the Confederacy). They contended that African Americans had an equal opportunity, that is, a fifty-fifty probability, to elect a representative of their choice (operationalized as African American Democrat) in a district in which African Americans constituted only 40.3 percent of the VAP, and they concluded that "black candidates seem to have a fair chance of winning, even in districts with a white majority (so called minority-minority districts)" (1996, 804). Their analysis, however, excluded the presence of Hispanics, which is critical to their estimate (see Lublin 1999). This is because the districts that no doubt had the greatest impact on the estimates (the three with the smallest African American VAP to elect an African American in 1992—the Eighteenth and Thirtieth in Texas and the Twenty-third in Florida) were 48.6, 47.1, and 45.7 percent African American in VAP. These were all *majority-minority* districts, however, when the Hispanic VAP within them was added to that of African Americans. There were only two districts in the South in which the VAP was in the 30 percentage point range (Mississippi's Fourth at 36.5 percent and Virginia's Fifth at 30.7 percent). In their response to Lublin's analysis, Epstein and O'Halloran found the inclusion of Hispanics in their analysis still resulted in equal opportunity points of 48.6, 46.6, and 42.5 for the 1992, 1994, and 1996 elections (1999, 188). But these estimates concerned the probability of electing an African American or a Hispanic and did not address the issue that Lublin raised, which concerned what it takes to elect an African American. It also needs to be noted that the concept of an "equal opportunity to elect" in the analysis concerns the opportunity within a district within a plan, not within a plan itself, which is the referent for equal opportunity in Section 2 of the VRA.

References

Aistrup, Joseph A. 1996. *The Southern Strategy Revisited: Republican Top-Down Advancement in the South*. Lexington: University Press of Kentucky.

Barone, Michael, and Grant Ujifusa. 1989. *The Almanac of American Politics 1990*. Washington, D.C.: National Journal.

———. 1991. *The Almanac of American Politics 1992*. Washington, D.C.: National Journal.

———. 1993. *The Almanac of American Politics 1994*. Washington, D.C.: National Journal.

Bartley, Numan V., and Hugh D. Graham. 1975. *Southern Politics and the Second Reconstruction*. Baltimore: Johns Hopkins University Press.

Bass, Jack, and Walter DeVries. 1976. *The Transformation of Southern Politics: Social Change and Political Consequence since 1945*. New York: Basic Books.

Beachler, Donald W. 1995. "Racial Gerrymandering and Republican Gains in Southern House Elections." *Journal of Political Science* 23: 65–86.

———. 1998. "Racial and Partisan Gerrymandering: Three States in the 1990s." *American Review of Politics* 19: 1–16.

———. 2000. "A Tale of Two Decades: Southern House Elections in the 1980s and 1990s." *Southeastern Political Review* 28: 353–69.

Black, Earl, and Merle Black. 1987. *Politics and Society in the South.* Cambridge: Harvard University Press.

———. 1992. *The Vital South: How Presidents Are Elected.* Cambridge: Harvard University Press.

———. 2002. *The Rise of Southern Republicans.* Cambridge: Harvard University Press.

Brace, Kimball, Bernard Grofman, and Lisa Handley. 1987. "Does Redistricting Aimed to Help Blacks Necessarily Help Republicans?" *Journal of Politics* 49: 169–85.

Bullock, Charles S. 1995a. "Affirmative Action Districts: In Whose Faces Will They Blow Up?" *Campaigns and Elections* 16: 22–23.

———. 1995b. "The Gift That Keeps on Giving? Consequences of Affirmative Action Gerrymandering." *American Review of Politics* 16: 33–39.

Bullock, Charles S., and Richard E. Dunn. 1999. "The Demise of Racial Redistricting and the Future of Black Representation." *Emory Law Journal* 48: 1209–53.

———. 2003. "White Voter Support for Southern Black Congressional Candidates." *American Review of Politics* 24: 249–65.

Bullock, Charles S., III, and Mark J. Rozell, eds. 1998. *The New Politics of the Old South: An Introduction to Southern Politics.* Lanham, Md.: Rowman and Littlefield.

Cameron, Charles, David Epstein, and Sharyn O'Halloran. 1996. "Do Majority-Minority Districts Maximize Substantive Representation in Congress?" *American Political Science Review* 90: 794–812.

Canon, David T. 1999. *Race, Redistricting, and Representation: The Unintended Consequences of Black Majority Districts.* Chicago: University of Chicago Press.

Edsall, Thomas B., and Mary D. Edsall. 1991. *Chain Reaction: The Impact of Race, Rights, and Taxes on American Politics.* New York: Norton.

Engstrom, Richard L. 1995. "Voting Rights Districts: Debunking the Myths." *Campaigns and Elections* 16: 24, 46.

———. 1986. "Repairing the Crack in New Orleans' Black Vote: VRA's Results Test Nullifies 'Gerryduck.'" *Publius* 16: 109–21.

———. 1988. "Black Politics and the Voting Rights Act, 1965–1982." In *Contemporary Southern Politics: Continuity and Change,* ed. James Lea. Baton Rouge: Louisiana State University Press.

———. 2001. "The Political Thicket, Electoral Reform, and Minority Voting Rights." In *Fair and Effective Representation? Debating Electoral Reform and Minority Rights,* ed. Mark E. Rush and Richard L. Engstrom. Lanham, Md.: Rowman and Littlefield.

Engstrom, Richard L., Stanley A. Halpin Jr., Jean A. Hill, and Victoria M. Caridas-Butterworth. 1994. "Louisiana." In *The Quiet Revolution in the South: The Impact of the Voting Rights Act 1965–1990,* ed. Chandler Davidson and Bernard Grofman. Princeton: Princeton University Press.

Engstrom, Richard L., and Jason F. Kirksey. 1998. "Race and Representational Districting in Louisiana." In *Race and Redistricting in the 1990s,* ed. Bernard Grofman. New York: Agathon Press.

Epstein, David, and Sharyn O'Halloran. 1999. "A Social Science Approach to Race, Redistricting, and Representation." *American Political Science Review* 93: 187–91.

Fenno, Richard F., Jr. 2000. *Congress at the Grassroots: Representational Change in the South, 1970–1998.* Chapel Hill: University of North Carolina Press.

———. 2003. *Going Home: Black Representatives and Their Constituents.* Chicago: University of Chicago Press.

Frymer, Paul. 1999. *Uneasy Alliances: Race and Party Competition in America.* Princeton: Princeton University Press.

Gaddie, Ronald Keith. 2004. "The Texas Redistricting, Measure for Measure." *Extensions*, 19–24.

Glaser, James M. 1996. *Race, Campaign Politics, and the Realignment in the South.* New Haven: Yale University Press.

Grofman, Bernard, and Lisa Handley. 1998. "Estimating the Impact of Voting-Rights-Related Districting on Democratic Strength in the U.S. House of Representatives." In *Race and Redistricting in the 1990s*, ed. Bernard Grofman. New York: Agathon Press.

Gronke, Paul, and J. Matthew Wilson. 1999. "Competing Redistricting Plans as Evidence of Political Motives: The North Carolina Case." *American Politics Quarterly* 27: 147–76.

Hagens, Winnett. 1998. "The Politics of Race: The Virginia Redistricting Experience, 1991–1997." In *Race and Redistricting in the 1990s*, ed. Bernard Grofman. New York: Agathon Press.

Havard, William C., ed. 1972. *The Changing Politics of the South.* Baton Rouge: Louisiana State University Press.

Hill, Kevin A. 1995. "Does the Creation of Majority Black Districts Aid Republicans? An Analysis of the 1992 Congressional Elections in Eight Southern States." *Journal of Politics* 57: 384–401.

Hill, Kevin A., and Nicol C. Rae. 2000. "What Happened to the Democrats in the South? U.S. House Elections, 1992–1996." *Party Politics* 6: 5–22.

Key, V. O., Jr. 1949. *Southern Politics in State and Nation.* New York: Knopf.

Knuckey, Jonathan O. 2001. "Racial Resentment and Southern Republican Voting in the 1990s." *American Review of Politics* 22: 257–77.

Lamis, Alexander P. 1984. *The Two-Party South.* New York: Oxford University Press.

———. 1999. *Southern Politics in the 1990s.* Baton Rouge: Louisiana State University Press.

Lublin, David. 1997. *The Paradox of Representation: Racial Gerrymandering and Minority Interests in Congress.* Princeton: Princeton University Press.

———. 1999. "Racial Redistricting and African American Representation: A Critique of 'Do Majority-Minority Districts Maximize Substantive Black Representation?'" *American Political Science Review* 93: 183–86.

———. 2004. *The Republican South: Democratization and Partisan Change.* Princeton: Princeton University Press.

Lublin, David, and D. Stephen Voss. 2000a. "Boll-Weevil Blues: Polarized Congressional Delegations into the 21st Century." *American Review of Politics* 21: 427–50.

————. 2000b. "Racial Redistricting and Realignment in Southern State Legislatures." *American Journal of Political Science* 44: 792–810.

Martinez, J. Michael, William D. Richardson, and Ron McNinch-Su, eds. 2000. *Confederate Symbols in the Contemporary South*. Gainesville: University Press of Florida.

Matthews, Donald R., and James W. Prothro. 1966. *Negroes and the New Southern Politics*. New York: Harcourt, Brace and World.

McKee, Seth C. 2002. "Majority Black Districts, Republican Ascendancy, and Party Competition in the South, 1988–2000." *American Review of Politics* 23: 123–39.

Moreland, Laurence W., and Robert P. Steed, eds. 1997. *The 1996 Presidential Election in the South: Southern Party Systems in the 1990s*. Westport, Conn.: Praeger.

Moreland, Laurence W., Robert P. Steed, and Tod A. Baker, eds. 1987. *Blacks in Southern Politics*. New York: Praeger.

————. 1991. *The 1988 Presidential Election in the South: Continuity amidst Change in Southern Party Politics*. New York: Praeger.

Niemi, Richard G., and Alan I. Abramowitz. 1995. "Partisan Redistricting and the 1992 Congressional Elections." *Journal of Politics* 56: 811–17.

Overby, L. Marvin, and Robert B. Brown. 2002. "Race, Redistricting, and Re-Election: The Fate of White Incumbent Democrats in the 1994 Congressional Elections." *American Review of Politics* 23: 337–53.

Overby, L. Marvin, and Kenneth M. Cosgrove. 1996. "Unintended Consequences? Racial Redistricting and the Representation of Minority Interests." *Journal of Politics* 58: 540–50.

Petrocik, John R., and Scott W. Desposato. 1998. "The Partisan Consequences of Majority-Minority Districts in the South, 1992 and 1994." *Journal of Politics* 60: 613–33.

Scher, Richard K. 1997. *Politics in the New South: Republicanism, Race and Leadership in the Twentieth Century*. Armonk, N.Y.: M. E. Sharpe.

Sellers, Patrick J., David T. Canon, and Matthew M. Schousen. 1998. "Congressional Redistricting in North Carolina." In *Race and Redistricting in the 1990s*, ed. Bernard Grofman. New York: Agathon Press.

Shafer, Byron E., and Richard C. Johnston. 2001. "The Transformation of Southern Politics Revisited: The House of Representatives as a Window." *British Journal of Political Science* 31: 601–25.

Shotts, Kenneth W. 2001. "The Effect of Majority-Minority Mandates on Partisan Gerrymandering." *American Journal of Political Science* 45: 120–35.

Smith, Stephen Samuel, Karen M. Kedrowski, and Joseph M. Ellis. 2004. "Electoral Structures, Venue Selection, and the (New?) Politics of School Desegregation." *Perspectives* 2: 795–801.

Squire, Peverill. 1995. "The Partisan Consequences of Congressional Redistricting." *American Politics Quarterly* 23: 229–40.

Steed, Robert P., and Laurence W. Moreland, eds. 2002. *The 2000 Presidential Election in the South: Partisanship and Southern Party Systems in the 21st Century*. Westport, Conn.: Praeger.

Steed, Robert P., Laurence W. Moreland, and Tod A. Baker, eds. 1985. *The 1984 Presidential Election in the South: Patterns in Southern Party Politics.* New York: Praeger.

———. 1994. *The 1992 Presidential Election in the South: Current Patterns of Southern Party and Electoral Politics.* Westport, Conn.: Praeger.

Streb, Matthew J. 2002. *The New Electoral Politics of Race.* Tuscaloosa: University of Alabama Press.

Swain, Carol M. 1995, enlarged ed. *Black Faces, Black Interests: The Representation of African Americans in Congress.* Cambridge: Harvard University Press.

Swain, John W., Stephen A. Borrelli, and Brian C. Reed. 1998. "Partisan Consequences of the Post-1990 Redistricting for the U.S. House of Representatives." *Political Research Quarterly* 51: 945–67.

Swansbrough, Robert H., and David M. Brodsky, eds. 1988. *The South's New Politics: Realignment and Dealignment.* Columbia: University of South Carolina Press.

Tate, Katherine. 2003. *Black Faces in the Mirror: African Americans and Their Representatives in the U.S. Congress.* Princeton: Princeton University Press.

Voss, D. Stephen, and David Lublin. 2001. "Black Incumbents, White Districts: An Appraisal of the 1996 Congressional Elections." *American Politics Research* 29: 141–82.

Walsh, Bill. 2005. "Demos Split on Electoral Strategy in the South." *Times-Picayune* (New Orleans), February 20, 2005.

Yarbrough, Tinsley E. 2002. *Race and Redistricting: The Shaw-Cromartie Cases.* Lawrence: University Press of Kansas.

★ **Chapter 5** ★

Writing about Women in Southern Politics

Penny M. Miller and Lee R. Remington

IN 1949 V. O. KEY WROTE his seminal *Southern Politics in State and Nation,* a work that played a major role in describing and explaining the politics of the South in the years leading up to the civil rights movement and that continues to be a valuable resource for those who study southern politics. Unfortunately, Key did not consider the political impact of a major class of citizens—women. Thus, the formulation of a realistic picture of southern politics should not begin, and certainly should not end, with the work of V. O. Key. Instead, this chapter provides a multilayered examination of the literature on women in southern politics while also suggesting avenues for future research in this field.

Unhappily, there is no abundance of information about women in southern politics. Books and articles on women in politics tend either to examine the nation as a whole or to focus on particular states. It is commonly acknowledged, however, that politics in the South is "different," and studies often include a South versus non-South control variable (Ford and Dolan 1995). Why, then, has so little been written about women in southern politics? The most obvious reason is the relatively low level of involvement by women in southern politics. The South has fewer female officeholders than other parts of the United States, so scholars wishing to study women in politics may look away from the region because more information is available elsewhere. Table 5.1 provides an illustration of the underrepresentation of women in southern politics.

Why should we care about the role of women in southern politics? Much of the research on women in southern politics has been carried out by only a small number of scholars, which has resulted in a lack of

Table 5.1: Status of Women in the South and Border States

| State | Women in State Legislatures in 2005[1] | | Women in 2004 Elected Offices Composite Index[2] | Women Voting in 1998 and 2000[3] |
	Percent	Rank	IWPR State Rank	IWPR State Rank
Alabama	10.0	49	32	12
Arkansas	16.3	37	30	36
Delaware	33.9	2	5	30
Florida	23.8	22	29	40
Georgia	18.2	33	33	47
Kentucky	12.3	48	47	34
Louisiana	16.0	40	14	27
Maryland	34.0	1	12	16
Mississippi	12.6	46	49	23
Missouri	21.3	26	24	10
North Carolina	22.9	25	18	39
Oklahoma	14.8	43	38	35
South Carolina	8.8	50	50	13
Tennessee	17.4	34	41	42
Texas	19.9	30	22	49
Virginia	14.3	45	46	44
West Virginia	15.7	42	39	43

1. Center for the American Woman and Politics, Eagleton Institute of Politics, Rutgers University, "Women in State Legislatures 2005 Fact Sheet."
2. Institute for Women's Policy Research (IWPR), "The Status of Women in the States—2004" (2005), accessed at www.iwpr.org/states2004. The composite index is based on the number of female statewide elected officials, state legislators, and congresspeople.
3. Ibid.

diversity in the literature. Many topics have been touched upon, but few specific issues have been deeply investigated. Still, as there is ample information concerning women as the "invisible" majority in U.S. politics, a regional focus on the unique politics of the South is quite important. As more women enter the political arena, their impact (past and future) on southern politics is an area of research needing to be explored.

The Common Body of Literature
on Women in U.S. Politics

Much of the writing on women in southern politics draws on a common body of work dealing with women's political participation, representation, and involvement in campaigns and elections. This detailed, nationwide research remains to be replicated in the South. The classic nationwide study of women in politics is Virginia Sapiro's *The Political Integration of Women* (1983). Recent works include the second edition of Susan Carroll's *Women as Candidates in American Politics* (1994), Barbara Burrell's *A Woman's Place Is in the House* (1994), Robert Darcy, Susan Welch, and Janet Clark's *Women, Elections, and Representation* (1994), Sue Thomas's *How Women Legislate* (1994), and Lois Duke Whitaker's *Women in Politics: Outsiders or Insiders?* (1999). Other important resources include the works of Malcolm Jewell and Marcia Lynn Whicker, as well as Wilma Rule, all of whom focus on women in state legislatures (Jewell and Whicker 1993; Rule 1990). Another important contribution to the study of women is M. Margaret Conway, Gertrude Steuernagel, and David Ahern's *Women and Political Participation: Cultural Change in the Political Arena* (1997).

Among these nationwide studies, there is a growing interest in how female officeholders differ from males. Some scholars have shown that women legislators are more likely than men to focus on "women's issues" (Saint-German 1989; Thomas and Welch 1991) and to serve on legislative committees that deal with welfare, education, and children's issues (Considine and Deutchman 1994). Legislatures with more female members pass more legislation devoted to the interests of women, children, and families (Thomas and Welch 1991). Women who chair legislative committees tend to be facilitators and less likely to pursue zero-sum outcomes (Thomas 1994), whereas men are more controlling (Kathlene 1994). Women devote more time than men to constituency service (Thomas 1992). One study even showed that the public sees women as more capable of handling social issues such as the environment, education, and health care, while men are perceived as better at handling security, military, and economic issues (Koch 1999). Finally, Kim Fridkin Kahn's 1996 work, *The Political Consequences of Being a Woman: How Stereotypes Influence the Conduct and Consequences of Political Campaigns,* attempts to explain the low representation of women in higher political offices (see also Bullock and Maggiotto 2003).

All in all, ample information is available concerning women on a national scale. Although the national focus on women is important, a need remains to focus on specific regions as well. This is because the South is renowned for its traditionalistic political culture, history of single-party politics, and traditional gender role expectations. Research has shown that women who enter the southern political arena, and those who are already in it, share experiences different from those of women in other parts of the country (Greene and Wall 2000a, 391–92). It is the very uniqueness of this region that makes its study valuable to political science. We hope that these national studies can serve as templates for more focused research designs.

Women Officeholders and Electing Women to Public Office

Some scholars have undertaken the challenge of studying specific regions and have provided more focused findings concerning female political candidates and officeholders. Deanne Nuwer's "Southern Women Legislators and Patriarchy in the South" (2000) reviewed research on women in Congress and in state legislatures. She discussed how patriarchal influences have excluded women from southern politics. Other scholars, such as Terry L. Gilmour and Penny M. Miller, have limited their focus to individual southern states. Gilmour's "The Women of the Texas Legislature—Through the Eyes of Journalists" (2000) examined the participation and progress of women in Texas politics. She found that even though women did not run for office intending to "represent" women, they ended up focusing on women's issues once in office. Miller's "The Silenced Majority: Glacial Movement of Women into Kentucky Politics" (2000) showed how scarce female participation is in Kentucky politics. The intermittent impact of Kentucky women as voters, appointed officeholders, members of boards and commissions, party activists, lobbyists, and campaign contributors historically has lagged behind national averages. Also, the role Kentucky women play as elected representatives—local, state, and national officeholders—remains among the most muted in the nation. Miller attributed this shortage of participation to the state's traditionalistic political culture, the powerful inertia of incumbency at all levels, and the entrenched "good old boy network" that dominates Kentucky politics (2000, 499).

A comprehensive data collection on women in southern legislatures is found in Joanne Hawks and Carolyn Staton's "On the Eve of Transition: Women in Southern Legislatures, 1946–1968" (1999). Convention holds that after their involvement in the war effort during World War II, women supposedly reembraced the traditional roles they had left behind. Hawks and Staton noted, however, that between 1946 and 1968 almost one hundred women entered legislatures in the traditional South. Unfortunately, the media seemed to ignore their legislative achievements, focusing instead on their domestic and feminine natures. Another interesting article is "'Winning in My Own Back Yard': County Government, School Board Positions Steadily More Attractive to Women Candidates" by Susan MacManus, Charles Bullock, Frances Akins, Laura Jane Hoffman, and Adam Newmark (1999). In this work the authors gathered data from Georgia and Florida that showed that although more women won county and school district offices in the early 1990s, there was still a glass-ceiling effect overall.

In "Female Candidate Success in Runoff Primaries," Charles S. Bullock and Michael Maggiotto (2003) researched women's success in Georgia in runoff primaries (required by some states when none of the candidates receives an electoral majority) in gaining nominations for statewide and local offices. Relying on data from a series of primaries, they tested the proposition that runoff elections disadvantage women. Runoff elections have been attacked as discriminatory against black and female candidates by individuals such as Jesse Jackson and former NOW president Eleanor Smeal. Smeal reviewed eight nomination contests in which women led the primary field in six, but lost the runoffs (Bullock and Maggiotto 2003, 3). This prompted Smeal to observe that runoffs give no assistance to female candidates. Bullock and Maggiotto provide the most extensive examination of whether women do experience discrimination in runoff primaries. Interestingly, they found that runoff elections do not disadvantage women. Although more women are being elected to office, however, proportional representation has not been fulfilled in Congress, in any state legislature (Rule 1999), or in most local governments (MacManus et al. 1999).

Many attempts have been made to explain women's underrepresentation in elective office, and most studies focus on electoral structures. One structure that is often cited and studied is districting. For instance, researchers have found that at-large elections do not necessarily impede women from winning office. In fact, some suggest that women do better in at-large or multimember systems because some voters are more willing to support a woman for one of the positions, since she will not be their *only* representative (Carroll 1985; Darcy, Welch, and Clark 1994; Karnig and Welch 1979; Welch and Studlar 1990). Still, others have found no evidence that women are either advantaged or disadvantaged by at-large elections (Bullock and MacManus 1991; Bullock and Maggiotto 2003; Welch and Herrick 1992).

In "The Effects of Member Gender and Constituency Characteristics on Southern Congressional Voting Behavior, 1972–2000," Daniel Green (2003) explored how attributes such as gender influence the roll call voting behavior of officeholders. Green found that though gender did play a statistically significant role in explaining voting behavior (females were more liberal than their male colleagues), other factors such as ideology, partisan identification, district composition, and the race of the member had stronger effects. These results reinforce the previous findings of other scholars (Darcy and Schramm 1977; Vega and Firestone 1995; Welch 1985). Green also noted that the majority-minority redistricting of the early 1990s in the South led to the election of a large number of female legislators. The impact that this increased number of female legislators might have on southern politics is an area ripe for research.

It is clear from existing research that women have made great strides in southern politics since World War II. More women are entering the political arena and succeeding. The literature also shows, however, that southern politics is still rampant with networks of "good old boys," patriarchs, and glass ceilings. Perhaps future research will be able to show how the "political female boom" of the early 1990s has resulted in noticeable changes in southern politics.

Women in Southern State Party Politics and Policy Preferences among Southern Party Elites

Many articles and book chapters have focused on the changing roles of women in Southern state party politics. One of the most interesting of these is Janet Clark, Charles Hadley, and Robert Darcy's "Political Ambition among Men and Women State Party Leaders" (1989). Using data from the 1984 State Convention Delegate Project collected under the direction of Robert P. Steed, Laurence W. Moreland, and Tod A. Baker (which included survey data from state party convention participants in six southern states), the authors researched whether countersocialization theory (which they defined as the "view that few women participate as political leaders; therefore, these few likely had some socialization experience that countered the prevailing norms of female political quiescence") explains why women and men decide to enter the political arena and run for public office (Clark, Hadley, and Darcy 1989, 195). In the survey southern male and female state convention delegates were asked about their desire to run for public office and about their political experiences. Although they found men to be more politically ambitious than women, Clark and her colleagues did not find that politically active women have socialization experiences different from those of the rest of the population. Interestingly, they found that "the hypothesis that a childhood in the South results in the inculcation of traditional norms against women's political participation receives no support whatsoever" (Clark et al. 1989, 203). Their findings are in line with Sapiro's thesis that adult experiences are more important sources of countersocialization for both men and women than are childhood experiences (1983). Finally, the authors suggested further study of structural barriers to the election of women, instead of simply blaming the attitudes of women.

In a related study, "The Changing Roles of Women in Southern State Party Politics," Darcy, Clark, and Hadley (1990) looked to see whether traditional gender roles (men in instrumental roles and women in expressive roles) have been carried over into the roles of men and women as political party activists. They did not find a connection with these traditional gender roles. Their evidence suggested, however, that Democratic women are more involved than Republican women in both instrumental and expressive activities. They also found that southern women had at least as much political ambition as women nationwide, and southern Democratic women were much more ambitious than southern Republican women. And though Democratic women may be more ambitious, the authors stated that they may have trouble translating their ambition into electoral success: Democratic women tend to have far more liberal views than the general southern electorate.

Another important article in this area is Harold Clarke, Frank Fiegert, and Marianne Stewart's "Different Contents, Similar Packages: The Domestic Political Beliefs of Southern Local Party Activists" (1995). The authors investigated the political beliefs of Democratic and Republican local party activists in eleven southern states. They found that the beliefs of both groups are structured by government involvement in the economy and society, traditional values, and women's rights and roles. Not surprisingly, they found that Republicans took more conservative positions than Democrats on specific issues. Further, there was less subgroup diversity among Republicans concerning government involvement and traditional values issues than among Democrats. It is the political beliefs of Democrats (not Republicans), however, that vary geographically. Deep South Democrats were more conservative than those in border states (Clarke et al. 1995).

In "The Importance of Attitudes toward Women's Equality: Policy Preferences among Southern Party Elites" (1997), Christine Day and Charles Hadley explored reasons for the gender gap in policy preferences among southern political party activists. To do this, they surveyed southern county-level political party activists and national convention delegates to test for gender differences in attitudes. They found that female party activists were more liberal than males on most issues and described themselves as more ideologically liberal. Further, they found that the gender gap is wider among Democrats than among Republicans. When controlling for attitudes toward women's equality with men, gender differences in policy preferences were insignificant or even reversed, with nonfeminist women taking more conservative positions than men. Day and Hadley concluded that the gender gaps they found on domestic and foreign-policy issues are not simply a function of women's socioeconomic status or economic autonomy from men. Instead, the gaps are more attributable to respondents' commitment to women's equality with men. Thus, it is the commitment to women's equality, rather than gender itself, that leads to general policy liberalism among activists. These findings are aligned with previous research on the gender gap in policy preferences. Other researchers have also found that women tended to be more liberal on most issues, to be more opposed to higher defense spending and use of force, and to be more supportive of environmental protection, government regulation, and social programs and that the gender gap in policy preferences tended to be greater among political elites than the general public.

A 1998 study entitled "Gender Differences in Careers and Policy Preferences" by William Hulbary, Anne Kelly, and Lewis Bowman looked specifically at the gender gap in the South. The authors noted that southern women are in a position to alter the traditional southern "politics as usual" attitude at the grassroots level. Using data from the 1991 Southern Grassroots Party Activists Project (a survey of a sample of precinct leaders across the eleven states of the old Confederacy; see

Hadley and Bowman 1998), the authors uncovered a link among gender, party, difference in background (demographic characteristics and socioeconomic status), and political career (experience, recruitment, and incentives). They also found that differences in political ideology and issues within the parties were associated with gender, socioeconomic status, and age. Specifically, they noted that when gender differences did emerge, it was because of issues directly affecting women personally, socially, or economically. Further, they found that gender differences tended to be greater among Democrats than among Republicans. Female Democratic activists in the South tended to be more liberal (especially those with more education and higher-status jobs) than male Democrats. Likewise, women Republicans moderated their party's conservatism, making the issue gap between Republican males and females smaller. Finally, the authors suggested that gender and differences in background, ideology, and issues might be changing southern political parties and candidates.

It should be noted that Hulbary and his coauthors also pointed out the importance of county party organizations, which have opened up opportunities for women to emerge as political activists. Women bring more diversity to party attitudes and career goals. This leads to an awareness by the party that the inclusion of women in party organizations may enhance efforts to gain more votes for the party. Especially at the grassroots level, women are (sometimes silently) transforming the organization of parties. But there remains room for further research concerning the gender gap, especially as to how it relates to southern politics.

Studies of Individual States

Much research has focused on specific states within the South. For instance, the University of Nebraska Press has published a series of volumes about the government and politics of specific states that includes limited information about women in those states. At present seven such books are available that focus on southern and border states: Alabama (Thomas and Stewart 1988), Arkansas (Blair 1988), Kentucky (Miller 1994), Mississippi (Krane and Shaffer 1992), North Carolina (Fleer 1994), Oklahoma (Morgan, England, and Humphreys 1991), and West Virginia (Brisbin, Dilger, Hammock, and Mooney 1997).

Articles addressing state-specific phenomena are quite diverse. For example, in a 1979 article entitled "Women in Florida," Joan Carver looked at how the traditional attitudes that had limited women's opportunities had diminished in Florida. She pointed to the movement of nonsoutherners to the state after World War II, which resulted in the formation of two female cultures—a native conservative culture in the northern part of the state and a culture more receptive to change in central and southern Florida. She found that it was this latter group that led the way for change for Florida women. Women have made progress toward full equality since 1960 by moving political power away from the northern part of the state (Carver 1979).

In "'What Women Wanted': Arkansas Women's Commissions and the ERA" (2000), Janine Parry discussed the creation of the Arkansas Governor's Commission on the Status of Women (GCSW) in 1964. Parry traced the GCSW's work and its support of the equal rights amendment (ERA). Though the GCSW was active during the 1970s, as the support for the ERA faded (the Arkansas legislature never ratified the ERA), so did support for the women's commission.

In her recent article on Kentucky politics, "The Slow and Unsure Progress of Women in Kentucky Politics," Penny Miller (2001) noted that women constituted 51 percent of the state's population but held only 11 percent of the seats in the General Assembly and only 18 percent of the state's 6,610 elective offices. Women have had most success at the local level as circuit court and county clerks, positions traditionally held by females across the South. As Miller noted also in her earlier article (2000), for a variety of cultural and psychological reasons male and female voters have viewed men as better suited to public office. Studies show that women are expected to prove their competence, electability, and toughness, while men are assumed to have these qualities (Dolan 1997; Huddy and Terkildsen 1993). Other influencing factors that have been observed include the power of incumbency, the limited role of political party recruitment of female candidates, escalating campaign costs, the rise of negative campaigning, stereotypical attitudes about politics as a male domain, the lack of women willing to run, the lack of female role models and mentors, the lack of training in public affairs and fundraising, and differential treatment by the media. Kentucky's traditionalistic political culture exacerbates many of these factors.

On a positive note, Miller (2001) noted that as more women have graduated from Kentucky's law schools, Kentucky women have made historic inroads in the male-dominated judiciary at all levels in the 1990s and early 2000s. Miller concluded that the future well-being of women in Kentucky is intricately tied to the increased development of women as public leaders.

Women and the Judiciary

As more women enter the legal profession, studying women and the judiciary is a relatively new yet necessary phenomenon in political science. In "A Woman of Many Firsts: The Honorable Lenore Prather" (2000), Diane Wall recounted the career of Mississippi's first female state supreme court justice. She related Prather's journey to the state supreme court, comparing and contrasting her experiences with those of her judicial colleagues. More important, Wall compared Prather's decision making to that of other female jurists serving on state supreme courts in the South. She found that Justice Prather was unique, for Prather maintained a centrist position among her colleagues and wrote few solo dissents during her tenure on the court. These findings are in contrast to other scholars' findings that state female jurists are located at their courts' ideological extremes and often write solo dissents (Allen and Wall 1993).

In addition to that article, Wall has written a number of works on women and the judiciary, particularly in relation to the South. These include "Judicial Incumbency: The Case of the Mississippi Supreme Court, 1932–1985" (1987), "Elite Female Justices' Decision Making within the South" (Wall and Allen 1987b), "Female Supreme Court Justices' Behavior within the South" (Wall and Allen 1988), "The Behavior of Women State Supreme Court Justices: Are They Tokens or Outsiders?" (Wall and Allen 1987a), and "Unanticipated Outcomes of Voting Rights Act Litigation in Mississippi: Women and Minorities in a Judicial Election" (Wall and Geter 1989).

In her article "The Role of Gender in Judicial Campaigns: North Carolina Trial Court Races" (2000), Traciel Reid examined how gender affected the 1998 North Carolina trial judge campaigns (trial court judges are elected in that state). She found that although women did not have trouble raising money for their campaigns, they still had to face other obstacles, such as the influence of political parties. This work is important because it is the first study to show how gender affects state and local judicial campaigns. Though Reid's results are limited to North Carolina, her study paves the way for future research on female judicial candidates.

Ronald Stidham, Robert Carp, and C. K. Rowland's "Women's Rights before the Federal District Courts, 1971–1977" (1983) is another useful component of the literature on women and the judiciary. The authors analyzed opinions by federal district judges (both in and outside the South) in women's rights and racial minority discrimination cases from 1971 through 1977. They found that petitioners in women's rights cases were slightly more likely to win than litigants from other disadvantaged groups. Further, they found no real differences in how northern and southern judges decided women's rights cases, but they did find that a judge's political party was an important variable in how such cases were decided.

Research on women and the judiciary is relatively new to political science. Therefore, it is no surprise that there is little of it that focuses only on southern judicial politics. The study of southern women and the judiciary is thus a vital future research opportunity waiting to be undertaken.

Black Women in Southern Politics

An important regional focus is the impact of black women on southern politics. Various studies have looked at the impact of black women in politics, though not necessarily only in the South. For instance, in "Black Women in Politics: The Puzzle of Success" (1988), Robert Darcy and Charles Hadley, in examining data from the 1984 State Convention Delegate Project (the survey of state party convention participants in twelve states, including six southern states, mentioned earlier), noted that, interestingly, most of the black women attending the state conventions in the twelve states were Democrats from the South (88 percent). While examining the sources of political ambition among state Democratic Party activists in the South, they found little difference in the effect of background factors between whites and blacks. Further, they found that blacks were no more favorable toward women in politics than whites were. Darcy and Hadley also found that greater ambition among black women is suggested by a greater proportion of black than white women activists from comparable socioeconomic backgrounds. In fact, although black women were still proportionately underrepresented in elected public offices, they made greater gains than white women in election to mayoral, state legislative, and congressional offices in the 1970s and 1980s.

Overall, Darcy and Hadley (1988) found that the reason for the electoral success of black women appeared to be their greater political ambition, something that may be attributed to involvement in the civil rights movement. Another explanation for black female political success could be found in the new opportunities resulting from the Voting Rights Act of 1965 as well as favorable judicial decisions that created black-majority political districts. The authors concluded by suggesting that the political success of black women requires greater attention.

In "Election Systems and the Representation of Black Women in American State Legislatures" (1993), Robert Darcy, Charles Hadley, and Jason Kirksey noted that blacks and women were underrepresented in American elected offices. At the local and the state legislative levels, however, the underrepresentation of blacks was almost entirely due to the underrepresentation of black women. According to the researchers, "Black men have achieved or exceeded parity between their population proportions and their proportions among elected officials; therefore, the under-representation of blacks and women are one and the same" (1993, 73). In "Asserting the Political Self: Community Activism among Black Women Who Relocate to the Rural South" (2000), Christopher Mele addressed the politicization of urban, working-class black women who left urban areas and relocated to small towns in the Southeast. Using participant observation techniques and interviews, Mele focused on how newcomers in three counties in southeastern North Carolina became politically active and how the local political culture influenced their activist experiences.

Women's Involvement in the Civil Rights Movement

Although the literature on this subject is primarily historical in nature, it is still highly relevant to the current study of women in southern politics. Lynne Olson's *Freedom's Daughters: The Unsung Heroines in the Civil Rights Movement from 1830 to 1970* (2001) was the first comprehensive history of the role of women in the civil rights movement. Olson began by noting that the fight for civil rights started much earlier than the 1950s and 1960s. In fact, the political activism of women was prominent from the first days of the abolitionist and suffragist movements to the more recent women's liberation movement. In chronicling this history, Olson examined the lives of more than sixty courageous women.

The first scholarly study focused on black women in the civil rights movement as it developed in the middle of the twentieth century—*Women in the Civil Rights Movement: Trailblazers and Torchbearers 1941–1965* (1993), edited by Vicki Crawford, Jacqueline Rouse, and Barbara Woods—contains a number of essays addressing the multiple roles women held during the civil rights movement. These articles include surveys of black women's roles as well as examinations of the struggles of particular groups of women during events such as the Montgomery bus boycott. Some articles within this work address the achievements of such individuals as Fannie Lou Hamer and Septima P. Clark.

Useful works more limited in scope include Clarice T. Campbell's *Civil Rights Chronicle: Letters from the South* (1997), in which she published letters she wrote in the early 1960s to family and friends during her campaign to end segregation. The letters are a valuable primary source documenting this volatile period.

Similarly, Constance Curry's 2000 volume, *Deep in Our Hearts*, examined the lives of nine women who committed themselves to the southern freedom movement during the 1960s. It contains first-person accounts, including testimonies involving the early days of the Student Nonviolent Coordinating Committee (SNCC), Students for a Democratic Society, the Albany Freedom Ride, voter registration drives and lunch counter sit-ins, Freedom Summer, the 1964 Democratic convention, and the rise of Black Power and the women's movement.

In *Going South: Jewish Women in the Civil Rights Movement* (2001), Debra Schultz discussed the impact of northern, middle-class Jewish women who participated in freedom rides, organized voter registration drives, and set up freedom schools in the South in the early 1960s. Most of the women in this study worked with SNCC. *Sisters in the Struggle* (2001), edited by Bettye Collier-Thomas and V. P. Franklin, documented African American women's impact upon social reform movements in the United States in the twentieth century. This book highlighted black women's dominant role in fighting for racial and gender equality. Examples of such women include Ella Baker, who helped found SNCC in 1960; Fannie Lou Hamer, who used her own personal anguish to establish her public persona; and Septima Clark, who created the "citizenship school" networks to teach poor black southerners to read and write and to help them register to vote. The book also described the roles of black women in the Mississippi Freedom Democratic Party, the Black Panther Party, and the Free Joan Little movement in the 1970s. It included the personal tales of prominent African American women, such as Rosa Parks, Charlayne Hunter-Gault, and Dorothy Height. Most important, the book analyzed the many roles black women in the civil rights movement took on, including the formulation of a new black feminism movement.

Information concerning the impact that women had on the civil rights movement in the South is abundant. These are just a few of the many works highlighting the great contributions of females in the civil rights movement.

Biographies and Autobiographies

Unfortunately, the large body of biographical and autobiographical works on individual women in the South cannot be discussed in detail in this chapter. What follows is but a sample of the many interesting and notable works in this genre.

In "Lindy Boggs: A Democrat for All Seasons" (2000), Judith Haydel and Thomas Ferrell examined the life and political career of the first woman elected to the U.S. House of Representatives from Louisiana and the first southerner to serve as ambassador to the Vatican. Though she delayed pursuing her political ambitions until after her husband's death, Boggs felt that women should actively engage in politics. This article examined the impact of Boggs's family background, Catholicism, and relationship with the various factions of the Democratic Party on her career in politics.

Several books have been written about Georgia Davis Powers and Mae Street Kidd, two prominent women who served in the Kentucky legislature. Powers became the first African American of either gender to serve in the Kentucky senate and was a leading advocate for blacks, women, children, the poor, and the disabled. Kidd was the first woman to serve on the powerful Rules Committee and advocated decent housing for minorities and the poor. Powers related her life in her autobiography, *I Shared the Dream: The Pride, Passion and Politics of the First Black Woman Senator from Kentucky* (1995). Wade Hall's *Passing for Black: The Life and Careers of Mae Street Kidd* (1997) is a fascinating biography of Kidd's life.

More generally, see the Web sites maintained by the University of California at Berkeley ("American Women: Biographical Sources") and Duke University ("Reference Sources for Women's Studies").

Conclusion: A Research Agenda

When it comes to studying women in southern politics, this chapter has shown that it is not a matter of what information is already available.

Instead, it is a matter of what is *not* available. For anyone interested in studying women in politics in general, or women in southern politics in particular, the following research issues are begging to be tackled. First, notwithstanding the increased political success of women in the early 1990s, no one has researched how the Year of the Woman has affected southern politics. The election of more and more female legislators, especially at the congressional level, is new to southern political affairs and requires thorough analysis. Further, we need to discover why structural barriers that hinder the election and fund-raising efforts of women, including the glass-ceiling effect, still exist in the South. In addition, although the gender gap has been researched with regard to its national effects, more needs to be done on how it affects southern politics particularly.

The study of women in roles other than legislators also needs attention. Traciel Reid showed how gender affected the judicial campaigns and election outcomes in North Carolina (2000). Her work can be expanded to include the impact of women jurists in all southern states. Similarly, there has been only limited attention paid to southern women as lobbyists. While Anthony Nownes and Patricia Freeman's "Female Lobbyists: Women in the World of 'Good Ol' Boys'" (1998) found evidence of women lobbyists' becoming more assimilated into the "good old boys" lobbying networks and having more opportunities for influencing state politics, their data were limited to three states and only one of those, South Carolina, was in the South. In short, women play a variety of roles in the political process—interest group representatives, campaign contributors, party officials—all of which could be part of an expanded research agenda (Miller 2001). Also, to echo a point made in Richard Scher's discussion in this book (chapter 3), more attention to the contemporary role of women in the civil rights movement is desirable.

Further, other research issues within American society could be fruitfully pursued more extensively in the South. For example, Jay Barth and Marvin Overby (2003) compared regional attitudes toward gay men and lesbians and found the South to be distinctive in the manner in which contact with gay men and lesbians operated as a tool for social change. Moreover, they found an inverse relationship between southerners' attitudes toward gays and lesbians and the percentage of gays and lesbians in their communities. Thus, while increased contact with gay men and lesbians positively alters attitudes toward those groups in the United States generally, the authors concluded the same might not be true for the South. With the increasing emergence of the gay rights movement, studying how gay and lesbian rights might affect southern politics is another research possibility. This policy-related research from the perspective of women in the South could be broadened to include the impact of government programs relating to welfare (and welfare reform) and to health care (and health care reform).

We hope that some of these research issues will be undertaken and new relationships discovered concerning women in southern politics. This chapter has summarized major contributions to the literature on women in southern politics. More important, it has established a research agenda for future southern politics scholars to follow. Perhaps one day the available literature on women in southern politics will be so abundant as to fill an entire book.

Note: Much of the information for the section on the literature on women in U.S. politics was obtained from the special issue on women in wouthern politics, *Southeastern Political Review,* edited by Kathanne Greene and Diane Wall (2000b), and from Bullock and Maggiotto (2003).

References

Allen, David W., and Diane E. Wall. 1993. "Role Orientations and Women State Supreme Court Justices." *Judicature: The Journal of the American Judicature Society* 77: 156–65.

"American Women: Biographical Sources." Women's Studies Collection. University of California at Berkeley. Accessed at www.lib.berkeley.edu/Collections/Womstu/wsbios.html.

Barth, Jay, and Marvin Overby. 2003. "Are Gay Men and Lesbians in the South the New 'Threat'? Regional Comparisons of Contact Theory." *Politics and Policy* 31: 1–19.

Blair, Diane D. 1988. *Arkansas Politics and Government: Do the People Rule?* Lincoln: University of Nebraska Press.

Brisbin, Richard A., Jr., Robert Jay Dilger, Allan S. Hammock, and Christopher Z. Mooney. 1997. *West Virginia Politics and Government.* Lincoln: University of Nebraska Press.

Bullock, Charles S., III, and Susan A. MacManus. 1991. "Municipal Electoral Structure and the Election of Councilwomen." *Journal of Politics* 53: 75–90.

Bullock, Charles S., III, and Michael A. Maggiotto. 2003. "Female Candidate Success in Runoff Primaries." *Women and Politics* 24: 1–18.

Burrell, Barbara. 1994. *A Woman's Place Is in the House: Campaigning for Congress in the Feminist Era.* Ann Arbor: University of Michigan Press.

Campbell, Clarice T. 1997. *Civil Rights Chronicle: Letters from the South.* Jackson: University Press of Mississippi.

Carroll, Susan J. 1994, 2nd ed. *Women as Candidates in American Politics.* Bloomington: Indiana University Press.

Carver, Joan S. 1979. "Women in Florida." *Journal of Politics* 41: 941–55.

Clark, Janet, Charles D. Hadley, and R. Darcy. 1989. "Political Ambition among Men and Women State Party Leaders." *American Politics Quarterly* 17: 194–207.

Clarke, Harold D., Frank B. Fiegert, and Marianne C. Stewart. 1995. "Different Contents, Similar Packages: The Domestic Political Beliefs of Southern Local Party Activists." *Political Research Quarterly* 48: 151–68.

Collier-Thomas, Bettye, and V. P. Franklin, eds. 2001. *Sisters in the Struggle: African-American Women in the Civil Rights–Black Power Movement.* New York: New York University Press.

Considine, Mark, and Iva Ellen Deutchman. 1994. "The Gendering of Political Institutions: A Comparison of American and Australian State Legislators." *Social Science Quarterly* 75: 854–66.

Conway, M. Margaret, Gertrude A. Steuernagel, and David Ahern. 1997. *Women and Political Participation: Cultural Change in the Political Arena.* Washington, D.C.: Congressional Quarterly Press.

Crawford, Vicki L., Jacqueline Anne Rouse, and Barbara Woods, eds. 1993. *Women in the Civil Rights Movement: Trailblazers and Torchbearers 1941–1965.* Bloomington: Indiana University Press.

Curry, Constance, ed. 2000. *Deep in Our Hearts: Nine White Women in the Freedom Movement.* Athens: University of Georgia Press.

Darcy, Robert, Janet Clark, and Charles D. Hadley. 1990. "The Changing Roles of Women in Southern State Party Politics." In *Political Parties in the Southern States: Party Activists in Partisan Coalitions,* ed. Tod A. Baker, Charles D. Hadley, Robert P. Steed, and Laurence W. Moreland. New York: Praeger.

Darcy, Robert, and Charles D. Hadley. 1988. "Black Women in Politics: The Puzzle of Success." *Social Science Quarterly* 69: 629–45.

Darcy, Robert, Charles D. Hadley, and Jason F. Kirksey. 1993. "Election Systems and the Representation of Black Women in American State Legislatures." *Women and Politics* 13: 73–89.

Darcy, Robert, and S. Schramm. 1977. "When Women Run against Men." *Public Opinion Quarterly* 41: 1–12.

Darcy, Robert, Susan Welch, and Janet Clark, eds. 1994, 2nd ed. *Women, Elections and Representation.* Lincoln: University of Nebraska Press.

Day, Christine L., and Charles D. Hadley. 1997. "The Importance of Attitudes toward Women's Equality: Policy Preferences among Southern Party Elites." *Social Science Quarterly* 78: 672–87.

Dolan, Kathleen A. 1997. "Gender Differences in Support for Women Candidates: Is There a Glass Ceiling in American Politics?" *Women and Politics* 17: 27–41.

Fleer, Jack D. 1994. *North Carolina Government and Politics.* Lincoln: University of Nebraska Press.

Ford, Lynn, and Kathleen Dolan. 1995. "The Politics of Women State Legislators: A South/Non-South Comparison." *Southeastern Political Review* 23:
333–48.

Gilmour, Terry L. 2000. "The Women of the Texas Legislature—Through the
Eyes of Journalists." *Southeastern Political Review* 28: 469–98.

Green, Daniel. 2003. "The Effects of Member Gender and Constituency Characteristics on Southern Congressional Voting Behavior, 1972–2000." *Politics and Policy* 31: 80–104.

Greene, Kathanne W., and Diane E. Wall. 2000a. "Women in Southern United
States Politics." *Southeastern Political Review* 28: 389–95.

———, eds. 2000b. Special issue on women and southern politics, *Southeastern Political Review* 28.

Hadley, Charles D., and Lewis Bowman, eds. 1998. *Party Activists in Southern
Politics: Mirrors and Makers of Change.* Knoxville: University of Tennessee
Press.

Hall, Wade H. 1997. *Passing for Black: The Life and Careers of Mae Street
Kidd.* Lexington: University Press of Kentucky.

Hawks, Joanne V., and Carolyn Ellis Staton. 1999, 3rd ed. "On the Eve of Tran-
sition: Women in Southern Legislatures, 1946–1968." In *Women in Politics:
Outsiders or Insiders?* ed. Lois Duke Whitaker. Upper Saddle River, N.J.:
Prentice-Hall.

Haydel, Judith, and Thomas H. Ferrell. 2000. "Lindy Boggs: A Democrat for
All Seasons." *Southeastern Political Review* 28: 427–47.

Huddy, Leonie, and Nayda Terkildsen. 1993. "Gender Stereotypes and the Perception of Male and Female Candidates." *American Journal of Political
Science* 37: 119–47.

Hulbary, William E., Anne E. Kelly, and Lewis Bowman. 1998. "Gender Dif-
ferences in Careers and Policy Preferences." In *Party Activists in Southern
Politics: Mirrors and Makers of Change,* ed. Charles D. Hadley and Lewis
Bowman. Knoxville: University of Tennessee Press.

Jewell, Malcolm, and Marcia Lynn Whicker. 1993. "The Feminization of Leadership in Legislatures." *PS: Political Science and Politics* 26: 705–12.

Kahn, Kim Fridkin. 1996. *The Political Consequences of Being a Woman: How
Stereotypes Influence the Conduct and Consequences of Political Campaigns.* New York: Columbia University Press.

Karnig, Albert, and Susan Welch. 1979. "Sex and Ethnic Differences in Municipal Representation." *Social Science Quarterly* 60: 465–81.

Kathlene, Lyn. 1994. "Power and Influence in State Legislative Policymaking:
The Interactions of Gender and Position in Committee Hearing Debates."
American Political Science Review 88: 560–76.

Key, V. O., Jr. 1949. *Southern Politics in State and Nation.* New York: Knopf.

Koch, Jeffrey. 1999. "Candidate Gender and Assessments of Senate Candidates." *Social Science Quarterly* 80: 84–96.

Krane, Dale, and Stephen D. Shaffer. 1992. *Mississippi Government and Politics: Modernizers versus Traditionalists.* Lincoln: University of Nebraska
Press.

MacManus, Susan A., Charles S. Bullock III, Frances E. Akins, Laura Jane Hoffman, and Adam Newmark. 1999, 3rd ed. "'Winning in My Own Back Yard': County Government, School Board Positions Steadily More Attractive to Women Candidates." In *Women in Politics: Outsiders or Insiders?* ed. Lois Duke Whitaker. Upper Saddle River, N.J.: Prentice-Hall.

Mele, Christopher. 2000. "Asserting the Political Self: Community Activism among Black Women Who Relocate to the Rural South." *Sociological Quarterly* 41: 63.

Miller, Penny M. 1994. *Kentucky Politics and Government: Do We Stand United?* Lincoln: University of Nebraska Press.

———. 2000. "The Silenced Majority: Glacial Movement of Women into Kentucky Politics." *Southeastern Political Review* 28: 499–529.

———. 2001. "The Slow and Unsure Progress of Women in Kentucky Politics." *Register of the Kentucky Historical Society* 99: 249–84.

Morgan, David R., Robert E. England, and George G. Humphreys. 1991. *Oklahoma Politics and Policies: Governing the Sooner State.* Lincoln: University of Nebraska Press.

Nownes, Anthony J., and Patricia K. Freeman. 1998. "Female Lobbyists: Women in the World of 'Good Ol' Boys.'" *Journal of Politics* 60: 1181–1201.

Nuwer, Deanne. 2000. "Southern Women Legislators and Patriarchy in the South." *Southeastern Political Review* 28: 449–68.

Olson, Lynne. 2001. *Freedom's Daughters: The Unsung Heroines in the Civil Rights Movement from 1830 to 1970.* New York: Scribner.

Parry, Janine A. 2000. "'What Women Wanted': Arkansas Women's Commissions and the ERA." *Arkansas Historical Quarterly* 59: 265–98.

Powers, Georgia Davis. 1995. *I Shared the Dream: The Pride, Passion and Politics of the First Black Woman Senator from Kentucky.* Far Hills, N.J.: New Horizon Press.

"Reference Sources for Women's Studies." Duke University Libraries. Accessed at scriptorium.lib.duke.edu/women/refbib.html.

Reid, Traciel V. 2000. "The Role of Gender in Judicial Campaigns: North Carolina Trial Court Races." *Southeastern Political Review* 28: 551–84.

Rule, Wilma. 1990. "Why Are More Women State Legislators?" *Western Political Quarterly* 43: 437–48.

———. 1999, 3rd ed. "Why Are More Women State Legislators?" In *Women in Politics: Outsiders or Insiders?* ed. Lois Duke Whitaker. Upper Saddle River, N.J.: Prentice-Hall.

Saint-Germain, Michelle A. 1989. "Does Their Difference Make a Difference? The Impact of Women on Public Policy in the Arizona Legislature." *Social Science Quarterly* 50: 42–61.

Sapiro, Virginia. 1981. "Research Frontier Essay: When Are Interests Interesting? The Problem of Political Representation of Women." *American Political Science Review* 75: 701–16.

———. 1983. *The Political Integration of Women.* Urbana: University of Illinois Press.

Schultz, Debra L. 2001. *Going South: Jewish Women in the Civil Rights Movement.* New York: New York University Press.

Stidham, Ronald, Robert A. Carp, and C. K. Rowland. 1983. "Women's Rights before the Federal District Courts, 1971–1977." *American Politics Quarterly* 11: 205–19.

Thomas, James D., and William H. Stewart. 1988. *Alabama Government and Politics*. Lincoln: University of Nebraska Press.

Thomas, Sue. 1992. "The Effects of Race and Gender on Constituency Service." *Western Political Quarterly* 45: 169–80.

———. 1994. *How Women Legislate*. New York: Oxford University Press.

Thomas, Sue, and Susan Welch. 1991. "The Impact of Gender on Activities and Priorities of State Legislators." *Western Political Quarterly* 44: 445–56.

Vega, Arturo, and Juanita M. Firestone. 1995. "The Effects of Gender on Congressional Behavior and the Substantive Representation of Women." *Legislative Studies Quarterly* 20: 213–22.

Wall, Diane E. 1987. "Judicial Incumbency: The Case of the Mississippi Supreme Court, 1932–1985." *Southeastern Political Review* 15: 111–35.

———. 2000. "A Woman of Many Firsts: The Honorable Lenore Prather." *Southeastern Political Review* 28: 531–50.

Wall, Diane E., and David W. Allen. 1987a. "The Behavior of Women State Supreme Court Justices: Are They Tokens or Outsiders?" *Justice Systems Journal* 12: 232–45.

———. 1987b. "Elite Female Justices' Decision Making within the South." Paper presented at the annual meeting of the Southern Political Science Association, Charlotte, N.C.

———. 1988. "Female Supreme Court Justices' Behavior within the South." *Mississippi Association for Women in Higher Education: A Collection of Papers* 2:48–68.

Wall, Diane E., and Mary Geter. 1989. "Unanticipated Outcomes of Voting Rights Act Litigation in Mississippi: Women and Minorities in a Judicial Election." Paper presented at the annual meeting of the American Political Science Association, Atlanta.

Welch, Susan. 1985. "Are Women More Liberal Than Men in the U.S. Congress?" *Legislative Studies Quarterly* 10: 125–34.

Welch, Susan, and Rabekah Herrick. 1992. "The Impact of At-Large Elections in the Representation of Minority Women." In *United States Electoral Systems: Their Impact on Women and Minorities*, ed. Wilma Rule and Joseph F. Zimmerman. New York: Greenwood.

Welch, Susan, and Donley Studlar. 1990. "Multi-Member Districts and the Representation of Women: Evidence from Britain and the United States." *Journal of Politics* 52: 391–412.

Whicker, Marcia, and Malcolm E. Jewell. 1998. "The Feminization of Leadership in State Legislatures." In *Women and Elective Office: Past, Present and Future*, ed. Sue Thomas and Clyde Wilcox. New York: Oxford University Press.

Whitaker, Lois Duke. 1999, 3rd ed. *Women in Politics: Outsiders or Insiders?* Upper Saddle River, N.J.: Prentice-Hall.

★ **Chapter 6** ★

Reflections on Scholarship in Religion and Southern Politics

Ted G. Jelen

OVER THE PAST GENERATION, the study of religion and politics in the South has undergone a profound transformation. Once the province of specialists in an arcane subfield of the discipline, religious politics is now a central concern to analysts of political life in the American South. Indeed, I am aware of no credible account of the 2000 or 2004 presidential election that does not assign a central role to religious differences among voters. It might well be argued that the principal difference between the "red" states (carried by Republican George W. Bush in both elections) and the "blue" states (carried by Democratic candidates Al Gore and John Kerry, respectively) is the "faith gap" between voters for whom matters of faith are quite salient and their more secular counterparts in the electorate. With issues such as relations with Islamic nations, gay marriage, private school tuition vouchers, and "faith-based initiatives" on the political agenda, it seems likely that religiously based cleavages will animate political conflict in the United States for some time to come.

My purpose in this chapter is to highlight some of the impressive work done on religion and southern politics in the past quarter century or so and to suggest promising lines of future inquiry. The field of religion and politics contains numerous unanswered questions. Moreover, the integration of religious variables into other streams of research on southern politics remains incomplete.

The study of religion and southern politics contains two general themes, to which I will refer as a "Master Narrative" and a series of "sub-

141

narratives." The Master Narrative involves the mobilization and realignment of white southern evangelicals. This group has changed rapidly from a Democratic segment of the population, with traditionally low levels of political participation and voting turnout, to one that is strongly identified with the Republican Party. Indeed, the evangelical vote is among the most loyal components of the Republican coalition, and the preponderance of white evangelicals in many parts of the South is a major source of Republican support.

The subnarratives are accounts of the political behavior of religious groups that lie outside the white evangelical majority in the South. Catholics, Jews, mainline Protestants, African American evangelicals, seculars, and citizens from outside the Judeo-Christian tradition all constitute consequential minorities in parts of the South. Indeed, religious pluralism, rather than white evangelical domination, appears to be the rule in southern "megastates" such as Texas, Florida, and Georgia, and the presence of such actual and potential voters in these states, so rich in electoral votes, poses a formidable strategic challenge for presidential candidates. Moreover, it is necessary to regard members of regional religious minorities as objects as well as participants in the political process. For example, it is important to learn how white evangelical voters, or voters from different religious minorities, reacted to the candidacy of John Kerry, a Roman Catholic, or Joseph Lieberman, an observant Orthodox Jew.

To date, attention to religious variables has been limited to scholars who study the region (for a prominent early exception, see Baker, Steed, and Moreland 1983; more recently, see Clark and Prysby 2004). It can be expected, however, that recent political developments (such as the presidential elections of 2000 and 2004) will cause scholars from outside the religion and politics specialty to pay closer attention to religious variables.

Models of Religious Influence

The recent popularity of economic models in the sociology of religion poses an interesting set of questions for the study of religious politics in the South. The religious composition of the South differs from that of the rest of the country, and there are important intraregional variations within the South as well. The religious environment (or "market") under investigation in a particular study might well affect the extent and manner to which religious beliefs and memberships influence political phenomena.

Perhaps the simplest model of religious influence is an *additive* model. Under this conception, religious attributes are characteristics of individuals and, therefore, assume political importance in settings in which citizens with particular characteristics are numerous. Thus, if white evangelicals are more prevalent in Mississippi than in Massachusetts and if evangelicalism is associated with restrictive attitudes toward abortion or with affiliation with the Republican Party, we might expect Mississippians to be more pro-life or more pro-Republican than residents of Massachusetts, even if the relationship between evangelicalism and political attitudes is the same in both states.

Despite the attractive parsimony of the additive model, it seems likely to be an oversimplification. It is possible (and indeed likely) that individual religious attributes might have effects on the attitudes and behavior of other citizens who are not necessarily adherents of a particular religious tradition. In other words, religious variables may have an impact on political contexts (what Wilcox, Rozell, and Green 2003 have termed "group ecology") that cannot be attributed simply to the aggregation of individuals.

One possible set of contextual effects might relate to what Peter Berger (1967) has termed the "sacred canopy." The sacred canopy hypothesis suggests that once there exists a critical mass of citizens who hold particular values (religious or otherwise), such people may provide political cues for people outside the value tradition. This phenomenon, which Alexis de Tocqueville ([1835, 1840] 1945) pejoratively termed the "tyranny of the majority" and which Elisabeth Noelle-Neumann (1984) characterized as the "spiral of silence," is thought to embody a sort of reverse Gresham's law of political discourse, whereby popular ideas drive unpopular ones out of circulation. For example, nonevangelicals in the South may be reluctant to express socially liberal opinions and indeed may come to change those views in the absence of social reinforcement. The general point is that locally or regionally dominant groups may impose informal (but very important) limits on the range of politically acceptable viewpoints, which may serve to isolate or to socialize those who hold minority attitudes.

Conversely, the existence of dissident viewpoints may occasion attitudinal or behavioral countermobilization. The *pluralism* hypothesis might suggest that local religious minorities may reaffirm their distinctive religious identities and emphasize, rather than conceal, their minority status. Indeed, a clear implication of the "supply-side" model of religious adherence is that congregations of locally unpopular denominations will engage in aggressive "product differentiation," which may well have implications for the political attitudes of their members. This, in turn, may occasion countermobilization from other denominations (this is analogous to V. O. Key's 1949 "black belt" thesis, in which he suggested that the salience of racial issues in the South was directly related to the concentration of African Americans within a particular jurisdiction). To take a remote example, the Catholicism of the Democratic presidential candidate John F. Kennedy in 1960 seems to have occasioned the activation of religious identification as a political force among Protestants and Roman Catholics alike (Converse 1966). The general point here is that religious *differences* may generate political distinctions and may define both opponents and allies. To the extent that religious influence in politics is a variable, religious diversity may well provide the roots of explanation for such variation.

As it happens, there exists empirical evidence supporting all three models. Several studies have shown that, with respect to attitudes toward abortion (Cook, Jelen, and Wilcox 1993) and the availability of abortion services (O'Connor and Berkman 1995), a strong Catholic presence in a particular state is likely to occasion a pro-choice countermobilization. That is, some non-Catholics in heavily Catholic states appear to reject the possibility of Catholic political influence by taking a position opposite to that taken by the Church (Faux 1988). O'Connor and Berkman, however, found no such pro-choice reaction to a strong state evangelical presence, as the effects of evangelicalism on abortion politics seem mostly additive. Similarly, Conger (2003) showed that the apparent influence of evangelicals within state Republican parties is greatest in non-southern states, in which evangelicals are a clear minority. This finding provides at least indirect support for the pluralism hypothesis.

The precise manner in which religion influences political contexts seems likely to depend on the nature of the religious market, the characteristics of the issue under consideration, and, what is perhaps most crucial, the group being socialized. In an earlier work (Jelen 1981) I reported substantial regional differences in tolerance toward unpopular minorities (communists, atheists, homosexuals, for example). In examining these regional contrasts across religious subgroups, I found support for the sacred canopy hypothesis among secular respondents. The "unchurched" in the South bore a much closer resemblance to evangelicals than did their northern counterparts. However, mainline Protestants responded in a manner most consistent with the pluralist hypothesis, in that the mainline-evangelical contrast was much more pronounced inside than outside the South. It may be that the sacred canopy model has its greatest applicability among secular citizens, who likely lack frequent interaction to reinforce their beliefs. Unlike observant Christians, religious "nones" (excluding, of course, members of nondenominational churches such as the Willow Creek Association) do not gather on Sunday mornings to reaffirm their shared theological noncommitments and do not experience comparable opportunities for political learning (Wald, Owen, and Hill 1988; Jelen 1992). Conversely, southern Jews, Roman Catholics, mainline Protestants, and African American Protestants appear to provide possible support for a more pluralistic model, since their shared religious experiences may insulate them from the dominant political culture.

The Master Narrative: The Political Mobilization of White Southern Evangelicals

In the study of religion and southern politics, the most important finding (from both scholarly and pragmatic perspectives) is the mobilization and realignment of white evangelicals. The general contours of the story are, of course, well known. The American South had been, for most of its post–Civil War history, a solidly Democratic region, with voting turnout lower than the rest of the country and a heavy concentration of native-born, white, evangelical Protestants. The Solid South experienced only occasional interruptions at the presidential level, such as the presidential elections of 1928 (in which southern support for the GOP candidate, Herbert Hoover, likely had a strong religious component) and 1952. (See below for a discussion of the religious basis of third-party movements.) Even in such anomalous years, the South generally remained solidly Democratic at the sub-presidential level. For most of the period between Reconstruction and the Great Society, white evangelicals were likely to identify with the Democratic Party or to be politically disengaged. Evangelicalism was long associated with an otherworldly orientation in which devout believers were encouraged to eschew political involvement (Wilcox 1989).

By most accounts the more or less permanent realignment of

southern evangelicals is generally thought to have begun at the level of presidential elections and only gradually diffused to support for GOP candidates for lower offices (Lamis 1984; Aistrup 1996; Bullock and Rozell 2003; for a contrary view see Aldrich 2000). Changes in political behavior seem to have begun in 1972, with the extremely negative reaction of cultural conservatives to the candidacy of George McGovern. Similarly, the turnout of white evangelicals was partly mobilized by the presidential candidacy of an avowed evangelical, Jimmy Carter, in 1976 (Wilcox 1989).

Black and Black (2002) have argued, however, that southern Republicanism was made a permanent part of the political landscape with the presidency of Ronald Reagan. Reagan's support for morally traditionalist attitudes on such issues as abortion and gay rights undoubtedly sealed the connection between white southern evangelicals and the Republican Party. Since the end of the Reagan administration, southern evangelicals have generally supported Republican presidential candidates and have extended their support for the GOP to lower offices.

While the realignment of white southern evangelicals has attained the status of conventional wisdom, there are a number of outstanding issues that would merit further investigation. One important question relates to the political style of evangelical activists and the possible electoral consequences of differences in the presentation of political ideas that are based on religion. It has often been argued that religious activists are more likely than other political leaders to assume a "purist" stance toward political matters. Politically mobilized evangelicals are considered likely to take extreme positions on issues of personal morality and to eschew compromise with more liberal viewpoints. At the level of political activists, the evidence is decidedly mixed. Some observers (Hadley 1994; Prysby 2004; Clark 2005) have provided evidence of a more purist orientation among religiously motivated political activists or of more extreme issue positions (Steed, Moreland, and Baker 1983), whereas others (Wilcox, Rozell, and Gunn 1996) suggest that although such intraparty differences certainly exist, their extent may be limited.

Moreover, it is not clear that stylistic differences between religiously motivated political activists and their more secular counterparts actually have electoral consequences of any sort. Elsewhere I have shown that voters who identify with the Republican Party and who hold liberal positions on divisive social issues such as abortion and capital punishment tend to remain loyal to Republican candidates with whom they disagree

(Jelen and Chandler 2000a). This tendency toward party loyalty, which is not as widely shared among Democratic identifiers, seems uniform across national regions (Jelen and Chandler 2000b). Thus, the question of whether religious activists bring an especially strident or uncompromising style to their political participation remains open and worthy of extensive further investigation.

A second scholarly issue relates to geographic differences in the effects of religion on political behavior across the South. Clearly, the importance of religion as a factor in the outcome of elections is a variable, and it seems likely that the impact of religious attitudes and memberships might differ across areas of the South. It is possible that the canopy model of religious socialization is correct, and religious effects are strongest in settings in which evangelical Christians have a clear majority. Members of doctrinally conservative denominations may receive reinforcement for their viewpoints in the absence of contradictory social cues (Sprague 1982; Huckfeldt and Sprague 1987). Conversely, the cultural conservatism of many evangelicals may be activated by the presence of creeds or lifestyles that lie outside the dominant religio-cultural tradition, as the pluralism model might predict. In other words, some evangelicals living in or near Atlanta or Austin may connect their religious beliefs and political attitudes in a very direct way when confronted with the existence of an active and visible gay community in those cities. Similarly, self-identification as an evangelical (or as a Southern Baptist) might be more salient within high concentrations of Roman Catholics, such as in southern Louisiana or southern Texas.

Obviously, a central issue in assessing the role of religious context in the relationship between religious variables and political behavior involves the selection of the geographic unit in which religious politics is likely to be most (or least) salient. One can imagine analyses conducted at the level of the congregation, the neighborhood, the county, or the state. An interesting first cut at this might be to compare the behavior of white evangelicals in megastates such as Florida, Texas, and (perhaps) Georgia with those in the rest of the South. An interesting question here is the extent to which religious diversity activates (or demobilizes) religiously based political activity.

A third set of questions involves variation in the political role of religion across time. The steady shift of white evangelicals to the GOP provides the backdrop to a dynamic of candidates and issues that vary across elections. While we know a great deal about the factors affecting the outcomes of specific elections (and the role of religion in accounting for such results), there is relatively little work done that involves comparisons across time.

By way of illustration, we are constantly reminded that the three most recent Democratic presidents were southerners. To what extent do white evangelicals contribute to these Democratic victories, and to what extent does that contribution vary across elections? Although both Jimmy Carter and Bill Clinton were Southern Baptists, it seems intuitively plausible to hypothesize that their respective appeals to culturally conservative white evangelicals might have been quite different.

On the Republican side, there are interesting studies to be done about GOP politics in South Carolina. Although the Palmetto State is often characterized as one in which evangelical Protestants are unusually influential and in which the Christian Right has great influence (Guth 2000), the South Carolina primary has occasionally been hazardous to Republican conservatives who have hoped to advance insurgent candidacies by prevailing there. Both the evangelical Pat Robertson (1988) and the conservative, pro-life Catholic Pat Buchanan (1992, 1996) pinned their hopes for the Republican presidential nomination on unrealized success in South Carolina. Indeed, the recent history of the South Carolina primary has suggested that the state has served as something of a firewall, in which previously vulnerable frontrunners reestablished their status as favorites for the GOP nomination. Future research might well address the question of why South Carolina, which would seem to be very promising territory for presidential candidates who make religiously based appeals, is not more hospitable to culturally conservative candidates in the state's quadrennial primary election.

Finally, it would seem useful to investigate the relationships between standard social issue attitudes and other issue positions among white evangelicals in the South. A typical research strategy to assess the political importance of religion in a particular population is to contrast the role of religious variables (church attendance, doctrinal orthodoxy, denominational membership) and attitudes that seem "naturally" related to religion (such as abortion, gay rights) with the role of attitudes toward race relations, foreign affairs, or economic issues (see, for example, Green, Kellstedt, Smidt, and Guth 2003). Indeed, one recent article (Hood, Kidd, and Morris 2004) dismissed the role of evangelicalism in accounting for the rise of southern Republicanism. As evidence of the supposed irrelevance of evangelical religion to party realignment among white southerners, Hood and his colleagues presented the results of a multivariate model in which the effects of Republican voting for president are controlled. Such model specification is, at the very least, controversial.

In particular, there is some work that suggests that the importance of white evangelicals to the political culture of the South may help us understand that hardy perennial issue of southern politics: race relations. An extensive historical literature suggests that religion provided a moral basis for slavery and, later, for segregation, but more recent empirical research has challenged such findings. In one study (Jelen, Kellstedt, and Wilcox 1990) religiously observant white evangelicals were found to have very "warm" feelings toward blacks. An ambitious study by Emerson and Smith (2000) has shown, however, that though many white evangelicals desire improved race relations and racial equality, the individualistic theology associated with evangelicalism makes it difficult for white religious conservatives to accept or understand structural explanations for poverty and perceived discrimination among African Americans. We understand very little about the political consequences of this apparent disjunction between the goals and beliefs of white evangelicals concerning race relations.

A more general point here is that future analyses of religious politics in the South would do well to devote some attention to the role of religion in attitude structure. Do southern evangelicals have distinctive ways of thinking about race or international politics? How are issue saliences related across religious groups? Since leaders of Christian Right organizations routinely take public positions on issues not directly related to questions of personal morality, it seems reasonable to inquire more deeply into the attitudes of religious mass publics. Though the manifest effect of religion on attitudes toward, say, military spending or race relations may be quite limited, religious variables may have subtle yet important effects on the manner in which attitudes are organized.

Finally, the interaction between religion and political institutions seems a promising avenue for future research. As is now well known, white evangelicals are *realigning* in a Republican direction, while much of the rest of the electorate is *dealigning*, or moving to a less partisan orientation. At the aggregate level, this would suggest that white evangelicals in the South and elsewhere constitute an increasing share of the Republican vote in any given election. Such compositional change in the GOP coalition may have effects on institutional arrangements, which, in turn, may affect the behavior of political leaders and voters alike.

One possible such set of relationships might involve the causes and effects of differences in legislative redistricting. It has been suggested (McDonald 1998) that, in a dealigning electorate, parties in state legislatures appear to engage in "mini-max" strategies, in which parties seek to protect their electoral bases rather than create a large number of districts in which the party can compete. That is, in an electorate in which the electoral choices (and turnout) of large numbers of voters are increasingly uncertain, legislative parties may seek to maximize the number of legislative districts (either for the U.S. House or for state legislative chambers) that are "safe" for the party in question.

Thus, the American South may be experiencing this reinforcing phenomenon: as white evangelicals align themselves with the Republican Party, such voters become increasingly important in the calculations of GOP strategists. To reduce the uncertainty associated with an increasingly Independent (in the partisan sense) electorate, Republican leaders (when they are able) will seek to create districts that are safe for Republican candidates. If the assumption is that the Republican electorate is becoming more and more religious and religiously conservative, it follows that an increasing number of GOP legislators will owe their electoral success to white evangelicals (see Fiorina, Abrams, and Pope 2004).

If this causal chain of reasoning is at least plausible, it may follow that the legislative wing of the Republican Party will consist of a critical mass of legislators (state legislators or U.S. representatives) who are accountable to white evangelical constituencies and, therefore, have electoral incentives to place social issues on the political agenda (Jelen 2000; Layman 2001).

The state of Texas may provide a testing ground for these conjectures. As a result of the 2002 elections, the Republican Party made important gains in both houses of the Texas state legislature and, indeed, came to command majorities in both chambers. As a result, the legislature sought to redraw the legislative districts in the state (presumably to the enhanced advantage of Republican candidates), and the revised map was upheld by the U.S. Supreme Court. If the foregoing argument connecting evangelical realignment to legislative redistricting is substantially correct, we should witness an increase in the number of legislators who are beholden to evangelical constituencies. This, in turn, should occasion a corresponding increase in bills introduced in the Texas state legislature or by Texas representatives in the U.S. House that deal with such religiously charged social issues as abortion, gay rights, and school prayer.

The main substantive finding, then, in research on religion and southern politics is the mobilization and realignment of white southern evangelicals. As scholars within an academic discipline, we have only begun to mine the implications of this important development in the region. Future research will likely emphasize temporal and geographical variations in the political role played by evangelical Protestants, as well as the implications of partisan change in the electorate for elite-level behavior.

Subnarrative I: Religion and the Political Empowerment of African Americans

Any complete account of the political role of religion in the South must, of course, take into account the complex relationship between religion and race. As I noted earlier, our understanding of the relationship between religious beliefs and racial attitudes among southern whites is, to say the least, incomplete. Conversely, while many analysts of race relations in the South have pointed to the central role of religious institutions in the civil rights movement and religion's more complex role in subsequent racial politics, we still lack an adequate understanding of the role of religion in the ever-changing relationship between race and religion in the states south of the Mason-Dixon line.

Again, the broad contours of the literature are quite familiar. Many analysts had long assumed, in a Marxian tradition, that religion served as a political "opiate," which encouraged African Americans to accept an unjust social and economic order. Religion (specifically Christianity) was thought to inculcate otherworldly orientations in which African Americans were encouraged to divert their attention from the inequities of this world and toward the promised rewards of the next (for an overview of this literature, see Harris 1999). The history of the civil rights movement suggests, however, that the net effect of religion among southern African Americans is likely to be one of political empowerment (ibid.).

Much of the leadership of the civil rights movement in the mid-twentieth century was recruited from the ranks of the African American clergy (Morris 1984; Branch 1988, 1999). Thus, civil rights activists followed the *Reverend* Martin Luther King Jr., the *Reverend* Andrew Young, or the *Reverend* Ralph Abernathy. In the era between *Plessy v. Ferguson* (1896) and *Brown v. Board of Education* (1954), the ministry was often the only path to community leadership available to educated African Americans. Thus, in the crucial decades of the 1950s and 1960s religion provided a vital resource in the struggle to change relations between the races in the American South.

At the level of the laity, more recent studies have suggested that religion is an important source of "social capital" for African Americans, in that participation in religious organizations (such as congregations) is an efficient means by which ordinary citizens can learn political skills and acquire politically relevant personal values. Indeed, Verba, Scholzman, and Brady (1995) have suggested that churches are often the only source of social capital for citizens whose circumstances are otherwise disadvantaged. To take a single example, active participation in religious organizations is a strong predictor of voting turnout among African Americans (Wilcox and Gomez 1990).

An important and generally unexplored area of the relationship between religion and political behavior among southern blacks, however, is the study of religion as a source of cleavage within the African American community and as a source of division within the Democratic Party. Barth (2004) has shown that African American activists in the Democratic Party in the South are measurably more conservative on social issues than their white counterparts. Calhoun-Brown (2002) has demonstrated similar conservatizing effects of religion among the African American laity. Though some African American congregations offer explicitly political messages (which increase support for the Democratic Party, turnout, and so on), more otherworldly congregations tend to inculcate conservative attitudes on such issues as abortion, gay rights, and sexual morality. To the extent that such social issues occupy prominent positions on the political agenda (which, of course, varies from election to election), religion may be a double-edged sword: the black church, writ large, may be a fertile source of Democratic activists, but it may also be an important source of intraparty conflict.

The question of why the political consequences of religion may vary across subgroups of southern African Americans is also worthy of further study. For example, it has been suggested that the effects of religion on political attitudes are strongest among older blacks, many of whom may have direct memories of the civil rights movement. Thus, the potential exists for a generational cleavage between older, more socially conservative African Americans and younger, more secular blacks, who may take more liberal positions on issues. It may also be the case that intraracial religious differences have political consequences. Whereas the extent of adherence to Islam among African Americans should not be exaggerated (Smith 2002), the effects of the presence of a highly visible black Muslim community in particular local contexts might be quite interesting. Does the possibility of religious competition within local African American communities serve as a source of political mobilization (as local religious minorities may provide outlets for previously unarticulated grievances), or might such competition cause Christian congregations to focus more directly on manifestly spiritual matters?

The general points to be made here are that, first, religion has historically been an important resource for southern African Americans and continues to provide political capital for the black community, and, second, it is no longer appropriate (if it ever was) to regard the African American community as a political or religious monolith. As relations between the races continue to evolve, religion may provide a set of circumstances in which intraracial differences are created or attenuated.

Subnarrative II: Religious Politics among Southern Nonevangelicals

It goes without saying that confining one's attention to evangelical Protestants (whether white or African American) in studies of politics would represent a gross oversimplification. Nevertheless, scant scholarly attention has been paid to the political role of nonevangelicals in the region. This represents an unfortunate gap in the literature because minority religions can affect political behavior in the South in at least two distinctive ways. First, groups such as Roman Catholics, Jews, Muslims, and secular citizens can serve as cognitive objects for the regional evangelical majority. That is, religious beliefs and feelings can be politically activated by the visible presence of cultural or theological outgroups. Second, members of nonevangelical faiths (or nonfaiths) are actual or potential citizens in their own right, and may affect policy deliberations or election outcomes through their own political participation. Thus, southerners from outside the dominant regional religious tradition may profitably be viewed as objects or subjects and may assume political importance in either or both of these roles.

Catholics

A large and growing literature has suggested that American Catholics remain distinctive in their political behavior. White Catholics have moved steadily into the GOP column over the past generation (Prendergast 1999), but they remain considerably more likely to identify with the Democratic Party than are white Protestants (Bendyna 2000; Brewer 2003). Moreover, the Republicanism of white Catholics does not seem related to religiosity or attitudes toward issues of personal morality (Leege 1996; Jelen 1997). Finally, there does seem to exist something of a "Catholic ethic" (Tropman 1995; Bendyna 2000), which suggests greater economic liberalism among white Catholics. These characteristics, along with the sheer size of the Catholic population, make it likely that Catholics have had, and will continue to have, a major impact on politics in the South (for a contrasting view, see Mockabee 2004).

The political importance of Roman Catholicism in the American South is most often considered in the context of the special case of Louisiana. Owing to its unique history, Louisiana is the one southern state that has always had a substantial Roman Catholic population, mostly concentrated in the heavily populated southern portion of the state. Traditionally, the Catholic vote was a source of party faction during Louisiana's history as a one-party state (Williams [1969] 1981; Bass and DeVries [1976] 1995). There have been few systematic analyses of Louisiana Catholics as a component of two-party competition in recent years, however. It seems possible that the Catholic vote in Louisiana is a source of partisan inertia (Louisiana has been slower to shift to the GOP than most southern states; Hadley and Knuckey 1997) as well as providing support for policy liberalism in issues involving economics, foreign policy, and race.

Obviously, as large portions of the American population move to the Sun Belt, the effects of Catholicism on political competition are virtually certain to affect southern states other than Louisiana. Since the 1960 election (Converse 1966) there have been few systematic studies of anti-Catholicism, a sentiment that was often thought quite common in the region (for an overview, see Perl and Bendyna 2002). It remains to be investigated whether the remnants of anti-Catholicism still exist among southern evangelicals (black or white) and whether such residual attitudes have political consequences (Cook, Jelen, and Wilcox 1993). It would be interesting, for example, to learn whether Pat Buchanan's Catholicism hurt him with socially conservative voters in southern Republican primaries in 1992 or 1996. Moreover, there has been very little work on the effects of context on the political attitudes of Catholics in the South. In most of the region Catholics remain a minority faith, yet there is little in the way of systematic evidence as to whether southern Catholics adopt the prevailing attitudes of their regional and local contexts (the canopy hypothesis) or whether a sense of social and political distinctiveness among southern Catholics has the effect of mobilizing the political implications of their religion (the pluralism effect). To illustrate, it would be interesting to know whether the opposition of Catholic clergy to the death penalty is softened or enhanced among Catholics who reside in states in which the death penalty is frequently imposed (such as Texas).

Thus, the political behavior of white Catholics in the South provides a fertile field of potential hypotheses, which is for the most part as yet untilled. Moreover, not all Catholics are white (or, more to the point, Anglo). Hispanics, taken collectively, are perhaps the fastest growing segment of the population in the United States, and most Hispanics have roots in nations that are traditionally Roman Catholic. The Hispanic population is large, consequential, and incompletely integrated into the American party system. These characteristics make the study of the effect of religion on the political behavior of Hispanic Catholics most promising.

Again, it may be useful to consider the effects of Hispanics on the political attitudes of other Americans. Questions of immigration (legal and illegal) are always salient in American politics, and they are likely to be particularly prominent in states that share a border with Mexico. Although concerns over immigration are usually considered to have an economic basis, there are, to my knowledge, no studies of the religious basis of attitudes toward immigration. Is it possible that latent anti-Catholicism is manifested in opposition to accommodations for immigrants from Mexico? Would such opposition differ on other grounds across different religious groups?

When considering possible religious bases of the political behavior of southern Hispanics, it might be useful to examine possible religious differences among diverse national communities. Are Cuban Americans more religious or more susceptible to religious appeals than Americans of Puerto Rican or Mexican descent? To what extent are smaller communities of immigrants from Central American nations religiously distinctive? While it seems obvious that the politics of Hispanic voting is likely to be quite different in Texas (with a Hispanic population primarily Mexican) from that in Florida (with large, politically consequential communities of Cubans and Puerto Ricans), there has been little investigation of the extent to which religiosity is a source of political integration or mobilization among these different groups.

Moreover, the fact that some Hispanic communities contain many members who are not citizens or who have only recently become citizens provides a potentially large dynamic element in the electoral politics of such megastates as Florida and Texas. While Hispanics have generally been supporters of the Democratic Party, the political inexperience of some Hispanic voters suggests that the GOP may be able to make substantial gains among citizens of Hispanic descent. Indeed, the elections of George W. Bush as governor of Texas are thought to be partly attributable to his limited but consequential success among Mexican American voters. It is possible that Hispanic Catholics are attracted to the social conservatism of the GOP. Further, not all Hispanics are Catholic; a number of studies (Hallum 2002) have shown that increasing numbers of Hispanics have converted to evangelical Protestantism, with Pentecostal denominations being particularly popular among Central Americans. A socially and perhaps economically conservative Hispanic element in the electorate of Texas (and perhaps Florida as well) could bode well for long-term Republican prospects in the region.

Jews

The vice presidential candidacy of Joseph Lieberman in the 2000 election represents something of a watershed in American politics generally and, perhaps, particularly in the study of southern politics. One plausible if perhaps cynical explanation for the selection of Lieberman as Al Gore's running mate suggests that Lieberman was placed on the ticket in the hopes that he could deliver the votes of Jewish retirees living in Florida and, therefore, Florida's electoral votes.

The Lieberman candidacy raises some general questions about the role of Jews in southern politics. Although a very small minority of southern voters, Jews may well play important roles in southern political behavior in certain contexts and in specific electoral situations. In particular, the importance of the Jewish vote in Florida is self-evident to most analysts of American politics. As urbanization and northern migration to the Sun Belt continue, the presence of Jews may assume greater political importance in such states as Texas and (perhaps) Georgia.

A few recent studies (Kane, Craig, and Wald 2001; Cohen 2005) have suggested that anti-Semitism is no longer a salient force among southerners, although the possibility remains that prejudice against Jews may be an important factor in certain state and local elections. It has also been shown (Wald and Sigelman 1997) that Jewish political attitudes have little in common with those of southern evangelicals. Some studies (Weisberg and Sylvan 2003) have suggested that higher-income Jews as well as Jews for whom the status of Israel is very important have a tendency toward ideological conservatism, but these relationships have not to date resulted in appreciably higher levels of Republican identification for Jews in or out of the South.

Mainline Protestants

Many analysts of religion and politics in the United States (Roof and McKinney 1987; Jelen 1993) have suggested that mainline Protestants have moved from the mainline to the sideline of American public life (for a contrasting view, see Wuthnow and Evans 2002). While it seems unlikely that Methodists, Presbyterians, or Episcopalians represent distinctive outgroups for southern evangelicals, their presence and political activity may have important political consequences for the region.

Traditionally, mainline Protestant denominations have been the source of an emphasis on social justice, in which the primary message of Scripture is thought to be ethical rather than doctrinal (Guth, Green, Smidt, Kellstedt, and Poloma 1997). Unlike seculars (to be discussed below), observant mainliners (no matter how scarce) may provide a source of support for social and economic liberalism, and mainline denominations may insulate their members against the socializing effects of the dominant evangelical culture. Thus, even in the absence of large numbers, mainline congregations may provide settings in which dovish foreign policy views or permissive viewpoints on lifestyle issues may be expressed by clergy and held by laity despite their relative unpopularity in the region. If the canopy model of religious socialization is substantially correct, the existence of politically distinctive mainline churches may provide alternative voices to the community conversation. Even if the actual influence of such clergy is limited by a lack of theological resources, such as a shared belief in an inerrant Bible (see Jelen 1993), the political importance of mainline laypeople may exceed their actual numbers.

Conversely, mainline denominations may occasion political conflict by increasing the salience of highly emotional issues. For example, the controversy within the Episcopal Church over the ordination of a gay bishop (Associated Press 2003) may well place the issue of gay rights on the political agenda, which in turn may alter the dynamics of electoral politics. The general point is that, even in the status of a theological minority (I leave it to the reader to digest the irony of the potentially oxymoronic concept of a "mainline minority"), southern mainline Protestantism may leaven the influence of evangelicalism on the political culture of the region.

Seculars

While church membership, religious observance, and orthodox religious belief are more common in the South than in other parts of the country, the southern electorate does include a substantial segment of religiously uncommitted (or "unchurched") citizens (Kellstedt and Green 1993). Indeed, the number of such people residing in the South can be expected to increase as the population shifts southward and westward. It is not clear that seculars would constitute a politically cohesive segment of the electorate in the South or elsewhere since there is no obvious secular equivalent of attendance at religious services. Unchurched citizens do not, as a rule, have occasion to gather to reaffirm their common religious (or irreligious) perspectives. Thus, it is an empirical question as to whether southern seculars are more or less likely to adopt the prevailing political culture.

Nevertheless, it seems clear that secular citizens might well provide support for liberal positions on social issues such as abortion or gay rights. The political influence of socially liberal seculars might serve to soften the cultural conservatism of the dominant evangelical political culture. Conversely, the presence of highly visible supporters of a woman's right to choose or gay marriage might well stimulate a countermobilization among evangelicals or other conservative people of faith. Again, the extent of such countermobilization may well depend on local political contexts. Is the salience of an issue such as gay marriage greater in Atlanta, where gays and supporters of gay rights might be relatively visible, or in Greenville, South Carolina, where public expression of support for gay rights might be less conspicuous? The general point here is that the presence of a critical mass of secular citizens in a local political context may increase the salience of issues that would otherwise be left off the political agenda.

One obvious aspect of secularism that deserves continued attention is the role of the unchurched in occasioning support for third parties. It has often been observed that the Dixiecrat presidential candidacy of Strom Thurmond in 1948 and the American Independent Party candidacy of George Wallace in 1968 may well have been harbingers of the shift of the southern electorate toward the Republican Party. But the assertion that support for Wallace in 1968 and for Nixon and Reagan in subsequent elections is part of the same general phenomenon is, at least, controversial. As we have seen, an important component of southern realignment is the mobilization of religious conservatives, with white evangelicals being a growing component of the GOP coalition. However, some excellent work has been done by Gilbert, Peterson, Johnson, and Djupe (1999), which suggests that support for third parties is most common among the unchurched, regardless of the ideological nature of the minor-party candidacy. (Presumably, few observers would be surprised to learn that Ralph Nader's supporters were less religious than other southern voters.) Thus, the Wallace and Thurmond campaigns may not have represented an intermediate stop for southern conservatives moving from the Democratic to the Republican Party, but instead may constitute a phenomenon generally independent of the more permanent trend of evangelical realignment. If this is correct, it follows that secular voters constitute an important "slack" resource that may make political insurgencies more viable in and outside the South. Although an analysis of the consequences of third-party voting is well beyond the scope of this chapter, few political scientists would deny the importance of minor parties in altering the policy agenda of politics in the United States. A low or nonexistent commitment to organized religion may indicate a more general social and political marginality that, in turn, may provide resources for candidates who seek to exert influence from outside the two-party system.

Outside the Judeo-Christian Tradition

It has become something of a cliché to note that the United States is becoming religiously more diverse and that increasing numbers of Americans are adherents of faiths not part of the Judeo-Christian tradition. The South surely is no exception to this generalization. Although the actual numbers of members of such non-traditional faiths should not be exaggerated (Smith 2002), many immigrants from Asia and the Middle East have become quite visible in numerous communities in and out of the South.

Again, it is appropriate to view new immigrants from Asia and Africa as both subjects and objects. It is often the case that the presence of highly visible foreigners evokes negative reactions among natives of the United States or of a particular region. Under some circumstances, such anti-immigrant sentiment may have a religious basis. For example, in the early twenty-first century, many Americans hold negative attitudes toward and stereotypes about Muslims, and the presence of a new mosque in a formerly "Christian" community may increase the salience of foreign policy or questions of immigration.

Perhaps more important, the growing presence of immigrants from cultures outside the Judeo-Christian tradition has enormous potential for electoral politics inside and outside the South. As such immigrant communities grow, they represent an increasing pool of politically inexperienced, potentially mobilizable voters. Newly minted citizens from Iraq, the People's Republic of China, and the Philippines have no obvious connection to the Republican or the Democratic Party in the United States, and they may be ripe for recruitment by either party. This dynamic of population replacement has the potential for profound alteration of the party system. In the South the political mobilization of non-Western immigrants may be preceded by the religious mobilization of these same people. It seems likely that people who would emigrate from Asia, Africa, or the Middle East were poorly integrated into their communities in their home countries, and they may therefore be available for recruitment into denominations indigenous to their new surroundings. In the South this most likely means that non-Western immigrants present opportunities for evangelical denominations and, indirectly, the Republican Party. If the "party of nonvoters" comes to have a distinctive religious complexion in the American South, changes in the party system may not be far behind.

Conclusion

As I hope this chapter has made clear, religion in the study of southern politics is of cardinal importance, and scholars who seek to understand the political life of the region can ignore the political role of the sacred only at their own intellectual peril. At various points in this chapter, I have attempted to suggest promising lines of future inquiry that build on the excellent but incomplete work already done.

Perhaps the main lesson to be learned from this review is that religious organizations are not primarily political in nature. While religious belief, practice, and organization often have important political consequences, religion, as practiced in most of the United States, is essentially a spiritual matter, with political considerations being of secondary importance. The political meanings of particular theological beliefs or traditions are thus matters of "time, place, and circumstance."

What this means is that context matters. It makes a difference whether one is religious, how one is religious, but, perhaps most important, *where* one is religious. The religious ecology of a particular jurisdiction is likely to make a great deal of difference for the effects of religious variables on political behavior. The nature of the religious market and the style of religious socialization are variables, and we are only beginning to understand the ways that individual religious characteristics interact with social environments.

Further complicating the enterprise is the fact that religious belief performs a variety of political functions. The political consequences of, say, evangelical Protestantism are likely to be quite different in a southern mill town concerned with rising unemployment and foreign competition (Grammich 1999) from what they are in a university town in which marijuana has been discovered on the local campus. Religious beliefs and memberships can be sources of political mobilization or demobilization, social criticism, or political legitimacy. Religion can function as either a centripetal or centrifugal force in southern politics.

Nevertheless, analysts of southern politics should not be discouraged by the apparent complexity and instability of the study of political religion. No serious analysis of southern political behavior can be complete without attention to the religious factor, and the political importance of religion in the American South shows no sign of abating.

Note: A version of this chapter was presented at the 2004 Citadel Symposium on Southern Politics in Charleston, S.C. Thanks to Robert Steed, Laura Olson, and John Clark for valuable comments on that earlier version of this chapter.

References

Aistrup, Joseph A. 1996. *The Southern Strategy Revisited: Republican Top-Down Advancement in the South.* Lexington: University Press of Kentucky.
Aldrich, John. 2000. "Southern Parties in State and Nation." *Journal of Politics* 62: 643–70.

Associated Press. 2003. "Anglicans Start Landmark Summit on Gay Priests." Accessed at www.nytimes.com/2003/10/15/international/15CND-Anglican. html.

Baker, Tod A., Robert P. Steed, and Laurence W. Moreland, eds. 1983. *Religion and Politics in the South: Mass and Elite Perspectives*. New York: Praeger.

Barth, Jay. 2004. "The Continuing Role of Race in Southern Party Organizations." In *Southern Political Party Activists: Patterns of Conflict and Change, 1991–2001*, ed. John A. Clark and Charles L. Prysby. Lexington: University Press of Kentucky.

Bass, Jack, and Walter DeVries. [1976] 1995. *The Transformation of Southern Politics: Social Change and Political Consequence since 1945*. Athens: University of Georgia Press.

Bendyna, Mary E. 2000. "The Catholic Ethic in American Politics: Evidence from Survey Research." Ph.D. dissertation, Georgetown University.

Berger, Peter. 1969. *The Sacred Canopy: Elements of a Sociological Theory of Religion*. Garden City, N.Y.: Anchor.

Black, Earl, and Merle Black. 2002. *The Rise of Southern Republicans*. Cambridge: Harvard University Press.

Branch, Taylor. 1988. *Parting the Waters: America in the King Years, 1954–63*. New York: Simon and Schuster.

———. 1999. *Pillar of Fire: America in the King Years, 1963–65*. New York: Touchstone Books.

Brewer, Mark D. 2003. *Relevant No More? The Catholic/Protestant Divide in American Electoral Politics*. Lanham, Md.: Rowman and Littlefield.

Bullock, Charles S., III, and Mark J. Rozell. 2003, 2nd ed. "Southern Politics in the Twenty-first Century." Introduction to *The New Politics of the Old South: An Introduction to Southern Politics*, ed. Charles S. Bullock III and Mark J. Rozell. Lanham, Md.: Rowman and Littlefield.

Calhoun-Brown, Allison. 2002. "This Side of Jordan: Black Churches and Partisan Political Attitudes." In *Understanding Public Opinion*, ed. Barbara Norrander and Clyde Wilcox. Washington, D.C.: Congressional Quarterly Press.

Clark, John A. 2004. "Religion: Culture Wars in the New South." In *Southern Political Party Activists: Patterns of Conflict and Change, 1991–2001*, ed. John A. Clark and Charles L. Prysby. Lexington: University Press of Kentucky.

Clark, John A., and Charles L. Prysby, eds. 2004. *Southern Political Party Activists: Patterns of Conflict and Change, 1991–2001*. Lexington: University Press of Kentucky.

Cohen, Jeffrey E. 2005. "The Polls, Religion and the 2000 Election: Public Attitudes toward Joseph Lieberman." *Presidential Studies Quarterly* 35: 387–402.

Conger, Kimberly. 2003. "Evangelicals: Outside the Beltway." *Religion in the News* 6: 7, 17.

Converse, Philip E. 1966. "Religion and Politics: The 1960 Election." In *Elections and the Political Order*, ed. Angus Campbell, Philip E. Converse, Warren E. Miller, and Donald E. Stokes. New York: John Wiley and Sons.

Cook, Elizabeth, Ted G. Jelen, and Clyde Wilcox. 1993. "Catholicism and Abortion Attitudes in the American States: A Contextual Analysis." *Journal for the Scientific Study of Religion* 32: 223–30.

Emerson, Michael O., and Christian Smith. 2000. *Divided by Faith: Evangelical Religion and the Problem of Race in America.* New York: Oxford University Press.

Faux, Marian. 1988. Roe v. Wade: *The Untold Story of the Landmark Supreme Court Decision that Made Abortion Legal.* New York: Macmillan.

Fiorina, Morris P., with Samuel J. Abrams and Jeremy C. Pope. 2004. *Culture War? The Myth of a Polarized America.* New York: Pearson/Longman.

Gilbert, Christopher P., David A. M. Peterson, Timothy R. Johnson, and Paul A. Djupe. 1999. *Religious Institutions and Minor Parties in the United States.* Westport, Conn.: Praeger.

Grammich, Clifford. 1999. *Local Baptists, Local Politics: Churches and Communities in the Middle and Upland South.* Knoxville: University of Tennessee Press.

Green, John C., Lyman A. Kellstedt, Corwin E. Smidt, and James L. Guth. 2003, 2nd ed. "The Soul of the South: Religion and Southern Politics at the Millennium." In *The New Politics of the Old South: An Introduction to Southern Politics,* ed. Charles S. Bullock III and Mark J. Rozell. Lanham, Md.: Rowman and Littlefield.

Green, John C., Mark J. Rozell, and Clyde Wilcox, eds. 2003. *The Christian Right in American Politics: Marching to the Millennium.* Washington, D.C.: Georgetown University Press.

Guth, James L. 2000. "South Carolina: Even in Zion the Heathen Rage." In *Prayers in the Precincts: The Christian Right in the 1998 Elections,* ed. John C. Green, Mark J. Rozell, and Clyde Wilcox. Washington, D.C.: Georgetown University Press.

Guth, James L., John C. Green, Corwin E. Smidt, Lyman A. Kellstedt, and Margaret M. Poloma. 1997. *The Bully Pulpit: The Politics of Protestant Clergy.* Lawrence: University Press of Kansas.

Hadley, Charles D. 1994. "Louisiana: The Continuing Saga of Race, Religion, and Rebellion." In *The 1992 Presidential Election in the South: Current Patterns of Southern Party and Electoral Politics,* ed. Robert P. Steed, Laurence W. Moreland, and Tod A. Baker. Westport, Conn.: Praeger.

Hadley, Charles D., and Jonathan O. Knuckey. 1997. "Louisiana: Laissez les bon temps rouler?" In *The 1996 Presidential Election in the South: Southern Party Systems in the 1990s,* ed. Laurence W. Moreland and Robert P. Steed. Westport, Conn.: Praeger.

Hallum, Anne Motley. 2002. "Looking for Hope in Central America: The Pentecostal Movement." In *Religion and Politics in Comparative Perspective: The One, the Two, and the Many,* ed. Ted G. Jelen and Clyde Wilcox. New York: Cambridge University Press.

Harris, Frederick C. 1999. *Something Within: Religion in African-American Political Activism.* New York: Oxford University Press.

Hood, M. V., III, Quentin Kidd, and Irwin R. Morris. 2004. "The Reintroduction of the *Elephas Maximus* to the Southern United States: The Rise of Republican State Parties, 1960–2000." *American Politics Research* 32: 68–101.

Huckfeldt, Robert, and John Sprague. 1987. "Networks in Context: The Social Flow of Political Information." *American Political Science Review* 81: 1197–1216.

Jelen, Ted G. 1981. "Sources of Political Intolerance: The Case of the American South." In *Contemporary Southern Political Attitudes and Behavior,* ed. Robert P. Steed, Laurence W. Moreland, and Tod A. Baker. New York: Praeger.

———. 1992. "Political Christianity: A Contextual Analysis." *American Journal of Political Science* 36: 692–714.

———. 1993. *The Political World of the Clergy.* Westport, Conn.: Praeger.

———. 1997. "Culture Wars and the Party System: Religion and Realignment, 1972–1992." In *Culture Wars: Critical Reviews of a Popular Thesis,* ed. Rhys H. Williams. New York: Aldine de Gruyter.

———. 2000. *To Serve God and Mammon: Church-State Relations in American Politics.* Boulder, Colo.: Westview.

Jelen, Ted G., and Marthe A. Chandler. 2000a. "Culture Wars in the Trenches: Short-Term Forces in Presidential Elections, 1968–1996." *American Review of Politics* 21: 69–87.

———. 2000b. "The Effects of Wedge Issues on Presidential Voting, 1972–1996: A Regional Comparison." Paper presented at The Citadel Symposium on Southern Politics, Charleston, S.C.

Jelen, Ted G., Lyman A. Kellstedt, and Clyde Wilcox. 1990. "Religion and Racism: Some New Evidence for an Old Problem." Paper presented at the annual meeting of the Association for the Sociology of Religion, Washington, D.C.

Kane, James G., Stephen C. Craig, and Kenneth D. Wald. 2001. "Religion and Presidential Politics: A List Experiment." Paper presented at the annual meeting of the American Political Science Association, San Francisco.

Kellstedt, Lyman A., and John C. Green. 1993. "Knowing God's Many People: Denominational Preference and Political Behavior." In *Rediscovering the Religious Factor in American Politics,* ed. David C. Leege and Lyman A. Kellstedt. Armonk, N.Y.: M. E. Sharpe.

Key, V. O., Jr. 1949. *Southern Politics in State and Nation.* New York: Knopf.

Lamis, Alexander P. 1984. *The Two-Party South.* New York: Oxford University Press.

Layman, Geoffrey. 2001. *The Great Divide: Religious and Cultural Conflict in American Political Parties.* New York: Columbia University Press.

Leege, David C. 1996. "The Catholic Vote: Can It Be Found in Church?" *Commonweal* 123: 11–18.

McDonald, Michael. 1998. "Redistricting, Dealignment, and the Political Homogenization of the House of Representatives." Paper presented at the annual meeting of the American Political Science Association, Boston.

Mockabee, Stephen T. 2004. "The Changing Catholic Voter." Paper presented at the annual meeting of the Midwest Political Science Association, Chicago.

Noelle-Neumann, Elisabeth. 1984. *The Spiral of Silence: Public Opinion, Our Social Skin.* Chicago: University of Chicago Press.

O'Connor, Robert E., and Michael B. Berkman. 1995. "Religious Determinants of State Abortion Policy." *Social Science Quarterly* 76: 447–59.

Perl, Paul, and Mary E. Bendyna. 2002. "Perceptions of Anti-Catholic Bias and Political Party Identification among U.S. Catholics." *Journal for the Scientific Study of Religion* 41: 653–68.

Prendergast, W. B. 1999. *The Catholic Voter in American Politics: The Passing of the Democratic Monolith.* Washington, D.C.: Georgetown University Press.

Prysby, Charles L. 2004. "Purists versus Pragmatists: Orientations among Southern Political Party Activists." In *Southern Political Party Activists: Patterns of Conflict and Change, 1991–2001,* ed. John A. Clark and Charles L. Prysby. Lexington: University Press of Kentucky.

Roof, Wade Clark, and William McKinney. 1987. *American Mainline Religion.* New Brunswick: Rutgers University Press.

Smith, Tom W. 2002. "Religious Diversity in America: The Emergence of Muslims, Buddhists, Hindus, and Others." *Journal for the Scientific Study of Religion* 41: 577–85.

Sprague, John. 1982. "Is There a Micro Theory Consistent with Contextual Analysis?" In *Strategies of Political Inquiry,* ed. Elinor Ostrom. Beverly Hills: Sage.

Steed, Robert P., Laurence W. Moreland, and Tod A. Baker. 1983. "Religion and Party Activists: Fundamentalism and Politics in Regional Perspective." In *Religion and Politics in the South: Mass and Elite Perspectives,* ed. Tod A. Baker, Robert P. Steed, and Laurence W. Moreland. New York: Praeger.

Tocqueville, Alexis de. [1835, 1840] 1945. *Democracy in America.* Ed. and trans. Phillips Bradley. New York: Vintage Books.

Tropman, John E. 1995. *The Catholic Ethic in American Society: An Exploration of Values.* San Francisco: Jossey-Bass.

Verba, Sidney, Kay Lehman Scholzman, and Henry E. Brady. 1995. *Voice and Equality: Civic Voluntarism in American Politics.* Cambridge: Harvard University Press.

Wald, Kenneth D., Dennis Owen, and Samuel S. Hill. 1988. "Churches as Political Communities." *American Political Science Review* 82: 531–48.

Wald, Kenneth D., and Lee Sigelman. 1997. "Romancing the Jews: The Christian Right in Search of Strange Bedfellows." In *Sojourners in the Wilderness: The Christian Right in Comparative Perspective,* ed. Corwin E. Smidt and James M. Penning. Lanham, Md.: Rowman and Littlefield.

Weisberg, Herbert F., and Donald A. Sylvan. 2003. "Social Justice and Self-Interest: Explaining Liberalism among American Jews." Paper presented at the annual meeting of the American Political Science Association, Philadelphia.

Wilcox, Clyde. 1989. "The New Christian Right and the Mobilization of the Evangelicals." In *Religion and Political Behavior in the United States,* ed. Ted G. Jelen. New York: Praeger.

Wilcox, Clyde, and Leopoldo Gomez. 1990. "Religion, Group Identification, and Politics among American Blacks." *Sociological Analysis* 51: 271–83.

Wilcox, Clyde, Mark J. Rozell, and John C. Green. 2003. "The Meaning of the March: A Direction for Future Research." In *The Christian Right in American Politics: Marching to the Millennium*, ed. John C. Green, Mark J. Rozell, and Clyde Wilcox. Washington, D.C.: Georgetown University Press.

Wilcox, Clyde, Mark J. Rozell, and Roland Gunn. 1996. "Religious Coalitions in the New Christian Right." *Social Science Quarterly* 77: 543–58.

Williams, T. Harry. [1969] 1981. *Huey Long*. New York: Vintage Books.

Wuthnow, Robert, and John H. Evans, eds. 2002. *The Quiet Hand of God: Faith-Based Activism and the Public Role of Mainline Protestantism*. Berkeley: University of California Press.

★ **Chapter 7** ★

Population Shifts Change a Region's Politics

The Old South Morphs into the New

Susan A. MacManus
With the assistance of Brittany L. Penberthy
and Thomas A. Watson

Coon dogs and kudzu. Banjos and biscuits. For years, the American South was as distinct from the rest of the nation as Jupiter from Mars. No more. The Rust Belt exodus and the Sun Belt renaissance have brought a host of new faces to the region, and the Wal-Mart-izing of the nation's suburbs has left stretches of Mobile, Ala., and Charleston, S.C., indistinguishable from the outskirts of Milwaukee and Cheyenne, Wyo.

—Margaret Edds, *Tallahassee Democrat*, June 16, 2003.

WRITING ABOUT THE SOUTH'S POLITICS requires one to write about the area's population metamorphosis. Population in-migration and shifts within the region (and within individual states) have dramatically altered the southern political landscape and increased the South's clout at the national level. With each election cycle comes a new flurry of writings from academics and journalists describing how the region has changed in its politics and population makeup. (See tables 7.1 and 7.2 for state-by-state presidential voting patterns and population growth rates.)

The linkage between population shifts and political change has been assumed by writers more than it is has been empirically demonstrated.

167

Table 7.1: Vote for Democratic Presidential Candidate in Southern States, 1952–2004

	AL	AR	FL	GA	LA	MS	NC	SC	TN	TX	VA	US
1952	64.6	55.9	45.0	69.7	52.9	60.4	53.9	50.7	49.7	46.7	43.4	44.4
1956	56.5	52.5	42.7	66.4	39.5	58.2	50.7	45.4	48.6	44.0	38.4	42.0
1960	56.8	50.2	48.5	62.5	50.4	36.3	52.1	51.2	45.8	50.5	47.0	49.7
1964	--	56.1	51.1	45.9	43.2	12.9	56.2	41.1	55.5	63.3	53.5	61.1
1968	18.7	30.4	30.9	26.7	28.2	23.0	29.2	29.6	28.1	41.1	32.5	42.7
1972	25.5	30.7	27.8	24.6	28.4	19.6	28.9	27.7	29.7	33.3	30.1	37.5
1976	55.7	65.0	51.9	66.7	51.7	49.6	55.2	56.2	55.9	51.1	48.0	50.1
1980	47.4	47.5	38.5	55.8	45.7	48.1	47.2	48.1	48.4	41.4	40.3	41.0
1984	38.3	38.3	34.7	39.8	38.2	37.4	37.9	35.6	41.6	36.1	37.1	40.6
1988	39.9	42.2	38.5	39.5	44.1	39.1	41.7	37.6	41.5	43.3	39.2	45.6
1992	40.9	53.2	39.0	43.5	45.6	40.8	42.7	39.9	47.1	37.1	40.6	43.0
1996	43.2	53.7	48.0	45.8	52.0	44.1	44.0	44.0	48.0	43.8	45.1	49.2
2000	41.6	45.9	48.8	43.0	44.9	40.7	43.2	40.9	47.3	38.0	44.4	48.4
2004	37.0	45.0	47.0	41.0	42.0	40.0	44.0	41.0	43.0	38.0	45.0	48.0

Sources: Richard M. Scammon, Alice V. McGillivray, and Rhodes Cook, *America Votes 25: A Handbook of Contemporary American Election Statistics* (Washington, D.C.: Congressional Quarterly Press, 2003); 2004 data accessed at www.CNN.com/ELECTION/2004.
Note: In 1964 the national Democratic candidates were not represented on the Alabama ballot.

Table 7.2: Southern States' Population Growth Rate, 1940–2000

	AL	AR	FL	GA	LA	MS	NC	SC	TN	TX	VA
1940–1950	8.1	-2	46.1	10.3	13.5	-0.2	13.7	11.4	12.9	20.2	23.9
1950–1960	6.7	-6.5	78.7	14.5	21.4	-0.05	12.2	12.5	8.4	24.2	19.5
1960–1970	5.4	7.7	37.1	16.4	11.9	1.8	11.6	8.7	10.1	16.9	17.2
1970–1980	13.1	18.9	43.5	19.1	15.4	13.7	15.7	20.5	16.9	27.1	14.9
1980–1990	3.8	2.8	32.7	18.6	0.4	2.2	12.8	11.7	6.2	19.4	15.8
1990–2000	10.1	13.7	23.5	26.4	5.9	10.5	21.4	15.1	16.7	22.8	14.4

Sources: U.S. Bureau of the Census, *Statistical Abstract of the United States* (Washington, D.C.: U.S. Department of Commerce), for appropriate years.

The more journalistic writers have tended to focus on the election at hand, making the literature more cross-sectional than longitudinal in design, and on a specific state, making it more a case study than comparative.

Political scientists have generally described changes in population composition and inferred that these shifts affect political outcomes. Thus, they use demographics to paint a picture of the setting in which the politics they are investigating take place. Scholars whose research relies on empirical models often include demographic variables from a single census (such as the percentage of blacks in 2000, or population growth rate between 1990 and 2000) but rarely include variables from multiple censuses. Part of the explanation for this is that census definitions have constantly changed and become more refined since the 1950s.

As a result, there is a sparse literature systematically linking shifts in demographics with political changes in the South[1] over the entire past half century. The population mobility literature, largely written by demographers, has come in spurts; it usually peaks in the period immediately following the release of new census data. This literature is much more extensive than that *directly* tying together population shifts with changes in the region's politics. The latter, where it exists, has generally been written by political scientists.

The bulk of this chapter chronologically traces the writings of demographers; we hope it will be helpful for understanding some of the trends observed elsewhere in this book.

From V. O. Key Jr. to the Present: Demographics Matter

In the late 1940s, when V. O. Key Jr. wrote *Southern Politics in State and Nation,* he was deeply aware of the importance of the region's demography. He noted that

> the South's heritage from crises of the past, its problem of adjustment of *racial* relations on a scale unparalleled in any western nation, its *poverty* associated with an *agrarian* economy which in places is almost feudal in character, the long habituation of many of its people to nonparticipation in political life—all these and *other social characteristics* both influence the nature of the South's political system and place upon it an enormous burden. (Key 1949, 4)

He described the South as an "unfathomable maze formed by tradition, caste, race, poverty" but admitted that the region was changing (ibid., 664). Population in-migration was creating animosity, he said, between recent immigrants from the North (urban, laboring classes) and white, native-born southerners (rural, agricultural).

The census variables that Key relied heavily upon included population growth rate, nativity (percent born outside each southern state), race (percent white, percent black), residential location (percent urban, percent living on farms), income (average per capita income), and education (rural illiteracy rates).

Southern politics scholars today still focus on many of the same variables but add to the list age breakdowns, statistics on foreign-born residents, more detailed analyses of regions from which in-migrants have arrived, the changing central city–suburban mix within metropolitan areas, and shifts in residential housing segregation patterns. U.S. census data, especially on mobility and nativity, have become more precise and more accessible, a development that has launched the burgeoning fields of applied demographics (Kintner, Merrick, Morrison, and Voss 1994) and promoted the geographical mapping of demographic and political characteristics. Growth has clearly affected some southern states more than others. Migration levels—in-migration and out-migration—vary both across and within states.[2]

The Movers: Who, Why, When, and Where?

Americans are a highly mobile population. Approximately 20 percent of the population moves every year. Historically, most movers relocate within a county or state rather than to another region or from another country.

Many of the writings about population shifts since World War II focus on the age, race, gender, marital status, income, and education of those who move, along with why, when, and where they go. Most are reports by the U.S. Bureau of the Census. Examples include *Current Population Reports* and *Census Special Reports* (with various authors— Wan He, Jason P. Schachter, Jesse McKinnon, Roberta R. Ramirez, G. Patricia de la Cruz, Eric C. Newberger, Andrea E. Curry, among others). An additional rich source of data analysis and discussion is the reports developed through academic institutions such as the University of Michigan Population Studies Center and through policy planning organizations such as the Brookings Institution (again with a variety of authors, including William H. Frey, Edward L. Glaeser, Jessie Shapiro, Jacob L. Vigdor, Paul D. Gottlieb). Finally, some more extended academic analyses appear in such journals as *Demography* and *Population Research and Policy Review,* with the occasional book-length treatment in the mix. These reports and analyses provide the foundation for those works that examine the political consequences of population movement for southern politics.

Unfortunately, the Census Bureau's annual population survey data, collected since 1948, cannot be disaggregated to individual states because the surveys generating the figures are based on a sample of households. Nevertheless, these data can give us insights into who moves, why, and when, and they offer some occasional opportunities to see more specifically how the South has been affected.

Who Moves?

A review of the Census Bureau's *Current Population Reports* over time shows that mobility statistics and their analyses have become more detailed and sophisticated. They also reveal some similarities and dissimilarities across the decades in who the movers are.

Since the early 1950s certain patterns stand out: those most likely to move are usually young (early twenties), often unemployed, unmarried (single, divorced, separated) or newly married, nonwhite, with low-to-moderate incomes, and above-average levels of education. By the 1960s the reports were singling out the South as the region experiencing the most population mobility (Bureau of the Census 1964).

By the early 1970s the census-based mobility studies showed residential mobility rates to be highest among young persons in their twenties, blacks, unemployed men, and newly married persons. Long-distance migration rates were highest for male college graduates (Bureau of the Census 1972). In the early 1980s movers living in the South were most likely to have moved between states (Bureau of the Census 1983). Metropolitan areas gained more immigrants than nonmetropolitan areas.

By the early 1990s metropolitan areas were drawing people from nonmetropolitan areas, suburbs from central cities and rural areas. Suburb-to-suburb moves increased. The South continued to experience a net in-migration of persons from other regions (Long and Hansen 1975), benefiting from industries moving to the South because of tax incentives and lower labor costs, the availability of home air-conditioning, better educational opportunities, and successes of the civil rights movement (Long 1988).

Analyses of mobility patterns during the 1990s and early 2000s focused more on those in-migrating from abroad, specifically Asians and Hispanics. Studies during this time also reported that better-educated, more affluent persons tended to move longer distances and were more likely to choose suburbs as their new residential location (Schachter 2001).

Why?

Beginning in 1998, the Census Bureau's Current Population Survey began asking respondents why they moved. The survey classified the reasons into four categories: family-related, employment-related, housing-related, and other (such as education, climate, health). The reasons for relocating differed depending upon the time period and the age of the mover. Interregional moves were more likely to be job-related, while intra-urban moves tended to be housing-related. Poorer persons were somewhat more likely to move for family- than for work-related reasons (see Schachter 2001, 1). Long-distance changes of address were most common among highly educated persons, young persons, and retirees.

When and Where?

Research shows that not everyone chooses the same time of the year to move. Studies based on the Census Bureau's Survey of Income and Program Participation (SIPP)[3] found that one-third of all moves took place during June, July, and August. The longer the move, the more likely the move was to occur during this period (Hansen 1998, 3). Moves from abroad, however, were more likely to occur during the winter months than domestic moves.

SIPP data revealed that "blacks, Hispanics, and non-citizens were less likely than non-Hispanic whites and citizens to move during the summer months, while people with a bachelor's degree were more likely to move during the summer than those less educated" (Schachter and Kuenzi 2002, 3). Older people were more prone to move after school started than were younger persons, although not by much (Hansen 1998, 2). Predictably, "for people moving within and to the South, the fall months were a less popular time to move" (Schachter and Kuenzi 2002, 5).

The timing of moves (summer particularly) has important political ramifications for fall elections, especially state and local elections held in non–presidential election years. In high-growth areas, mobility may help explain lower turnout rates in off-year elections, since we know that it takes a while for newcomers to feel informed enough about state and local politics to vote.

Four Major Groups of In-Migrants

A sizable body of writing, primarily by demographers, has focused on large groups of in-migrants and the areas from which they have come. The South's growth over the past half century has been fueled by (1) in-migration from other countries, particularly countries in Latin and South America; (2) in-migration of African Americans of southern heritage leaving northern states and returning home; (3) in-migration of retirees from other regions of the United States attracted by warmer weather, lower taxes, cheaper land, and lower housing costs; and (4) in-migration of younger, better-educated, U.S.-born persons from outside and within the region attracted to the South by an expanding job market. Obviously, not every state has been equally affected by all four types of new arrivals.

Foreign-born Moving to the South

From the outset it is important to note that Census Bureau definitions and measurement of the foreign-born population have evolved across several censuses (see Malone, Baluja, Costanzo, and Davis 2003, 1). The literature tracking the incidence and impact of foreign-born in-migrants is relatively recent. More detailed census racial and ethnic classifications have yielded more in-depth analyses of specific population subsets and prompted writers to caution against assumptions of homogeneity within broad categories.

In recent years, specifically from 1990 to 2000, the growth rate of the foreign-born was higher in the South (88 percent) than in the United States as a whole (57 percent). By 2000 the South was home to more than one-fourth of all foreign-born persons in the United States. Most were from Latin America (63.0 percent), and the remainder were from Asia (19.0 percent), Europe (11.5 percent), Africa (3.6 percent), North America (2.6 percent), and Oceania (0.3 percent) (Malone et al. 2003, 7). Census Bureau studies clearly show considerable "diversity within the foreign-born population with regard to year of entry, citizenship status, and country of origin" (He and Schachter 2003, 3). Political scientists increasingly take these same elements into account when describing immigrant politics.

The states heavily affected by new residents from foreign countries are, in the words of demographers like William Frey, "immigrant magnet" states or "melting pots." Among the eleven states of the Confederacy, two have foreign-born population proportions higher than the U.S. average (2000 figures): Florida (16.7 percent) and Texas (13.9 percent). All the deep South states except Louisiana, however, have recently experienced growth rates in their foreign-born populations that exceed that of the United States at large (Malone et al. 2003, 3).

The foreign-born population of the United States is younger than the population in general, although in the South the senior figure is higher (Kritz and Nogle 1994; Zavodny 1999). Among older foreign-born, "the presence of immigrant networks and communities is a primary determinant of geographic location of residence or internal migration" (He 2002, 5). It is also often the key to understanding naturalization rates.

Compared with other regions of the United States, the South has the lowest proportion of foreign-born who are naturalized citizens (37.4 percent). That proportion is down from 39.6 percent in 1990 (Malone et al. 2003, 3). Among southern states, just three have a higher proportion of naturalized foreign-born residents than the U.S. average (40.3 percent) in 2000: Louisiana (48.4 percent), Florida (45.2 percent), and Virginia (40.8 percent). The lowest proportions are in North Carolina (26.2 percent), Georgia (29.3 percent), and Arkansas (29.6 percent). Citizenship statistics like these are important because eligibility to vote has played a major role in reapportionment and redistricting debates and litigation following the 1990 and 2000 censuses, as states have struggled to meet equal opportunity requirements of the Voting Rights Act.

In considering citizenship, one must remember that the foreign-born population does not remain static. Growth in a state's foreign-born population "occurs through movement from abroad or through foreign-born migrants' secondary migration from elsewhere in the United States after their initial arrival" (He and Schachter 2003, 3). Newly arrived immigrants are more likely to settle in traditional or established gateway cities such as New York, Los Angeles, San Francisco, Chicago, and Miami. Five new gateway cities are emerging, four of which are in the South: Atlanta, Charlotte, Fort Worth–Arlington, and Orlando (Singer 2003). Long-term foreign-born residents are more likely to leave gateway cities. Three southern metro areas—Atlanta, Dallas, and Orlando—rank among the top five gainers of secondary foreign-born residents in the 1990s (Frey 2002, 13).

Recent foreign-born immigrants to the United States are more likely to have come from Asia and Latin America than from Europe (Perry and Schachter 2003, 2). Latinos who came to the South in the 1990s had Florida and Texas (71 percent) as their main destinations (Frey 2001c, 4), but five other southern states—Alabama, Arkansas, Georgia, North Carolina, and Tennessee—also saw tremendous growth in their Hispanic populations.

Before the 1980s Latinos tended to settle in Texas, California, and New York. In the 1980s "the first significant shift in permanent Latino settlement patterns" occurred when Hispanics moved from Texas to the Midwest. In the 1990s the shift reverted to the deep South, though Texas and Florida were still part of the pattern (Torres 2000, 2). Florida experienced a big influx of Cubans in the 1960s and again in 1980 (the Mariel boatlift). In the 1980s and 1990s refugees from Nicaragua, Honduras, El Salvador, and Haiti escaped from wars and economic upheavals by heading to Miami (ibid., 3). In general, Florida had the highest net migration gain of Hispanics from 1995 to 2000, followed by Nevada, Arizona, and Georgia (Schachter 2003, 10).

In noting these shifts, scholars repeatedly warn against treating Hispanics as a monolithic group, particularly in politics. "While Hispanics share a cultural heritage from a Spanish-speaking country, differences in nationality, politics, religion, level of education, skills, and language use exist among the Hispanic subgroups such as Mexican American, Mexican, Salvadorian, Nicaraguan, Cuban, Dominican, and Puerto Rican" (Torres 2000, 1). Florida's Hispanic populations are proof positive: Cubans and non-Cubans do not always vote alike (Moreno 2004).

The same warnings apply to analyses of Asians[4] and Pacific Islanders. Neither group is homogeneous; "each comprises many groups who are different in language, culture, and length of residence in the United States" (Reeves and Bennett 2003, 1). As of March 2002, 18.9 percent of the nation's Asians and Pacific Islanders called the South home, ranking the region second behind the West, where a majority reside (51.1 percent).

African Americans Moving to the South

Race has been a thread running through the entire fabric of writings on southern politics. Beginning in the 1970s and accelerating into the 1990s, scholars focused more of their attention on a major shift in migration patterns—the return of middle-class blacks to the South. Black gainer states have been the old Cotton Belt or Black Belt states of Alabama, Georgia, North Carolina, South Carolina, and Tennessee (Frey 2000). New writings have also focused on the growing suburbanization of the black population. Blacks moving to the South fall into three groups: (1) middle-class persons drawn to the booming New South economies; (2) working-class persons who were turned away from manufacturing restructuring in the North; and (3) retirees (ibid., 2).

This reverse migration has been fueled by an attraction to "a booming economy, warmer climate, historical roots and a growing middle-class black population" (Bayer and Bonilla 2001). Blacks moving from the North to the South are settling in suburbs, "contributing to a decline in residential segregation in those areas" (ibid., 2). The 2000 census showed that minorities made up 27 percent of the suburban population, up from 19 percent in 1990 ("The New Black Flight" 2002).

Residential integration is at a higher level in the South and West than elsewhere. Black-nonblack neighborhood segregation declined considerably in Atlanta, Orlando, Jacksonville, Norfolk, and Houston over the past twenty years (Frey 2001c, 4). As the demographer William Frey noted, "The improved segments of the black population are moving to the fastest-growing parts of the country, and that's where economic progress is being seen."

Retirees Moving to the South

Retirees fueled the growth of Sun Belt states like Florida beginning in the 1970s and 1980s and, more recently, in other southern states such as Mississippi, North Carolina, and Georgia. A growing number of these states have aggressively recruited retirees, especially younger, healthier, wealthier, and better-educated retirees who spend disproportionately large amounts of their disposable income in the local economy (MacManus 2000). Gone are the days when "old" was simply anyone sixty-five or older. Scholars from various disciplines, including political science, have begun to make major distinctions between the mobility patterns and politics of the younger-old and the older-old.

Studies of older movers' migration patterns from 1995 to 2000 have found that states gaining older migrants usually were in close proximity to or had milder climates than the states with net losses of older migrants. The most "senior magnet" states, as measured by net migration rates, were Florida, 56.9; South Carolina, 33.6; North Carolina, 22.1; Georgia, 18.1; and Tennessee, 15.2 (see He and Schachter 2003). Only one southern state, Louisiana, suffered a net loss of older migrants in the late 1990s.

A newly emerging pattern in some states is the out-migration of the oldest old ("return migration"). For example, between 1995 and 2000, Florida experienced a net out-migration of those aged eighty-five and over (He and Schachter 2003, 8). Wan He and Jason Schachter note that "at the oldest ages, many older people who initially moved away at retirement may have returned to their states of origin, perhaps to be closer to family or simply to return home" (ibid.).

Within individual states, older movers are leaving highly congested areas and relocating to more rural areas that are proximate to metro areas. These patterns have been particularly noticeable in Florida and Arkansas (ibid., 10). For example, older residents in Florida are leaving south Florida and moving to southwest and central Florida. In Arkansas they have moved from southwestern to northwestern areas. Obviously, such intrastate migration patterns can greatly alter a state's local politics: seniors are high-turnout voters whose needs and priorities may differ from those of other age groups (MacManus 1996, 2000).

Some seniors move to the suburbs to be near enough to medical care but out of the crowded inner city. In the late 1990s and early 2000s writings identifying a "racial *generation* gap" in the suburbs, particularly in "melting pot" metro areas, began to appear. In these suburbs "over half of younger residents are non-white or Hispanic, while only a third of older residents are" (Frey 2003, 1). In 2000 in the South, racial generation gaps (measured as the difference between the percentage of a minority population that is under thirty-five and the percentage that is over thirty-five) were widest in the suburbs of West Palm Beach–Boca Raton (26 percent) and Fort Lauderdale (21.7 percent). Frey notes that the changing race-age structure of suburbs is relatively new but may heighten tensions between the generations over a community's taxing and spending policies (ibid., 12).

Gender differences are significant among southern seniors. Within the older population women outnumber men, but men are more likely than women to be married, be living with their spouses, and have a bachelor's degree or higher (Smith 2003). The sheer political clout of older women is greater than that of older men; there are simply more women than men voters in this cohort (MacManus 2000). In general, older widows are more dependent upon government income security programs than older widowers, especially among foreign-born seniors (He 2002, 11).

U.S. Natives Moving to the South

The South has experienced a higher domestic net migration rate of native-born residents than all other regions.[5] Younger, better-educated, middle-class, U.S.-born suburbanites, disproportionately white, have moved from "expensive, congested suburbs of the Northeast and California coastal metropolises" to states Frey calls "domestic migrant magnets." Georgia, North Carolina, Tennessee, Texas, and Florida rank among the top 1990s gainers. (During the 1990s Georgia, the Carolinas, and Tennessee increased their white voting age populations by more than twice the national rate.) These states "are attractive because of their growing economies, relatively low cost of living, and their climatic or environmental amenities" (Frey 2002, 6).

Young adults between the ages of twenty-five and thirty-nine are movers, especially young, single, college-educated adults who are "more willing to relocate in order to meet economic or lifestyle demands than married individuals, who could be contained by location preferences of a spouse" (Franklin 2003b, 1). Southern states with positive net migration rates by this important demographic group are Georgia (150.5), North Carolina (50.2), Texas (48.7), Florida (40.1), Virginia (38.4), and Tennessee (15.2). Among the twenty metropolitan statistical areas with the highest domestic migration rates for young, single, and college-educated persons, ten are in the South, including three of the top five (Naples, Florida; Charlotte–Gastonia–Rock Hill, North Carolina–South Carolina; and Atlanta, Georgia).

Five states experienced negative net migration rates by this demographic group between 1995 and 2000: South Carolina, Arkansas, Alabama, Louisiana, and Mississippi.

As we have noted, the same states that are attracting young, single, college-educated persons are also attracting more foreign-born residents, especially Hispanics, who fill construction, service, and retail jobs created by growth in these areas (Frey 2002; Suro and Singer 2002). Overall, "states with net in-migration of natives from other states usually had net in-migration of foreign born, too" (He and Schachter 2003, 7). The booming states of the South, particularly the South Atlantic, obviously fit this pattern.

Linking Demographic Shifts, Political Participation, and Partisan Leanings

Most of the literature on population mobility has been generated by demographers rather than by political scientists, as we have noted. The most extensive work to date on the direct link between population mobility and politics is Thad Brown's *Migration and Politics: The Impact of Population Mobility on American Voting Behavior* (1988). Brown relied heavily on National Election Studies survey data from 1952 to 1980, rather than on Census Bureau data, to examine the effect of migration on the voting behavior of Americans. (Regrettably, there is no regional breakdown of the analysis.)

Brown asked this empirical question: "[Do] individuals change at all politically, change gradually in the years after migration, or change quickly at the time of migration?" (1988, 146). His findings:

Migrants (movers) are different from nonmigrants, especially at the time of migration. They are better educated and more affluent. Even in the years after they move, they tend to attain higher incomes than nonmigrants.

At the time of their migration, movers appear to be less involved and committed to politics than nonmigrants, primarily because movers tend to be younger; the voter turnout rates and levels of party attachment are weaker among movers.

Over time migrants end up participating and voting "in a fashion similar to that of nonmigrants."

Most of the variability in migrants' political participatory and electoral attributes is accounted for by the social, economic, and demographic characteristics of migrants, and not by specific migration-related attributes, *with the exception of those who move across a regional boundary.*

The migration across regional boundaries is critical to thinking about changes in southern politics. Why? Because Brown concludes that migration "turns projected partisans into political independents," dealigns voters from political parties, and opens the political system to the possibility of long-term political change. "As a result of geographical mobility, individuals become susceptible to political change and new political movements," Brown argues (1988, 153).

Brown's findings contradict those reached by University of Michigan researchers several decades earlier: "Political socialization forms virtually permanent political loyalties that immunize migrants from the force of new political environments, however persuasive those new environments might be" (ibid., 10, describing the findings of Converse 1966). These studies attributed the changing politics of the South, namely the erosion of Democratic strength, to out-migration of southern Democrats (often blacks moving north) and the in-migration of northern, middle-class Republican professionals moving south after World War II as the region's economy recovered. These in-migrant Republicans did not change their party affiliations (Converse 1966).

The debate has continued over whether migration loosens an individual's pre-move political party attachments. But now the debate has been extended to the effect of in-migration on natives and nonmovers: Do in-migrants with different party attachments over time create a more competitive political environment, thereby loosening the party attachments of nonmigrants? The answer to the question varies across states because the characteristics of in-migrants differ considerably, as do the socioeconomic status and party attachments of natives and longtime residents. Some states are stronger magnets than other states for certain racial or ethnic and age groups with different socioeconomic attributes (income, education).

Another question that has resurfaced is whether movers seek out locations populated by politically like-minded individuals. Converse (1966), Brown (1988), and others concluded that decisions to move are politically neutral and driven more by economics and personal circumstances than politics. This premise is increasingly coming under attack, particularly with regard to older movers (with stronger partisan attachments) and the more affluent (of all races and ethnicities), who have the economic means to be more selective in their relocation decisions; they often choose areas that are more politically homogeneous in their voting patterns and populated by persons in-migrating from the same countries or states. In Florida, for example, retirees moving from the Northeast generally take up residence in south Florida in heavily Democratic areas like Broward County, whereas retirees from the Midwest are more likely to move to central and southwest counties with larger concentrations of Republican senior voters.

Shifts in Population Composition Affect
Politics and Coalition Building

Political scientists who study southern politics have focused most of their attention on the political consequences of shifts in the racial and ethnic composition of the region's population. Key forever linked race and politics and treated the relationship as more powerful than geography (urban versus rural) or economic status (rich versus poor), although not mutually exclusive from either: "In its grand outlines the politics of the South revolves around the position of the Negro. It is at times interpreted as a politics of cotton, as a politics of free trade, as a politics of agrarian poverty, or as a politics of planter and plutocrat. . . . [But] in the last analysis, the major peculiarities of southern politics go back to the Negro. Whatever phase of the southern political process one seeks to understand, sooner or later the trail of inquiry leads to the Negro"(1949, 5).

Key's state-by-state analysis of the South focused on white political power in areas with large concentrations of blacks—the Black Belts. His conclusion? "The character of the politics of individual states will vary roughly with the Negro proportion of the population" (ibid.).

Today Key's thesis has been expanded to include newly arrived racial and ethnic groups (Hispanics, Asians and Pacific Islanders, and others). Changes in the relative size of a racial or ethnic group affect each group's electoral successes.

Effects of Black Population Growth

In some states with large metropolitan centers and wide social distance in such areas as education and income between whites and minorities, growth in the black population has prompted white flight to the suburbs and beyond. Politically and racially driven population redistribution patterns have resulted in more residentially segregated housing patterns and more majority-minority communities and legislative districts. The result has been the election of more minorities to congressional, state, and local legislative bodies, particularly from single-member districts.

There is much debate over the extent to which the emergence of middle-class blacks and their movement to suburbia have narrowed the black-white "social distance," promoted more residential integration, and resulted in less racially polarized voting patterns. An analysis of racial segregation in three hundred metropolitan statistical areas using 2000 census redistricting files found that black-nonblack segregation levels were at their lowest point since 1920 and that "the 1990s continued a three-decade trend towards decreasing segregation throughout the U.S." (Glaeser and Vigdor 2001, 1). But the analysis did not look at segregation levels in multiracial communities. The study did, however, find that the West and the South were more integrated than the Northeast and Midwest and concluded that "metropolitan areas that are growing quickly have had sharper declines in segregation than metropolitan areas that are stagnant (ibid., 6). Austin, Texas, and Raleigh-Durham, North Carolina, were singled out as areas with "remarkably low and declining segregation levels."

Effects of Hispanic Population Growth

There is a growing concern that Hispanics are becoming more residentially segregated, often because of language. Some recent studies have found that Hispanic-white segregation increased significantly over the 1990s in southern metro areas such as Raleigh-Durham, Atlanta, Charlotte, Nashville, and Greensboro (Frey 2002, 9). The proportion of Hispanics who speak only Spanish at home or who do not speak English well has increased in these places. This population trend has prompted political parties and candidates to use different media outlets (Spanish-language television and radio) to target this concentrated ethnic group. It appears to be working. Hispanic turnout rates are rising and more Hispanics are getting elected at all levels.

Population Changes Affect Coalition Building

Population groups express their needs and preferences in many ways, including their political affiliation and participation. Often two or more groups band together in a coalition to achieve similar political aims. Coalition building can become volatile when population mobility is high, particularly in multiracial settings in heavily urbanized states. Coalitions may shift in racial or ethnic composition and over time, depending on demographic changes that alter group size. In coalition building the goal is always political victory.

Survey data, including exit polls, have uncovered a wide range of coalitions in the South: liberal whites with blacks; blacks and Hispanics versus non-Hispanic whites; Hispanics and non-Hispanic whites versus blacks.[6] But survey data have also shown that among racial and ethnic groups, blacks are by far the most politically cohesive.

Lingering Questions and the Need for Future Research

Two big questions still remain regarding the nature of the link between population mobility and regional politics. First, do in-migrants to the South maintain their pre-move political leanings, thereby changing the overall political landscape, or is it the reverse? Second, are individual decisions to move truly politically neutral? Political scientists have done little to definitively answer either of these population mobility questions over the past fifty years.

The increasingly melting pot nature of the South highlights the need to conduct more research into the mobility patterns and decisions of specific racial and ethnic groups. For example, political scientists have paid little attention to the political preferences and participation rates of minorities, especially African Americans, returning to the South or moving into the suburbs. The impact of upward mobility on the politics of minorities has also been grossly understudied. So, too, has the impact of mobility on coalition building.

More research is also needed on generational shifts in mobility patterns. A key question with major political consequences is whether baby boomers will decide to stay put or relocate once they retire. If they decide to relocate, will they move to the same high-growth, warm-climate states their parents did? Or will they move to less crowded, more rural areas outside metropolitan areas? The sheer size of the baby boomer generation ensures that their mobility decisions have the potential to greatly alter the face of state and local politics. Generation-based frictions are likely to surface.

The bottom line is that political scientists need to analyze more carefully the individual-level data that are driving the aggregate-level growth-rate figures. By better understanding the numbers behind the numbers, we will get a clearer picture of the impact of population growth and mobility on a region's politics.

Notes

1. By southern states, we (like many other southern politics scholars) refer to the eleven states of the Confederacy (Alabama, Arkansas, Florida, Georgia, Louisiana, Mississippi, North Carolina, South Carolina, Tennessee, Texas, and Virginia), unless we are citing Census Bureau regional statistics. The South (and its three subregions) as defined by the Census Bureau includes more than the eleven states of the Confederacy, as follows: the South Atlantic Division includes the District of Columbia, Virginia, West Virginia,

North Carolina, South Carolina, Georgia, and Florida; the East South Central Division includes Kentucky, Tennessee, Alabama, and Mississippi; and the West South Central Division includes Arkansas, Louisiana, Oklahoma, and Texas.

2. The Census Bureau defines *migration* as "moves that cross jurisdictional boundaries." Movement into and out of the United States is *international* migration. *Domestic,* or *internal,* migration is the "movement of people within national boundaries" (for example, moves that cross state, division, or region boundaries within the United States). *In-migration* is "migration into an area during a given period." *Out-migration* is "migration out of an area during a given period" (see Franklin 2003a, 1; Schachter, Franklin, and Perry 2003, 1). Gross in-migration and out-migration figures are actual numbers of movers. *Net in-migration* indicates that more movers entered an area than left during a specified time. *Net out-migration* means the reverse (He and Schachter 2003). Moves within a jurisdiction are referred to as *residential mobility*.

3. The Survey of Income and Program Participation is a longitudinal survey of people who are at least fifteen years old, conducted at four-month intervals by the U.S. Census Bureau (Schachter and Kuenzi 2002, 10).

4. The U.S. Census Bureau defines Asians as persons "having origins in any of the Far East, Southeast Asia, or the Indian subcontinent including, for example, Cambodia, China, India, Japan, Korea, Malaysia, Pakistan, the Philippine Islands, Thailand, and Vietnam" (Reeves and Bennett 2003, 1).

5. The West's net domestic migration rate from 1995 to 2000 was 2.1 percent; for the Northeast it was –24.6, and for the Midwest it was –9.9. The U.S. Census Bureau defines domestic migration as movement within the United States that crosses jurisdictional boundaries. Net migration is the difference between in-migration and out-migration during a given time. A positive net in-migration indicates that more migrants entered an area than left during that time. A negative net in-migration means that more migrants left an area then entered it (He and Schachter 2003, 5).

6. There is little research on Asians in coalitions because of the relatively small size of the population in most southern states and communities.

References

Bayer, Angela, and Joshua Bonilla. 2001. "Executive Summary: Our Changing Nation." *Population Resource Center*. Washington D.C.: Population Resource Center.

Black, Earl, and Merle Black. 2002. *The Rise of Southern Republicans.* Cambridge: Harvard University Press.

Brown, Thad A. 1988. *Migration and Politics: The Impact of Population Mobility on American Voting Behavior.* Chapel Hill: University of North Carolina Press.

Bureau of the Census. 1953. "Mobility of the Population of the United States April 1952 to April 1953." *Current Population Reports* P-20, no. 49, December 1.

186   Susan A. MacManus

———. 1964. "Mobility of the Population of the United States April 1961 to April 1962." *Current Population Reports* P-20, no. 127, January 15.

———. 1972. "Mobility of the Population of the United States March 1970 to March 1971." *Current Population Reports* P-20, no. 235, April.

———. 1983. "Geographical Mobility: March 1980 to March 1981." *Current Population Reports* P-20, no. 377, January.

Converse, Philip E. 1966. "The Concept of the Normal Vote." In *Elections and the Political Order,* ed. Angus Campbell, Philip E. Converse, Warren E. Miller, and Donald E. Stokes. New York: John Wiley and Sons.

DeAre, Diana. n.d. "Geographical Mobility: March 1990 to March 1991." *Current Population Reports* P-20, no. 463.

Edds, Margaret. 2003. "Dixie Still Whistles a Different Political Tune." *Tallahassee Democrat,* June 16.

Fix, Michael, Jeffrey S. Passel, and Kenneth Sucher. 2003. "Trends in Naturalization." *Immigrant Families and Workers,* brief no. 2, September.

Franklin, Rachel S. 2003a. "Domestic Migration across Regions, Divisions, and States: 1995 to 2000." *Census 2000 Special Reports,* CENSR-7, August.

———. 2003b. "Migration of the Young, Single, and College Educated: 1995 to 2000." *Census 2000 Special Reports,* CENSR-12, November.

Frey, William H. 2000. "Regional Shifts in America's Voting-Aged Population: What Do They Mean for National Politics?" *Research Report No. 00–459.* Ann Arbor: University of Michigan Population Studies Center.

———. 2001a. "Census 2000 Shows Large Black Return to the South, Reinforcing the Region's 'White-Black' Demographic Profile." *Research Report No. 01–473.* Ann Arbor: University of Michigan Population Studies Center.

———. 2001b. *Melting Pot Suburbs: A Census 2000 Study of Suburban Diversity.* Brookings Census 2000 Series. Washington, D.C.: Brookings Institution Center on Urban and Metropolitan Policy.

———. 2001c. "Migration to the South Brings U.S. Blacks Full Circle." *Population Today* 29, no. 4.

———. 2002. "Census 2000 Reveals New Native-Born and Foreign-Born Shifts Across U.S." *Population Today* 30, no. 6.

———. 2003. "Boomers and Seniors in the Suburbs: Aging Patterns in Census 2000." Brookings Census 2000 Series. Washington, D.C: Brookings Institution Center on Urban and Metropolitan Policy.

Glaeser, Edward, and Jessie Shapiro. 2001. *City Growth and the 2000 Census: Which Places Grew, and Why.* Washington, D.C.: Brookings Institution Center on Urban and Metropolitan Policy.

Glaeser, Edward L., and Jacob L. Vigdor. 2001. *Racial Segregation in the 2000 Census: Promising News.* Washington, D.C.: Brookings Institution Center on Urban and Metropolitan Policy.

Guillory, Ferrel, and John Quinterno. 2003. "New Politics in a Metropolitan South." *South Now,* no. 5, September.

Hansen, Kristin A. 1998. "Seasonality of Moves and Duration of Residence," *Current Population Reports,* P70–66.

He, Wan. 2002. "The Older Foreign-Born Population in the United States: 2000." *Current Population Reports*, P23–211, September.

He, Wan, and Jason P. Schachter. 2003. "Internal Migration of the Older Population: 1995 to 2000." *Census 2000 Special Reports*, August.

Hetzel, Lisa, and Annetta Smith. 2001. "The 65 Years and Over Population: 2000." *Census 2000 Brief*, C2KBR/01–10, October.

Key, V. O., Jr. 1949. *Southern Politics in State and Nation*. New York: Knopf.

Kintner, Hallie J., Thomas W. Merrick, Peter A. Morrison, and Paul R. Voss, eds. 1994. *Demographics: A Casebook for Business and Government*. Boulder, Colo.: Westview Press.

Kritz, Mary M., and June Marie Nogle. 1994. "Nativity Concentration and Internal Migration among the Foreign-Born." *Demography* 31: 509–24.

Long, Larry E. 1988. *Migration and Residential Mobility in the United States*. New York: Russell Sage Foundation.

Long, Larry H., and Kristin A. Hansen. 1975. "Trends in Return Migration to the South." *Demography* 12: 601–14.

MacManus, Susan A. 1996. *Young v. Old: Generational Combat in the 21st Century*. Boulder, Colo.: Westview Press.

———. 2000. *Targeting Senior Voters*. Lanham, Md.: Rowman and Littlefield.

Malone, Nolan, Kaari F. Baluja, Joseph M. Costanzo, and Cynthia J. Davis. 2003. "The Foreign-Born Population: 2000." *Census 2000 Brief*, C2KBR-34, December.

Moreno, Dario. 2004. "Florida's Hispanic Voters: Growth, Immigration, and Political Clout." In *Florida's Politics: Ten Media Markets, One Powerful State*, ed. Kevin Hill, Susan MacManus, and Dario Moreno. Tallahassee: Florida Institute of Government.

"The New Black Flight: Guess Who's Coming to the Suburbs." 2002. Editorial, *Wall Street Journal*, included in *WSJ Opinion Journal* (April 27, 2002), accessed at www.opinionjournal.com/editorial/feature.html?id=105001990.

Perry, Marc J., and Jason P. Schachter. 2003. "Migration of Natives and the Foreign Born: 1995 to 2000." *Census 2000 Special Reports*, August.

Reeves, Terrance, and Claudette Bennett. 2003. "The Asian and Pacific Islander Population in the United States, March 2002." *Current Population Reports*, P20–540, May.

Schachter, Jason P. 2001. "Why People Move: Exploring the March 2000 Current Population Survey." *Current Population Reports*, P23–204, May.

———. 2003. "Migration by Race and Hispanic Origin: 1995 to 2000." *Census 2000 Special Reports*, CENSR-13, October.

Schachter, Jason P., Rachel S. Franklin, and Marc J. Perry. 2003. "Migration and Geographic Mobility in Metropolitan and Nonmetropolitan America: 1995 to 2000." *Census 2000 Special Reports*, CENSR-9, August.

Schachter, Jason P., and Jeffrey J. Kuenzi. 2002. "Seasonality of Moves and the Duration and Tenure of Residence: 1996." U.S. Census Bureau, Population Division Working Paper Series no. 69, December.

Schmidley, A. Dianne. 2001. "Profile of the Foreign-Born Population in the United States: 2000." *Current Population Reports*, P23–206, December.

Schmidley, A. Dianne, and Campbell Gibson. 1999. "Profile of the Foreign-Born Population in the United States: 1997." *Current Population Reports,* P23–206.

Singer, Audrey. 2003. "The New U.S. Demographics." PowerPoint presentation to the Funders Network on Population, Reproductive Health and Rights, Brookings Institution Center on Urban and Metropolitan Policy, November 10.

Smith, Denise. 2003. "The Older Population in the United States: March 2002." *Current Population Reports,* P20–546, April.

Stack, Carol. 1996. *Call to Home: African Americans Reclaim the Rural South.* New York: Basic Books.

Suro, Roberto, and Audrey Singer. 2002. "Latino Growth in Metropolitan America: Changing Patterns, New Locations." *Census 2000 Survey Series.* Washington, D.C.: Brookings Institution and Pew Hispanic Center.

Taylor, Melissa, and James Carroll. 2002. "The Changing Population in the U.S.: Baby Boomers, Immigrants, and Their Effects on State Government." *Trends Alert.* Lexington, Ky.: Council of State Governments, December.

Torres, Cruz C. 2000. "Emerging Latino Communities: A New Challenge for the Rural South." *The Rural South: Preparing for the 21st Century.* Monthly report from the Southern Rural Development Center), no. 12, August.

Zavodny, Madeline. 1999. "Determinants of Recent Immigrants' Locational Choices." *International Migration Review* 33: 1014–30.

★ Chapter 8 ★

Issues, Ideology, and Political Opinions in the South

Patrick R. Cotter, Stephen D. Shaffer, and David A. Breaux

ARE SOUTHERNERS DIFFERENT? If they are, why are they different?

The research most directly concerned with examining public opinion in the South has sought to answer one or both of these questions. Our purpose here is to review this research with the goal of identifying what conclusions currently can be reached regarding the nature and causes of southern distinctiveness in the area of public opinion. Further, our review will point to the additional steps needed to determine fully and accurately if, and why, southerners are different.

The public opinion research investigating whether southerners are different from citizens living elsewhere in the country covers a wide variety of topics. As a consequence, it is necessary to concentrate here on a specific part of the regional distinctiveness literature—published studies that, as a central part of their analyses, have compared the political issue opinions and ideological leanings of southerners to those of other citizens. Studies investigating other important political topics, such as the party identifications, voting preferences, or levels of political participation of southerners, are not examined here. Further, our examination of political issue opinions is limited to those dealing with domestic policy concerns. Research examining regional differences in foreign policy–related issues is limited and somewhat dated. For one study in this area, see Hero (1965).

This review will also generally not include studies that have investigated regional differences in less directly political topics, even though

189

these concerns may influence the issue opinions or ideological leanings of southerners. Thus, research investigating regional differences in areas such as level of violence (Hackney 1969; Gastil 1971; Loftin and Hill 1974; Dixon and Lizotte 1987; Ellison 1991; Flynn 1994; Nisbett and Cohen 1996; Clarke 1998), use of leisure time (Marsden, Reed, Kennedy, and Stinson 1982), divorce (Glenn and Shelton 1985), authoritarianism (Williams 1966), English usage (Tillery, Wikle, and Baily 2000), religious involvement (Stemp 1987; Hunt and Hunt 2001) is not examined here.

Similarly, studies that examine regional differences generally are not closely examined here (see, for example, Glenn and Simmons 1967; Glenn 1967, 1974; Weakliem and Biggert 1999; Griswold and Wright 2004). Such investigations show that regional differences exist. They provide, however, limited information concerning the specific ways in which the South is or is not different from other parts of the country.

Finally, an electronic search of post-1950 political science and sociology journals, using as keywords "South" and the name of either of the two major sources of national public opinion data—the National Election Studies and the General Social Survey—identifies several hundred studies examining issue opinions or ideological leanings. Most of these studies are only tangentially—rather than centrally—concerned with southern public opinion or regional differences. Their interest in region is restricted to its use as a data analysis control variable. Consequently, the findings of these studies are not included in this review, though cataloging the findings of these projects regarding the influence of region would be a useful endeavor.

The studies that are reviewed here are all interested in examining whether the opinions of southerners are different from those of others. Most of the studies are also interested in at least speculating about the reasons for the differences found between the South and other parts of the country. The studies reviewed here approach the topic of southern distinctiveness from roughly three different perspectives.

First, several of the studies (for example, Beck and Lopatto 1982; Hawkey 1982, 1988; Cotter and Stovall 1990) investigate the issue opinions and ideological leanings of southerners as a means of gaining insight into the region's changing politics. More generally, these studies are concerned with examining whether it is correct to characterize the South broadly as politically distinct or, more specifically, as a region "in which conservatism flourishes and liberalism withers" (Black and Black 1987, 213).

Second, other studies are primarily concerned with the concept of region (for example, Reed 1974; Hurlbert 1989; Weakliem and Biggert 1999; Rice, McLean, and Larsen 2002). These investigations examined the issue opinions and ideological leanings of southerners in order to document the existence of regional differences and to determine the influence of modernizing trends in the media, the economy, and other areas of social life on these variations.

Finally, a third category of studies is primarily concerned with investigating public attitudes about specific issues. Regional differences are examined in these studies to determine if and why opinions about the issue in question vary from one location to another. Not surprisingly, given the topic's importance in both southern and national political history, many of the studies in this category have investigated regional differences in race-related issues (for example, Middleton 1976; Schuman, Steeh, Bobo, and Krysan 1997). In more recent years, possibly because of a declining importance of race on the nation's political agenda, researchers have devoted more attention to studying regional differences in social or cultural issues such as abortion, school prayer, or gender roles (for example, Mezey 1983; Feig 1990; Rice and Coates 1995).

Methodological Characteristics

Methodological characteristics of the studies we review are important because they affect what conclusions can be drawn about how southerners differ from others. More important, they affect the explanations offered concerning the causes of southern distinctiveness.

Where Is the South?

A necessary first step in studying any aspect of southern politics, including public opinion, is to define where the region's boundaries are and thus determine which states or areas are included in the South. In *Southern Politics in State and Nation,* the publication normally treated as the benchmark in the subfield, V. O. Key advocated a direct and relatively simple approach to determining what constitutes the region (1949, 11). Specifically, he argued that if the purpose is to study southern politics, then a measure of political behavior should be the basis of identifying the region. Key argued that "the critical element in the southern political system has been solidarity in national politics." Thus, determining which states to include in the South should be based upon their "consistency of attachment to the Democratic party nationally" (ibid., 10).

Using this partisan consistency standard, Key found that the eleven states of the former Confederacy were the only ones that had not gone "Republican more than twice in the presidential elections from 1876 to 1944 (both inclusive)" (ibid.). Thus, Key stipulated that the South consisted of Alabama, Arkansas, Florida, Georgia, Louisiana, Mississippi, North Carolina, South Carolina, Tennessee, Texas, and Virginia.

The partisan consistency test also meant, according to Key, that border states such as Delaware, Kentucky, Maryland, Missouri, and West Virginia were not part of the region (ibid., 10n2). Nor was Oklahoma. This assertion was made despite the fact that at the time of Key's writing, the Sooner State had, since its admission to the Union, supported the GOP in only two presidential elections. Rather, Key argued that Oklahoma was not part of the South since Republican strength there was much higher than that then found in the eleven states of the former Confederacy (ibid.). Thus, in the end Key's definition of the South was based on two measures of political behavior: party strength and presidential election outcomes.

Key recognized that there were other ways to define the South. For example, without mentioning any specific names, he acknowledged the work being done by sociologists at the University of North Carolina (for example, Odum 1936). "Indices of illiteracy, maps of the distribution of cotton production, averages of per-capita income, and scores of other statistical measures could be used to delimit the region" (Key 1949, 11). Similarly, in apparent reference to W. J. Cash (1941) and possibly others, Key stated that other analysts "have tried to delimit the South in terms of psychological attitudes and have spoken of 'the mind' and 'the spirit' of the South."

Still, Key argued, political behavior was the best measure of what constituted the South. The reason for this was "that the regional cast of political attitude has a reality and a being over and beyond all the underlying social and economic characteristics that can be pictured in endless tabulations, correlations, and graphic representations" (Key 1949).

The question of how to define the South was revisited by Charles D. Hadley in 1981. In particular, he considered the question of how researchers analyzing the results of national opinion surveys should define the South. Hadley pointed out that much of the existing non-survey-based research on southern politics employed Key's eleven-state definition of the region. Thus, for reasons of comparability, Hadley argued, researchers using national surveys to study public opinion in the region should use this same measure of the South (1981, 400). (For more recent, alternative approaches to determining regional boundaries, see Reed 1973, 1974, 1982, 1991b; Shortridge 1987, 1989; Reed, Kohls, and Hanchette 1990.)

How have researchers studying southern public opinion defined the South? Table 8.1 shows the methodological characteristics of published studies that examined the opinions and ideological leanings of southerners. We can see, first, that these studies have used a variety of definitions for the region. Consequently, it is difficult sometimes to draw generalizations concerning public opinion in the region. Moreover, relatively few have used Key's definition of the South. Instead, most have used a broader, census-based definition of the region. By this measure, the South consists of the eleven former Confederate states as well as Delaware, the District of Columbia, Kentucky, Maryland, Oklahoma, and West Virginia. Consequently, as Hadley (1981) warned, there is often a lack of connection between public opinion research and studies of other aspects of southern politics.

Table 8.1 also suggests that the source of a researcher's data is the primary factor influencing how he or she defines the South. Specifically, most of the studies using, or coming close to using, Key's definition of the South employ data collected in a National Election Study (NES) survey. Those using the broader definition are generally based on General Social Survey (GSS) data.

The reason for this data-based difference in definition of the region is that (with the exception of the 1948 study) NES surveys have included a measure of each respondent's home state. Further, all the former Confederate states except Tennessee (which is treated as a border state) constitute a single category of the region variable in the national NES survey. Thus, with the NES data it is easy, and methodologically justifiable, to construct a measure of the South that is close to Key's definition of the region. Moreover, at minimum methodological costs (that is, combining Tennessee with the other Confederate states), it is possible with NES data to create a measure of the South that exactly matches Key's definition.

In contrast, publicly available GSS data sets do not include a measure of respondents' home states. Rather, the most detailed available geographic measure is the respondent's census division. Consequently,

Table 8.1: Methodological Characteristics of Studies Examining Differences in Public Opinion between the South and Other Regions

Publication	South Operationalized	Comparisons Made	Population Studied
Hawkey 1982	Confederate South[1]	South/non-South	Adults
Hawkey 1988	Confederate South	South/North[2]	Adults
Cotter and Stovall 1990	Confederate South	South/non-South	Adults/whites
Carmines and Stanley 1990	Confederate South[3]	South/non-South	Whites[3]
Beck and Lopatto 1982	Confederate South minus Tenn.	South/non-South	Adults
Kuklinski, Cobb, and Gilens 1997	Confederate South minus Tenn.	South/non-South	Whites
Ladd and Hadley 1978	Confederate South plus Ky. and Okla.	Four regions	Adults
Hyman and Sheatsley 1964	Census South[4]	South/non-South	Whites
Sheatsley 1965	Census South	South/non-South	Whites
Glenn and Simmons 1967	Census South	South/non-South and four regions	Whites
Glenn 1967	Census South[3]	South/non-South	Adults
Greeley and Sheatsley 1971	Census South	South/non-South	Whites
Glenn 1974	Census South[3]	South/non-South	Adults
Reed 1974	Census South[5]	South/non-South	Whites
Middleton 1976	Census South	Four census regions[6]	Adults/whites
Condran 1979	Census South	South/non-South	Whites
Holloway and Robinson 1981	Census South	South/non-South	Whites
Jelen 1982	Census South	South/non-South	Adults
Mezey 1983	Census South	South/non-South	Adults
Abrahamson and Carter 1986	Census South	Four census regions	Adults
Wilson 1986	Census South	South/non-South	Whites
Tuch 1987	Census South	South/non-South	Whites[3]
Firebaugh and Davis 1988	Census South	South/non-South	Whites

Table 8.1: Methodological Characteristics of Studies Examining Differences in Public Opinion between the South and Other Regions (*continued*)

Publication	*South Operationalized*	*Comparisons Made*	*Population Studied*
Hurlbert 1989	Census South	Seven census regions and South/non-South	Whites
Ellison and Musick 1993	Census South	South/non-South	Adults
Rice and Coates 1995	Census South	South/non-South	Adults
Jelen 1996	Census South	South/non-South	Whites
Quillian 1996	Census South	South/non-South	Whites
Glaser and Gilens 1997	Census South	South/non-South	Whites
Rice and Pepper 1997	Census South	South/non-South	Whites
Schuman, Steeh, Bobo, and Krysan 1997	Census South	South/non-South	Whites
Hurlbert and Bankston 1998	Census South	Seven census regions and South/non-South	White/black adults
Weakliem and Biggert 1999	Census South[7]	Varies	Varies
Rice, McLean, and Larsen 2002	Census South	South/non-South and four regions	Adults/whites
Powers et al. 2003	Census South	South/non-South	White/black adults
Feig 1990	Not identified	South/non-South	Adults
Kellstedt 1990	Not identified	South/non-South	White Protestant evangelicals

[1] Alabama, Arkansas, Florida, Georgia, Louisiana, Mississippi, North Carolina, South Carolina, Tennessee, Texas, and Virginia.

[2] North refers to "those areas of the country which made up the northern forces during the Civil War period. The West is excluded from analysis" (Hawkey 1988, 37).

[3] Inferred from publications cited.

[4] Confederate states plus Delaware, Washington, D.C., Kentucky, Maryland, Oklahoma, and West Virginia.

[5] In analyzing American Institute of Public Opinion data, Reed defines the South as including the eleven Confederate states and Kentucky and Oklahoma (Reed 1974, 103).

[6] Also conducts separate analyses among border and Confederate states.

[7] This study also uses a measure based on nine census divisions, as well as one of the South that includes the former Confederate states (except Texas) and Kentucky (Weakliem and Biggert 1999, 872, 883).

researchers using GSS data cannot construct a measure corresponding to Key's politically based definition of the region. They are required to define the South more broadly, as consisting of the South Atlantic, East South Central, and West South Central census divisions. (Weakliem and Biggert 1999, 883n7, however, said that, upon their request, the National Opinion Research Center at the University of Chicago, which conducts the GSS, provided them with data identifying each respondent's home state.)

Relatively few of the researchers employing the census-based measure of the South offer a substantive justification for this measure. Those who do (Hurlbert 1989; Rice and Pepper 1997; Hurlbert and Bankston 1998) argue that the broader definition probably works against finding statistically significant regional differences, and thus is a conservative approach to data analysis. What implications the use of the broader definition of the South has on explaining any regional differences is not discussed.

Different Compared to What?

Table 8.1 also shows that most studies examined here rely on a relatively simple approach to the question of southern distinctiveness. In particular, most of the investigations compare the South to the rest of the country—typically labeled as the North or the non-South. The South versus non-South design is appealing since it is simpler from a data-management perspective, it conserves the number of cases available for analysis, and it avoids the problem of having to delineate the boundaries of nonsouthern regions. Further, combining the remainder of the country into one non-South category can be statistically justified by arguing that this is also a conservative approach to data analysis, since it minimizes the number of statistically significant differences found.

It is not, however, altogether clear that combining nonsouthern states into one category is justifiable. Researchers studying nonsouthern parts of the country, such as the Midwest or New England states, often note how "their" region varies from other sections of the country (Donnelly 1940; DeGrazia 1954; Fenton 1957, 1966; Lockard 1959; Jonas 1969; Shortridge 1989; Marchant-Shapiro and Patterson 1995). John Shelton Reed is one of the few researchers who offered a substantive justification for aggregating the rest of the country into the non-South (1974, 117n23). In particular, he argued that the results presented by Norval Glenn and J. L. Simmons (1967) showing the "relative homogeneity of the non-southern regions [provide] a rationale for grouping them as the 'non-South.'" In their study Glenn and Simmons divided the country into four census regions and then examined regional differences, among younger and older respondents, in responses to questions drawn from several Gallup Poll studies and one National Opinion Research Center survey. On many, but not all, of these items the South had the fewest number of "liberal" responses. On a number of the items examined by Glenn and Simmons, however, the difference in liberalism between the South and the most similar nonsouthern region was about equal to or less than the variation among the three nonsouthern regions. Thus, after we inspect Glenn and Simmons's findings, it is not altogether obvious how Reed reached his conclusion.

Which Citizens?

Another methodological decision for studies examining regional differences in public opinion involves which citizens are studied. Most studies examined here are based on samples of the entire population. As part of their investigations, some of these studies separately examined the opinions of regional natives and migrants. But unlike some studies of partisan change in the South (Hadley 1981), attention is not limited to native southerners. Additionally, some studies of regional differences in public opinion limit their analyses to whites. Most, but not all (Glenn and Simmons 1967; Reed 1974; Hurlbert 1989; Rice and Pepper 1997), of the studies taking this approach are concerned with examining attitudes about race-related topics.

Regional Differences in Issues and Ideology

We take an issue-based approach in reviewing the findings of studies that, as a central part of their analyses, have compared the political opinions and ideological leanings of southerners to those of other citizens, including studies that address self-described ideology, attitudes toward New Deal– and social welfare–type issues, race, political tolerance, and cultural issues. We conclude this section by considering how best to account for the changing pattern of southern regional differences and similarities in issue attitudes and ideological orientations.

Self-described Ideology

The South is often depicted, by both commentators and researchers, as a politically conservative region (see, for example, Black and Black 1987;

for a different viewpoint, see Carleton 1946). Findings concerning the self-described political ideologies of southerners, however, suggest that this portrayal generally is not accurate (Ladd and Hadley 1978; Holloway and Robinson 1981; Beck and Lopatto 1982; Hawkey 1988; Cotter and Stovall 1990; Carmines and Stanley 1990). In particular, most studies examining political ideology have found that southerners are more likely than others to identify themselves as conservatives. Nevertheless, a close examination of regional differences found in this area shows that even though they may be statistically significant, differences are substantively small. Further, there is some indication that in recent years regional differences in self-described ideologies may have gotten smaller (Hawkey 1988; Carmines and Stanley 1990).

To examine self-identified ideological differences between the South and non-South before the NES started asking the self-placement question in 1972, Earl Hawkey (1988) created an ideology scale that combined respondents' responses to how "warmly" they felt toward the groups labeled "liberal" and "conservative." Though southerners were consistently more conservative than were nonsoutherners from 1962 through 1980, by 1976 the regional differences were so small that they failed to achieve statistical significance. Hawkey also pointed out that regional convergence was due more to changes among northerners than among southerners, as the non-South became somewhat more conservative over this period while the South changed very little. Using the ideological self-placement question in the four presidential election years from 1972 to 1984 and examining only whites, Edward Carmines and Harold Stanley (1990) combined the strong, not very strong, and moderate-to-slightly conservative groups. They found that the regional gap in conservatism in 1980 and 1984 was about half what it had been in the previous two presidential election years. By 1984, for instance, 47 percent of southern whites identified with the conservative term, compared to 41 percent of nonsouthern whites.

Most studies found that fewer than half of southerners label themselves as conservatives, even when those who say that they do not think about themselves in ideological terms, or are undecided about their ideological leanings, are deleted from the analysis. These patterns are found even when attention is limited to white southerners or white middle-class southerners (Cotter and Stovall 1990).

Rather than focusing on aggregate ideological differences between the regions, a more fruitful area for future research may be how ideology relates to other theoretically important subjects. For instance, party identification differences in the political ideologies of nonsouthern whites were evident throughout the 1972–84 presidential election years, as conservatives were much more likely to be Republican compared to liberals (Carmines and Stanley 1990). Such partisan differences between ideological groupings of southern whites only gradually emerged over this time frame. While a majority of conservative white southerners in 1972 regarded themselves as Democrats, by 1976 this grouping was evenly split between the two parties, and by 1980 and 1984 a majority of conservative white southerners regarded themselves as Republicans (ibid.). The 61 percent of conservative white southerners who in 1984 regarded themselves as Republicans, however, remained lower than the 74 percent of conservative white nonsoutherners who called themselves Republicans, which suggests that the partisan realignment of ideological groups in the South had not yet been completed. It was not until 1992 that 72 percent of conservative white southerners regarded themselves as Republicans, a proportion that remained high at 76 percent in 1996 (Knuckey 2001).

Attitudes about Social Welfare Issues

Another area where the conservative label generally does not apply to the South involves opinions about social welfare or New Deal–type issues. Everett Carll Ladd and Charles D. Hadley found that during Roosevelt's presidency, white southerners "were the regional group most supportive of New Deal initiatives" (1978, 131). By the mid-1970s, however, the South was no longer the region most likely to support these types of initiatives. Rather, Ladd and Hadley reported that the "South was the most liberal section of the country during the New Deal and is now the most conservative, while the Northeast has moved to the liberal pole" (ibid., 166).

Other, more recent studies, however, have generally found few differences between southerners and others in opinions regarding domestic social welfare issues such as guaranteed jobs or health care (Holloway and Robinson 1981; Beck and Lopatto 1982; Hawkey 1982, 1988; Mezey 1983; Hurlbert 1989; Cotter and Stovall 1990; Rice and Pepper 1997; Rice, McLean, and Larsen 2002). Examining GSS data collected from 1972 through 2000, Tom Rice, William McLean, and Amy Larsen (2002) identified all statistically significant differences between southerners and nonsoutherners on numerous social and political issues. They examined data in various issue areas to see how many years during this period were characterized by statistically significant regional differences. Inasmuch as not all issues were included in all the surveys, however, the number of years with comparable data varied from issue to issue. They found that southerners were more conservative than nonsoutherners on education spending in only four of twenty-two years and were more conservative than nonsoutherners on environmental spending in only three years; no significant differences emerged in the other years. No regional differences existed on health care spending in nineteen years: southerners were more conservative in two years but more liberal in the most recent year, 2000. No regional differences existed in welfare spending preferences in nineteen years, and while the South was more liberal in the three other years, those years were all in the 1970s. On spending for the poor, a question asked in only fourteen of the years, no significant regional differences existed in ten years, and the other four years were split equally between the South being more conservative and more liberal than the non-South (ibid.). More broadly, Jeanne S. Hurlbert and William B. Bankston looked at the general issue of government spending and found that in 1994 southerners were generally more conservative in this area than were nonsoutherners (1998, 184). This pattern was largely the result of differences between southerners and residents of the Northeast and Middle Atlantic regions.

Racial Attitudes

Public opinion researchers have devoted considerable attention to examining citizens' race-related attitudes and behaviors. For both substantive and methodological (that is, the number of cases available for analysis) reasons, most of these studies have focused on the opinions and actions of whites. Overall, research in this area generally shows that white southerners are different from their counterparts in other regions, although the differences in racial attitudes between white southerners and others are diminishing.

The most comprehensive—in terms of topics examined, time period investigated, and data sources analyzed—study of racial attitudes in the United States was conducted by Howard Schuman, Charlotte Steeh, Lawrence Bobo, and Maria Krysan (1997). Although this study does not completely meet our standard of having as its central concern a comparison of the opinions across regions, it nonetheless provides much highly useful information about the race-related opinions of white southerners. Further, the findings reported by Schuman and his colleagues are generally quite consistent with the results of other studies that were more focused on the attitudes of white southerners (Hyman and Sheatsley 1964; Sheatsley 1965; Greeley and Sheatsley 1971; Middleton 1976; Ladd and Hadley 1978; Condran 1979; Holloway and Robinson 1981; Beck and Lopatto 1982; Hawkey 1982, 1988; Mezey 1983; Wilson 1986; Tuch 1987; Firebaugh and Davis 1988; Hurlbert 1989; Ellison and Musick 1993; Jelen 1996; Quillian 1996; Hurlbert and Bankston 1998; Rice, McLean, and Larsen 2002). This consistency is not surprising, given that the different studies generally analyze the same data sets.

Overall, Schuman and his coauthors found that, in the country as a whole, white support for the principle of racial equality has increased over time so that now there is a high level of support for this position. In contrast, whites generally expressed less support for government actions to implement the principle of racial equality. Further, relatively little change has occurred in attitudes about implementation efforts. Additionally, they found that the response of whites to integrated situations in schools and residential settings was affected by the racial makeup of their situation. They also found that whites most frequently explained blacks' disadvantages by referring to lack of motivation or willpower. Discrimination was less frequently cited as an explanation for the position of blacks in society. Finally, whites generally opposed affirmative action programs or policies if they involved preferential treatment for blacks.

With regard to regional differences, Schuman and his colleagues (and other researchers) found that white southerners and nonsoutherners generally held different opinions about race-related topics. In particular, white southerners were more opposed than others to racial integration and government assistance to blacks. White southerners also held more negative views of African Americans and the civil rights movement and were more likely than others to give individual-based explanations for racial differences. Most studies have found, however, that regional differences in racial opinions are generally getting smaller over time.

More specifically, Schuman and his colleagues concluded that, beginning with the earliest survey data, in the area of school integration "there has been a sizable gap between attitudes in the South and the North, though both regions have shown essentially the same type of change over time." For example, in 1942, 2 percent of southern whites, compared to 42 percent of nonsouthern whites, said that black and white children should go to the same rather than separate schools (Schuman et al. 1997, 109).

During the last half century support for school integration has increased throughout the country, and differences in opinions between the South and the North have diminished, though they have not disappeared. Thus, by 1985 about 86 percent of white southerners and 96 percent of white nonsoutherners favored white and black children's going to the same school. Schuman and his colleagues further argued that the regional convergence was "due largely to the fact that acceptance of the principle of integrated schools in the North is approaching 100 percent, thus creating a ceiling constraint" (ibid.). Throughout the country support for school integration was positively related to education. Further, "the least-educated Southerners remain distinctly lower in acceptance of the principle of integrated schooling" than others, including their counterparts outside the South. "The most-educated southerners," however, "have moved to the level of the most-educated Northerners" (ibid., 110).

Nearly identical trends were found regarding opinions about other race-related issues such as "principles of equal treatment in employment, in public accommodations and seating on public transportation" (ibid., 111). Similarly, southerners were found to be more likely than others "to claim that whites have the right to keep blacks out of a neighborhood" (ibid., 113). Again, however, opposition to residential integration has diminished over time in both the South and the non-South. With this shift, regional differences have diminished. Indeed, level of education was found to have a greater influence on opinions about this issue than was region (ibid.). The same general patterns of increasing support and diminishing regional differences were also found when respondents were asked about support for a qualified black candidate for president, interracial marriage, and segregation generally (ibid., 114, 115–16, 119).

Somewhat different results were found when Schuman and his colleagues examined questions asking about federal government action to implement racial equality. In particular, they found that since the 1960s white southerners have expressed "modest but stable or even slightly rising support for federal intervention" in school integration (ibid., 127). In contrast, support for federal activity in this area has declined among whites elsewhere in the country. As a result, the "two regions began to converge by the end of the 1970s, but they did so in the form of a low level of support for the implementation of school desegregation" (ibid., 127–28).

When subjects were asked about federal government implementation efforts in the field of public accommodations, Schuman and his
coauthors found that opinions showed "clear regional and education
differences: support for implementation is more positive in the North
and more positive as education increases" (ibid., 133). Still, "the gap in
implementation by region" has decreased since the mid-1960s. A similar pattern was found regarding the implementation of residential integration. "Differences by region and educational levels are crystal clear
through the entire time span: Northerners and more educated persons
support open housing laws more than do Southerners and the less educated" (ibid., 134).

Schuman and his colleagues also examined the results of survey
questions asking "white Americans how they themselves would feel or
act in particular situations that involve racial integration" (ibid., 139). In
particular, these "social distance" items asked citizens how they would
feel or react in situations involving such things as sending their children to school or residing in neighborhoods with a few or many blacks.
Overall, the results of these questions indicate that "Southern respondents generally show less acceptance of personal involvement in desegregated situations, but the regional differences have tended to decrease
in recent years. This decrease occurs most strikingly for acceptance of
token school integration; a large North-South difference in earlier decades—no doubt due to the heritage of legal segregation of schools in
the South—virtually disappeared by the 1980s" (ibid., 153).

Some regional differences were also found when whites were asked
to account for racial differences. In particular, surveys showed that white
southerners were more likely than others to mention lower black ability and motivation and less likely to mention educational disadvantages
or discrimination (ibid., 164). Similarly, "Northerners tend to perceive
more discrimination than do Southerners," though regional differences
were not large in this area (ibid., 166).

White southerners were less likely than others to support federal
government expenditures to assist blacks (ibid., 178). "Regional differences tend to disappear," however, on questions asking about "preferential treatment" for blacks in areas such as employment and school
admission (ibid., 182). Moreover, among whites throughout the country,
support for preferential treatment policies and programs was low.

Finally, Schuman and his colleagues reported that throughout the
country whites increasingly said that the civil rights movement was mov-

ing at about the "right speed" (ibid., 190). Southerners, however, were more likely to say the civil rights movement was going "too fast." Similarly, Sheatsley (1965) found that white southerners were more likely than others to see civil rights as a state rather than a national issue. He also found that there were few regional differences in whether a respondent reported being personally affected by the civil rights movement. Most said that they had not been affected.

As we noted earlier, most studies find that opinions, especially regarding the principle of racial equality, have changed over time in the direction of higher support. James H. Kuklinski, Michael D. Cobb, and Martin Gilens (1997), however, questioned this conclusion. In particular, they reported the results of a study, based on an unobtrusive measure, that suggest that racial attitudes may not have changed over time. Rather, they argued, social desirability concerns have made citizens less willing to publicly state their real opinions about race. While this research is certainly imaginative and interesting, the study's concept of social desirability is not altogether convincing. In particular, Kuklinski and his colleagues failed to document the existence of a social desirability problem in measuring racial attitudes. Using their unobtrusive technique (and some apparently ex post facto statistical procedures), they found that 42 percent of white southerners were "angry" about "a black family moving in next door," compared to 0 percent of white nonsoutherners. They also found that 98 percent of white southerners were angered by "black leaders asking for affirmative action," compared to only 41 percent of white nonsoutherners. What were not presented, however, were survey results based on questions directly asking respondents if they would be angry if a black family moved in next door or if a black leader voiced support for affirmative action. Thus, the presence and magnitude of social desirability remained uncertain, since it is not possible to determine if the findings of the unobtrusive measures were higher or lower than those that might be obtained from direct questions.

In fact, there is some evidence that suggests that the technique Kuklinski, Cobb, and Gilens used does not produce results different from those found through more direct questioning. For example, the results of the 1996 NES survey, presented by Schuman and his coauthors (1997, 175), show that about 90 percent of white southerners said that they opposed affirmative action. The authors also reported that there was little regional variation in opinions about this topic. The difference between this finding and the results of the Kuklinski, Cobb, and Gilens unobtrusive measure can be explained as easily and reasonably by the basis of differences in question wording as by the presence of social desirability. Similarly, with regard to the housing question, Kuklinski and his colleagues themselves cited the results of a 1976 survey that showed that "a large majority of white southerners admitted to preferring an entirely white neighborhood" (1997, 325).

Some of the studies examining regional differences in racial attitudes have sought to identify what types of southerners are more or less supportive of racial integration. Herbert H. Hyman and Paul Sheatsley (1964) found that among white southerners support for racial integration was higher in areas that had experienced desegregated schools, among those who had lived in the North, among better-educated citizens, and, generally, among younger citizens. Sheatsley (1965) reported similar patterns of opinions. In particular he found that among white southerners support for integration was highest among younger, nonnative, Catholic, moderately religious, more educated, higher-income, and white-collar citizens. Andrew W. Greeley and Paul Sheatsley (1971) also found that among white southerners, younger citizens were most supportive of integration. Kuklinski and his colleagues (1997) found that southern white males were much more likely to express anger over a black family moving next door than were southern white females, while no significant differences in expressed anger existed between age or education groups among white southerners.

In his analysis of a 1964 National Opinion Research Center survey, Russell Middleton (1976) found that native white southerners were the most racially prejudiced, while native white nonsoutherners were the least prejudiced. Interestingly, Middleton also reported finding "only slight regional variations" in prejudice regarding Jews, Catholics, and immigrants (1976, 102). He found migrants to be in an intermediary position—southern migrants and nonsouthern migrants had about the same level of prejudice. Thomas C. Wilson (1986), James M. Glaser and Martin Gilens (1997), and Tom W. Rice and Meredith L. Pepper (1997) also reported similar findings regarding the racial attitudes of regional natives and migrants.

Glenn Firebaugh and Kenneth Davis (1988) suggested that the decline in antiblack prejudice among white southerners is best explained by a combination of cohort replacement and, to a lesser extent, attitude change. Clearly, younger white southerners are less prejudiced than the older generation, so their movement into the population as the older generation passes away produces a less prejudiced white southerner over time. Migration, Firebuagh and Davis argued, is not a major source of the changes that have occurred in southern public opinion regarding race.

Tolerance

Closely related to the issue of race is a concern with political tolerance, typically defined as a willingness to allow unpopular groups to exercise their constitutional rights or civil liberties. Researchers examining public opinion regarding tolerance have frequently found regional differences. Mark Abrahamson and Valerie Carter reported that "people in the East and West tend to give more tolerant replies than people in the South and Midwest, though the most pronounced differences are usually between residents of the South and all others" (1986, 290). Other studies, in some cases examining white respondents only, have also found lower levels of tolerance in the South. These differences remain even after statistically controlling for factors such as education, age, and gender (Holloway and Robinson 1981; Jelen 1982; Mezey 1983; Ellison and Musick 1993; Rice and Pepper 1997; Hurlbert and Bankston 1998; Rice, McLean, and Larsen 2002). Additionally, Jelen (1982), Ellison and Musick (1993), and Rice, McLean, and Larsen (2002) reported findings indicating that southerners may be more tolerant toward right-wing (militarist or racist, for example) than left-wing (such as atheist, communist, or homosexual) groups.

As is true of attitudes about racial issues, however, the level of regional distinctiveness in tolerance is growing smaller (Rice and Pepper 1997; Rice, McLean, and Larsen 2002). Migration is one possible reason for this decline. Ellison and Musick (1993) used the 1988 GSS survey to examine regional differences in overall tolerance as well as tolerance toward specific left-wing (atheist, communist, and homosexual) and right-wing (militarist and racist) groups. They found that even after controlling for a number of social and demographic characteristics, native southerners were less tolerant than native nonsoutherners. Further, they found that those who had moved to the South were similar in tolerance to native nonsoutherners. Thus, Ellison and Musick argued, "migration into the South from other areas of the country may be moderating some aspects of the attitudinal distinctiveness that has historically characterized the region" (1993, 386).

Several studies have explored whether the lower level of tolerance among southerners is the result of the religious characteristics of the region's citizens. Ted Jelen reported that southerners' lower level of tolerance toward atheists, communists, and homosexuals was best "explained by the high incidence of religious fundamentalism" within the region (1982, 76). Ellison and Musick found that "members of fundamentalist denominations and frequent churchgoers are less tolerant than other persons" (1993, 386). They also found, however, that regional differences in tolerance toward left-wing groups remained even after taking into account these variables. Yet when examining tolerance toward right-wing groups, Ellison and Musick reported a different pattern. "In part because regional differences in tolerance of right-wing groups are relatively modest to begin with, the inclusion of theological conservatism and other religious controls" had the impact of reducing "these differences in tolerance of right-wing groups to statistical nonsignificance" (ibid., 389).

Attitudes about Cultural Issues

Recent decades have seen an apparent growth in the political importance of social or cultural issues. The specific concerns in this area are not easily clustered. Further, researchers examining regional differences have focused more attention on some cultural issues than others. Therefore, we have arbitrarily grouped these issues under four topics: crime and criminal justice, gender roles, morality, and school prayer.

Overall, researchers have found regional differences on many, but not all, of the cultural issues examined here, and southerners typically have more conservative or traditional views than others. And though there are some exceptions, the research findings provide little evidence that regional differences are diminishing.

Crime and Criminal Justice.   Regional differences are found on several issues dealing with crime and the criminal justice system. For example, southerners are generally more opposed than others to gun control proposals, though this difference may be getting smaller (Ladd and Hadley 1978, 171; Holloway and Robinson 1981, 233; Hurlbert 1989, 259; Hurlbert and Bankston 1998, 177; Rice, McLean, and Larsen 2002, 210). Attitudes about the death penalty and the leniency of the courts, however, do not vary substantially across regions (Holloway and Robinson 1981, 233; Mezey 1983, 16; Hurlbert 1989, 259; Rice, McLean, and Larsen 2002, 210). There is some indication that among whites only southerners are becoming more supportive of the death penalty (Rice, McLean, and Larsen 2002, 210).

Gender Roles. Regional differences occur on issues of women's role in politics. For example, Rice, McLean, and Larsen (2002) found that southerners were generally more likely than others to say that men should run the country and that men were better suited for politics. Similarly, nonsoutherners typically were more likely to say that they would vote for a woman for president. In her study of regional differences among whites only, Jeanne Hurlbert found that "southerners asserted more often that men are better suited for politics than women, and that women should run their homes and let men run the country. They also said more often that they were unwilling to vote for a qualified female candidate for President" (1989, 259). Tom Rice and Diane Coates reported similar findings. And, like Hurlbert, they further found that "when it comes to women in politics, Southerners definitely hold more traditional views, even after controlling for a host of socioeconomic factors" (Rice and Coates 1995, 752). They also reported, however, that on questions about women in politics, as well as other items dealing with gender roles, southerners had "become substantially more egalitarian over time" (ibid.). (See also Rice, McLean, and Larsen 2002.)

On other issues related to gender roles, such as whether women should have the same rights as men or if women should be employed outside the home, research generally reveals little or no variations across regions (Holloway and Robinson 1981; Beck and Lopatto 1982; Hawkey 1982; Mezey 1983; Hurlbert 1989; Rice and Coates 1995; Powers, Suitor, Guerra, Shackelford, Mecom, and Gusman 2003).

Among southerners, Rice and Coates found that black men generally had the most conservative gender role attitudes and black women generally held the least conservative attitudes (1995, 748–49). White men and women typically fell in between, with the men holding somewhat more conservative attitudes than women, although these patterns varied somewhat by specific gender role questions. Black men generally held "the most conservative views about employed women and women in politics, and white men tend to hold the most conservative views about employed mothers" (ibid., 748). Black women had the "most liberal views about employed mothers and women in politics" (ibid., 749). Finally, Rice and Coates found that white women were more conservative than white men about women in politics (ibid.). (For additional research in this area, see Powers et al. 2003.) The greater polarization of gender role attitudes between the sexes among African Americans as compared to whites suggests a fascinating subject for future research, which would require a more intensive study of African American values made possible by a larger sampling of minorities than is normally found in national surveys.

In their study of white respondents only, Tom Rice and Meredith Pepper (1997) reported that the most conservative gender role attitudes were found among native southerners, and native nonsoutherners were generally the least conservative. Regional migrants fell in between these extremes; native southerners who migrated north had more traditional views than native nonsoutherners who moved to the South.

Future research should explore how regional differences in gender role attitudes shape the political systems of southern states. For instance, interstate differences in in-migration may affect the representation of women in public office. As late as 2003, for example, fewer than 15 percent of Alabama and Mississippi state legislators were women, compared to over 20 percent of Florida lawmakers. Perhaps these representational differences can be attributed to the more than 70 percent of Alabama and Mississippi residents who were born in their states, compared to the mere 33 percent of native Floridians.

Morality.   Regional differences are frequently found on political issues touching on questions of morality. (See Kellstedt 1990 for an examination of regional differences on cultural issues among white evangelical Protestants.) In particular, Rice, McLean, and Larsen reported that "southern attitudes about sexual matters are almost always more conservative than non-southern attitudes, particularly with regard to homosexual relations" (2002, 206). Similarly, they found that southerners held "more conservative views" on issues involving abortion and pornography, but not on sex education in the public schools, providing birth control to teenagers, or ease of obtaining a divorce. Controlling for factors such as education, income, age, race, and gender reduced but did not eliminate regional differences on these issues (ibid., 210–13). Several other researchers (Mezey 1983; Hurlbert 1989; Hurlbert and Bankston 1998) reported generally similar results. Finally, the analysis conducted by Rice, McLean and Larsen suggested that little change has occurred in the regional differences found on such morality issues (2002, 206). Future research should seek to explain why regional differences persist on moral issues, perhaps by controlling for a greater number of religious variables. Such variables may include the political activism of religious interest groups, the number of active churchgoers when studying differences between states or regions, and the number of intensely religious individuals and fundamentalists when doing individual-level analyses.

School Prayer. Researchers have consistently found that southerners are more religiously active and more likely to hold conservative religious beliefs than others (see, for example, Reed 1974; Rice, McLean, and Larsen 2002). Thus, it is not surprising that researchers have also consistently found regional differences regarding the issue of school prayer (Mezey 1983; Rice, McLean, and Larsen 2002). In perhaps the most thorough study of regional differences in opinions over this issue, Douglas Feig (1990) found that southerners were more supportive than others of school prayer when it was framed as a "free exercise of religion" question ("What do you think—schools should be allowed to start each day with a prayer, or religion does not belong in the schools?"). Regional differences in attitudes about school prayer were not found when it was presented as an "antiestablishment" issue ("The U.S. Supreme Court has ruled that no state or local government may require the reading of the Lord's Prayer or Bible verses in public schools. What are your views on this—do you approve or disapprove of the court's ruling?"). Specifically, Feig reported that a free exercise question asked in the 1984 NES survey found that about 86 percent of southerners, compared to about 64 percent of nonsoutherners, supported school prayer. In contrast, an antiestablishment item asked in the 1985 GSS found less difference in support for school prayer between southerners (61 percent) and nonsoutherners (53 percent).

Feig further found that attitudes about school prayer were affected by several variables, including a number of religious-related characteristics, such as church attendance, importance of religion, and views of the Bible. Consequently, he argued that the regional difference found when the school prayer issue is presented as an issue related to the free exercise of religion is the result of two factors. First, "those groups which are less supportive of school prayer make up a smaller portion of the population in the South than is the case in the non-South" (ibid., 103). Second, "these same groups, in the South, are much more supportive of school prayer than their counterparts in the non-South" (ibid., 104). Thus, when the question is framed as a free exercise issue, "in the South there is a pervasive support for public school prayer which manifests itself even within those groups of individuals which one would expect to be opposed to that practice" (ibid., 103). When school prayer is presented as an antiestablishment issue, however, the second condition identified does not occur.

Causes of Southern Distinctiveness

Are southerners different? The research reviewed here shows that with regard to some political topics, especially those dealing with cultural issues, the answer to this question is yes. Yet in other domains, such as racial attitudes, the answer is less clear; southerners were once different but are increasingly similar to citizens living elsewhere in the country. Finally, in still other realms, such as self-described ideology or opinions about social welfare policies, the research results reviewed here show that southerners are not different from residents of other regions.

This overall mixed pattern of findings makes it difficult to draw a single, simple, or unqualified conclusion about southern public opinion. From the perspective of public opinion results, it is not proper, as is frequently done, to label the South as a generally conservative or traditional region. Yet there are specific elements of southern public opinion to which such labels are legitimately applied.

Moreover, the mixed pattern of findings concerning southern public opinion makes answering the question of why southerners are different both more difficult and more interesting. In particular, understanding the sources of southern distinctiveness requires explaining why the region varies from other regions with regard to some but not all topics. It also requires accounting for variations in levels of distinctiveness across time.

The results of the studies examined here consistently show that when public opinion in the South does differ from opinion in other regions, differences are not the result of variations in the compositions of populations. Rather, these studies show that differences, though sometimes diminished in size, remain even when a variety of individual characteristics, such as education, income, age, and gender, are statistically taken into account.

Further, none of the studies reviewed here suggests that the process of opinion formation is fundamentally different among southerners from that among nonsoutherners. Mezey, for example, concluded that "although the mind of the South may be somewhat distinctive from that of the rest of the nation, it functions and responds to environmental factors in much the same way as the mind of the non-South" (1983, 23). (For a similar conclusion see Middleton 1976.) Still, as Feig's (1990) findings regarding the school prayer issue show, while the same factors may affect opinions across regions, their relative influence may be greater or lesser in the South than elsewhere. Similarly, John Shelton Reed argued that one source of southern distinctiveness is a variation in the influence of different socialization agents across regions (1974, 87). Culturally conservative agents, such as the family and church, are, Reed argued, more influential in the South than elsewhere, while less traditionally oriented forces, such as schools and the media, are less important.

A difference in political culture is often used to explain southern distinctiveness (see, for example, Middleton 1976; Hurlbert 1989; Rice, McLean, and Larsen 2002). The specific character of the South's political culture has generated considerable speculation. (See, for example, Simpkins 1947; Key 1955; Havard 1972; Reed 1974, 1991a; Bartley 1976; Eubanks 1988. For discussions and analyses of the political culture concept see, for example, Elazar 1966; Patterson 1968; Johnson 1976; Erikson, McIver, and Wright 1987; Nardulli 1990; Lieske 1993; Wilson 1997; Wedeem 2002.) To date, however, little has been done empirically to identify or test the importance of political culture, except for Charles Johnson's (1976) work. Empirically testing Daniel Elazar's concept of political culture, Johnson found that southern states were especially likely to possess traditionalistic cultures and that such cultures were related to limited government activities and to limited popular participation in politics.

In a 1955 discussion of whether the partisan politics of the South would remain distinctive, V. O. Key almost reluctantly suggested that "there may well be sets of basic attitudes with a special strength in the region that can be counted on to have for some time a continuing effect in unifying the section in national affairs" (175). He further suggested that in some cases, "these views may be limited largely to the echelons of political leaderships." In other instances these attitudes "may well have been fixed in mass attitudes by the preaching of generations of politicians" (ibid.).

Key's argument suggested that southern distinctiveness in public opinion might result from the character of information flowing from the region's leaders to the general public. Ellison and Musick took a similar position in discussing the reasons for the higher level of intolerance in the South. In particular, they suggested that the differences across regions in these attitudes may be the result of southerners' experiencing "long-term exposure to a wide range of intolerant messages" (1993,

393). (Jelen 1982 also suggests this possibility.) The flow-of-information argument is appealing because it provides a way to account for varying levels of regional distinctiveness across both time and issue areas. Unfortunately, few studies have thoroughly examined regional differences in the content of the mass media or other politically relevant information sources. The few studies that have examined this topic have generally had a relatively narrow scope in terms of time or topics investigated (see, for example, Carter 1957; Breed 1958; Higbie 1964).

Finally, regardless of whether regional differences in public opinion are directly attributed to a unique political culture or the flow of particular information from leaders to citizens, the ultimate source of southern distinctiveness is "a product of the history and character of the people" (Key 1955, 175). If this view is correct—and it is one that most researchers seem to acknowledge—then questions arise regarding how southern distinctiveness in public opinion has been investigated. In particular, if regional differences are the product of historical events and patterns, it is not clear how this topic is appropriately studied using a measure of region that includes both Confederate and border states. To take an extreme example, Maryland and Mississippi certainly share some common historical experiences and patterns (such as the institution of slavery); however, there are many other experiences often cited in explaining southern distinctiveness (such as joining the Confederacy or experiencing Reconstruction) that they do not have in common. In sum, in studying southern distinctiveness in public opinion, we believe that Key's politically based definition is the most appropriate measure of the South. Similarly, it is probably more appropriate when studying southern distinctiveness to compare the South to specific regions of states that have relatively common historical experiences rather than to the non-South at large.

References

Abrahamson, Mark, and Valerie J. Carter. 1986. "Tolerance, Urbanism and Region." *American Sociological Review* 51: 287–94.

Bartley, Numan V. 1976. "The South and Sectionalism in American Politics." *Journal of Politics* 38: 239–57.

Beck, Paul Allen, and Paul Lopatto. 1982. "The End of Southern Distinctiveness." In *Contemporary Southern Political Attitudes and Behavior: Studies and Essays*, ed. Laurence W. Moreland, Tod A. Baker, and Robert P. Steed. New York: Praeger.

Black, Earl, and Merle Black. 1987. *Politics and Society in the South*. Cambridge: Harvard University Press.

Breed, Warren. 1958. "Comparative Newspaper Handling of the Emmett Till Case." *Journalism Quarterly* 35: 291–98.

Carleton, William G. 1946. "The Conservative South—A Political Myth." *Virginia Quarterly Review* 22: 179–92.

Carmines, Edward G., and Harold W. Stanley. 1990. "Ideological Realignment in the Contemporary South: Where Have All the Conservatives Gone?" In *The Disappearing South? Studies in Regional Change and Continuity*, ed. Robert P. Steed, Laurence W. Moreland, and Tod A. Baker. Tuscaloosa: University of Alabama Press.

Carter, Roy E., Jr. 1957. "Segregation and the News: A Regional Content Study." *Journalism Quarterly* 34: 3–18.

Cash, Wilbur J. 1941. *The Mind of the South*. New York: Knopf.

Clarke, James W. 1998. "Without Fear or Shame: Lynching, Capital Punishment and the Subculture of Violence in the American South." *British Journal of Political Science* 28: 269–89.

Condran, John G. 1979. "Changes in White Attitudes toward Blacks: 1963–1977." *Public Opinion Quarterly* 43: 463–76.

Cotter, Patrick R., and James Glen Stovall. 1990. "The Conservative South?" *American Politics Quarterly* 18: 103–19.

DeGrazia, Alfred. 1954. *The Western Public: 1952 and Beyond*. Stanford: Stanford University Press.

Dixon, Jo, and Alan J. Lizotte. 1987. "Gun Ownership and the 'Southern Subculture of Violence.'" *American Journal of Sociology* 93: 383–405.

Donnelly, Thomas C., ed. 1940. *Rocky Mountain Politics*. Albuquerque: University of New Mexico Press.

Elazar, Daniel. 1966. *American Federalism: A View from the States*. New York: Thomas Y. Crowell.

Ellison, Christopher G. 1991. "An Eye for an Eye? A Note on the Southern Subculture of Violence Thesis." *Social Forces* 69: 1223–39.

Ellison, Christopher G., and Marc A. Musick. 1993. "Southern Intolerance: A Fundamentalist Effect?" *Social Forces* 72: 379–98.

Erikson, Robert S., John P. McIver, and Gerald C. Wright Jr. 1987. "State Political Culture and Public Opinion." *American Political Science Review* 81: 797–813.

Eubanks, Cecil L. 1988. "Contemporary Southern Politics: Present State and Future Possibilities." In *Contemporary Southern Politics*, ed. James F. Lea. Baton Rouge: Louisiana State University Press.

Feig, Douglas G. 1990. "Dimensions of Southern Public Opinion on Prayer in Schools." In *The Disappearing South? Studies in Regional Change and Continuity*, ed. Robert P. Steed, Laurence W. Moreland, and Tod A. Baker. Tuscaloosa: University of Alabama Press.

Fenton, John H. 1957. *Politics of the Border States*. New Orleans: Hauswer Press.

———. 1966. *Midwest Politics*. New York: Holt, Rinehart and Winston.

Firebaugh, Glenn, and Kenneth E. Davis. 1988. "Trends in Antiblack Prejudice, 1972–1984: Region and Cohort Effects." *American Journal of Sociology* 94: 251–72.

Flynn, Clifton P. 1994. "Regional Differences in Attitudes toward Corporal
Punishment." *Journal of Marriage and the Family* 56: 314–24.

Gastil, Raymond D. 1971. "Homicide and a Regional Culture of Violence."
American Sociological Review 36: 412–27.

Glaser, James M., and Martin Gilens. 1997. "Interregional Migration and Political Resocialization: A Study of Racial Attitudes under Pressure." *Public
Opinion Quarterly* 61: 72–86.

Glenn, Norval D. 1967. "Massification versus Differentiation: Some Trend Data
from National Surveys." *Social Forces* 46: 172–80.

———. 1974. "Recent Trends in Intercategory Differences in Attitudes." *Social
Forces* 52: 395–401.

Glenn, Norval D., and Beth Ann Shelton. 1985. "Regional Differences in Divorce in the United States." *Journal of Marriage and the Family* 47: 641–
52.

Glenn, Norval D., and J. L. Simmons. 1967. "Are Regional Cultural Differences
Diminishing?" *Public Opinion Quarterly* 31: 176–93.

Greeley, Andrew W., and Paul B. Sheatsley. 1971. "Attitudes toward Racial Integration." *Scientific American* 225: 13–19.

Griswold, Wendy, and Nathan Wright. 2004. "Cowbirds, Locals, and the Dynamic Endurance of Regionalism." *American Journal of Sociology* 109:
1411–51.

Hackney, Sheldon. 1969. "Southern Violence." In *The History of Violence in
America*, ed. Hugh Davis Graham and Ted Robert Gurr. New York: Ban-
tam.

Hadley, Charles D. 1981. "Survey Research and Southern Politics: The Implications of Data Management." *Public Opinion Quarterly* 45: 393–401.

Havard, William C. 1972. "The South: A Shifting Perspective." In *The Changing Politics of the South,* ed. William C. Havard. Baton Rouge: Louisiana
State University Press.

Hawkey, Earl W. 1982. "Southern Conservatism 1956–1976." In *Contemporary
Southern Political Attitudes and Behavior: Studies and Essays,* ed. Laurence W. Moreland, Tod A. Baker, and Robert P. Steed. New York: Praeger.

———. 1988. "Public Opinion in the South Today." In *Contemporary Southern
Politics,* ed. James F. Lea. Baton Rouge: Louisiana State University Press.

Hero, Alfred O. 1965. *The Southerner and World Affairs.* Baton Rouge: Louisiana State University Press.

Higbie, Charles E. 1964. "Book Reviewing and Civil Rights: The Effect of Regional Opinion." *Journalism Quarterly* 41: 385–94.

Holloway, Harry, and Ted Robinson. 1981. "The Abiding South: White Attitudes and Regionalism Reexamined." *Perspective on the American South:
An Annual Review of Society, Politics and Culture* 1: 227–52.

Hunt, Larry L., and Matthew O. Hunt. 2001. "Race, Region, and Religious Involvement: A Comparative Study of Whites and African Americans." *Social Forces* 80: 605–31.

Hurlbert, Jeanne S. 1989. "The Southern Region: A Test of the Hypothesis of Cultural Distinctiveness." *Sociological Quarterly* 30: 245–66.

Hurlbert, Jeanne S., and William B. Bankston. 1998. "Cultural Distinctiveness in the Face of Structural Transformation: The 'New' Old South." In *The Rural South since World War II*, ed. R. Douglas Hurt. Baton Rouge: Louisiana State University Press.

Hyman, Herbert H., and Paul B. Sheatsley. 1964. "Attitudes toward Desegregation." *Scientific American* 211: 16–23.

Jelen, Ted G. 1982. "Sources of Political Intolerance: The Case of the American South." In *Contemporary Southern Political Attitudes and Behavior: Studies and Essays*, ed. Laurence W. Moreland, Tod A. Baker, and Robert P. Steed. New York: Praeger.

———. 1996. "The Effect of Economic Individualism and Racial Stereotyping on Attitudes toward Racial Policies: A Regional Comparison." *American Review of Politics* 17: 113–27.

Johnson, Charles A. 1976. "Political Culture in American States: Elazar's Formulation Examined." *American Journal of Political Science* 20: 491–509.

Jonas, Frank W., ed. 1969. *Politics in the American West*. Salt Lake City: University of Utah Press.

Kellstedt, Lyman A. 1990. "Evangelical Religion and Support for Social Issue Policies: An Examination of Regional Variation." In *The Disappearing South? Studies in Regional Change and Continuity*, ed. Robert P. Steed, Laurence W. Moreland, and Tod A. Baker. Tuscaloosa: University of Alabama Press.

Key, V. O., Jr. 1949. *Southern Politics in State and Nation*. New York: Knopf.

———. 1955. "The Erosion of Sectionalism." *Virginia Quarterly Review* 81: 161–79.

Knuckey, Jonathan. 2001. "Ideological Realignment and Partisan Change in the American South." *Politics and Policy* 29: 337–58.

Kuklinski, James H., Michael D. Cobb, and Martin Gilens. 1997. "Racial Attitudes and the 'New South.'" *Journal of Politics* 59: 323–49.

Ladd, Everett Carll, Jr., and Charles D. Hadley. 1978, 2nd ed. *Transformations of the American Party System: Political Coalitions from the New Deal to the 1970s*. New York: W. W. Norton.

Lieske, Joel. 1993. "Regional Subcultures of the United States." *Journal of Politics* 55: 888–913.

Lockard, Duane. 1959. *New England State Politics*. Princeton: Princeton University Press.

Loftin, Colin, and Robert H. Hill. 1974. "Regional Subculture and Homicide: An Examination of the Gastil-Hackney Thesis." *American Sociological Review* 39: 714–24.

Marchant-Shapiro, Theresa, and Kelly D. Patterson. 1995. "Partisan Change in the Mountain West." *Political Behavior* 17: 359–78.

Marsden, Peter V., John Shelton Reed, Michael D. Kennedy, and Kandi M.

Stinson. 1982. "American Regional Culture and Differences in Leisure Time Activities." *Social Forces* 60: 1023–49.

Mezey, Michael L. 1983. "The Minds of the South." In *Religion and Politics in the South: Mass and Elite Perspectives,* ed. Tod A. Baker, Robert P. Steed, and Laurence W. Moreland. New York: Praeger.

Middleton, Russell. 1976. "Regional Differences in Prejudice." *American Sociological Review* 41: 94–117.

Nardulli, Peter F. 1990. "Political Subcultures in the American States: An Empirical Examination of Elazar's Formulation." *American Politics Quarterly* 18: 287–315.

Nisbett, Richard E., and Dov Cohen. 1996. *Culture of Honor: The Psychology of Violence in the South*. Boulder, Colo.: Westview Press.

Odum, Howard W. 1936. *Southern Regions of the United States*. Chapel Hill: University of North Carolina Press.

Patterson, Samuel C. 1968. "The Political Cultures of the American States." *Journal of Politics* 30: 187–209.

Powers, Rebecca S., J. Jill Suitor, Susana Guerra, Monisa Shackelford, Dorothy Mecom, and Kim Gusman. 2003. "Regional Differences in Gender-Role Attitudes: Variations by Gender and Race." *Gender Issues* 21: 40–54.

Quillian, Lincoln. 1996. "Group Threat and Regional Change in Attitudes toward African-Americans." *American Journal of Sociology* 102: 816–60.

Reed, John Shelton. 1973. "'The Cardinal Test of a Southerner': Not Race but Geography." *Public Opinion Quarterly* 37: 232–40.

———. 1974. *The Enduring South: Subcultural Persistence in Mass Society*. Chapel Hill: University of North Carolina Press.

——— 1982. "The Cardinal Test of a Southerner?" In *One South: An Ethnic Approach to Regional Culture*, ed. John Shelton Reed. Baton Rouge: Louisiana State University Press.

———. 1991a. "New South or No South? Regional Culture in 2036." In *The South Moves into Its Future: Studies in the Analysis and Prediction of Social Change*, ed. Joseph S. Himes. Tuscaloosa: University of Alabama Press.

———. 1991b. "The South: What Is It? Where Is It?" In *The South for New Southerners*, ed. Paul D. Escott and David R. Goldfield. Chapel Hill: University of North Carolina Press.

Reed, John Shelton, James Kohls, and Carol Hanchette. 1990. "The Dissolution of Dixie and the Changing Shape of the South." *Social Forces* 69: 221–33.

Rice, Tom W., and Diane L. Coates. 1995. "Gender Role Attitudes in the Southern United States." *Gender and Society* 9: 744–56.

Rice, Tom W., William P. McLean, and Amy J. Larsen. 2002. "Southern Distinctiveness over Time, 1972–2000." *American Review of Politics* 23: 193–220.

Rice, Tom W., and Meredith L. Pepper. 1997. "Region, Migration, and Attitudes in the United States." *Social Science Quarterly* 78: 83–95.

Schuman, Howard, Charlotte Steeh, Lawrence Bobo, and Maria Krysan. 1997, rev. ed. *Racial Attitudes in America: Trends and Interpretations*. Cambridge: Harvard University Press.

Sheatsley, Paul B. 1965. "White Attitudes toward the Negro." In *The Negro American*, ed. Talcott Parsons and Kenneth B. Clark. Boston: Houghton Mifflin.

Shortridge, James R. 1987. "Changing Usage of Four American Regional Labels." *Annals of the Association of American Geographers* 77: 325–36.

———. 1989. *The Middle West: Its Meaning in American Culture*. Lawrence: University Press of Kansas.

Simpkins, Francis B. 1947. "The Everlasting South." *Journal of Southern History* 13: 307–22.

Stemp, Roger W. 1987. "Regional Contrasts within Black Protestantism: A Research Note." *Social Forces* 66: 143–51.

Tillery, Jan, Tom Wikle, and Guy Bailey. 2000. "The Nationalization of a Southernism." *Journal of English Linguistics* 28: 280–94.

Tuch, Steven A. 1987. "Urbanism, Region, and Tolerance Revisited: The Case of Racial Prejudice." *American Sociological Review* 52: 504–10.

Weakliem, David L., and Robert Biggert. 1999. "Region and Political Opinion in the Contemporary United States." *Social Forces* 77: 863–86.

Wedeem, Lisa. 2002. "Conceptualizing Culture: Possibilities for Political Science." *American Political Science Review* 96: 713–28.

Williams, J. Allen. 1966. "Regional Differences in Authoritarianism." *Social Forces* 45: 273–77.

Wilson, Richard W. 1997. "American Political Culture in Comparative Perspective." *Political Psychology* 18: 483–502.

Wilson, Thomas C. 1986. "Interregional Migration and Racial Attitudes." *Social Forces* 65: 177–86.

Chapter 9

Presidential Elections and the South

Harold W. Stanley

THE CONNECTION BETWEEN THE SOUTH and presidential electoral politics since World War II has been the central focus of most scholarly work on the South and the presidency over the past half century or so. Although some literature has addressed presidential decision making during the civil rights era of the 1950s and, especially, the 1960s, this has been primarily a recounting of the effort to extend full citizenship rights to black southerners and is, therefore, more properly categorized as a part of the literature that focuses on presidential decision making regardless of region. Even that literature, however, tends to underscore electoral politics as the major connection between the presidency and the South. For example, there are frequent extended discussions of how presidents approached the development of civil rights policy positions with a sharp eye on how those positions might affect their ability to attract votes in the South—see, for example, the later discussion in this chapter of Lyndon Johnson's recognition of the consequences of his signing the 1964 Civil Rights Act for his—and other Democrats'—electoral chances in the region (Black and Black 1992).

The electoral focus is understandable. Inasmuch as the presidency is a national office, there is relatively little about its contemporary institutional structure and operation that is uniquely regional. Thus, the electoral context frames most of the research on the connections between the presidency and southern politics qua southern politics, and it is mainly that research that concerns us in this chapter.

One useful way of grouping this research is to divide it into two broad, frequently overlapping categories. First, there is a body of literature that examines presidential elections in the South from the perspective of specific elections. Early examples include Donald Strong's *The 1952 Presidential Election in the South* (1955) and Bernard Cosman's *Five States for Goldwater* (1966). More recent examples include the series of studies of the 1984–2000 presidential elections in the South edited by Robert Steed, Laurence Moreland, and Tod Baker (Steed, Moreland, and Baker 1986, 1994; Moreland, Steed, and Baker 1991; Moreland and Steed 1997; Steed and Moreland 2002). Although he included more than one election in the 1990s, Alexander Lamis's *Southern Politics in the 1990s* (1999) can also be placed in this category in light of its extended but relatively focused discussion of presidential electoral politics during that decade.

All these studies presented data and analyses aimed at clarifying voting patterns in the South in specific elections. What is perhaps more significant is that they also set those elections in a broader historical context that attempted, generally successfully, to identify how those elections fit into the larger patterns of regional political change. Thus, for example, Strong and Cosman both discussed an emerging Republican presidential vote in the South in the early 1950s and mid-1960s, respectively, that pointed to more generalized party transformation. Although (as I will discuss later in this chapter) the bases of Republican support in those elections differed in important ways, both elections demonstrated a growing willingness on the part of white southerners to desert the Democratic Party, at least in presidential elections. The development of presidential Republicanism in the South and its contribution to broader partisan change continued to be a major focus of the later studies of specific elections as well.

The second broad category of literature includes those studies that take a longer view of how presidential politics in the South evolved historically. In some instances presidential elections are contributing but secondary elements of a broader discussion of southern political change. For example, Earl Black and Merle Black in their landmark 1987 study, *Politics and Society in the South,* included one chapter devoted to presidential politics as a key indicator of the wide-ranging social, economic, demographic, and political changes in the region. Again in their 2002 book, which focused mainly on southern congressional politics (*The Rise of Southern Republicans*), the Blacks included related material on presidential elections to advance the general theme of partisan transformation. From a slightly different angle, Nicol Rae paid significant attention to presidential electoral politics in the South as an integral part of his examination of southern factionalism within the national Democratic Party in *Southern Democrats* (1994).

In fact, it is difficult to find any broad examination of southern partisan change during the period since World War II that did not in some way consider presidential elections as a significant element of that change. The prime examples include the usual suspects: *The Changing Politics of the South* edited by William Havard (1972), *Southern Politics and the Second Reconstruction* by Numan Bartley and Hugh Graham (1975), *The Transformation of Southern Politics* by Jack Bass and Walter DeVries (1976), *Southern Republicanism* by Louis Seagull (1975), and *The Two-Party South* by Alexander Lamis (1988). A more recent addition to the list is David Lublin's *The Republican South: Democratization and Partisan Change* (2004). A number of these books highlight the importance of Republican success in capturing presidential votes in the South as a means of gaining an electoral foothold in the region, but special mention should be made of Kevin Phillips's *The Emerging Republican Majority* (1969) and Joseph Aistrup's *The Southern Strategy Revisited: Republican Top-Down Advancement in the South* (1994) for their emphasis on the Republicans' strategic calculations in the 1960s. It was a conscious design to peel off southern white votes as a base of long-term Republican growth in the South. Aistrup in particular noted how success in presidential elections paved the way for a slower climb to competitiveness for Republicans in subnational elections over the last quarter of the century.

Finally, the most extensively developed overview of presidential electoral politics in the South over the past half century is Earl Black and Merle Black's *The Vital South: How Presidents Are Elected* (1992). Not only did the Blacks provide a thorough discussion of the details of presidential elections in the post–World War II South, but they placed this discussion in the context of national politics over the same period and also in a broader historical framework that ranged back well into the 1800s. In the process they presented a strong case for viewing the changes in southern presidential voting as important for understanding southern politics but also as important for understanding national politics. Their concluding sentence captured the central theme: "Above all, this is a portrait of a *vital* South, a region once again at the center of struggles to define winners and losers in American politics" (ibid., 366).

This is not an exhaustive listing of the work on presidential elections and the South; other materials will be cited in the following discussion. The rich body of work on presidential elections and southern politics often varies in emphasis, detail, time frame, and interpretative analysis, but collectively it tells an important story critical to understanding political patterns in the region. The remainder of this chapter offers an overview of that story.

Before Goldwater

In the years after World War II the southern states, once solidly Democratic, began undergoing a lengthy political shift. In 1952 four southern states backed the Republican presidential candidate. Rather than proving aberrational—as was the case in 1928 when five southern states defected rather than back the Democratic nominee, Governor Alfred E. Smith of New York—political forces inside and outside the South transformed the South, establishing competitive two-party politics, initially at the presidential level.

In *The Rise of Southern Republicans*, Earl Black and Merle Black emphasized the transforming roles of two Republican presidential candidates, Barry Goldwater in 1964 and Ronald Reagan in the 1980s. Goldwater's presidential bid marked the first time more southern whites voted Republican than Democratic. The Reagan years marked the first time more southern whites identified themselves as Republicans than as Democrats, which laid the foundation for Republican advances below the presidential level in the 1990s (Black and Black 2002, 205).

The Goldwater breakthrough followed a major federal intervention in race relations, the Civil Rights Act of 1964, an act that scrambled the political calculus of the South. President Lyndon Johnson, a Democrat, had made passage of the Civil Rights Act of 1964 a memorial to the assassinated President John Kennedy. No longer could solid southern attachment to the Democratic Party seem the best means of preventing federal interference with race relations in the South. The solidly Democratic South had rested on just such a notion, contrasting the Democrats as the party of and for the South with the Republican Party as the party of President Abraham Lincoln, the Civil War, and Reconstruction.

President Franklin Roosevelt's New Deal had set in motion the potential for conflict within the New Deal support coalition, because that coalition included both blacks and southern whites. Yet the notion that the Democratic Party would best protect white supremacy in the South had begun seriously unraveling in 1948 with President Harry Truman's endorsement of a civil rights program as he sought reelection. If the Democratic Party would not preserve southern race relations, a fundamental justification for one-party politics would be lost, and the way to two-party competition would be opened. In 1948 the Independent candidacy of Strom Thurmond of South Carolina gave voice to white southerners opposed to civil rights who wished to defect from the Democratic ticket. Thurmond carried four deep South states—Alabama, Louisiana, Mississippi, and South Carolina—and gained 39 electoral votes. Truman defeated Governor Thomas Dewey of New York 303 to 189. Such third-party candidacies can be viewed as halfway houses that facilitate the move of voters from identification with and support of one party to another.

In 1952 and 1956 the Democratic presidential nominee, Governor Adlai Stevenson of Illinois, did not repeat Truman's endorsement of a strong civil rights plank, but many southern voters did not return to their Democratic loyalties. Instead, they found reason to like General Dwight David Eisenhower, the Republican candidate and World War II commander. "'Ike' was the personification of a genial, non-threatening Republican . . . [who] could attract conservative Democrats and independents and carry several southern states" (Black and Black 2002, 207–9). Unlike Dewey in 1948 and previous Republicans, Eisenhower actively campaigned for southern votes and secured four of the largest southern states (Florida, Tennessee, Texas, and Virginia) in 1952. In 1956 he won these four states again and even added Louisiana.

Nor did the 1960 contest between Republican Vice President Richard Nixon and Democratic Senator John Kennedy draw sharp contrasts between the two in terms of civil rights. Nevertheless, the Solid South's Democratic ties were fraying. In 1960 Nixon carried Florida, Tennessee, and Virginia. The addition of Senator Lyndon Johnson to the Democratic ticket as ice president helped Democrats retake Texas, without which Kennedy would not have had an Electoral College majority.

Race, while central to southern politics, was not the only issue in southern presidential politics propelling some white voters toward the Republicans. Some southern voter disenchantment in 1952–60 with the Democratic Party and its presidential candidates could be traced back to President Roosevelt's New Deal. Conservative Democrats, and they were numerous among southern Democrats, could find much to dislike in the more progressive politics of the New Deal. A developing and broad-ranging ideological misfit between conservative southern Democrats and the national Democratic Party would help produce a reconfiguration of party support in the South (Lamis 1999, 5, 7).

This ideological reconfiguration was not rapid. Between 1952 and 1980 many southern whites, considering themselves staunch Democrats, would defect in their presidential voting either to Governor George Wallace of Alabama, an Independent candidate in 1968, or to the Republican candidate. These were the latter-day equivalents to V. O. Key's "strange political schizophrenic, the presidential Republican," who made up the Republican base in the 1940s, along with "mountain Republicans" and "Negro Republicans." But Key noted that these three parts added up to very little. For decades the Republican Party had not been seriously seeking southern Electoral College votes. Key, writing in 1949, said the Republican Party in southern states "scarcely deserves the name of party. It wavers somewhat between an esoteric cult on the order of a lodge and a conspiracy for plunder in accord with the accepted customs of our politics." Rather than seeking to win elections in the South, Republican officials would raise funds for contests in more doubtful states in the non-South (Key 1949, 278, 277, 296).

The Republican Party in the late-1940s South was not a robust political organization, but political trends in the region augured brighter days ahead for the party. In 1952 Alexander Heard, a principal research assistant to Key in *Southern Politics*, published *A Two-Party South?* Heard's analysis set out the long-term trends at work in the South. According to Heard, prospects for an invigorated Republicanism rested with changes brought on by economic and social developments. The shift from a rural, agricultural orientation to an urban and industrial society should alter the bases of political controversy in the South. Liberal factions within the state Democratic parties should eventually become stronger partly because of the increasing political organization of blacks and workers. Conservative Democrats would be driven to seek refuge in the Republican Party as third-party efforts and continued loyalty to the Democratic Party lost favor. The growth of a sizable urban middle class, subject to Republican as well as Democratic appeals, should nourish a two-party politics. The increasing competitiveness should realign the parties along liberal and conservative dimensions in line with the national parties (Heard 1952, 128–29, 245–49).

It is fitting that Key's other research assistant, Donald Strong, extended Heard's analysis with his exploration of the 1952 election in *The 1952 Presidential Election in the South* (1955). In this publication, and again in his *Urban Republicanism in the South* (1960), Strong found evidence supporting the expectation that Republican support in the 1950s was emerging in many of the sectors Heard had identified (for example, the white urban middle class).

Goldwater: A Choice, Not an Echo

Unlike the 1952, 1956, and 1960 campaigns, the 1964 presidential contest offered voters stark differences on civil rights. Senator Goldwater had voted against the Civil Rights Act of 1964, arguably for reasons of principle rather than racism or political opportunity. For southern whites opposed to change from white supremacy and segregation, Goldwater's opposition to the Civil Rights Act gave them a choice.

Shortly after signing the Civil Rights Act of 1964, President Johnson reportedly told an aide: "I think we just delivered the South to the Republican Party for a long time to come" (Black and Black 1992, 6). Subsequent presidential politics proved Johnson more prophetic than wrong.

The issue of race provided Republicans with an opportunity to expand their support among white southerners. Before Goldwater, Republicans had earned a considerable share of the black vote, particularly in 1956 after *Brown v. Board of Education* (1954). In 1960 this support ebbed a bit. The black vote, where it did not split evenly, went predominantly Democratic. Democrats had regained black support without significantly estranging white supporters. The Republican loss in 1960 was particularly vexing for Republicans; they had not gained white votes and had lost black votes. "Nixon had received only 33.4 percent of the vote in the black-belt counties in 1960, yet he was clearly more conservative, especially on racial matters, than was Kennedy" (Bartley and Graham 1975, 95). A Republican Party postmortem on 1960 statewide losses in Virginia and North Carolina, in which Republicans had run progressive campaigns with no race-baiting, pinpointed a paradox ripe with implications for future Republican strategy: Democratic victories rested on "the support of an unnatural coalition—Negroes demanding change in the pattern of race relations and those most strongly opposed to departure from the pattern" (ibid.). Since the black vote was small, writing off black voters to pick up white segregationist votes was not, at the time, particularly costly. In 1961 Goldwater had put it expressively: "We're not going to get the Negro vote as a bloc in 1964 and 1968, so we ought to go hunting where the ducks are" (Tindall 1972, 60). Hunt they did.

Survey research indicates "Goldwater was perceived by southern whites as a defender of segregation, even to a point well beyond any which the Senator actually took" (Converse 1966, 241). Goldwater carried the deep South states of Alabama, Georgia, Louisiana, Mississippi, and South Carolina. He won the deep South but lost every other state except Arizona, his home state. As Bernard Cosman discussed in some depth in *Five States for Goldwater* (1966), Goldwater swept the southern areas of high black population in the Black Belt counties, the areas of the South most resistant to black advancement, in which few blacks voted before the Voting Rights Act of 1965. Black Belt counties gave Goldwater greater support than did traditional Republican counties or urban areas.

Southern whites were not the only ones paying attention to the candidates' stances on civil rights. For blacks the 1964 choice between Johnson the Democrat and Goldwater the Republican, along with the clear identification of the national Democratic Party as the stronger advocate of civil rights in 1964 and later, established strong ties to the Democratic Party that have endured. Before 1964 the positions of the Democratic and Republican parties had not been clearly differentiated on civil rights. In 1964 and afterward they were (Carmines and Stimson 1989). In the five southern states Goldwater carried, between 62 and 93 percent of the voting age blacks had been unregistered in 1964 (Bass and DeVries 1976, 29). In the years that followed, blacks in even these most racially resistant areas of the South gained an effective right to vote with passage and enforcement of the Voting Rights Act of 1965. And their votes were cast with a strong attachment to the Democrats.

Wallace, Nixon, Reagan, and a Southern Strategy

Federal interventions in civil rights and the Democratic Party's more progressive positions led many southern whites to reconsider their political preferences. Regarding the rise in the 1960s in Republican voting, one South Carolinian discounted the apparent partisan shift in voting: "There ain't that many Republicans in South Carolina, just a lot of mad Democrats" (Tindall 1972, 71). Many of these "mad Democrats" defected from their partisan ties, some backing Governor George Wallace of Alabama, some backing Republican candidates.

Wallace, a highly skilled and ambitious politician, called for federal defiance as exemplified by his "stand in the schoolhouse door"—an unsuccessful attempt to prevent desegregation of the University of Alabama in June 1963. His defiant rhetoric struck a chord. And he sought to expand his support base beyond Alabama. Wallace entered three Democratic presidential primaries in 1964 to challenge President Johnson politically and to show support for his views outside the South. Wallace lost each primary but secured almost 43 percent of the vote in the last one, in Maryland. In July 1964, three days after Republicans nominated Goldwater and less than three weeks after President Johnson signed the Civil Rights Act of 1964, Wallace withdrew, bowing to the reality that Goldwater's running as the Republican nominee had eclipsed the justification for his candidacy (Carter 1995).

Wallace returned to run for president in 1968, not as a Democrat in the primaries but as an Independent in the general election, giving voice again to southern whites who had found a temporary home with Goldwater in 1964. The Wallace candidacy threatened to deny either the Republican Nixon or the Democratic Vice President Hubert Humphrey a majority in the Electoral College, which would throw the election into the House of Representatives. Wallace fell short, securing 46 electoral votes from five southern states (Alabama, Arkansas, Georgia, Louisiana, and Mississippi). Nixon won 301 electoral votes, Humphrey only 191; 270 votes constituted a majority of the Electoral College. Opinion polling revealed that two-thirds of the 1968 Wallace voters would have backed Nixon had Wallace not run (Bartley 1970, 108). Humphrey won only one southern state (Texas), and Nixon won five.

In 1968 Republicans backed away from the blunt, toxic approach to racial issues that had characterized Goldwater's campaign. The outer South, less scarred by racial anxieties, would make a more feasible target; GOP gains in the outer South spilled over as the deep South evolved (Phillips 1969, 205). Nixon himself had proclaimed in 1966: "Republicans must not go prospecting for the fool's gold of racist votes" (Bass and DeVries 1976, 29). And again: "Southern Republicans must not climb aboard the sinking ship of racial injustice. They should let the Southern Democrats sink with it, as they have sailed with it" (Tindall 1972, 69). Noble sentiments these, but when made in 1966 the Republican choice was not so much one of climbing aboard as one of jumping off.

For his 1968 presidential campaign Nixon fashioned a "southern strategy" that sought to strike a responsive chord in the South, at least those southern states outside the deep South. In early spring 1968 Nixon and southern Republican strategists came to an understanding of a southern strategy that two journalists characterized like this: "If I'm president of the United States, I'll find a way to ease up on the federal pressures forcing school desegregation—or any other kind of desegregation" (Murphy and Gulliver 1971, 2).

Nixon's comeback win of the presidency in 1968 was predicated in part on this southern strategy, personified by Senator Strom Thurmond of South Carolina. The southern strategy sought to profit politically from racial resentment without driving away more moderate support. The political logic behind the Republican strategy was set forth in Kevin Phillips's *The Emerging Republican Majority* (1969). Phillips, Nixon's main electoral analyst and strategist, optimistically lumped together Nixon and Wallace support to divine trends in the political tides. As his book developed in some detail, Phillips saw the southern strategy as a key ingredient in a national electoral strategy that would have long-term payoffs for the party. Phillips's analysis has since been recognized as one of the most prescient writings on American partisan politics in the post–World War II era. Indeed, these long-term implications would later be examined by Joseph Aistrup in *The Southern Strategy Revisited: Republican Top-Down Advancement in the South* (1994), in which he would connect Republican growth in the South to the strategic seeds sowed in the late 1960s.

When Wallace returned in 1972 to run again for president, he ran as a Democrat, something the Nixon administration was keen to encourage. (Nixon had surreptitiously aided Wallace in his comeback bid for governor in Alabama in 1970, a fact that came out with the Watergate investigations.) Nixon realized a politically potent Wallace offered real prospects for dividing Democrats nationally. The shooting of Wallace in May 1972 effectively ended his potency in national politics, although he did run for president again in 1976 in the Democratic primaries, only to be eclipsed by a fellow southerner, Governor Jimmy Carter of Georgia.

In 1952 Eisenhower had broken through the solidly Democratic South: "The watershed election for presidential Republicanism was the contest of 1952, which clearly established the G.O.P. as the respectable party of the urban and suburban affluent whites in the South's large and small cities and a visible threat in presidential elections in the South" (Bartley and Graham 1975, 86; cf. Strong 1955). One estimate is that Eisenhower secured 50 percent of the southern white vote in 1952 and close to that in 1956. Eisenhower's candidacy attracted to the GOP southern members enthusiastic about electoral victory. Republican organizations increasingly resembled true party organizations with electoral ambitions for state and national office rather than a closed group focused on federal patronage.

Eisenhower ran well in the South's metropolitan regions, drawing from the growing urban and suburban middle class (Black and Black 2002, 209). Aggregate analysis reveals that presidential Republicanism made the greatest gains in metropolitan areas during the Eisenhower years. Nixon's 1960 campaign continued the trend; he was most successful in metropolitan areas (and traditional mountain Republican areas, as Ike had been). Goldwater upset the trend, gaining greater percentages of support in Black Belt counties than in traditional Republican counties or metropolitan areas. The trend returned with Nixon's 1968 campaign, although the conclusion must be hedged a bit since urban areas then contained a large number of blacks who had begun to vote and who backed the Democrats (Strong 1971, 239, 256).

In 1972, against the Democratic presidential nominee Senator George McGovern, Nixon swept the South, something that had not occurred since 1944, except in 1944 a Solid South was Democratic. Only five of the eleven southern states had cast electoral votes for the Republican presidential candidate since 1880 (Florida, North Carolina, Texas, and Virginia in 1928 and Tennessee in both 1920 and 1928).

Republican prospects for party building down South (as well as across the nation) were set back by the Watergate scandal. Gerald Ford took over as president, declaring "the long national nightmare" was over. Governor Jimmy Carter of Georgia, the Democratic presidential nominee in 1976, symbolized a political nightmare for Republicans and a dream candidate for Democrats: a moderate southerner who could mobilize black voter turnout and support as well as secure substantial white voter support in the South and across the nation. Such biracial coalitions had proven effective at the state level, enabling southern Democrats to win office and turn back the rising Republican challenge (Lamis 1999, 8–9). Prospects were strong for Democratic presidential wins, too.

Carter's regional roots appealed to white southern voters in ways that President Johnson's Texas ties had not in 1964. Carter carried every southern state except Virginia and narrowly won the presidency. Carter's 1976 campaign proved alluring, but his presidency proved off-putting, marked as it was by poor economic performance combined with foreign policy crises (Black and Black, 1992, 307–12). Chief among the crises was what one nightly network news program regularly called "America Held Hostage," as U.S. embassy employees were held captive in Iran during the final year of Carter's presidency.

Governor Ronald Reagan, favored by the Republican right, had challenged incumbent President Gerald Ford for the Republican nomination in 1976, coming close to toppling the sitting president. In 1980 Reagan gained the Republican presidential nomination and defeated Carter's reelection bid. This time Carter lost every southern state except his home state of Georgia (Black and Black 2002, 212–14).

Reagan's presidency strengthened the Republican Party in the South in ways that won converts to the party among many former Democratic supporters. This bolstered the Republican presence in the South and promised larger gains later below the presidential level, a promise realized during the 1990s. As Black and Black wrote of Reagan: "Ronald Reagan's presidency legitimized the Republican party for many white southerners. His southern legacy was immense. . . . His optimistic conservatism and successful performance in office made the Republican party respectable and useful for millions of southern whites. Many of them, for the first time in their lives, began to think of themselves as Republicans. . . . By realigning white conservatives and dealigning white moderates, Reagan produced a partial realignment of the southern white electorate" (ibid., 206, 370). In 1984 Reagan won reelection in a landslide. Carter's vice president, Walter Mondale of Minnesota, captured the Democratic presidential nomination in 1984, and Reagan—as Nixon had in 1972—swept every southern state (Stanley 1986).

The rise of the religious right in the 1980s, firmly tied to the Republican Party and prominent in the South, aided Republican prospects even as it added tensions within the Republican coalition (Black and Black 2002, 214–15, 227–29, 250–51).

A key Republican campaign operative, Lee Atwater, in 1981 explained the evolving role of race for Republicans:

> You start out in 1954 by saying "Nigger, nigger, nigger." By 1968 you can't say "nigger"—that hurts you. Backfires. So you say stuff like forced busing, states' rights, and all that stuff. You're getting so abstract now you're talking about cutting taxes, and all these things you're talking about are totally economic things and a by-product of them is blacks get hurt worse than whites.

And subconsciously maybe that is part of it. I'm not saying that. But I'm saying that if it is getting that abstract, and that coded, that we are doing away with the racial problem one way or the other. You follow me—because obviously sitting around saying, "we want to cut this," is much more abstract than even the busing thing *and* a hell of a lot more abstract than "Nigger, nigger." (July 8, 1981, interview quoted in Lamis 1988, 26; cf. Black and Black 1992, 8, and Edsall and Edsall 1991, 3–4)

The South Reforms the Presidential Selection Process

Many southern Democratic Party and elected officials were tiring of Democratic presidential candidates with limited appeal to southern whites. Before the 1988 presidential caucuses and primaries, southern Democrats, spearheaded by the Southern Legislative Council, sought to schedule each southern state's caucus or primary for Super Tuesday, March 8. (The first "Super Tuesday," in 1980, had been created when Alabama and Georgia agreed to move their primary dates earlier to join Florida to provide incumbent President Carter with friendly southern settings after Senator Edward Kennedy of Massachusetts was expected to win the early events of Iowa and New Hampshire.) With the southern states uniting to stage a mammoth one-day nominating event, it was hoped that Super Tuesday would raise the profile of southern voters in Democratic presidential nominating politics, benefit more moderate Democratic candidates, and thus help stop the movement of southern whites toward presidential Republicanism.

Those were the hopes, but the reality differed dramatically. In Republican primaries marked by substantially increased turnout, Vice President George H. W. Bush swept the southern states, cementing the Republican nomination. Among Democrats, Governor Michael Dukakis of Massachusetts won two states (Florida and Texas), the black civil rights activist Reverend Jesse Jackson won five (Alabama, Georgia, Louisiana, Mississippi, and Virginia), and Senator Al Gore of Tennessee won three (Arkansas, North Carolina, and Tennessee). This was not the result more moderate southern Democrats had envisioned. Disappointment with the 1988 results and the ultimate nomination of Michael Dukakis led several southern states to back off the regional primary. In 1992 four states (Alabama, Arkansas, North Carolina, and Virginia) moved the primary to a later date, turning their backs on the attempt to make southern clout felt early in the nomination process. A fifth southern state, Georgia, moved earlier in the calendar, snagging greater media and candidate attention as the curtain-raiser for the six southern states remaining in Super Tuesday. (South Carolina Republicans had shown the advantages of such timing in 1988.) By 1996 only four southern states remained on Super Tuesday (Louisiana, Mississippi, Tennessee, and Texas). South Carolina and Georgia scheduled primaries before Super Tuesday, which served as gateway primaries to the South (Clark and Haynes 2002, 25; Stanley 1997).

Bush, Clinton, and Bush

The state-by-state analyses of the presidential elections in the South from 1984 through 2000 in the Praeger series of books edited by Robert Steed, Laurence Moreland, and Tod Baker, coupled with similar state-by-state analyses of the presidential elections of the 1990s edited by Alexander Lamis, paint a vivid picture of developments over the past two decades. Moreover, these works addressed regionwide concerns regarding the presidential nomination process we have just examined.

Vice President Bush won the election in 1988, turning back Governor Michael Dukakis of Massachusetts. Bush, as Reagan had in 1984, swept the South. White southern voters—as they had with Humphrey in 1968, McGovern in 1972, and Mondale in 1984—again demonstrated little affinity for nonsouthern left-of-center Democratic presidential candidates. Significant numbers of southern electoral votes had previously gone for such a candidate—Senator John F. Kennedy in 1960—but those days were gone. The Bush campaign successfully targeted Dukakis as a Democratic symbol of "the various accumulated Democratic party stigmas that . . . [had produced] a national partisan reshuffling favorable to the GOP"—such as being weak on defense, opposed to the death penalty, and soft on crime. The Bush campaign may not have aired the most notorious Willie Horton ad, but they did air television ads attacking Governor Dukakis for "a Massachusetts prison furlough program in which a convicted murderer named Willie Horton, released for a weekend during Dukakis' tenure, fled and later committed rape" (Lamis 1999, 401–2).

Governor Bill Clinton of Arkansas proved a more resilient Democratic nominee, positioning himself as more of a centrist, a "new Democrat." Clinton and his running mate, Senator Al Gore of Tennessee, drew a sharp contrast with previous Democratic images, stating in an early television ad: "They are a new generation of Democrats, Bill Clinton and Al Gore. And they don't think the way the old Democratic party did. They've called for an end to welfare as we know it, so welfare can be a second chance, not a way of life. They've sent a strong signal to criminals by supporting the death penalty. And they've rejected the old tax and spend politics" (quoted in Lamis 1999, 34). The end of the cold war in 1989 helped, blunting the stigma of Democrats as being too soft on defense (ibid., 402). And Clinton hammered hard at the economic recession under President Bush and defeated the incumbent with 370 electoral votes to 168.

Yet neither for election in 1992 nor reelection in 1996 did Clinton, a moderate Democrat from the South, prove capable of repeating Carter's near-sweep of the southern states in 1976. Clinton carried four southern states in 1992 and again in 1996: Arkansas, Louisiana, and Tennessee in both elections, and Georgia in 1992 and Florida in 1996.

In 1996 Clinton turned back Senator Robert Dole, 379 electoral votes to 159. Democrats had an all-southern ticket in 1992 and 1996 with Clinton and Gore, but rather than battling to take back the South, the all-southern ticket put together enough Electoral College votes to win in the non-South. In neither 1992 nor 1996 did electoral votes from the southern states provide a margin crucial for the Democratic victory.

In 1996 as in 1992, the South was not a vital region in presidential politics. Bill Clinton's victories could have weathered losing every one of the Electoral College votes he secured from the southern states—fifty-one in 1996, thirty-nine in 1992. Ironically, an all-southern Democratic ticket proved electable in 1992 and 1996, but it did not require southern electoral votes. The Democratic Party had two southerners as presidential and vice presidential nominees, but their appeal outside the South, not a strong southern base, made victory attainable (Stanley 1997, 223).

Both 1992 and 1996 featured third-party bids by billionaire Ross Perot. Despite Perot's Texas ties, his Independent candidacy proved less appealing in the South than in the non-South. Nationwide Perot pulled in almost 19 percent of the popular vote. In the South Perot averaged just under 16 percent (Lamis 1999, 36). Third parties with impact on southern politics have tended to articulate populist themes that resonate with traditional southern culture rather than progressive themes such as those Perot advanced in 1992 and 1996 (Green 1997, 35).

President Clinton took strides to reshape politics. He signed welfare reform into law, and he declared that the era of big government was over. In many respects he was a different kind of Democrat. Clinton's presidency offered hopes for resuscitating Democratic presidential prospects in the South, but Clinton had baggage. His failed health care program in 1994 smacked of big government; its failure eroded Clinton's claims to be a "new Democrat" and helped Republicans win congressional majorities in 1994 (Lamis 1999, 42–43). Personal scandal and impeachment proceedings added bite to an increasingly polarized politics, and even his own vice president, Al Gore, used Clinton only minimally in his 2000 bid for the presidency. Kevin Phillips, commenting on the declining southern white voters' affection for Democrats, noted that "each time the Democrats have had a southern president who disappointed Dixie, the party has paid the price—LBJ in 1964–68, Carter in 1980, and most recently Clinton" (Phillips 2004). Gore, hailing from Tennessee, failed to carry even a single southern state in 2000. Winning his home state or even Clinton's Arkansas would have sufficed to put Gore in the winner's circle.

In 2000 Gore did not resonate with southern whites as Clinton had in 1992 and 1996 or even as Carter had in 1976. Governor George W. Bush of Texas proved more likable and appealing. Gore evoked strong support among black voters in the South, as in the nation, but his more liberal positions did not resonate with southern whites (Stanley 2002, 225).

In 2000 Bush campaigned as a "compassionate conservative," seeking to soften the hard-edged positions often associated with some of the more conservative Republicans. Bush thought Republicans needed to "put a compassionate face on our conservative philosophy [because] people think oftentimes that Republicans are mean-spirited folks. Which is not true, but that's what people think." Bush, pointing to his record in Texas, claimed that without abandoning conservative ideology or alienating core Republican voters, he was capable of reaching out to Hispanics, blacks, and working-class Catholics (ibid.).

Bush's outreach contrasted vividly with previous Republican campaigns that relied on a southern strategy to secure overwhelming support from white voters to offset strong opposition among minority voters. Nixon, Reagan, and even the elder Bush had relied on such a strategy. Ralph Reed, a former political operative of the religious right, then a consultant to the Bush campaign, put it bluntly: "This is a very different party from the party that sits down on Labor Day and cedes the black vote and cedes the Hispanic vote, and tries to drive its percentage of the white vote over 70 percent to win an election" (ibid., 226).

"Compassionate conservatism" may not have won Bush very many votes from minorities, but it probably benefited him among white moderates. As one analyst noted before the election: "He doesn't come across as one of these southern, Christian Coalition, right-wing-nut Republican candidates. So white suburbanites, especially white suburban women, who are looking for someone who is reasonable can support him" (David Bositis, quoted in ibid., 226–27).

In 2000 Bush's southern state victories had "depended heavily on religious constituencies, especially observant evangelical Protestants, the prime constituency of the Christian Right and the core of traditional southern Protestantism" (Green 2002, 11). In 2004 Republicans solidified their support among white evangelical, fundamentalist, and Pentecostal voters. The "churchgoing white South" was counted as critical to the 2004 Bush victory (Phillips 2004).

Conclusion

Noting that every one of the nine times between 1932 and 1988 that one party captured all or most of the South's electoral votes, that party won, Black and Black concluded that "as the united south goes, so goes the nation" (Black and Black 1992, 344).

In recent decades southern electoral votes have mostly gone overwhelmingly to the Republicans, adding to the Republican margin of victory without being critical to that victory. Only in the past two presidential elections have southern electoral votes made the difference between losing and winning. Bush swept the southern states in 2000 and again in 2004 (although critics still argue over the 2000 vote count in Florida). Republican presidential candidates had previously swept the South in 1972, 1984, and 1988. Yet none of those previous Republican wins while sweeping the South depended on southern electoral votes. Also, Reagan's near-sweep of southern states in 1980 was not required for his victory. Had every southern state remained solidly Democratic in 1972, 1980, 1984, and 1988, Nixon, Reagan (twice), and George H. W. Bush would still have won. Not so in 2000 and 2004. Southern electoral votes, solidly Republican, proved crucial for the two George W. Bush wins.

Another perspective on how Democratic presidential candidates have fared in 1968 and later with southern electoral votes is that only two of three southerners—Carter and Clinton, but not Gore—have won southern electoral votes. In four elections Carter and Clinton carried a southern state nineteen times out of a possible total of forty-four. Of the five nonsouthern Democratic presidential candidates—Humphrey, McGovern, Mondale, Dukakis, and Kerry—only one won a southern state (Humphrey won Texas in 1968). Put differently, these nonsouthern Democratic candidates carried a southern state once out of a possible total of fifty-five times.

In the aftermath of the 2004 elections, what does a retrospective view suggest about Democratic presidential prospects? Virginia has not voted Democratic for president since 1964. Five southern states (Alabama, Mississippi, North Carolina, South Carolina, and Texas) have not voted Democratic since 1976. Georgia last voted Democratic in 1992, Florida in 1996—neither Florida nor Georgia backed Clinton in both his presidential elections. Three states last backed a Democrat in 1996 (and also backed Clinton in 1992)—Arkansas, Louisiana, and Tennessee. Put differently, Virginia has voted Republican for president in the last ten elections; Alabama, Mississippi, North Carolina, South Carolina, and Texas have voted Republican seven straight times; Georgia three times; and Arkansas, Louisiana, and Tennessee twice.

Should Democrats write off the South in presidential campaigns or seek to win the hearts and minds of voters in southern states? One school of thought holds that Democrats are doomed without a presidential candidate capable of securing southern electoral votes. (In 2003 Howard Dean urged the wooing of southern whites, stating that he wanted the votes of southern whites with Confederate flags on their pickup trucks. This colorful but awkward wording attracted flak; lost was the larger point that Dean thought Democrats had winning economic and substantive arguments about why such voters should be siding with Democrats.) If Democrats write off the South, conceding southern states and over a quarter of the electoral votes to the Republicans, they will be forced to carry two-thirds of the electoral votes in the non-South. Yet Democrats could win without the South. If Gore had carried New Hampshire (as Kerry did in 2004), he would have won a majority of the Electoral College. Indeed, across the nation, the states Democrats carried each time in the four presidential elections between 1992 and 2004 now total 248 of the 270 electoral votes needed for a majority. The corresponding figure for Republicans is 135.

Electoral College majorities would be within reach for the Democrats if their base states could be supplemented with southern electoral votes, but recent history reveals the distinct, sizable advantage Republican presidential candidates have enjoyed in courting and carrying southern states.

References

Aistrup, Joseph. 1994. *The Southern Strategy Revisited: Republican Top-Down Advancement in the South*. Lexington: University Press of Kentucky.

Bartley, Numan V. 1970. *From Thurmond to Wallace: Political Tendencies in Georgia 1948–1968*. Baltimore: Johns Hopkins University Press.

Bartley, Numan V., and Hugh D. Graham. 1975. *Southern Politics and the Second Reconstruction*. Baltimore: Johns Hopkins University Press.

Bass, Jack, and Walter DeVries. 1976. *The Transformation of Southern Politics: Social Change and Political Consequence since 1945*. New York: Basic Books.

Black, Earl, and Merle Black. 1987. *Politics and Society in the South*. Cambridge: Harvard University Press.

———. 1992. *The Vital South: How Presidents Are Elected*. Cambridge: Harvard University Press.

———. 2002. *The Rise of Southern Republicans*. Cambridge: Harvard University Press.

Carmines, Edward G., and James A. Stimson. 1989. *Issue Evolution: Race and the Transformation of American Politics*. Princeton: Princeton University Press.

Carter, Dan T. 1995. *The Politics of Rage: George Wallace, the Origins of the New Conservatism, and the Transformation of American Politics*. New York: Simon and Schuster.

Clark, John, and Audrey Haynes. 2002. "The 2000 Presidential Nomination Process." In *The 2000 Presidential Election in the South: Partisanship and Southern Party Systems in the 21st Century*, ed. Robert P. Steed and Laurence W. Moreland. Westport, Conn.: Praeger.

Converse, Philip E. 1966. "On the Possibility of Major Political Realignment in the South." In *Elections and the Political Order*, ed. Angus Campbell, Philip E. Converse, Warren E. Miller, and Donald E. Stokes. New York: John Wiley and Sons.

Cosman, Bernard. 1966. *Five States for Goldwater: Continuity and Change in Southern Presidential Voting Patterns*. Tuscaloosa: University of Alabama Press.

Edsall, Thomas Byrne, and Mary D. Edsall. 1991. *Chain Reaction: The Impact of Race, Rights, and Taxes on American Politics*. New York: W. W. Norton.

Green, John. 1997. "The Third Party South: Minor Parties in Southern Elections, 1892–1996." In *The 1996 Presidential Election in the South: Southern Party Systems in the 1990s*, ed. Laurence W. Moreland and Robert P. Steed. New York: Praeger.

————. 2002. "Believers for Bush, Godly for Gore: Religion and the 2000 Election in the South." In *The 2000 Presidential Election in the South: Partisanship and Southern Party Systems in the 21st Century*, ed. Robert P. Steed and Laurence W. Moreland. Westport, Conn.: Praeger.

Havard, William C., ed. 1972. *The Changing Politics of the South*. Baton Rouge: Louisiana State University Press.

Heard, Alexander. 1952. *A Two-Party South?* Chapel Hill: University of North Carolina Press.

Key, V. O., Jr. 1949. *Southern Politics in State and Nation*. New York: Knopf.

Lamis, Alexander P. 1988, expanded ed. *The Two-Party South*. New York: Oxford University Press.

————, ed. 1999. *Southern Politics in the 1990s*. Baton Rouge: Louisiana State University Press.

Lublin, David. 2004. *The Republican South: Democratization and Partisan Change*. Princeton: Princeton University Press.

Moreland, Laurence, and Robert P. Steed, eds. 1997. *The 1996 Presidential Election in the South: Southern Party Systems in the 1990s*. New York: Praeger.

Moreland, Laurence, Robert P. Steed, and Tod A. Baker, eds. 1991. *The 1988 Presidential Election in the South: Continuity amidst Change in Southern Party Politics*. New York: Praeger.

Murphy, Reg, and Hal Gulliver. 1971. *The Southern Strategy*. New York: Scribner.

Phillips, Kevin. 1969. *The Emerging Republican Majority*. New Rochelle, N.Y.: Arlington House.

————. 2004. "All Eyes on Dixie." *American Prospect* 15: 24–28.

Rae, Nicol C. 1994. *Southern Democrats*. New York: Oxford University Press.

Seagull, Louis. 1975. *Southern Republicanism*. New York: John Wiley and Sons.

Stanley, Harold W. 1986. "The 1984 Presidential Election in the South: Race and Realignment." In *The 1984 Presidential Election in the South: Patterns of Southern Party Politics*, ed. Robert P. Steed, Laurence W. Moreland, and Tod A. Baker. New York: Praeger.

————. 1997. "The South and the 1996 Presidential Election: Republican Gains among Democratic Wins." In *The 1996 Presidential Election in the South: Southern Party Systems in the 1990s*, ed. Laurence W. Moreland and Robert P. Steed. Westport, Conn.: Praeger.

————. 2002. "The South in the 2000 Elections." In *The 2000 Presidential Election in the South: Partisanship and Southern Party Systems in the 21st Century*, ed. Robert P. Steed and Laurence W. Moreland. Westport, Conn.: Praeger.

Steed, Robert P., and Laurence W. Moreland, eds. 2002. *The 2000 Presidential Election in the South: Partisanship and Southern Party Systems in the 21st Century*. Westport, Conn.: Praeger.

Steed, Robert P., Laurence W. Moreland, and Tod A. Baker, eds. 1986. *The*

1984 Presidential Election in the South: Patterns of Southern Party Politics. New York: Praeger.

———. 1994. *The 1992 Presidential Election in the South: Current Patterns of Southern Party and Electoral Politics.* Westport, Conn.: Praeger.

Strong, Donald. 1955. *The 1952 Presidential Election in the South.* Tuscaloosa: University of Alabama Bureau of Public Administration.

———. 1960. *Urban Republicanism in the South.* Tuscaloosa: University of Alabama Press.

———. 1971. "Further Reflections on Southern Politics." *Journal of Politics* 33: 239–56.

Tindall, George B. 1972. *The Disruption of the Solid South.* New York: W. W. Norton.

★ Chapter 10 ★

Congress and the South

Stanley P. Berard

THE SOUTH HAS ALWAYS PLAYED a distinctive role in the U.S. Congress. Since the middle of the twentieth century that role has been characterized by change as well as distinctiveness. At the end of World War II the South constituted a minority faction within the majority Democratic Party, a faction that used its institutional position to thwart many of the policy initiatives of that party. By the 1980s the civil rights movement and the growth of two-party competition had transformed southern politics to the point where southern Democrats were pivotal to the formation of both Democratic and conservative majority coalitions. Finally, by the early twenty-first century the realignment of southern party politics placed southerners in the vanguard of a Republican congressional majority.

How has political science understood these interactions between southern politics and congressional politics? A review of the literature that touches on this subject is necessarily selective, drawing from two streams of scholarship. Of obvious importance are works on southern politics that address congressional behavior. In congressional studies, literature that explicitly treats the South as a unit of analysis or as a major explanatory variable deserves the closest attention, but one should place this work in the context of broader explanations of Congress.

Almost any review of postwar Southern politics must begin with V. O. Key's *Southern Politics in State and Nation;* this one begins with Key's treatment of Congress at midcentury.

The South in Congress at Midcentury: V. O. Key's *Southern Politics*

V. O. Key's classic study established the benchmark against which all subsequent studies of southern politics are judged. This statement is true in two senses. The study's thorough empiricism and insightful conceptualization set a high standard for subsequent work, and its findings provided a baseline against which to measure political development in the South.

It was Key's contention that the one-party system in the South served the purpose of southern solidarity in national politics. The sole purpose of southern Democratic solidarity was to protect the southern system of racial segregation, in which political, social, and economic standing was denied to blacks. Southern politicians usually subordinated other issues to the race issue in national politics. When other issues did come to the fore, the whites of the plantation districts proved to be most committed to the racial status quo (Key 1949, 315–16).

To study the operation of southern solidarity in Congress, Key focused on roll call voting. He acknowledged that southern influence in Congress owed much to the operation of the seniority system, but he used roll call votes as a source of evidence of variation in southern solidarity and conservatism across issues. On votes where majorities of both northern and southern Democrats opposed a majority of Republicans, it is notable that southern Democrats usually displayed greater cohesion than their northern Democratic colleagues, especially in the Senate. Almost half the partisan Senate votes Key studied demonstrated southern Democratic support for the president's positions on international trade, war preparations, and the postwar settlement (ibid., 352–53, 376–77).

In the late 1930s observers began to note the occasional appearance of a conservative coalition of southern Democrats and Republicans in roll call voting. Labor-related issues turned up most frequently among the votes on which this alignment occurred. A review of Key's evidence indicates that southerners were less cohesive in their support of the conservative position on the general concept of wages and hours legislation than on specific exemptions for industries tied to agriculture and on limiting the ability of unions to disrupt war production. He identified rural and agrarian conservatism as the most durable basis for the conservative coalition (ibid., 355–59, 374–75).

Not only did southern Democratic conservatism vary across issues; it also varied across individuals. Senators with more populist appeals who attracted support from rural upland areas (such as Hugo Black and Lister Hill of Alabama) tended to be more supportive of the New Deal than those whose base of support was in the more conservative Black Belt regions. Senators elected with the support of identifiably liberal (Huey Long and Allen Ellender of Louisiana) or conservative (Carter Glass and Harry F. Byrd of Virginia) factional organizations tended to represent those views in their roll call votes (ibid., 360–67). In the House the districts whose representatives were most likely to vote with the national Democrats against the conservative coalition were those with substantial urban populations. Representatives of upland districts with few blacks were also more likely to support national Democratic positions than those from the Black Belt (ibid., 378–80).

Whatever their differences on economics, however, southern Democrats were united in opposition to federal action on civil rights. When southern Democrats supported a position at a rate of 90 percent against majorities of both northern Democrats and Republicans, race was almost always the issue. For example, southerners voted against allowing black soldiers to vote in primary elections, against prohibiting poll taxes for federal elections, and against antilynching measures (ibid., 351, 371–72). Southern members of Congress were far more unified in their opposition to black civil rights than in their opposition to organized labor or expanded social welfare benefits. At the height of partisan conflict over the New Deal, race was the issue of ultimate importance in shaping the role of the South in Congress.

The central concern of *Southern Politics in State and Nation* was not the functioning of Congress, but how the distinctive patterns of southern politics were reflected in congressional behavior. The next work to pose this question across a broad range of issues appeared nearly twenty years later (Shannon 1968). In the intervening two decades the southern politics literature addressed the rise of Republicanism in urban congressional voting (Heard 1952; Strong 1960; Cosman 1967) and the potential implications of black voter mobilization for the representation of black interests in legislatures (Matthews and Prothro 1966; Keech 1968). Scholars pursuing either line of inquiry devoted substantial attention to the impact of these phenomena on the internal workings of Congress.

The 1950s and 1960s: Responsible Parties and Behavioralism in Congressional Studies

The theory of responsible party government gave shape to much of the congressional literature of the 1950s (American Political Science Association 1950). Scholars applying the emerging methods of roll call voting analysis generally concluded that although parties were weak in the United States compared to those in other nations, party was the single best predictor of roll call behavior in Congress. They generally sought to explain deviations from partisanship in terms of demographic characteristics of constituencies (Turner 1951; Truman 1959; Froman 1963; Mayhew 1966). The most persistent intraparty difference was that between northern and southern Democrats. The focus on responsible parties also inspired several studies of party leadership in Congress, which frequently addressed the constraints and opportunities faced by congressional leaders because of the policy differences between northern and southern Democrats (Bone 1956; Huitt 1961; Masters 1961; Robinson 1963; Ripley 1964, 1967; Froman and Ripley 1965; Peabody 1967; Jones 1968a, 1968b, 1970).

The impetus to develop general behavioral theories of Congress reduced the emphasis that scholars placed on the distinctive role of southerners. Duncan MacRae pioneered the application of psychometric methods, particularly Guttman scaling, to the analysis of roll call voting (MacRae 1958). This development laid the groundwork for Aage Clausen's "policy dimension" theory. Clausen used cross-Congress correlations among roll call scales constructed from the Eighty-third to Eighty-eighth Congresses (1953–64) to validate several enduring dimensions of congressional policy making: government management, social welfare, civil liberties, international involvement, and agricultural assistance. These data revealed a high degree of stability in members' policy attitudes, a finding that has been replicated by several roll call studies using a variety of measurement approaches over the years (Clausen 1967, 1973; Asher and Weisberg 1978; Stone 1982; Kingdon 1989, 274–78; Poole and Rosenthal 1997).

Scholars also applied sociological theories to congressional organization and behavior. Donald R. Matthews described the "folkways" of the U.S. Senate and the processes by which its members became socialized into the role expectations of senators (Matthews 1959, 1960; see also Huitt 1957). Roger Davidson studied the forces shaping the role orientations of House members (Davidson 1969). Richard Fenno and John Manley approached the House Appropriations and Ways and Means committees, respectively, as social systems within which leaders and followers interact according to socialized roles (Fenno 1962, 1966; Manley 1965, 1969, 1970; see also Huitt 1954). Studies of the seniority system generally placed more emphasis on the institutional functions it served than on its political consequences (Goodwin 1959; Polsby 1968;

Polsby, Gallaher, and Rundquist 1969; Hinckley 1971). Arguably, southern Democrats' longevity of service and their distinct policy preferences gave shape to the congressional norms and roles that these studies documented. Though a close reading of most of these works would support such an inference, it was not their central concern.

Congressional scholars did frequently note the ability of southerners to thwart liberal policy initiatives through a conservative coalition with Republicans, whether in committee or on the floor, and by using the seniority advantages they accrued by holding safe Democratic seats. A few works on the role of Congress in the political system regarded it as a central feature of American politics. James MacGregor Burns's *The Deadlock of Democracy* (1963) took a dim view of the divisions within both parties, while James Burnham's *Congress and the American Tradition* (1959) portrayed them as an extension of the Madisonian design of the political system.

Roll Call Studies and the Rise of the Conservative Coalition

A pair of studies by W. Wayne Shannon marked the next major effort after V. O. Key to give sustained attention to the behavior of southern Democrats and their role in the functioning of Congress. Shannon found that the conservative coalition had evolved from an occasional alliance into a "revolt" in the southern ranks of congressional Democrats against the policy initiatives of their party. In six House sessions in the 1950s and 1960s, the conservative coalition appeared at more than double the rate that Key had observed. On votes where majorities of both southern and northern Democrats opposed a majority of Republicans, the northern Democrats were more cohesive than the southerners—a reversal of the pattern Key had reported. Southern disaffection with northern Democratic positions extended beyond civil rights issues to include social welfare and foreign policy matters as well (Shannon 1968, 1972; see also Lerche 1964; Manley 1973).

Given the stability of congressional policy attitudes revealed by Clausen (1973) and in the absence of a critical electoral realignment reshaping the congressional parties during this period (Brady 1978, 1988), what could account for the declining rates of partisanship in roll call voting from the 1950s to the 1970s? Applying Clausen's issue categories, Barbara Sinclair provided a comprehensive exploration of voting alignments in Congress from the New Deal through the 1970s. The central insight informing Sinclair's work was that the composition of the issue agenda, itself shaped by the political and policy environment, influences the policy-making alignments observed in Congress (Sinclair 1977, 1981, 1982).

Sinclair showed that agenda change contributed to the increasing split between northern and southern Democrats. Southern Democrats provided a high level of support for New Deal legislation in response to the economic crisis of the 1930s, but their support for liberal social welfare provisions started to decline by the late 1940s, after the crisis had passed. The cold war and the Vietnam conflict changed the debate over internationalism in foreign affairs, and the rise of civil rights as a legislative issue transformed the civil liberties dimension. Southern Democratic agreement with northern Democrats on these issue dimensions declined precipitously during the 1950s and 1960s (Sinclair 1977, 1981, 1982).

Through the early 1960s southern Democrats continued to vote similarly to northern Democrats on the issue dimension that Clausen labeled "government management," which can best be described as the replacement of private with public discretion in the deployment of productive economic resources, typically through public works spending or business regulation. Even here, however, the degree of liberalism displayed by southern Democrats declined precipitously in the late 1960s and early 1970s. Until the 1960s growth-oriented policies dominated the economic agenda; during the 1960s the agenda shifted toward greater emphasis on regulation and limitation of business activities in the interest of consumer and environmental protection and energy conservation. By the early 1970s southern Democrats' liberal support scores on government management issues were not much higher than their scores on civil liberties issues (Sinclair 1981, 1982).

Whereas Sinclair's work took a global view of congressional voting alignments, David Brady and Charles Bullock specifically examined the conservative coalition between southern Democrats and Republicans in the House of Representatives. Using Clausen's validation techniques, they identified labor and social welfare as two issue dimensions around which the conservative coalition tended to form in the late 1930s and 1940s. In the 1950s those concerns were joined by civil liberties and foreign affairs as persisting dimensions of conservative coalition voting (Brady and Bullock 1980, 1981). Other studies of regional, partisan, and ideological coalitions in Congress include Schneider (1979) and Shaffer

(1980, 1982, 1987). Mack C. Shelley's study of the conservative coalition is notable for its extensive time series data on conservative coalition appearances and victories from 1933 to 1980 (Shelley 1983).

It is notable that the roll call studies that followed Clausen's approach did not emphasize the centrality of race to southern Democratic conservatism as Key and Shannon had. Civil rights issues were seldom the subject of floor votes, and they were subsumed under civil liberties in Clausen's classification. Studies that adopted Clausen's categories, as Sinclair's did, thus did not treat civil rights as a distinct issue dimension. Brady and Bullock did not find civil rights an enduring dimension among conservative coalition votes because federal civil rights legislation did not typically draw the Republicans into a conservative coalition with southern Democrats until the mid-1960s. Until then southern Democrats had generally stood alone against majorities of both northern Democrats and Republicans, but in the mid-1960s northern Republicans began voting with southern Democrats to weaken civil rights measures at the amendment stage (Black 1979).

Rational Theories and the Resurgence of Partisanship

The rise of the conservative coalition was associated with the decline of partisanship as a predictor of congressional behavior. Many studies documented this decline, and several of these explained it in relation to the decentralization of Congress and the decline of parties as electoral institutions over the course of the twentieth century (Brady, Cooper, and Hurley 1979; Collie and Brady 1985). Scholars became much less interested in the study of congressional party leadership, which now seemed relatively inconsequential to policy outcomes.

At the same time, rational approaches adapted from economics began to influence thinking about Congress. David Mayhew was explicit about the shift from sociological to economic theorizing. He argued that all the institutional arrangements in Congress, including party leadership roles and the functioning of the committee system, could be explained entirely in terms of their utility in promoting the reelection interests of individual members (Mayhew 1974). Rational approaches thus saw individual goals driving collective behavior. Congressional organization came to be explained as a means for distributing electorally useful benefits to members. In these distributive theories, the committee system and its associated norms of reciprocity and universalism were mechanisms to promote efficient logrolling among members with salient interests in different policy domains (Shepsle 1979; Weingast 1979).

This emerging rational perspective very likely influenced many congressional scholars' analyses of the probable impacts of the House reforms implemented by the Democratic caucus in the early 1970s. Representative Richard Bolling (D-Missouri), a member of the Rules Committee, detailed a central purpose of the reforms in *House Out of Order* (1966): to make committees more responsive to a majority of the party caucus. The changes would also empower the party leadership to move policy in a direction favored by a majority of the caucus. After the reforms were put into place in 1971–75, congressional observers made much of the reforms' tendency toward further decentralization of the House. Committee majorities and subcommittees were empowered at the expense of committee chairs, and so legislative power devolved to a larger number of representatives. Centralizing reforms, such as the election of committee chairs by the party caucus, caucus ratification of nominations by the Speaker to fill Democratic seats on the Rules Committee, and the shift of committee assignment functions from the Democrats on Ways and Means to the Democratic Steering and Policy Committee, received less attention and were regarded as insufficient to counter the decentralizing forces (see, for example, Waldman 1980; Davidson 1981; Dodd and Oppenheimer 1981; Reiselbach 1986; see Rohde 1991a for a fuller discussion).

Counter to these expectations, the Democratic leadership in the House became progressively more active in controlling floor amendments by crafting special rules, using an expanded whip system to mobilize votes, and setting a policy agenda for the majority to pursue. Several studies by Barbara Sinclair documented this increased leadership activity and its role in shaping policy agendas and outcomes. Sinclair linked this trend to concern among Democratic caucus members about the effects of excessive individual activism on public policy, the need to respond to the aggressive Republican agenda under President Ronald Reagan, and the election of a larger proportion of national Democrats from southern constituencies (Sinclair 1983, 1989, 1995).

Rational approaches to Congress provided divergent explanations of the changing landscape. Gary Cox and Matthew McCubbins explained that the House majority party constitutes a "legislative cartel" in its control of the rules and delegation of authority to committees. Since the maintenance of the cartel is to the advantage of all its members, an empowered party leadership is a fixed feature of congressional organization. Party leaders are to use their discretion to enhance the party's reputation, which is always in the electoral best interest of all members of the party. The range of issues on which the party exerts leadership thus depends on the interests of the caucus members, but party leaders are always exerting some influence (Cox and McCubbins 1993). Keith Krehbiel, on the other hand, regarded the congressional parties as having no real impact; he argued that partisan outcomes simply reflect the level of within-party agreement and cross-party difference in members' policy preferences and that such outcomes can be predicted without any reference to the legislative party organizations (Krehbiel 1991, 1993).

Neither Krehbiel's nor Cox and McCubbins's approach incorporated the *sources* of preference heterogeneity within and between the parties in their explanations of partisan behavior. Thus, neither could have been used to *predict* the resurgence of partisanship. In contrast, explaining the sources of member preferences was a central concern of David W. Rohde's "conditional party government" theory. The degree of similarity among the constituencies represented by members of the same party was at the core of the theory's explanation of variations in congressional partisanship. The approach provided an analytical framework for addressing the interaction of constituency change and institutional arrangements. Since change in the behavior of southern Democrats figured so prominently in the resurgence of partisanship, conditional party government directed the attention of congressional scholarship to the electoral dynamics of the South. This distinguished Rohde's approach from practically all previous theoretical treatments of congressional behavior.

The Southern Transformation of Congressional Politics

Well before congressional scholars grappled with the resurgence of partisanship, Jack Bass and Walter DeVries had already noted that changes in the South and in Congress had reduced the conservatism of southern Democrats by the mid-1970s. Retirements in both chambers, coupled with the reformers' attack on the seniority system in the House, reduced the influence of southern Democrats in the committee system. At the same time, southern Democrats first elected in 1966 and after that compiled higher party unity scores than previous cohorts, whereas newer cohorts of southern Republicans amassed the most conservative voting

records in Congress. On the basis of interviews with members, Bass and
DeVries linked the new moderation among southern Democrats to the
expansion of the black electorate after the Voting Rights Act of 1965 and
the removal of segregation from the political agenda because of the successes of the civil rights movement (Bass and DeVries 1976).

The full implications for Congress of the transformation of southern politics did not come to fruition until the late 1980s. At that point
the resurgence of partisanship demanded explanation by congressional
scholars. Among the theories offered, it was David Rohde's model of
conditional party government that linked the congressional party resurgence to regional political change of the sort that Bass and DeVries had
outlined over a decade before.

Rohde's approach highlighted both members' policy preferences
and the actions of party leadership in explaining the role of parties in the
postreform House. If a high level of agreement on policy preferences
exists within the parties (especially the majority party) and if the level
of disagreement between the parties is also high, then the necessary
conditions exist for party government—the empowerment by caucus
members of their party leaders for the purpose of pursuing legislative
outcomes on which there is general agreement within the caucus. This
theory of conditional party government directs the attention of congressional scholars to both the level of policy agreement within the majority
party and the role of party leadership in guiding the legislative process
(Rohde 1991a).

Having identified increased similarity of policy preferences among
Democrats as a necessary condition for the resurgence of party leadership, Rohde argued that the similarity of preferences among party members is constrained by the degree of similarity among their constituencies.
Resurgent partisanship was thus rooted in constituency change, and the
most dramatic changes had occurred in the South. Building on the work
of Morris Fiorina (1974) and Richard Fenno (1978), Rohde emphasized
the role of electorally supportive subsets of the constituency in defining
each member's policy preferences. Though the mobilization of African
American voters and the growth of urban influence in southern House
districts profoundly changed southern congressional constituencies, the
rise of Republican electoral competition was crucial in reshaping the
primary and general election constituencies of southern Democrats. As
Republican candidates drew more support from conservatives, southern
Democrats retained supportive coalitions of blacks and relatively liberal

whites as their core constituents. The result was that southern Democrats now represented constituency preferences that were more similar than before to those of northern Democrats (Rohde 1991a, 1991b). Increased electoral competition also reduced southerners' ability to accrue seniority advantages, which in turn eroded their influence in the committee system (see Black and Black 1990).

In the most extensive use of survey data to test Rohde's theory, Stanley Berard reported that the reelection constituents of southern Democratic representatives—constituents who voted Democratic in congressional elections—were indistinguishable from Republican reelection constituents on a range of issues in the late 1960s and early 1970s. By the 1990s southern Democratic reelection constituents had moved to a position closer to northern Democrats than Republicans on economic issues, apparently the result of a shift in southern conservative support from Democratic to Republican congressional candidates. On civil rights and on cultural issues such as abortion and school prayer, however, southern Democratic reelection constituents continued to be closer to Republican reelection constituents than to northern Democrats. Southern Democratic representatives exhibited greater partisanship over time, but their rate of party support was higher on roll calls concerning economic issues than social issues, which is consistent with Rohde's emphasis on the conditional nature of partisanship. This pattern continued after the rise of the Republican congressional majority in the 1994 election (Berard 2001).

It was also the case that, even as they exhibited more partisan behavior on economic than moral or cultural issues, southern Democrats did move closer to the northern Democratic position on several issues on which there was little convergence between southern and northern Democratic reelection constituents. On some issues, such as abortion and civil rights, many southern Democrats appeared to cast votes in response to likely primary constituencies rather than simply represent the typical views of their reelection constituents (ibid.).

Tracking the effects on congressional partisanship of changing southern electoral coalitions sheds light on the manner in which electoral change influences congressional policy change. Members of Congress display a high degree of consistency in roll call voting over the course of their careers (Clausen 1973; Asher and Weisberg 1978; Stone 1982; Kingdon 1989; Poole and Rosenthal 1997). In a party realignment that is associated with a single critical election—where one or more social groups switch party allegiance and a new majority party takes control of Congress—it is new members who infuse Congress with new definitions of the policy stands that distinguish the parties (Brady 1978, 1988). The southern congressional realignment was not associated with a single critical election, however. Several studies addressed the question of whether the increasing partisanship of southern Democrats was due to the replacement of old cohorts by new members or to adjustment by returning members to the changing composition of their constituencies (Bullock 1981, 1985; Shaffer 1987; Rohde 1989; Whitby and Gilliam 1991; Hood and Morris 1998; Hood, Kidd, and Morris 1999; Berard 2001). The overall result of these studies is that both member replacement and adjustment have a role in translating electoral change into congressional policy deliberation.

It would be appropriate to study the relative contributions of member replacement and adjustment to the rise of conservative coalition support among southern Democrats in the 1960s. William C. Havard's edited volume *The Changing Politics of the South* (1972), as well as Numan Bartley and Hugh Graham (1975) and Earl Black and Merle Black (2002), provides extensive details of southern House and Senate elections that pitted supporters and opponents of the national Democratic Party against one another in party primaries during the 1950s and 1960s. In these contests national Democrats were frequently portrayed by their opponents as racial liberals and opponents of segregation. The replacement of arguably liberal members by conservatives in Democratic primaries as well as adjustment by old New Dealers to the rise of race as an issue in southern campaigns both appear to have contributed to the decline of partisanship among southern Democrats during these decades.

The role of the South in the partisan resurgence sheds light on yet another general question. If constituency forces drive congressional partisanship, do institutional arrangements or party leadership make any independent contribution? Rohde had argued that legislative party members in substantial agreement on a salient policy dimension (and facing opposition from outside the party) were likely to empower party leaders to enforce the party's collective interests. John Aldrich added the observation that in a situation where members' preferences are ordered on multiple dimensions, enforcement of the members' collective interests on a primary dimension would entail discouraging members from defecting to pursue their favored outcomes on secondary dimensions. With caucus support, party leaders can use some combination of sanctions and agenda manipulation to promote the collective policy interests of caucus members (Aldrich 1995).

Research on southern Democrats underscores the relevance of multiple issue dimensions and party leadership activities to understanding the role of the South in the partisan resurgence. Most notable were Nicol C. Rae's interviews with southern Democratic representatives and senators. Rae found that the southerners identified most closely with the national Democrats on economic and civil rights issues and were far less comfortable with their party caucus on moral and cultural issues (Rae 1994). See also Rohde (1993, 1994) on the persisting North-South differences among House Democrats on defense policy in the 1980s. At the same time, southern Democrats routinely admitted to helping the leadership on some legislation in recognition of the caucus's role in assigning chairmanships (Rae 1994). David Rohde also documented southern Democrats' responsiveness to efforts by party leaders to provide both rewards and cover for members who took electoral risks to support party positions (Rohde 1991a). Thus, both constituency forces and institutional arrangements shaped the resurgence of partisanship in Congress.

The Republican Era in Southern Congressional Politics

The elections of the early 1990s established a new era for the role of the South in Congress. Election outcomes and party switches transformed what had been a 77–39 Democratic advantage in the southern House delegation after the 1990 elections into a 71–54 Republican advantage after the 1996 elections. A net gain of 16 seats in 1994 gave the Republicans a majority of southern House seats for the first time since Reconstruction, and it gave them control of the House of Representatives for the first time in forty years. Net losses outside the South in 1996 and 1998 meant that Republicans' control of the House was increasingly dependent on their southern majority.

A similar transition occurred in the Senate. Republicans had held as many as half the South's Senate seats in the early 1980s, but their loss of four seats in 1986 reversed these gains. The 1994 elections gave Republicans a majority of the southern Senate delegation for the first time since Reconstruction, a majority they have held ever since. The 50–50 Senate deadlock after 2000 and the 51–49 Republican majority after 2002 resulted from a four-seat Republican majority in the South.

The most comprehensive assessment of the rise of southern con-

gressional Republicans is *The Rise of Southern Republicans,* by Earl
Black and Merle Black (2002). Their analysis traces the ideological realignment of southern whites' presidential voting and party loyalties and
links it to the emergence of Republican opportunities in House and Senate elections. Several factors combined in some measure to produce the
new partisan balance: the emergence of strong Republican candidates,
the ability to link Democratic candidates to President Bill Clinton (who
was especially unpopular in the region in 1994), and the effects of majority-
minority districting on the composition of congressional constituencies
(see also Hill and Rae 2000).

In addition to describing the historical bases of the Republican surge,
Black and Black provide a framework for understanding how the new
electoral dynamics of the South influence the character of southern representation in Congress. The "newest southern congressional politics"
produces three basic types of representation rooted in three distinct reelection constituencies. Under the "rule of black majorities," majority-
minority districts elect African American Democrats who display high
rates of party support in roll call voting. Under the "rule of white majorities," white voters control the election outcome and send Republicans
to Congress who also have high party support scores. Under the "rule
of biracial coalitions," overwhelming African American support and a
substantial minority of the white vote combine to elect white Democrats
who are generally moderate in their party voting and have a far wider
dispersion of party unity scores than either black Democrats or (white)
Republicans. Although majorities of southern whites normally can be
counted on to vote Republican in congressional elections, biracial coalitions are possible because the party loyalties and voting tendencies of
whites are divided along lines of income, religious conservatism, and
gender (Black and Black 2002, 244–56, 382–90).

Of these three reelection constituencies, the rule of biracial coalitions and the rule of black majorities have been studied extensively with
regard to their implications for congressional behavior. Our understanding is clearest with respect to the dynamics of biracial coalitions, which
dominated the southern congressional delegation during the partisan resurgence of the 1980s. Alexander Lamis in *The Two-Party South* (1984)
clearly articulated the importance of the black-white coalition to the
election of Democrats in the post–civil rights South and emphasized the
difficulty of straddling the ideological diversity of this coalition. White
and black southerners are similarly conservative on many social issues,

and white attitudes on economic issues tend to be more liberal at lower levels of income. Still, the gulf between African Americans and working-class whites on economic and racial issues tends to be greater than the difference between working-class and other whites on these matters (Lamis 1984; Black and Black 1987, 2002).

In Congress southern Democrats represent biracial reelection constituencies by taking a mix of partisan and conservative positions on different issues, by demonstrating their ties to conservative groups such as the "blue dog" Democratic-Republican congressional coalition, and by concentrating much of their legislative work on district issues. (On roll call voting across issues, see especially Rhode 1991a and Berard 2001.) Their behavior in Washington is closely related to their electoral strategies and their "presentation of self," to use Fenno's (1978) term, back home in the district. In case studies of five congressional campaigns in fairly rural districts during the 1980s, James Glaser (1996) demonstrated how white southern Democrats built winning coalitions by targeting different parts of their campaign message to white and black constituents. Glaser observed that the size of the potential African American vote, along with the historic association of black population with white conservatism in the rural South, established a variety of constraints and opportunities for southern Democrats to build and represent biracial electoral majorities.

The Representation of African Americans

By contrast with the representation of biracial coalitions, there has been less scholarly consensus on the implications of majority-minority districts for the representation of minority interests in Congress (see Richard Engstrom's detailed exploration of this topic in chapter 4 of this volume). Given the relatively large number of majority-minority districts created in the South during the 1990 round of redistricting, this question is crucial for understanding how the South is represented in Congress. Works by David Lublin and D. Stephen Voss in particular have focused on the net change in likely policy outcomes in the House resulting from majority-minority districting. On the one hand, African American representatives provide more liberal representation than do white southern Democrats, as measured by various roll call voting scores. On the other hand, the creation of majority-minority districts to elect African Americans deprives other districts of liberal voters. By removing African Americans

from surrounding districts, majority-minority districts potentially reduce
the attentiveness of white southern Democrats to black concerns. They
almost certainly enhance the prospects of Republican election victories.
Since roll call liberalism among white representatives increases with the
black share of district population, some studies indicate that the creation
of a larger number of "black-influence" districts at something less than
50 percent black would maximize the representation of African American
interests in Congress (Cameron, Epstein, and O'Halloran 1996; Lublin
1997; Epstein and O'Halloran 1999; Lublin and Voss 2000).

Several recent works go beyond roll call voting to examine other
representational behaviors, both in Washington and in the district. Carol
Swain pioneered this work with her case studies of white and black representatives from majority-minority districts (Swain 1993). Most work
that extends its vision to behavior off the floor, however, has called into
some question one of Swain's essential findings—that white liberals can
represent black interests as well as blacks can. Richard Fenno's study
of the representational style of four African American representatives
emphasizes the importance of their symbolic and organizational connections to blacks in their districts, connections that white representatives
would have great difficulty achieving (Fenno 2003).

David Canon (1999) studied African American representatives across
a range of legislative behaviors: roll call voting, bill sponsorship and co-
sponsorship, committee assignments, content of speeches and news-
letters, placement of district offices and staff, and coverage in black
newspapers. Black representatives showed greater attentiveness to black
constituent needs and to issues with a racial component than did white
representatives. White liberals cast votes similar to African Americans',
but nonracial issues dominated whites' other legislative activities.

Canon's most fundamental contribution was to our understanding of
representation under the rule of black majorities. African American politicians take a variety of approaches to representation. Applying developments in contemporary political theory to this variation, Canon noted
that some black politicians search for commonality across the racial divide in representing their constituents, whereas others seek to represent
difference. The commonality approach places priority on finding ways
to represent as many different constituencies as possible; the difference
approach focuses more exclusively on asserting the interests of black
constituents. The dynamics of Democratic primaries determine which
type of representation a majority-black district will receive. White voters

are in a position to tilt the outcome in favor of a candidate who pursues the politics of commonality. If a white candidate is in the primary field, however, the outcome is likely to favor a difference candidate (Canon 1999).

Katherine Tate's recent contribution to this literature is also notable. Her analysis was based on survey responses from the National Black Election Study and roll call voting data from the 104th Congress. She found that descriptive representation mattered to black constituents in their evaluation of representatives, but it did not result in precise congruence between black constituency opinion and roll call voting across all issue areas (Tate 2003). This finding echoes the variation across issue areas in the congruence between southern Democrats and their reelection constituents (Berard 2001), and it raises the question of the conditions under which African American representatives will be responsive to different subconstituencies or to partisan and organizational imperatives within Congress.

Representation by Republicans

The content and style of Republican representation has been the least carefully studied of the three broad types extant in southern congressional politics today. The rise of southern Republicans has exacerbated the partisan split in Congress by reducing the number of moderate Democrats while adding distinctly conservative members to the Republican caucus. Observers generally acknowledge also that southern Republicans provide uniformly conservative representation for their constituents. By various measures, their roll call voting is consistently the most conservative of any group in Congress, and the degree of variation in their party support scores is the smallest among any group of southern representatives (Black 1998, 605–7; Black and Black 2002, 382–90).

The conclusion of conservative Republican uniformity originates almost entirely in observation of the roll call voting record. Such uniformity is striking in view of the degree of diversity exhibited by Republican representatives. As a group Republican constituencies are the least diverse in the South, but in representing more than 60 percent of southern congressional districts, Republicans necessarily represent a greater range of constituency variation than they did before 1994. In their geographic constituencies, white majority districts vary in their urban, suburban, or rural character, in their economic characteristics, and in the role of minorities in politics. In their reelection constituencies, Republicans represent both economic and social conservatives, groups that do not always agree on issue priorities (Aistrup 1996, 143–66; Schneider 1998). The hypothesis that member behavior will reflect such diversity is worthy of exploration. If Republican roll call voting is highly uniform, perhaps other dimensions of representation will show more variation.

Studies of representation that rely on aggregated voting scores have limited usefulness in examining the question of how southern Republicans represent their constituencies. Keith Poole and Richard Rosenthal's excellent work has established that in the 1990s congressional roll call voting became polarized along a single liberal-conservative dimension to a greater degree than at any time since the 1890s and that a single dimension dominates most of the history of congressional roll call voting (Poole and Rosenthal 1997). Still, studies of roll call voting by African American (Tate 2003) and southern Democratic (Berard 2001) representatives reveal the gains to be made by examining variations in behavior across issue areas. Additionally, roll call voting is arguably only the final stage of a process that translates multidimensional constituency preferences into a revealed placement on this single voting dimension (Talbert and Potoski 2002). Richard Hall's analysis of member participation in committee work emphasizes the choices members make among competing issue priorities in allocating scarce time and staff resources (Hall 1995).

Are there variations in southern Republican representation in the "pre-floor" stages of representation? David Canon's study of African American representation provides a model for investigating this question, as does Wendy Schiller's study of U.S. Senate delegations. Schiller relied on a wide range of data, including roll call votes, committee assignments, bill sponsorships and cosponsorships, local media coverage, and campaign contributions, to address the representational agendas of pairs of U.S. senators from the same state. She found that same-state senators represent different policy agendas, have distinct reputations in the local media, and have different supportive constituencies, even when the senators are of the same party. Schiller explains that same-state senators have an incentive to establish distinct identities and electoral bases. Pairs of senators end up thereby representing the multidimensional interests of their state electorates (Schiller 2000). Schiller's work provides an approach for examining variations in the representation offered not only by pairs of southern senators, but also by sets of representatives—for instance, southern Republicans—who hail from constituencies that are deemed to be almost identical with regard to important constituency characteristics.

Richard Fenno has provided theoretical grounding on which to base expectations about variations in representational strategy. Building on his previous work (Fenno 1978, 1996), he has observed that legislators pursue representational strategies that are mixtures in some degree of two base strategies: a person-intensive strategy that emphasizes the representative's personal connections to constituents and a policy-intensive strategy that emphasizes the representative's involvement in policy making. The constituency context is one important factor shaping the member's representational strategy. In *Congress at the Grassroots* Fenno observed that the Georgia congressional district represented by Mac Collins, a Republican, in the 1990s had become less conducive to the person-intensive representational style that had been exhibited by Jack Flynt, the southern Democrat whom Collins succeeded and who had represented the district for about two decades. Rapid population growth and suburbanization reduced the viability of a person-intensive strategy and made a policy-intensive strategy more appropriate (Fenno 2000).

Collectively, the work of Canon, Schiller, and Fenno suggests avenues for studying variation in how the three broad types of southern constituencies—black majorities, white majorities, and biracial majorities—are represented. Following their example shows promise of deepening our understanding of representation. Such work would also demonstrate whether and how variations in southern politics continue to reflect themselves in Washington.

The South and Congressional Leadership

The Republican revolution in the South not only transformed how the South is represented in Washington; it also shifted partisan control of Congress from a liberal party in which moderate and conservative southerners were a deviant minority to a conservative party in which southerners arguably set the ideological tone. Black and Black note two important implications for congressional politics. One is that the rise of southern Republicans has made the contest for partisan control of Congress far more competitive than it was under most of the post–World War II era, especially in the House. Because Democrats will retain a secure base in the southern electorate for some time to come, Republicans will never have the sort of majority in the South that the Democrats had in the era of the Solid South. In addition, Republican seat gains in the South have tended to be partially offset by Democratic gains outside the South since the mid-1990s (Black and Black 2002).

The second implication of the rise of southern Republicans is its effect on the character of the Republican congressional party and its leadership. The South's role in the new Republican majority placed Senators Trent Lott (R-Mississippi) and Bill Frist (R-Tennessee) in the role of majority leader and gave southerners such as Phil Gramm (R-Texas) and Jesse Helms (R-North Carolina) important roles in specific policy areas. The impact on House leadership was even more striking. Republicans selected three southerners—Newt Gingrich (R-Georgia), Richard Armey (R-Texas), and Tom DeLay (R-Texas)—to hold the top three party leadership positions when they took control of the House after the 1994 elections.

The rise of southern Republican leadership gave rise to explanations of its significance. Black and Black observed that the House leadership of the 1990s was "far too southern, far too conservative, and, indeed, far too *southern conservative* to serve as a unifying force in the nation" (Black and Black 2002, 395–96, emphasis in original). Drawing on his study of the freshman class in the 104th Congress, Nicol Rae reported that southerners were a driving force in the policy direction taken by the Republican House leadership after the 1994 election. The southern ascendance ultimately produced tensions within the party between conservative purists and more electorally vulnerable nonsouthern moderates (Rae 1998, 2001).

Rae's observation that the Republican Party had become a "southern white conservative party" (2001, 149) emphasizes the continuing importance of southern distinctiveness in Congress. On the other hand, Ronald M. Peters has observed that the region was largely irrelevant in selecting Republican leaders in the 1990s. Southerners captured most of the Republican leadership positions, but they did so by winning contested elections in the conference for which they built coalitions across regional lines. Nonsouthern conservatives apparently viewed their own interests as fully consistent with southern leadership. By contrast, under Democratic control from the late 1930s to the late 1980s, both North and South had always been represented in party leadership in a carefully crafted balance that was necessary for satisfying all elements of the party caucus (Peters 2001).

In view of the decline of regional differences and the increased cohesion within both parties, Peters foresees that party leaders will no longer take distinct regional perspectives and that "the study of southern House leaders will merge into the topic of House leadership in general" (ibid., 132). Yet for Rae southern leadership helped redefine the Republican Party in Congress: the rise of southern Republicans cast conservatism in a southern mold. This impact might well be comparable to the impact southern Democrats were said to have on congressional norms and rules in the middle of the twentieth century. It is a comparison worth considering.

Conclusion

Two critical points helped define the literature addressing the South in Congress after the Second World War. In the quest for general theories that could explain congressional behavior, political scientists of both behavioral and rational bents gave insufficient theoretical weight to the importance of the South in shaping congressional norms and coalitions. It was only the resurgence of partisanship in the 1980s that brought theoretical scholarship on Congress to confront the centrality of the South. The Republican revolution of 1994 highlighted the importance of the South to the evolution of congressional politics, but it also eventually increased speculation that the South had now "nationalized" and no longer needed to be considered as a distinctive political region in understanding congressional politics.

This last assumption would divert scholarly attention from several promising lines of inquiry, especially regarding the relationship between representatives and their constituents and the integration of diverse constituencies into congressional party leadership. The particular mix of constituency perspectives offered by "the newest southern politics" gives a measure of diversity to both the Republican caucus and the Congressional Black Caucus, even if that diversity does not show itself clearly in aggregated roll call votes. The prospect that biracial coalitions will continue to provide a base for electing some number of white southern Democrats has implications not only for the diversity of representation in Congress but also for partisan control. Understanding southern politics continues to be an essential element of anticipating and explaining change in Congress.

References

Aistrup, Joseph A. 1996. *The Southern Strategy Revisited: Republican Top-Down Advancement in the South*. Lexington: University Press of Kentucky.

Aldrich, John. 1995. *Why Parties? The Origin and Transformation of Political Parties in America*. Chicago: University of Chicago Press.

American Political Science Association, Committee on Political Parties. 1950. "Toward a More Responsible Two-Party System." *American Political Science Review* 44:3 (supplement).

Asher, Herbert B., and Weisberg, Herbert F. 1978. "Voting Change in Congress: Some Dynamic Perspectives on an Evolutionary Process." *American Journal of Political Science* 22: 391–425.

Bartley, Numan V., and Hugh D. Graham. 1975. *Southern Politics and the Second Reconstruction*. Baltimore: Johns Hopkins University Press.

Bass, Jack, and Walter DeVries. 1976. *The Transformation of Southern Politics: Social Change and Political Consequence since 1945*. New York: Basic Books.

Berard, Stanley P. 2001. *Southern Democrats in the U.S. House of Representatives*. Congressional Studies Series, vol. 2. Norman: University of Oklahoma Press.

Black, Earl. 1998. "The Newest Southern Politics." *Journal of Politics* 60: 591–612.

Black, Earl, and Merle Black. 1987. *Politics and Society in the South*. Cambridge: Harvard University Press.

———. 2002. *The Rise of Southern Republicans*. Cambridge: Harvard University Press.

Black, Merle. 1979. "Regional and Partisan Bases of Congressional Support for the Changing Agenda of Civil Rights Legislation." *Journal of Politics* 41: 665–79.

Black, Merle, and Earl Black. 1990. "The South in the Senate: Changing Patterns of Representation on Committees." In *The Disappearing South? Studies in Regional Change and Continuity*, ed. Robert P. Steed, Laurence W. Moreland, and Tod A. Baker. Tuscaloosa: University of Alabama Press.

Bolling, Richard. 1966. *House Out of Order*. New York: Dutton.

Bone, Hugh A. 1956. "An Introduction to the Senate Policy Committees." *American Political Science Review* 50: 339–59.

Brady, David W. 1978. "Critical Elections, Congressional Parties, and Clusters of Policy Change." *British Journal of Political Science* 8: 79–99.

———. 1988. *Critical Elections and Congressional Policy Making*. Palo Alto: Stanford University Press.

Brady, David W., and Charles S. Bullock III. 1980. "Is There a Conservative Coalition in the House?" *Journal of Politics* 42: 549–59.

———. 1981, 2nd ed. "Coalition Politics in the House of Representatives." In *Congress Reconsidered*, ed. Lawrence C. Dodd and Bruce I. Oppenheimer. Washington, D.C.: Congressional Quarterly Press.

Brady, David W., Joseph Cooper, and Patricia A. Hurley. 1979. "The Decline of Party in the U.S. House of Representatives, 1887–1968." *Legislative Studies Quarterly* 4: 381–407.

Bullock, Charles S., III. 1981. "Congressional Voting and the Mobilization of a Black Electorate in the South." *Journal of Politics* 43: 662–82.

———. 1985. "Congressional Roll Call Voting in a Two-Party South." *Social Science Quarterly* 66: 789–804.

Burnham, James. 1959. *Congress and the American Tradition*. Chicago: H. Regnery.

Burns, James MacGregor. 1963. *The Deadlock of Democracy*. Englewood Cliffs, N.J.: Prentice-Hall.

Cameron, Charles, David Epstein, and Sharyn O'Halloran. 1996. "Do Majority-Minority Districts Maximize Substantive Black Representation in Congress?" *American Political Science Review* 90: 794–812.

Canon, David T. 1999. *Race, Redistricting, and Representation: The Unintended Consequences of Black Majority Districts*. Chicago: University of Chicago Press.

Clausen, Aage R. 1967. "Measurement Identity in the Longitudinal Analysis of Legislative Behavior." *American Political Science Review* 61: 1020–35.

———. 1973. *How Congressmen Decide: A Policy Focus*. New York: St. Martin's Press.

Collie, Melissa P., and David W. Brady. 1985, 3rd ed. "The Decline of Partisan Voting Coalitions in the House of Representatives." In *Congress Reconsidered*, ed. Lawrence C. Dodd and Bruce I. Oppenheimer. Washington, D.C.: Congressional Quarterly Press.

Cosman, Bernard. 1967. "Republicanism in the South: Goldwater's Impact upon Voter Alignment in Congressional, Gubernatorial, and Senatorial Races." *Southwest Social Science Quarterly* 48: 13–23.

Cox, Gary W., and Mathew D. McCubbins. 1993. *Legislative Leviathan: Party Government in the House*. Berkeley: University of California Press.

Davidson, Roger H. 1969. *The Role of the Congressman*. New York: Pegasus.

———. 1981. "Subcommittee Government: New Channels for Policy Making." In *The New Congress*, ed. Thomas E. Mann and Norman J. Ornstein. Washington, D.C.: American Enterprise Institute.

Dodd, Lawrence, and Bruce I. Oppenheimer. 1981, 2nd ed. "The House in Transition: Change and Consolidation." In *Congress Reconsidered*, ed. Lawrence C. Dodd and Bruce I. Oppenheimer. Washington, D.C.: Congressional Quarterly Press.

Epstein, David, and Sharyn O'Halloran. 1999. "Measuring the Electoral and Policy Impact of Majority-Minority Voting Districts: Candidates of Choice, Equal Opportunity, and Representation." *American Journal of Political Science* 43: 367–95.

Fenno, Richard F. 1962. "The House Appropriations Committee as a Political System: The Problem of Integration." *American Political Science Review* 56: 310–24.

———. 1966. *The Power of the Purse: Appropriations Politics in Congress*. Boston: Little, Brown.

———. 1973. *Congressmen in Committees*. Boston: Little, Brown.

———. 1978. *Home Style: House Members and Their Districts*. Boston: Little, Brown.

———. 1996. *Senators on the Campaign Trail: The Politics of Representation.* Norman: University of Oklahoma Press

———. 2000. *Congress at the Grassroots: Representational Change in the South 1970–1988.* Chapel Hill: University of North Carolina Press.

———. 2003. *Going Home: Black Representatives and Their Constituents.* Chicago: University of Chicago Press.

Fiorina, Morris P. 1974. *Representatives, Roll Calls, and Constituencies.* Lexington, Mass.: Lexington Books.

Froman, Louis. 1963. *Congressmen and Their Constituencies.* Chicago: Rand McNally.

Froman, Louis, and Randall Ripley. 1965. "Conditions for Party Leadership: The Case of the House Democrats." *American Political Science Review* 59: 52–63.

Glaser, James M. 1996. *Race, Campaign Politics, and the Realignment in the South.* New Haven: Yale University Press.

Goodwin, George, Jr. 1959. "The Seniority System in Congress." *American Political Science Review* 53: 412–36.

Hall, Richard L. 1995. *Participation in Congress.* New Haven: Yale University Press.

Havard, William C., ed. 1972. *The Changing Politics of the South.* Baton Rouge: Louisiana State University Press.

Heard, Alexander. 1952. *A Two-Party South?* Chapel Hill: University of North Carolina Press.

Hill, Kevin A., and Nicol C. Rae. 2000. "What Happened to the Democrats in the South? U.S. House Elections, 1992–1996." *Party Politics* 6: 5–22.

Hinckley, Barbara. 1971. *The Seniority System in Congress.* Bloomington: Indiana University Press.

Hood, M. V., III, Quentin Kidd, and Irwin L. Morris. 1999. "Of Byrd[s] and Bumpers: Using Democratic Senators to Analyze Political Change in the South, 1960–1995." *American Journal of Political Science* 43: 465–87.

Hood, M. V., III, and Irwin L. Morris. 1998. "Boll Weevils and Roll Call Voting: A Study in Time and Space." *Legislative Studies Quarterly* 23: 245–69.

Huitt, Ralph. 1954. "The Congressional Committee: A Case Study." *American Political Science Review* 48: 340–65.

———. 1957. "The Morse Committee Assignment Controversy: A Study in Senate Norms." *American Political Science Review* 51: 313–29.

———. 1961. "Democratic Party Leadership in the Senate." *American Political Science Review* 55: 333–44.

Jones, Charles O. 1968a. "Joseph G. Cannon and Howard W. Smith: An Essay on the Limits of Leadership in the House of Representatives." *Journal of Politics* 30: 617–46.

———. 1968b. "The Minority Party and Policy Making in the House of Representatives." *American Political Science Review* 62: 481–93.

———. 1970. *The Minority Party in Congress.* Boston: Little, Brown.

Keech, William R. 1968. *The Impact of Negro Voting: The Role of the Vote in the Quest for Equality.* Chicago: Rand McNally.

Key, V. O., Jr. 1949. *Southern Politics in State and Nation.* New York: Knopf.

Kingdon, John W. 1989, 3rd ed. *Congressmen's Voting Decisions*. Ann Arbor: University of Michigan Press.

Krehbiel, Keith. 1991. *Information and Legislative Organization*. Ann Arbor: University of Michigan Press.

———. 1993. "Where's the Party?" *British Journal of Political Science* 23: 235–66.

Lamis, Alexander P. 1984. *The Two-Party South*. New York: Oxford University Press.

Lerche, Charles O. 1964. *The Uncertain South*. Chicago: Quadrangle Books.

Lublin, David. 1997. *The Paradox of Representation: Racial Gerrymandering and Minority Interests in Congress*. Princeton: Princeton University Press.

Lublin, David, and D. Stephen Voss. 2000. "Boll-Weevil Blues: Polarized Congressional Delegations into the 21st Century." *American Review of Politics* 21: 427–50.

MacRae, Duncan, Jr. 1958. *Dimensions of Congressional Voting*. Berkeley: University of California Press.

Manley, John F. 1965. "The House Committee on Ways and Means: Conflict Management on a Congressional Committee." *American Political Science Review* 59: 927–59.

———. 1969. "Wilbur D. Mills: A Study in Congressional Influence." *American Political Science Review* 63: 442–64.

———. 1970. *The Politics of Finance: The House Committee on Ways and Means*. Boston: Little, Brown.

———. 1973. "The Conservative Coalition." *American Behavioral Scientist* 17: 223–47.

Masters, Nicholas A. 1961. "Committee Assignments in the House of Representatives." *American Political Science Review* 55: 345–57.

Matthews, Donald R. 1959. "The Folkways of the United States Senate: Conformity to Group Norms and Legislative Effectiveness." *American Political Science Review* 53: 1064–89.

———. 1960. *United States Senators and Their World*. Chapel Hill: University of North Carolina Press.

Matthews, Donald R., and James W. Prothro. 1966. *Negroes and the New Southern Politics*. New York: Harcourt, Brace and World.

Mayhew, David R. 1966. *Party Loyalty among Congressmen: The Difference between Democrats and Republicans*. Cambridge: Harvard University Press.

———. 1974. *Congress: The Electoral Connection*. New Haven: Yale University Press.

Peabody, Robert L. 1967. "Party Leadership Change in the United States House of Representatives." *American Political Science Review* 61: 675–93.

Peters, Ronald M., Jr. 2001. "Southern Party Leaders in the Postreform House." In *Eye of the Storm: The South and Congress in an Era of Change*, ed. John C. Kuzenski, Laurence W. Moreland, and Robert P. Steed. Westport, Conn.: Praeger.

Polsby, Nelson W. 1968. "The Institutionalization of the House of Representatives." *American Political Science Review* 62: 144–68.

Polsby, Nelson W., Miriam Gallaher, and Barry S. Rundquist. 1969. "The Growth of the Seniority System in the U.S. House of Representatives." *American Political Science Review* 63: 787–807.

Poole, Keith T., and Howard Rosenthal. 1997. *Congress: A Political-Economic History of Roll Call Voting.* New York: Oxford University Press.

Rae, Nicol C. 1994. *Southern Democrats.* New York: Oxford University Press.

———. 1998. *Conservative Reformers: The Republican Freshmen and the Lessons of the 104th Congress.* Armonk, N.Y.: M. E. Sharpe.

———. 2001. "The Conscience of the Revolution: Southern Influence in the House Republican 'Class of 1994.'" In *Eye of the Storm: The South and Congress in an Era of Change,* ed. John C. Kuzenski, Laurence W. Moreland, and Robert P. Steed. Westport, Conn.: Praeger.

Reiselbach, Leroy. 1986. *Congressional Reform.* Washington, D.C.: Congressional Quarterly Press.

Ripley, Randall B. 1964. "The Party Whip Organization in the House of Representatives." *American Political Science Review* 58: 561–76.

———. 1967. *Party Leaders in the House of Representatives.* Washington, D.C.: Brookings Institution.

Robinson, James A. 1963. *The House Rules Committee.* Indianapolis: Bobbs-Merrill.

Rohde, David W. 1989. "'Something's Happening Here; What It Is Ain't Exactly Clear': Southern Democrats in the House of Representatives." In *Home Style and Washington Work: Studies of Congressional Politics,* ed. Morris P. Fiorina and David W. Rohde. Ann Arbor: University of Michigan Press.

———. 1991a. *Parties and Leaders in the Postreform House.* Chicago: University of Chicago Press.

———. 1991b. "The Electoral Roots of the Resurgence of Partisanship among Southern Democrats in the House of Representatives." Paper presented at the annual meeting of the American Political Science Association, Washington, D.C.

———. 1993. "Partisanship, Leadership, and Congressional Assertiveness in Foreign and Defense Policy." In *The New Politics of American Foreign Policy,* ed. David A. Deese. New York: St. Martin's Press.

———. 1994. "Presidential Support in the House of Representatives." In *The President, the Congress, and the Making of Foreign Policy,* ed. Paul E. Peterson. Norman: University of Oklahoma Press.

Schiller, Wendy J. 2000. *Partners and Rivals: Representation in United States Senate Delegations.* Princeton: Princeton University Press.

Schneider, Jerrold E. 1979. *Ideological Coalitions in Congress.* Westport, Conn.: Greenwood Press.

Schneider, Paige. 1998. "Factionalism in the Southern Republican Party." *American Review of Politics* 19: 149–62.

Shaffer, William R. 1980. *Party and Ideology in the United States Congress.* Lanham, Md.: University Press of America.

———. 1982. "Party and Ideology in the U.S. House of Representatives." *Western Political Quarterly* 35: 92–106.

———. 1987. "Ideological Trends among Southern U.S. Democratic Senators:

Race, Generation, and Political Climate." *American Politics Quarterly* 15: 299–324.

Shannon, W. Wayne. 1968. *Party, Constituency, and Congressional Voting.* Baton Rouge: Louisiana State University Press.

———. 1972. "Revolt in Washington: The South in Congress." In *The Changing Politics of the South,* ed. William C. Havard. Baton Rouge: Louisiana State University Press.

Shelley, Mack C., II. 1983. *The Permanent Majority: The Conservative Coalition in the United States Congress.* Tuscaloosa: University of Alabama Press.

Shepsle, Kenneth A. 1979. "Institutional Arrangements and Equilibrium in Multidimensional Voting Models." *American Journal of Political Science* 23: 27–59.

Sinclair, Barbara. 1977. "Party Realignment and the Transformation of the Political Agenda: The House of Representatives, 1925–1938." *American Political Science Review* 71: 940–53.

———. 1981, 2nd ed. "Agenda and Alignment Change: The House of Representatives, 1925–1978." In *Congress Reconsidered,* ed Lawrence C. Dodd and Bruce I. Oppenheimer. Washington, D.C.: Congressional Quarterly Press.

———. 1982. *Congressional Realignment.* Austin: University of Texas Press.

———. 1983. *Majority Party Leadership in the U.S. House.* Baltimore: Johns Hopkins University Press.

———. 1989, 4th ed. "House Majority Party Leadership in the Late 1980s." In *Congress Reconsidered,* ed. Lawrence C. Dodd and Bruce I. Oppenheimer. Washington, D.C.: Congressional Quarterly Press.

———. 1995. *Legislators, Leaders, and Lawmaking: The U.S. House of Representatives in the Postreform Era.* Baltimore: Johns Hopkins University Press.

Stone, Walter J. 1982. "Electoral Change and Policy Representation in Congress: Domestic Welfare Issues from 1956–1972." *British Journal of Political Science* 12: 95–115.

Strong, Donald S. 1960. *Urban Republicanism in the South.* Tuscaloosa: University of Alabama Bureau of Public Administration.

Swain, Carol M. 1993. *Black Faces, Black Interests: The Representation of African Americans in Congress.* Cambridge: Harvard University Press.

Talbert, Jeffery C., and Matthew Potoski. 2002. "Setting the Legislative Agenda: The Dimensional Structure of Bill Cosponsoring and Floor Voting." *Journal of Politics* 64: 864–91.

Tate, Katherine. 2003. *Black Faces in the Mirror: African Americans and Their Representation in the U.S. Congress.* Princeton: Princeton University Press.

Truman, David. 1959. *The Congressional Party: A Case Study.* New York: John Wiley and Sons.

Turner, Julius. 1951. *Party and Constituency: Pressures on Congress.* Baltimore: Johns Hopkins University Press.

Waldman, Sidney. 1980. "Majority Leadership in the House of Representatives." *Political Science Quarterly* 95: 373–93.

Weingast, Barry R. 1979. "A Rational Choice Perspective on Congressional Norms." *American Journal of Political Science* 32: 245–62.

Whitby, Kenny J., and Franklin D. Gilliam Jr. 1991. "A Longitudinal Analysis of Competing Explanations for the Transformation of Southern Congressional Politics." *Journal of Politics* 53: 504–18.

★ Chapter 11 ★

Southern Governors and Legislatures

Branwell DuBose Kapeluck, Robert P. Steed, and Laurence W. Moreland

IN CONTRAST TO THE SUBSTANTIAL attention paid to the transforming effect of the civil rights era on southern politics, the continuing realignment of the southern electorate, and most other topics addressed in this volume, scholarly analyses of southern legislators and governors have been relatively sparse. Until the mid-1970s neither southern governors nor state legislatures were known for their strong leadership. In many of the southern states a traditionalistic political culture saw little role for government in society beyond defending the status quo, maintaining white supremacy, and protecting the interests of a relatively small number of county seat elites. In this environment it is not surprising that both governors and legislatures operated under a variety of cultural, legal, and constitutional restraints. As Black and Black summarized the pre–World War II situation: "The old southern politics went round and round in circles, seldom moving beyond the question of whether Jack or Jock would win public office. Essentially it was a politics of limited taxation, limited spending, and, above all, a determined resistance to any changes in the racial status quo" (1987, 8–9).

The works discussed in this chapter fall into roughly three categories. First, there are those studies that provide a baseline description of southern governors and state legislatures at about the time of World War II and the decade or so immediately thereafter. A second line of scholarly work looks specifically at southern political change as reflected in, or as influenced by, changes in the governorship or the legislature, especially those changes that ensued following the court-ordered redistricting and civil rights reforms of the mid-1960s. A third broad category of research focuses on the contemporary nature of southern gubernatorial and legislative organization and power, showing where the changes led and offering contrasts to the baseline descriptions of the studies in the first category. There is in all three categories a rich mixture of research ranging from case studies (primarily state-specific examinations of legislatures and biographies of various governors and legislative leaders) to national studies treating the South as a regional subset to studies focusing fully and exclusively on the South.

Baseline Studies

The research on southern governors and state legislatures in the immediate post–World War II period, not surprisingly, was largely descriptive of institutions that tended to be relatively weak and inefficient. A good early example is H. C. Nixon's "The Southern Legislature and Legislation" (1948). Nixon's description of southern legislatures was consistent with V. O. Key's (1949) contemporaneous observation; as Nixon summarized it, "The typical southern legislature . . . provides little voice for Republicans, inadequate representation for all urban people, no direct and little indirect participation for Negroes, and an open season for economic pressures from near and far" (Nixon 1948, 412). He also provided some useful perspective by including some comparisons with legislatures in other regions. Though he noted some interregional similarities (such as complex committee systems, lobbyist registration requirements, turnover rates), he also identified some striking differences, most of which clearly reflected the race-based, rural-dominated, one-party, low-output politics of the immediate postwar period in the South.

Little additional research on southern legislatures appeared until scholarly attention to the South was reignited in the 1960s with much of the focus on the effects of redistricting and a newly enfranchised southern black electorate on the office of the governor and the inevitable changes faced by southern legislatures. Even though this interest was prompted by the expectation that these changes in the external environment—for example, the 1962 *Baker v. Carr* decision—would lead to changes in the composition and power of state legislatures, the initial research still focused on how the legislatures looked as they stood on the verge of transition.

Perhaps the best example of this approach is Malcolm Jewell's revisiting of H. C. Nixon's work on southern state legislatures. In "State Legislatures in Southern Politics" (1964) Jewell provided a detailed review of the reapportionment process in the southern states and made several predictions regarding the effect of increased urban representation. Noting that southern metropolitan areas also contain significant concentrations of black voters, he suggested that southern legislatures could become more liberal in regard to social and economic issues. He indicated that the impact of greater black representation hinged on the degree to which southern legislatures were able to maintain at-large districting systems. In addition to increased black electoral power, Jewell also predicted the rise of the Republican Party in southern legislatures, particularly in the urban areas. Even at this early stage in southern realignment, Jewell pointed to advances in GOP strength in Kentucky, Florida, and Texas. Interestingly, the last two states also contained the largest urban populations in the region.

Jewell proposed that the relatively low level of conflict characteristic of southern legislatures was poised for change. Increased urban, black, and Republican representation portended growing factionalism within the Democratic Party, and he argued that Republican identifiers might oscillate between support for urban Democrats on racial issues and conservative Democrats on fiscal issues. Overall, Jewell's article is essential for its coverage of this period in southern legislative politics. In a farsighted observation Jewell suggested that genuine two-party competition might be realized in the southern states by the early 1970s.

Even with change on the horizon, however, examinations of state legislatures during the next decade often still focused on the persistence of traditional patterns. (We will discuss below an important exception, Jewell's extended examination of legislative change published in the mid-1960s.) This is shown in the Citizens Conference on State Legislatures' 1971 publication of *State Legislatures: An Evaluation of Their Effectiveness*. This study provided a thorough analysis of the fifty state legislatures. Though attention was not confined to the South, nor was there a special focus on regional legislative differences, this research was a valuable resource for scholars plotting institutional change in southern legislatures. On the basis of field interviews, institutional data, and survey responses, the study's authors presented a comprehensive portrait of state legislatures and constructed an index based on several criteria.

One of the primary analyses of this study was its ranking of "state legislative capability," in which it found southern states (with the notable exception of Florida) clustered at the low end of the scale, still occupying the same relative positions they had occupied for decades. Much of this low ranking was attributed to one-party dominance in the South. In short, even in the early 1970s, a period of dramatic change, some of the southern state legislative literature continued to spotlight persistent constraints rooted in the region's past.

This description of institutional limitations also characterized the literature on southern governors during this period. Cortez Ewing's 1948 article, "Southern Governors," is a good starting point for those interested in a descriptive treatment of the office. Ewing provided several tables that detailed the demographic, occupational, and educational characteristics of the southern governors as well as various constitutional provisions pertaining to governorship. The dry nature of these data was supplemented with historical observations that put these statistics in perspective. Ewing's article also contained two short case studies of what he considered the two "southern gubernatorial crises" of this era. The first of these was a short primer on the Louisiana Long dynasty. He covered in several pages the surreal rise of Huey Long to near dictatorial power up to his assassination in 1935. The second involved another important southern political family, the Talmadges of Georgia. This brief introduction highlighted two important characteristics of southern governors in the pre–civil rights era. First, Ewing illuminated the antipathy of Eugene Talmadge toward federal assistance during the New Deal era, quoting Talmadge's description of New Deal programs as "a combination of wet nursin', frenzied finance, downright communism an' plain damn foolishness" (Ewing 1948, 406). Some of this resentment may be ascribed to long-standing suspicion of the federal government among white southerners, but the author suggested Talmadge's real concern was with expanded rights of black citizens. At any rate, Talmadge's reaction to federal largesse under the New Deal provided a stark contrast to the attitude of the later governors of the "New South." Second, the discussion of the Talmadge machine brought to light the electoral strategies of governors under the dramatic malapportionment that was common to most southern states during this period.

Another early work on southern governors explored the power of southern governors to exercise the veto. Frank Prescott's "The Executive Veto in the Southern States" (1948), while largely a discussion of the growing adoption of the executive veto in the southern states, is a worthy contribution for those interested in the transformation of the governor's office in this region. In mild contrast to the prevailing viewpoint of the time, Prescott questioned the notion of the impotent southern governor and suggested that the increased use of the veto on policy grounds and for reasons of budgetary responsibility indicated a "gradually developing tendency to designate the governor as the 'third house' of the popular assembly" (Prescott 1948, 675).

The most exhaustive treatment of southern governors in this period, Coleman B. Ransone's *The Office of Governor in the South* (1951), returned to the theme of gubernatorial constraints. The author interviewed the governors, past governors, and other important state officials and staff in the eleven southern states and argued that the conventional view of the powerless southern governor was close to the mark. The majority of time in office was devoted to public relations. Southern governors, however, viewed their most important role as that of legislative leader, a view at odds with their perception of themselves as chief administrators. Ransone's interviews suggested that governing the bureaucracy was not of much interest to southern governors, nor did this task consume much of their time. Ransone followed up this descriptive appraisal of the southern governor with a number of suggestions intended to strengthen the office, though as one contemporary reviewer commented, the political cast of the office made it unnecessary—even pointless—to acquire the technical expertise required for efficient administration (Grant 1952).

There were, of course, individual exceptions to this general picture of weakness in the governorship. These figures often gained a good deal of attention because they stood in stark contrast to the norm and because they were usually colorful characters who did interesting, if sometimes eccentric, things. One such figure who looms large in the literature is the populist governor of Louisiana Earl Long. Michael J. Kurtz and Morgan D. Peoples's *Earl K. Long: The Saga of Uncle Earl and Louisiana Politics* (1990) is a good resource for scholars interested in the populist politics of the period. Long is an interesting subject for extended examination because of the complex political environment in which he operated. Unlike many other southern governors, Long included in his coalition African Americans, and as the authors note, he was the only significant southern governor to fight for black enfranchisement. Such was his support for Louisiana blacks that the racist White Citizens Council condemned him in 1959.

This progressive streak, however, was tempered by Long's well-known connections with organized crime. Despite this record, Long was well loved by the working class of Louisiana and devoted much of his career to improving health care, education, and social welfare in the state. The authors recounted these reforms and placed them in the unique political context of the state. Of particular interest to political scientists is Kurtz and Peoples's descriptive treatment of Long's skills in negotiation with the Louisiana legislature. Moreover, it becomes apparent that V. O. Key's depiction of the state as bifactionalized may not apply so well in Long's case, inasmuch as his leadership and ability to shape political realities often curbed factional allegiances.

As Richard Scher points out in *Politics in the New South* (which we discuss later in this chapter), governors such as Long were not the norm during this period. As was true of the literature on southern legislatures, then, the central thrust of work on the southern governorship during the period immediately following World War II emphasized institutional limitations. For both institutions the sweeping social, economic, and political changes from the early 1960s on would alter this focus.

Transformational Studies

As the 1960s unfolded, a host of changes led to an energized southern governorship and legislative branch. First, Supreme Court rulings on malapportionment resulted in an increased importance of southern urban centers. This, coupled with a substantial metropolitan black population, forced a reappraisal of elite and mass partisanship. Finally, population movement to the South and rising levels of prosperity tended to diminish interregional differences and even led some to question the notion of a distinctive South (Beck and Lopatto 1982, for example).

Malcolm Jewell was among the first to explore the connections between this changing political environment and southern state legislatures. Building on his 1964 article, he presented a considerably more exhaustive examination of southern legislative changes during the tumultuous 1960s period of reapportionment in *Legislative Representation in the Contemporary South* (1967). Here Jewell continued his analysis of southern party competition with a focus on eight states in the region (Alabama, Florida, Kentucky, Louisiana, North Carolina, South Carolina, Tennessee, and Texas) with data from at least four elections in each state between 1947 and 1964. The principal goal of this research was to understand the role of competitiveness in nonpartisan versus partisan electoral systems. Jewell's study looked at both primaries and general elections, though given the relative newness of Republican competition in the South, the bulk of his analysis centered on state legislative primaries. Measuring competition from five perspectives, he made several important findings. First, he found an inverse relationship between two-party competition and the level of competition within the Democratic Party primary. Though Jewell was unable to control for the effect of those state Democratic primaries that have runoffs (which may suppress candidates unlikely to achieve a majority of the vote), he suggested a desire for party unity might preclude an extensive slate of candidates. Moreover, his analysis revealed heightened competition for Democratic primaries in urban areas. Districts with high black population proportions also witnessed lower levels of party competition. Party competition was also related to the lack of an incumbent in the race. In short, Jewell brought attention to the importance of rethinking the nature of southern state legislatures in a period of rapid change.

The theme of party competition (or lack thereof) was revisited in Grau's (1981) study of state legislative primaries in fifteen states from 1972 to 1978. Even though his focus was not on southern states (only four states were southern), the analysis shed light on the centrality of two-party competition. Grau's research was anchored in Key's argument that for voter choice to be realized there must be at least two candidates in a primary. General election competition, while important, should be accompanied by rivalries within the two parties' respective primaries. As one would expect, a look at just the southern states during this period revealed less Republican primary competition. On the other hand, metropolitan districts, regardless of region, tended to have considerably higher levels of competition. Given the increasing urbanization of the South, Grau's analysis presaged increasing GOP strength in the region. Finally, a hint of a nascent repositioning of southern state Democratic legislative candidates was revealed in the higher incumbency loss rates in many of the region's Democratic primaries. Overall, Grau's research is important for identifying the early stages of partisan dislocation in the South of the early to mid-1970s.

A more recent examination of legislative elections and southern partisan change is found in David Lublin's *The Republican South* (2004). Lublin's book focused on the sweep of party transformation in the South over the past half century, but one of the main strengths of that discussion was his inclusion of a substantial amount of data on state legislative elections—well beyond what is usually found in such treatments—in his analysis. Incidentally, Lublin also included data on southern gubernatorial elections as a part of his investigation of changes in the southern party system. Additionally, as would be expected, he couched much of his discussion of southern state legislatures in terms of racial considerations related to districting and representation (for more detail, see Richard Engstrom's discussion in chapter 4 of this volume). In this sense, then, Lublin's analysis also stands as an example of how the state legislature literature addresses the larger issue of southern political and social change.

An illustrative case study examining the nature of legislative change in this period of turmoil is Mary DeLorse Coleman's *Legislators, Law, and Public Policy: Political Change in Mississippi and the South* (1993). Coleman presented a detailed discussion of the prolonged legal battle over black representation in the Mississippi legislature and offered some insights into the nature of white obstructionism. Although the legal battle was eventually won and blacks finally gained more representation, Coleman observed that this did not necessarily (or automatically) translate into significant policy gains for Mississippi blacks. Representation was a necessary first step, but the reality was that blacks were still a minority who had to deal with a long-established political process that was not often responsive to their agenda. Coleman clearly demonstrated, however, that even in deep South states the civil rights movement and the resulting change in the political landscape had, by the 1980s, altered the electoral and institutional equations for state legislatures.

Two additional case studies further illustrate the representational change within southern state legislatures as a consequence of 1960s era reapportionment, civil rights reforms, and the emergence of a viable Republican Party in the South.

Keith Hamm, Robert Harmel, and Robert Thompson's "Ethnic and Partisan Minorities in Two Southern State Legislatures" (1983) considered the effect of the influx of minorities and the increasing Republican presence in the Texas and South Carolina legislatures in the mid-1970s. The conventional wisdom is that these minority representatives, many of whom represented either newly enfranchised constituencies or voters who had undergone a change in partisanship, were likely to translate these new demands into greater levels of legislative activity and output. This is important research since we would expect a natural concomitant to changing patterns of representation would be a noticeable impact on the state legislative process. The authors found, however, that Republicans, Mexican Americans (in the case of Texas), and blacks were not more active in introducing bills and amendments, nor was their success rate (when controlling for seniority and positions of leadership) higher than that of majority representatives. This research was valuable in that it suggested that policy change following the transformation in the South to a competitive party system was muted. Moreover, the analysis provided a baseline and methodology useful for scholars wishing to revisit the question.

Robert Harmel, in "Minority Partisanship in One-Party Predominant Legislatures: A Five-State Study" (1986) continued and added to some of the conclusions drawn in Hamm, Harmel, and Thompson's examination of minority representation patterns in southern states. In this study Harmel focused on minority partisanship in one-party-predominant legislatures in five southern states (Alabama, Arkansas, Louisiana, Mississippi, and Texas). Employing both attitudinal and behavioral indicators derived from a mail survey sent to all Republican members of these legislatures in 1984, Harmel found Republicans beginning to vote more cohesively and also identified the emergence of informal party caucuses. Nevertheless, there was considerable variation among states, which he sought to explain by three contextual factors. First, the presence of a Republican governor, which might be thought to be related to greater party unity, is found to be unrelated to party cohesion and may actually lessen partisan fervor. Harmel suggested this was particularly the case in those states where Democratic legislators were relatively conservative. A second factor that Harmel explored was how the relative proportion of Republican members might influence the degree to which the legislative party flexed its partisan muscle. Again, evidence for this hypothesis was mixed at best. Perhaps the most important contextual factor in explaining Republican unity was treatment by the majority party leadership. Ill-treatment, particularly in conjunction with sizable Republican membership, was related to greater minority party solidarity. While Harmel's study left more questions than answers, the topic is certainly relevant for understanding the process by which an inchoate Republican Party grew in importance in the southern states. In its recognition of the slow but pervasive realignment in the South during the early 1980s, Harmel's study is of particular utility for scholars interested in tracing the behavior and perceptions of the relatively nascent Republican Party in that region.

Southern governorships also underwent significant change in the 1970s and into the 1980s. Much of the scholarly attention to this change focused on how the inclusion of blacks as active participants in the electoral process affected gubernatorial campaigns and elections. Prior to the 1960s civil rights reform, the issue received rather little scholarly attention. Because black political participation was stifled, there was little incentive for southern governors to solicit their support. The increase in black political participation following the civil rights reforms of the 1960s required a rethinking on the part of gubernatorial contenders, particularly Democrats. Indeed, Black and Black argue that "virtually all serious Democratic senatorial and gubernatorial candidates understood that black participation was an irreversible reality of southern electoral politics and that Democratic nominees needed solid black support to win general elections" (1987, 26). Additionally, some research gave attention to the impact of other changes, such as the rise of the middle class, increased urbanization, and in-migration.

Two early works by Earl Black explored the impact of these sorts of changes on the southern governorship. The first, "Southern Governors and Political Change: Campaign Stances on Racial Segregation and Economic Development, 1950–69," covered the reaction of southern governors to federal desegregation efforts from the relatively peaceful early 1950s through the turbulent electoral dislocations of the 1960s (Black, 1971). Black also examined the rapid economic growth that began during this period, a second component of the South's "social revolution," in light of the reaction by elite white politicians, namely, southern governors.

Black's approach was to examine patterns of gubernatorial election rhetoric. By reviewing newspaper coverage in the eleven states of the old Confederacy, he identified both regional differences (that is, deep South versus peripheral South) and temporal change in the campaign stances of successful southern governors on these two important issues. He also provided valuable data for scholars interested in understanding the evolution of elite southern attitudes toward race and economic development.

Focusing first on differences in racial campaign rhetoric, Black identified three categories of southern governor: the militant segregationist, the moderate segregationist, and the nonsegregationist. Not surprisingly, governors strongly committed to the maintenance of racial separation hailed largely from the deep South, though there were some exceptions. Black concluded that increasing black voting rates and federal intervention largely explain the decline in racial campaign appeals during this period.

Turning to economic change, Black established another typology, this one based on gubernatorial attitudes on the role of public education and the degree to which the candidate supported redistributive state programs. Using these two dimensions, Black created four categories: the marginalists (advocate neither increased education spending nor redistributive policy), the adaptives (focus on increased educational spending), the neo-populist marginalists (focus on redistributive policy), and the neo-populist adaptives (advocate both increased education spending and redistributive policy). In developing this categorization Black helped demonstrate the emergence of the contemporary New South governor.

Finally, Black showed substantial correlation between the two indicators of social change in the South. His analysis paid special attention to interregional differences. Overall, his work presented a wealth of empirical data and painted a compelling portrait of change among southern white political leaders.

Black's 1971 work was followed in 1976 with a more ambitious work, *Southern Governors and Civil Rights: Racial Segregation as a Campaign Issue in the Second Reconstruction,* which extended his analysis of southern governors and the issue of race to 1973. This exhaustive study covered eighty governorships and added considerable contextual data to his earlier investigation. Black included voting data for both Democratic first and second primaries and close general elections on a county-by-county basis. These data, complemented by county-level demographic data, enabled Black to uncover the sources of support for (and resistance to) segregationist candidates. He also explored further the link between gubernatorial racial attitudes and their approach to state economic development. In addition to the rich discussion of changing political rhetoric, Black's meticulous coverage of gubernatorial campaigns during this era—the book includes twenty-nine figures, fifty-four tables, and two appendices—has been an important resource for scholars seeking a thorough understanding of the response of southern governors to the dramatic changes of this period.

Earl and Merle Black included discussion of how southern social and economic change affected gubernatorial politics in their landmark 1987 study, *Politics and Society in the South*. They examined how various factors such as the rise of the middle class, urbanization, the increasing competitiveness of the Republican Party, and, especially, the inclusion of blacks in the southern electorate changed the nature of gubernatorial (and other) elections in the region. With regard to race, candidates rarely voiced overtly racist appeals, and Democrats in particular saw the need to develop some type of biracial coalition capable of producing enough votes to win statewide elections. Black and Black pointed out, however, that a narrow appeal to black voters alone was doomed to fail because whites were still in the majority in all southern states. Similarly, liberal positions were a hard sell in an electorate that was primarily moderate to conservative. Still, the game had changed, and blacks now were able to participate. Gubernatorial candidates had to acknowledge this in their campaigns, and governors had to at least think about the policy implications of their agenda for an expanded electorate.

A number of case studies of gubernatorial elections demonstrate and essentially confirm Black and Black's conclusions about how the changing political environment in the South affected gubernatorial politics. Three fairly recent works should serve to make the point.

Perhaps one of the most studied 1960s-era southern governors is the erstwhile segregationist George Wallace. Dan T. Carter's book *The Politics of Rage: George Wallace, the Origins of the New Conservatism, and the Transformation of American Politics* (1995) is a well-researched study of this complicated figure. Wallace not only was influential in Alabama, where he served four terms (five if you count the election of his wife, Lurleen), but also, as Carter argued, played a pivotal role in the realignment of southern whites from the Democratic Party to the GOP. Carter did an admirable job describing the way in which Wallace transformed the more typical use of overt racial appeals into rhetoric that cast civil rights reform as a generalized antipathy toward the federal government. Though considerable portions of this book dealt with Wallace's activities in Alabama, the general theme was national: Carter in his preface suggested the governor's career led to the "Americanization of Dixie and the Southernization of America" (1995, 14). Scholars interested in the transformation of the region to one with increased national influence will find *The Politics of Rage* a useful resource.

Whereas George Wallace attained prominence in Alabama and later on the national stage through his transformation of the race issue, North Carolina governor Terry Sanford built his reputation as a moderate on desegregation and avid support for education. John Drescher's *Triumph of Good Will* (2000) did a good job of documenting Sanford's rise to the governorship in 1960. Though Sanford served only one term, he was one of the first southern governors to secure office as a racial moderate opposing an avowed segregationist. Thus, he represented a break with the Old South and served as an example to other would-be New South governors of how to implement a winning campaign strategy devoid of racial appeals. Drescher, a longtime reporter for the *Charlotte Observer*, described in detail Sanford's 1960 campaign, with particular emphasis on his handling of the issue of race. Like most New South governors, Sanford was instrumental in improving the quality of education; however, Drescher spent relatively little time addressing this aspect of the governor's agenda. Scholars interested in this topic should read Sanford's own book *But What about the People?* (1966), in which he described his educational program and his contribution to public education in North Carolina. Sanford's book *Storm over the States* (1967), in which he proposed a reorganization of state governments in light of changing intergovernmental relationships, also illustrated his progressive outlook.

The contrast between such governors as Wallace and Sanford during this transformational period, and the resulting changed direction for the southern governorship, is also demonstrated in Randy Sanders's book, *Mighty Peculiar Elections* (2002). Sanders examined races for governor in two deep South states (South Carolina and Georgia) and two peripheral South states (Arkansas and Florida) in 1970, the first gubernatorial election year in which African American voters turned out in high numbers. This surge in black voter participation, Sanders argued, led to a change in the electoral strategies of gubernatorial candidates in these four states that moved away from racial demagoguery toward a spirit of moderation.

Sanders's study fit well with Black and Black's assertion that the southern electoral landscape would have to accommodate black voters (1987). He began by describing the social and political milieu of the period leading up to the 1970 elections, with an emphasis both on the growing acceptance of integration among southern whites and on the apparent desire to rid the region of the stigma of racism. It was in this environment that politicians, such as the governors he examined, could portray themselves as "good men" and promise to move past the divisive racist dialogue and usher in a New South, or as some have termed it, a "Good South." Sanders then applied this thesis with an in-depth analysis of each of the four gubernatorial campaigns of 1970. Integrating evidence from personal interviews, media sources, archives, and personal papers, he made a convincing case that 1970 marked an important turning point in the transformation of the South and provided valuable insight into this pivotal period in southern politics.

Change in the South was not limited to elections. There were also some significant institutional changes in the office of governor during these decades. This was not the case only in the South. Perhaps the best book on the evolution of the state governor is Larry Sabato's *Goodbye to Good-Time Charlie: The American Governor Transformed, 1950–1975* (1978). Sabato documented the emergence of a new type of executive—younger, more experienced, and better educated—and he identified certain institutional reforms, such as longer terms and off-year elections, that led to a strengthened executive branch. Though Sabato's study was mainly concerned with national trends, the changing status of the historically weak southern governor was highlighted. This was particularly the case in the increasing willingness of southern governors to take advantage of the devolution of power during the beginning phase of "New Federalism," which in turn showed a reorientation toward greater policy responsiveness that stood in sharp contrast to the prevailing view of governors in the baseline period.

In summary, as southern politics changed dramatically after the early 1960s, parallel changes in legislative and gubernatorial elections and institutional arrangements also occurred, and these, in turn, led to increased scholarly interest, research, and writing. The result was an enlarged and enriched literature on southern governors and legislatures.

Southern Governors and State Legislatures: The Contemporary Picture

The focus in more recent works on southern state legislatures and governors has tended to describe them in the aftermath of the transformations summarized above and the degree to which they have come to resemble legislatures and governors in the rest of the country. Notable among these works is "Southern State Legislatures: Recruitment and Reform" by Lee E. Bernick, Patricia K. Freeman, and David M. Olson (1988). This is a case study limited to Tennessee, but it has broader implications for the South generally. The authors examined the processes through which southern state legislatures have become both more diverse and more professional. Much of this change, they argued, is due to a change in recruitment patterns. The authors' discussion of recruitment identified several factors that have led to a more heterogeneous southern legislative branch. First, increasing urbanization and industrialization along with higher incomes in the South have led to increased demands by citizens for competent public administration and a more effective legislature. Second, the rapid professionalization of southern state legislatures has made legislative careers possible for those traditionally excluded. Increased two-party competition has also improved the electoral prospects for previously marginalized portions of the southern state electorate. Finally, redistricting and black enfranchisement are important factors contributing to the changing face of southern state legislatures.

Bernick and his colleagues provided data suggesting that these changes in recruitment have resulted in a slow decline in Democratic dominance in the South, a decline likely to be exacerbated by ongoing growth in typically Republican suburban districts. Of particular note is the concomitant rise in Democratic dominance in nonsouthern state legislatures, which indicates an important regional dynamic. Though their data were confined to Tennessee, Bernick and his coauthors also revealed important changes in the social characteristics of southern state legislators. In the last half century, women and blacks have enjoyed gains, whereas lawyers have lost some of their traditional edge in the state legislature. Family connections, a traditional avenue to political office in the South, have also declined in importance.

The changes in recruitment patterns shown by Bernick and his colleagues have important implications for Republican strength in the South. Declines in Democratic fortunes in southern state legislatures have, if anything, increased since the 1980s. The Republican Party enjoyed substantial success during the 1990s and still maintains a competitive edge. Although a number of factors have contributed to GOP ascendancy, Earl Black and Merle Black (1987) suggested that, in the long term, support for Republican candidates would increase among educated and middle-class southern whites. Nancy Martorano, R. Bruce Anderson, and Keith Hamm provided an empirical test of this assertion in their analysis of southern statehouse seat contests (2000). They brought to the question a rich data set that included district-level data on such important variables as level of education, urban-suburban status, and racial characteristics. This analysis is particularly valuable for understanding Republican Party strategy in southern state legislative elections and how it has affected Democratic patterns of contestation. Overall, Martorano and her colleagues demonstrated that the Republican Party pays particular attention to demographic characteristics, especially the racial make-up of legislative districts.

Research on the effect of the changing southern political landscape on southern governorships includes Sabato's "New South Governors and the Governorship" (1988). Sabato's analysis addressed a number of enduring themes in southern politics. He provided a thorough treatment of the interplay of race and two-party competition. Linking the transformation of the southern governor to the rise in two-party competition, he argued that earlier Democratic dominance often led to a diminution of the governorship as little more than a "gold watch given for dedicated service to the party" (1988, 204). In contrast to the "Good-time Charlies" Sabato discussed in his earlier work (1978), governors of the New South, with some exceptions, were more professional in their approach to the office. Sabato attributed this metamorphosis to the creation of new majority coalitions that were precipitated by the upheaval of the mid-1960s. Echoing Black and Black and others, he argued that growing black electoral participation minimized the role of racism in southern politics and allowed a widening of the southern gubernatorial agenda. The reduced salience of race also led to the emergence of a new breed of southern governors. The governor of the New South, as Sabato also noted in his 1978 work, was typically young, well-educated, and more experienced than his segregationist predecessors. Sabato, however, was careful to note that despite the growing professionalization of the southern governorship, southern governors remained largely homogeneous—white, male, and Protestant.

Along with the impact of 1960s reforms and the consequent rise in two-party competition, Sabato provided insight into the changing relationship between the southern states and the federal government. Sabato discussed the increased willingness among southern governors to take advantage of federal assistance, given the decentralization of intergovernmental aid following the Great Society era. Much of this change Sabato attributed to a more efficient and invigorated southern state government. A strengthened executive, professionalized legislatures, and constitutional revisions have resulted in a southern state government more capable of assuming responsibilities heretofore left to federal government control.

One reflection of this transformation of southern governorships and legislatures can be seen in the changing patterns of interest-group activity and influence at the state government level by the 1980s. In *Interest Group Politics in the Southern States*, edited by Ronald Hrebenar and Clive Thomas (1992), scholars examining interest-group activity in all the southern states (and Kentucky) concluded that interest groups operated differently from the way they once did in response to a number of the same factors that are associated with changes in state political institutions: increased political participation by blacks and lower-income whites, the rise of the Republican Party and two-party competition, reapportionment of state legislatures, increased economic diversity and the decreasing importance of agriculture, increasing urbanization and the rise of the middle class, and increased demand for state and local governmental services.

Perhaps the best general overview of all elements of gubernatorial and legislative literature discussed here is found in Richard Scher's *Politics in the New South* (1997). While Scher's book is a broad text, the chapters devoted to governors and legislatures ably addressed the historical weaknesses of these institutions in the South, noted the few regional comparisons that set them in a larger national context, summarized the nature of the significant changes toward greater responsibility and increased professionalism in the period since 1970, and discussed their contemporary status in southern state governments that have become considerably more policy-oriented in the post–civil rights period. Moreover, Scher's discussion of governors and legislators also supported in important ways a key theme of his book, the partisan transformation of the South, as he presented electoral data showing the rising competitiveness of Republicans in contesting for these offices.

One of the major strengths of Scher's discussion is his classification of southern governors into four categories: the businessman, the populist, the demagogue, and the policymaker. As he pointed out, the scheme is not perfect and, since few governors represent pure types, there may well be reasonable disagreement over whether a particular governor has been classified correctly. Still, the typology is extremely useful because it serves to create order out of what is otherwise a tangle of (often) colorful individuals whose broad similarities and differences are difficult to discern. Additionally, and perhaps more important, this classification helps to illuminate in various ways the connections between governors and some of the key patterns in southern political history. Thus, identifying the businessman governor as the most numerous category helps explain both the historically conservative approach to state policy noted at the outset of this chapter and the widespread current popularity of governor-led initiatives to encourage economic development (such as the attraction of new industry) in the region. Similarly, Scher's argument that demagogues constitute the smallest category helps provide proper perspective and counterbalance to the widely held historical image that the vast majority of southern governors (and other political leaders) fit the stereotype of Senator Foghorn; at the same time this discussion underscores the disproportionate influence this type of governor had on southern politics during the period examined.

Given the historical importance of the election of a black governor in a southern state in illustrating the changed face of politics in the region, we include a discussion of two recent case studies on the 1989 election of L. Douglas Wilder as the first African American governor in the South (indeed, in the nation). These two works addressed what might well be considered the culmination of the movement of blacks into southern gubernatorial politics. Both *Claiming the Dream: The Victorious Campaign of Douglas Wilder of Virginia* (1990) by Margaret Edds and *Virginia's Native Son: The Election and Administration of L. Douglas Wilder* (2000) by Judson L. Jeffries described the personal political development, the electoral campaign strategy, and the short-term variables that led to Wilder's landmark victory. Though the interpretations differed on certain details, both books pointed to the necessity of combining the black vote with a sufficient white vote as a cornerstone of Wilder's electoral strategy. Fortunately for Wilder, he was a skilled campaigner and fund-raiser and a recognizable political figure, he enjoyed the support of a reasonably unified party and the endorsement of key Virginia Democrats, he ran at a time of Democratic strength in the state (the two previous governors, Charles Robb and Gerald Baliles, were Democrats), and he faced an opponent burdened by a divided party and a number of damaging issue positions, especially on abortion. Even so, Wilder barely won, which further underscores Black and Black's (1987) argument that the changed southern political landscape is still not very amenable to Democrats or liberals or those who rely primarily on black voter support.

Jeffries's book went beyond a description of the campaign and examined Wilder's administration. He argued that Wilder had some success on such issues as raising appropriations for Virginia's black colleges and professional schools and that he generally advanced a policy agenda that demonstrated his ability to use the powers of the office effectively (for an opposing interpretation of Wilder's administrative record, see McGlennon 2003). In any case, the research on gubernatorial elections in the South during the 1960s, 1970s, and 1980s fairly consistently pointed to dramatic change from the baseline period.

The product of the sweeping change of the post–World War II South, and the concomitant transformation of legislatures and governorships, is addressed effectively in our final case study, Laura van Assendelft's *Governors, Agenda Setting, and Divided Government* (1997). This book compared the interplay of governors and legislatures in two unified states (Georgia and Tennessee) and two divided states (Mississippi and South Carolina) in the mid-1990s. While the choice of southern states was not due to any particular interest in the South as a region, van Assendelft recognized the importance of selecting states that have "basic historical, cultural, and economic factors" in common (1997, 20). It is notable, however, that there is an implicit recognition that conclusions regarding the effect of divided government in the South are generally applicable to nonsouthern states. Significantly, van Assendelft's book is set *in* the South, but it is not *of* the South. And that is the critical point. The decline of southern distinctiveness had advanced far enough by the 1990s that the author felt comfortable using southern case studies not to advance our understanding of southern politics (though that is certainly a by-product of the discussion), but to advance our understanding of national politics at the state level. How far removed that is from the baseline studies reviewed earlier in this chapter!

Conclusion

It is understandable that scholarly interest in southern governors and legislatures peaked during the period of rapid and sweeping social, economic, demographic, and partisan change of the 1960s, 1970s, and 1980s. Before then there was relatively little to report beyond the case studies that highlighted colorful characters or unusual events. While these were interesting, the prevailing picture was of state governments with little power and little concern for significant policy initiatives, especially in contrast with other regions.

Change is typically more interesting than stasis. Consequently, as is true of many of the other topics covered in this book, the literature on southern governors and legislatures expanded as regional change affected in various ways legislative and executive politics. While the progression from the weak governor and torpid legislature of the 1950s and 1960s to the dynamic governor and energetic legislative branch of the so-called New South can be illuminated chronologically, it is useful to isolate several important themes developed in the relevant literature.

First, and probably foremost, are those changes stemming from the disruption of the old political order associated with civil rights reform and judicial decisions on malapportionment. Intimately connected with this is the ensuing southern realignment from a one-party Democratic system to a political constellation in which the GOP was able to establish a foothold and eventually become competitive, if not dominant. A third theme focuses on the rapid socioeconomic and demographic transformation that has tended to erode southern distinctiveness. As southern states have come more and more to resemble their nonsouthern counterparts, southern citizens have demanded more from their state governments. Finally, the changing context of intergovernmental relations in the post–World War II era altered long-held southern antipathy toward federal assistance. This was particularly the case once the issue of race had begun to fade from prominence (Scher 1997). Once we move beyond what we have termed the baseline studies, practically all the literature on southern legislatures and governors addressed one or more of these changes; in a sense, all pointed toward understanding New South state governments in terms of their dramatic transformations since the World War II period.

Fortunately for continued research on contemporary southern governors and legislatures, a wealth of highly accessible data is available. Along with the sources noted here, two additional ones deserve mention. First is the *Almanac of State Legislatures* (Lilley, DeFranco, and Diefenderfer 1994; Lilley, DeFranco, and Bernstein 1998), which contains an abundance of state district-level demographic data. Additionally, scholars conducting research on southern governors would be well advised to explore Thad Beyle's online data, which include downloadable files on gubernatorial campaign spending and various indices of governmental power. These types of data afford a good opportunity to develop analyses charting the outcomes of the changes begun in the earlier post–World War II era. For example, such central issues as whether the South is still a politically distinctive region—and, if so, how and why—can be addressed within the context of research on southern legislatures and governors. Such research would clearly be important in exploring the broader issue of how the South's politics fit into larger national patterns. The process of change is interesting; understanding where that change has led should be equally interesting and important. Considering the close connections between legislatures, governors, and the larger regional political environment demonstrated by the literature reviewed in this chapter, continued attention to these institutions in this context should be fruitful.

References

Beck, Paul Allen, and Paul Lopatto. 1982. "The End of Southern Distinctiveness." In *Contemporary Southern Political Attitudes and Behavior: Studies
and Essays*, ed. Laurence W. Moreland, Tod A. Baker, and Robert P. Steed.
New York: Praeger.

Bernick, E. Lee, Patricia K. Freeman, and David M. Olson. 1988. "Southern
State Legislatures: Recruitment and Reform." In *Contemporary Southern
Politics*, ed. James F. Lea. Baton Rouge: Louisiana State University Press.

Beyle, Thad. "SouthNow." Accessed at www.unc.edu/~beyle/.

Black, Earl. 1971. "Southern Governors and Political Change: Campaign Stances
on Racial Segregation and Economic Development, 1950–69." *Journal of
Politics* 33: 703–34.

———. 1976. *Southern Governors and Civil Rights: Racial Segregation as a
Campaign Issue in the Second Reconstruction*. Cambridge: Harvard University Press.

Black, Earl, and Merle Black. 1987. *Politics and Society in the South*. Cambridge: Harvard University Press.

Carter, Dan T. 1995. *The Politics of Rage: George Wallace, the Origins of the
New Conservatism, and the Transformation of American Politics*. New
York: Simon and Schuster.

Citizens Conference on State Legislatures. 1971. *State Legislatures: An Evaluation of Their Effectiveness; The Complete Report*. New York: Praeger.

Coleman, Mary DeLorse. 1993. *Legislators, Law, and Public Policy: Political
Change in Mississippi and the South*. Westport, Conn.: Greenwood Press.

Drescher, John. 2000. *Triumph of Good Will: How Terry Sanford Beat a Cham-
pion of Segregation and Reshaped the South*. Jackson: University Press of
Mississippi.

Edds, Margaret. 1990. *Claiming the Dream: The Victorious Campaign of Douglas Wilder of Virginia*. Chapel Hill, N.C.: Algonquin Books.

Ewing, Cortez A. M. 1948. "Southern Governors." *Journal of Politics* 10: 385–
409.

Grant, Daniel R. 1952. "The Office of Governor in the South: The Organization of the Executive Office of the Governor." *American Political Science
Review* 46: 244–45.

Grau, Craig H. 1981. "Competition in State Legislative Primaries." *Legislative
Studies Quarterly* 6: 35–54.

Hamm, Keith E., Robert Harmel, and Robert Thompson. 1983. "Ethnic and
Partisan Minorities in Two Southern State Legislatures." *Legislative Studies Quarterly* 8: 177–89.

Harmel, Robert. 1986. "Minority Partisanship in One-Party Predominant Legislatures: A Five-State Study." *Journal of Politics* 48: 729–40.

Hrebenar, Ronald J., and Clive S. Thomas, eds. 1992. *Interest Group Politics in
the Southern States*. Tuscaloosa: University of Alabama Press.

Jeffries, Judson L. 2000. *Virginia's Native Son: The Election and Administration of
Governor L. Douglas Wilder*. West Lafayette, Ind.: Purdue University Press.

Jewell, Malcolm E. 1964. "State Legislatures in Southern Politics." *Journal of Politics* 26: 177–96.

———. 1967. *Legislative Representation in the Contemporary South*. Durham, N.C.: Duke University Press.

Key, V. O., Jr. 1949. *Southern Politics in State and Nation*. New York: Knopf.

Kurtz, Michael L., and Morgan D. Peoples. 1990. *Earl K. Long: The Saga of Uncle Earl and Louisiana Politics*. Baton Rouge: Louisiana State University Press.

Lilley, William, III, Laurence J. DeFranco, and Mark F. Bernstein. 1998, 2nd ed. *The Almanac of State Legistlatures: Changing Patterns, 1990–1997*. Washington, D.C.: Congressional Quarterly Press.

Lilley, William, III, Laurence J. DeFranco, and William M. Diefenderfer III. 1994. *The Almanac of State Legislatures: State Data Atlas*. Washington, D.C.: Congressional Quarterly Press.

Lublin, David. 2004. *The Republican South: Democratization and Partisan Change*. Princeton: Princeton University Press.

Martorano, Nancy, R. Bruce Anderson, and Keith E. Hamm. 2000. "A Transforming South: Exploring Patterns of State House Seat Contestation." *American Review of Politics* 21: 201–23.

McGlennon, John J. 2003. "Party Activists in Virginia, 1991–2001: Finishing the Realignment Cycle." *American Review of Politics* 24: 197–211.

Nixon, H. C. 1948. "The Southern Legislature and Legislation." *Journal of Politics* 10: 410–17.

Prescott, Frank W. 1948. "The Executive Veto in Southern States." *Journal of Politics* 10: 659–75.

Ransone, Coleman B., Jr. 1951. *The Office of Governor in the South*. Tuscaloosa: University of Alabama Bureau of Public Administration.

Sabato, Larry. 1978. *Goodbye to Good-Time Charlie: The American Governor Transformed, 1950–1975*. Lexington, Mass.: Lexington Books.

———. 1988. "New South Governors and the Governorship." In *Contemporary Southern Politics*, ed. James F. Lea. Baton Rouge: Louisiana State University Press.

Sanders, Randy. 2002. *Mighty Peculiar Elections: The New South Gubernatorial Campaigns of 1970 and the Changing Politics of Race*. Gainesville: University Press of Florida.

Sanford, Terry. 1966. *But What about the People?* New York: Harper and Row.

———. 1967. *Storm over the States*. New York: McGraw-Hill.

Scher, Richard K. 1997, 2nd ed. *Politics in the New South: Republicanism, Race and Leadership in the Twentieth Century*. Armonk, N.Y.: M. E. Sharpe.

van Assendelft, Laura A. 1997. *Governors, Agenda Setting, and Divided Government*. Lanham, Md.: University Press of America.

Looking Back and Looking Forward

A Research Agenda for Southern Politics

John A. Clark

AS THE CHAPTERS IN THIS VOLUME make clear, the literature on southern politics is vast and continues to grow.

No other region has attracted as much attention, either collectively or in terms of the states individually. If, as V. O. Key suggested, "of books on the South there is no end" (1949, ix), this particular book does great service by placing much of the literature in context. Still, despite the best efforts of the authors of this volume, much of that literature was necessarily omitted because of space limitations or substantive concerns. What accounts for the vast literature that has developed on the topic? Parochial southerners might suggest that their region is simply more interesting than others. They may be right. The South continues to be a distinctive region, owing in part to the rapid changes that have taken place over the past half century and the impact of the region on national politics. In the section that follows, I develop those themes in the context of the chapters in this book. For now, it is worth pointing out that my own midwestern university library contains more than one hundred listings for "Southern States—Politics and Government" but only a dozen such listings for the "Middle West" and even fewer for "Northeastern States." Southern politics must be a topic of interest both within the region and beyond, or libraries would not spend scarce dollars acquiring books about the South.

On the supply side of the equation, the literature on southern politics reflects the tremendous diversity of the discipline of political science.

Nearly every research approach is represented, from biographies and single-case studies to large, data-based statistical studies using advanced quantitative methods to rational-choice analyses that employ formal modeling techniques. It is not simply the case that many scholars find the subject interesting; what is more, the subject can be appropriately studied from a wide variety of analytical perspectives that may appeal to readers of varying levels of skill and interest.

The authors of the previous chapters have placed their segments of literature into a useful context; they have highlighted the themes and noted the areas ripe for additional research. In this concluding chapter I will attempt to treat their chapters in the same way. Three themes quickly emerge: the dramatic change in the region and its politics, the continuing question of southern distinctiveness, and the relationship of the South to national politics. Not surprisingly, all three themes were identified or, in some cases, envisioned in Key's monumental work. Despite the volume of research since *Southern Politics in State and Nation* was published in 1949, there remain areas marked by an absence of scholarly inquiry or in need of additional study as circumstances change. This chapter closes with an examination of what that research agenda might look like.

Changes in the South and Its Politics

In his concluding chapter Key noted that the South was a diverse region; moreover, "the region is also changing. Its rate of evolution may seem glacial, but fundamental shifts in the conditions underlying its politics are taking place. All these changes drive toward a political system more completely in accord with the national ideas of constitutional morality" (1949, 664). In particular, he identified the decline in African American population (which has since been reversed), urbanization, and a shift from agriculture to industry as the primary economic engine. These demographic changes would not "automatically bring political change. They only create conditions favorable to change that must be wrought by men and women disposed to take advantage of the opportunity to accelerate the inevitable" (ibid., 674–75).

The "glacial" changes identified by Key occurred much more swiftly following the publication of his book. Dramatic population growth, especially in Florida and Texas but also elsewhere across the region, brought an influx of new residents from nonsouthern states and other countries. Notable among these new residents are expanding Hispanic populations. Trends in urbanization have accelerated to the point that a majority of every southern state but Mississippi is now urban. Proactive state governments and the pressures of a global economy have made the southern Sun Belt the new home of industry and business in many economic sectors (Cobb 1993; Cobb and Stueck 2005; see also chapter 7 of this volume).

Even more dramatic has been the change in the role played by African Americans in the region's politics. The 1964 Civil Rights Act and the 1965 Voting Rights Act were significant milestones in the transformation of the South. Some of the literature on this transformation is recounted in chapters 3 and 4 of this volume.

The political implications of these trends also have reshaped the South from what it was at the time of Key's work. Most notable, perhaps, are the increases in black elected officials (almost all of them Democrats) and the development of a competitive (and sometimes dominant) Republican Party. Both were almost nonexistent in Key's time, especially in the deep South states. Today African Americans and Republicans have all but crowded out the formerly dominant white Democrats in many areas.

Things that change are more interesting to study than things that remain the same. The changes taking place in the South were so dramatic—and so obvious—that they attracted the attention of a wide range of scholars. Some of them were no doubt native southerners who would have been interested in their local politics regardless of the larger implications of regional transformation. Others saw in these changes an opportunity to study political phenomena of interest to them in a quasi-experimental setting. It was not the South per se that grabbed their interest, but rather the changes taking place in its politics and political institutions.

I place myself in this second group. A native midwesterner, I completed graduate school in 1991 and took a faculty position at a southern university. My academic interests were in party realignment and the development of party organizations. What better place to study these things than in the South in the 1990s? They were not dry theoretical concepts in books and journals; instead, they were the topics of news stories in the local papers. My interest in southern politics developed not because I was interested in the South, but because the South was where my interests were playing themselves out.

The changes that have rocked the South have driven much of the scholarship on the region's politics since World War II. Literature dealing with social and demographic change is analyzed by Richard Scher (chapter 3), Richard Engstrom (chapter 4), and Susan MacManus (chapter 7). Central to these chapters is the role of race and race relations. As Key wrote, using the language of his day, "In its grand outlines the politics of the South revolves around the position of the Negro" (1949, 5). Changes in the position of African Americans in the South and throughout the country necessarily led to changes in the rest of the political system. Considerable work by political scientists remains to be done, as Scher notes, in comparing the civil rights movement to other social movements and grounding it in the rich theoretical traditions of our discipline.

Key (1949) anticipated the effect that these changes would have on the formerly one-party Democratic South. His work on realignment (1955, 1959) shaped the way scholars applied the concept to changes taking place both regionally and nationally. The topic of realignment is covered by Charles Prysby (chapter 1) and, with regard to southern evangelicals, by Ted Jelen (chapter 6). Key was concerned about the absence of party organizations in the region as well. Organizational development and two-party competition are clearly related, although the question of which came first may be impossible to untangle. Local parties on the whole were much weaker in the South than in the rest of the country a quarter century ago (Cotter, Gibson, Bibby, and Huckshorn 1984). Prysby and John McGlennon (chapter 2) chronicle the attempts by scholars to analyze local party development. Missing from most of the studies they cover is the ability to compare the region to the rest of the country to see whether the South has "caught up" in this area.

Finally, the way these changes have manifested themselves in the institutions of government are covered in other chapters of this volume. Penny Miller and Lee Remington (chapter 5) show that despite the impact of individual female political leaders, women remain underrepresented as elected officials in the South. Of the eleven states of the former Confederacy, only Florida was in the upper half of all states in terms of the percentage of women state legislators in 2004. Nevertheless, as Kapeluck, Steed, and Moreland report (chapter 11), southern legislatures have evolved into much more professional assemblies than they were at the time of Key's work. The role of the governor has been transformed as well, both in terms of power within the state and as a launching pad for national political careers. It is worth noting that Jimmy

Carter, Bill Clinton, and George W. Bush lacked Washington experience before winning the presidency. More work needs to be done on ways legislators adjust the organization and rules of their chambers in an era of two-party competition, especially in light of a government divided between executive and legislative branches and the transfer of majority power from one party to the other in the legislature itself.

It would be naïve to assume that no additional changes will occur in the South and its politics. Political scientists are well positioned to analyze these changes and their implications. Placing them in an appropriate historical and theoretical context will strengthen both our understanding of the South as a unique region and our general theories of political phenomena.

Is the South Distinctive?

Inherent in the research on southern politics is the assumption that the South is distinctive from the rest of the country. At times the assumption is implicit, at other times explicit, but it is usually tested only when the point of the argument is to show that it does or does not still hold. In other words, we assume the South is distinctive unless our point is to show that it is not.

The assumption is not without risk, as most of us who make it know but rarely acknowledge. It may not hold, and thus our assertions are rendered uninteresting or the scope of our findings is needlessly limited to a single region. Alternatively, we may conclude a pattern or relationship to be "a southern thing" without pushing deeper to discern what makes it so. The situation is nicely articulated by the journalist Edwin M. Yoder Jr. in his foreword to John Shelton Reed's *The Enduring South*:

> The artist, journalist, or historian who ponders the South for a living must at times be haunted, as I am, by the fear that the regional "differences" he traffics in are essentially obscurantist when you get down to it: elegantly so, it may be, but obscurantist all the same. . . . Each relies on an asserted differentness that mystifies some, infuriates others, and occasionally gives aid and comfort to sworn political enemies. If this regionalist is Southern-born, as he almost invariably is, he feels the differences in his bones. His is a search for definition and explanation. Yet in the dark of night, he contemplates his profession in terror: Is it per-

haps a sort of *trahison des clercs*? Is he dealing in tomfoolery or raising ancient spirits better left sleeping? Is he a cotton-patch Spengler, a Lysenko of the magnolia groves? (1972, xv)

V. O. Key opened his study of southern politics by stating that the South "remains the region with the most distinctive character and tradition" (1949, 1). He did not make the assumption of southern distinctiveness lightly, however. His operational definition of the South as the eleven states of the former Confederacy was grounded in distinctive patterns of presidential voting (ibid., 10). It is more than coincidence that those patterns corresponded with the shared history of secession from the Union during the Civil War and the contemporary characteristic of substantial populations of African Americans, but these underlying causes of presidential voting patterns did not impinge on Key's empirical operationalization.

Fortunately for those who study the region today, we know that the South remains distinctive in a number of ways. Dewey Grantham has identified several cultural patterns that display the persistent differences across regions in the domains of religion, physical violence, music, and literature (1994, 311–31). These and other regional peculiarities are familiar to readers of the journal *Southern Cultures* and consumers of popular culture. Similar differences have been documented in the realm of public opinion (Rice, McLean, and Larsen 2002). Nevertheless, we know that the South has undergone dramatic changes in a number of areas. Does the assumption of southern distinctiveness still hold in the political realm?

Most of the chapters in this volume reflect the implicit nature of the assumption in the literature they cover. For example, a weakness of most of the party activist literature analyzed by John McGlennon (chapter 2) is that only rarely can comparisons be made to the rest of the country. These studies (of which I was a part) provide insight into the changes taking place in the South, but they are unable to tell us whether the same patterns are present in local parties in other places. The difficulties (including the sheer cost) of expanding the scope of a survey from eleven states to fifty is considerable and the unwillingness to do so forgivable, but that does not overcome the limitations imposed by a strictly regional research design.

The question of southern distinctiveness is taken up most directly by Patrick Cotter, Stephen Shaffer, and David Breaux (chapter 8), who examine research on several dimensions of public attitudes. The evidence that the South is different is mixed, and the explanations for why it may (or may not) be different are varied. They conclude that the way in which people form their opinions is the same in the South as elsewhere, even if the factors that influence the content of those opinions may differ. It matters *why* the South may be different as much or more than *whether* it is.

As American society becomes increasingly nationalized, observers of southern politics must continue to question the assumption of southern distinctiveness. We soon may find more studies like that of Laura van Assendelft (1997, discussed in chapter 11 of this volume) that implicitly assume that the South is *not* distinctive and that findings from southern states can be generalized to the rest of the country.

The South and National Politics

While holding the South to be distinctive, V. O. Key was careful to ground his analysis in a broader, more national context. (Note that the full title of his book is *Southern Politics in State and Nation*, not just *Southern Politics*.) Key agreed in part with those southerners who were quick to condemn the North in their defense of their own region. He wrote: "In its shortcomings the South has all the failings common to the American states. The South after all is part of the United States, and everywhere state governments have a long way to go to achieve the promise of American democracy. . . . Southern politicians are also confronted by special problems that demand extraordinary political intelligence, restraint, patience, and persistence for their solution" (1949, 4). Key contended that the basic tenets of democracy, including expanded suffrage and competition between parties, should be applied more broadly in all states. Their notable absence in the South of the 1940s made the region useful for analysis from the perspective of democratic theory; its quirks and unique features made it appealing to a general audience (ibid., especially 298–311).

Key saw the South as the manifestation of potential failings in the rest of the country taken to the extreme. If the South could overcome its political pathologies, so could other states. More recently, however, Augustus Cochran (2001) has argued that the opposite transformation is taking place. For Cochran, the country as a whole has adopted a politics that increasingly resembles the formerly Solid South: a lack of debate over issues, the politics of personality, weakened party organizations, and the significance of money.

The influence of the South on the national political arena can be seen from two perspectives, both captured quite well in various chapters in this volume. First, the South can be seen as a special case because of its unique demographics (see chapter 7). As Richard Scher notes in chapter 3, the civil rights movement was both a regional and a national phenomenon. Some aspects, notably limited voting rights and Jim Crow laws, were more common in the South than elsewhere, and many of the bloody episodes of the struggle for civil rights took place across the South. School segregation and racial discrimination generally, on the other hand, were not limited to any one region of the country. Along the same lines, the drawing of majority-minority districts is one example of the redistricting battles taking place across the country; though more common in the South, minority-based districts have become a part of the political landscape in California and elsewhere (see chapter 4). As Ted Jelen notes in chapter 6, the realignment of social conservatives into the Republican Party and the culture wars dividing "red states" from "blue states" may be especially visible in the South, but the same trends are occurring in many parts of the country (see, for example, Layman 2001). We should heed the caution, though, that it is easy to overstate the differences between Republican red states and Democratic blue states, and many political commentators do just that. (A useful corrective may be found in Fiorina 2004.)

Second, the South as a region has had an important influence on national politics, and it continues to do so today. This influence is most easily recognized in the national institutions of Congress and the presidency. Stanley Berard (chapter 10) summarizes Key's discussion of the opposition of southern Democrats in the U.S. House and Senate to civil rights legislation, a pattern that has been altered as the southern electorate has changed and the parties have realigned. The Republican takeover of the House in 1994 had a particularly strong southern flavor.[1] In fact, the switch of party control of both chambers was made possible by Republican gains in the region. As Harold Stanley demonstrates (chapter 9), the Democratic Solid South has become strongly Republican in presidential politics. Republican nominees swept all eleven southern states in 1972, 1984, 1988, 2000, and 2004. The region's electoral votes were especially important to George W. Bush in 2000, as victory by Al Gore in Florida or his home state of Tennessee—or anywhere else, for that matter—would have denied Bush the presidency.

The South's role in the transformation of the presidential nominating system has not been fully appreciated by political scientists. For roughly a century, from Jackson's administration to the rule's abolition in 1936, a Democratic Party rule required that a candidate receive the support of two-thirds of national convention delegates to win the party's nomination. The two-thirds rule gave the southern states, acting in concert, the ability to block the nomination of a candidate whom they opposed (see Freidel 1971, 2716–27). The McGovern-Fraser reforms following the Democrats' tumultuous 1968 convention grew out of a need to establish clear rules for determining which delegates should be seated at the national convention. Conflicts arose in Mississippi in 1964 and in Mississippi and Georgia in 1968 when two slates of delegates demanded to be seated (Broder 1971, 3734–35; Bass and DeVries 1976). The new rules transformed presidential nominations into the candidate-centered process that we see today.[2]

More recently, various southern states have tried to alter the timing of their state primaries to affect the outcome of the nomination process. Their collective attempt to make an impact resulted in the "Super Tuesday" regional primary in 1988. In all, twenty states and the territory of Guam held their Democratic nomination contests on the same day. Of the southern states, only South Carolina did not hold its primary on Super Tuesday. Regional organizers hoped to propel a moderate southerner to the Democratic nomination; instead, the South's votes were split among three candidates. Although Super Tuesday failed to make the impact its Democratic designers envisioned, it did help Vice President George H. W. Bush sew up the Republican nomination (Hadley and Stanley 1989; Bullock 1991; Norrander 1992). In 1992, 1996, and 2000 the early South Carolina primary helped Republican front-runners fend off challenges following disappointing finishes in Iowa and New Hampshire. The Georgia primary helped catapult Arkansas's Governor Bill Clinton to the Democratic nomination in 1992. The primary date was moved up at the request of Governor Zell Miller, an early supporter of Clinton (Bullock 1994, 1997; Clark and Haynes 2002).

Whether the South continues to exert undue influence over national politics depends on its continued distinctiveness in the midst of regional change. The continued flow of jobs and people from the Rust Belt to the Sun Belt may slow as the costs of living equalize across regions and the costs of manufacturing drive jobs to other countries. Likewise, a new set of issue cleavages could replace the current red state–blue state division that favors the South when Republicans are in power. In the near future, though, it seems that the current "southernization" of national politics is likely to continue.

A Research Agenda for Southern Politics

The authors of these chapters have identified some aspects of their topics that deserve additional study, and I have highlighted some as well. Old questions need to be reexamined using new methodologies or different theoretical perspectives, and new questions are constantly being formulated.

Two topics not directly covered in this volume strike me as worthy of additional attention by political scientists. The first is race. The importance of race was certainly understood by Key, who wrote, "Whatever phase of the southern political process one seeks to understand, sooner or later the trail of inquiry leads to the Negro" (1949, 5). Each of the preceding chapters deals with race in some form or another, yet most of us fail to understand how the nuances of racial relations affect other aspects of politics. We often assume that the people we place into various racial categories all think and act the same way, yet our assumption is no more true today than it was in the pre–civil rights South. The study of race becomes more complicated when new groups such as Hispanic Americans enter the fray. The question of race has not been ignored, and in some topical areas such as the one addressed by Engstrom in chapter 4 it has been investigated extensively. As Scher suggests in chapter 3, however, it deserves more attention from political scientists.

A second topic in need of more attention is the role of interest groups in the politics of southern states. Relatively little systematic work has been done in this area.[3] The economic elite long exerted considerable influence in statehouses across the region. At one point these elites were primarily plantation owners; now they may be executives of multinational corporations. Business groups have lobbied to improve the quality of educational systems to expand the pool of skilled workers and to make it easier to recruit executives from elsewhere. Business leaders worked behind the scenes in South Carolina and Georgia to reduce the visibility of the Confederate battle flag, to give another example.

In addition to economic interests, other groups (both formal and informal) are deserving of systematic analysis. As Richard Scher notes in chapter 3, the civil rights movement should be compared to other types of social movements. Civil rights groups can be contrasted with the citizens' councils and other reactionary groups that formed to oppose civil rights. Groups associated with the religious right or organized labor may have varying degrees of success in different states.

Research on these and other topics can build on the themes identified earlier in this chapter. Questions of how the South is changing, whether it continues to be distinctive, and how the region influences national politics will shape research well into the future. When it comes to "writing southern politics," to paraphrase Key, there is not likely to be an end anytime soon.

Notes

1. Interestingly, the top two leaders, Newt Gingrich of Georgia and Richard Armey of Texas, were transplants to the South. Gingrich was an Army brat whose family moved to Georgia when he was in high school. Armey is a North Dakota native who moved to Texas to take a teaching job after graduate school. The third-ranked leader, Tom DeLay, is a lifelong Texan.

2. The reform movement and its consequences have been thoroughly analyzed. See, for example, works by Ranney (1975), Kirkpatrick (1976), Polsby (1983), and Shafer (1983).

3. There are a few exceptions, of course. For example, a book edited by Hrebenar and Thomas (1992) examined interest groups in each of the southern states in the 1980s.

References

Bass, Jack, and Walter DeVries. 1976. *The Transformation of Southern Politics: Social Change and Political Consequence since 1945*. New York: Basic Books.

Broder, David S. 1971. "Election of 1968." In *History of American Presidential Elections, 1789–1968*, ed. Arthur M. Schlesinger Jr. New York: Chelsea House.

Bullock, Charles S., III. 1991. "The Nomination Process and Super Tuesday." In *The 1988 Presidential Election in the South: Continuity amidst Change in Southern Party Politics*, ed. Laurence W. Moreland, Robert P. Steed, and Tod A. Baker. New York: Praeger.

———. 1994. "Nomination: The South's Role in 1992 Nomination Politics." In *The 1992 Presidential Election in the South: Current Patterns of Southern Party and Electoral Politics*, ed. Robert P. Steed, Laurence W. Moreland, and Tod A. Baker. Westport, Conn.: Praeger.

———. 1997. "The 1996 Presidential Nomination: Short and Sweet." In *The 1996 Presidential Election in the South: Southern Party Systems in the 1990s*, ed. Laurence W. Moreland and Robert P. Steed. Westport, Conn.: Praeger.

Clark, John A., and Audrey A. Haynes. 2002. "The 2000 Presidential Nominating Process." In *The 2000 Presidential Election in the South: Partisanship and Southern Party Systems in the 21st Century*, ed. Robert P. Steed and Laurence W. Moreland. Westport, Conn.: Praeger.

Cobb, James C. 1993, 2nd ed. *The Selling of the South: The Southern Crusade for Industrial Development, 1936–1990*. Urbana: University of Illinois Press.

Cobb, James C., and William Stueck, eds. 2005. *Globalization and the American South*. Athens: University of Georgia Press.

Cochran, Augustus B., III. 2001. *Democracy Heading South: National Politics in the Shadow of Dixie*. Lawrence: University Press of Kansas.

Cotter, Cornelius P., James L. Gibson, John F. Bibby, and Robert J. Huckshorn. 1984. *Party Organizations in American Politics*. New York: Praeger.

Fiorina, Morris P., with Samuel J. Abrams and Jeremy C. Pope. 2004. *Culture War? The Myth of a Polarized America*. New York: Pearson/Longman.

Freidel, Frank. 1971. "Election of 1932." In *History of American Presidential Elections, 1789–1968*, ed. Arthur M. Schlesinger Jr. New York: Chelsea House.

Grantham, Dewey W. 1994. *The South in Modern America: A Region at Odds*. New York: HarperCollins.

Hadley, Charles D., and Harold W. Stanley. 1989. "Super Tuesday 1988: Regional Results, National Implications." *Publius: The Journal of Federalism* 19: 19–37.

Hrebenar, Ronald J., and Clive S. Thomas, eds. 1992. *Interest Group Politics in the Southern States*. Tuscaloosa: University of Alabama Press.

Key, V. O., Jr. 1949. *Southern Politics in State and Nation*. New York: Knopf.

———. 1955. "A Theory of Critical Elections." *Journal of Politics* 17: 3–18.

———. 1959. "Secular Realignment and the Party System." *Journal of Politics* 21: 198–210.

Kirkpatrick, Jeane J. 1976. *The New Presidential Elite: Men and Women in National Politics*. New York: Russell Sage Foundation.

Layman, Geoffrey. 2001. *The Great Divide: Religious and Cultural Conflict in American Party Politics*. New York: Columbia University Press.

Norrander, Barbara. 1992. *Super Tuesday: Regional Politics and Presidential Primaries*. Lexington: University Press of Kentucky.

Polsby, Nelson W. 1983. *Consequences of Party Reform*. New York: Oxford University Press.

Ranney, Austin. 1975. *Curing the Mischiefs of Faction: Party Reform in America*. Berkeley: University of California Press.

Rice, Tom W., William P. McLean, and Amy J. Larsen. 2002. "Southern Distinctiveness over Time, 1972–2000." *American Review of Politics* 23: 193–220.

Shafer, Byron E. 1983. *Quiet Revolution: The Struggle for the Democratic Party and the Shaping of Post-Reform Politics*. New York: Russell Sage Foundation.

van Assendelft, Laura. 1997. *Governors, Agenda Setting, and Divided Government*. Lanham, Md.: University Press of America.

Yoder, Edwin M., Jr. 1972. Foreword to *The Enduring South: Subcultural Persistence in Mass Society*, by John Shelton Reed. Lexington, Mass.: Lexington Books.

Contributors

STANLEY P. BERARD is an assistant professor of political science at Lock Haven University of Pennsylvania.

DAVID A. BREAUX is a professor of political science and chair of the Department of Political Science at Mississippi State University.

JOHN A. CLARK is a professor of political science at Western Michigan University.

PATRICK R. COTTER is a professor of political science at the University of Alabama.

RICHARD L. ENGSTROM is Research Professor of Political Science at the University of New Orleans.

TED G. JELEN is a professor of political science at the University of Nevada at Las Vegas.

BRANWELL DUBOSE KAPELUCK is an assistant professor of political science at The Citadel.

SUSAN A. MACMANUS is a professor of political science at the University of South Florida.

JOHN J. MCGLENNON is a professor of government at the College of William and Mary.

PENNY M. MILLER is an associate professor of political science at the University of Kentucky.

LAURENCE W. MORELAND is a professor of political science at The Citadel.

BRITTANY L. PENBERTHY is an honors graduate of the University of South Florida and is currently a research associate at that institution.

CHARLES PRYSBY is a professor of political science at the University of North Carolina at Greensboro.

LEE R. REMINGTON is a Ph.D. candidate at the University of Kentucky.

RICHARD K. SCHER is Robin and Jean Gibson Professor of Political Science at the University of Florida.

STEPHEN D. SHAFFER is a professor of political science at Mississippi State University.

HAROLD W. STANLEY is Geurin-Pettus Distinguished Professor of American Politics and Political Economy at Southern Methodist University.

ROBERT P. STEED is a professor of political science at The Citadel.

THOMAS A. WATSON is an undergraduate student in political science at the University of South Florida.

Index

1928 elections, 145, 222
1948 elections, 159, 223
1952 elections, 145, 222, 223, 225, 226, 228
1956 elections, 223, 225
1960 elections, 144, 154, 223, 225, 229, 232, 281
1964 elections, x–xi, 2, 18, 222, 225–26, 227, 229, 234
1968 elections, 18, 159, 224, 227–28, 229, 232, 234, 235, 299
1970 elections, 281
1972 elections, 146, 228, 229, 230, 232, 235
1976 elections, 19, 146, 228, 229, 230, 233, 234
1978 senatorial election in Virginia, 44–45
1980 elections, 20, 222, 230, 234, 235
1984 elections, 222, 230, 231, 232, 235
1984 state convention delegate survey, 47, 124, 130
1986 elections, 253
1988 elections, 112n4, 231, 232, 235, 299
1989 election in Virginia, 286
1990 elections, 253
1992 elections, viii, 95, 96, 97, 98, 99, 101–4, 112n3, 112n6, 113n8, 113n10, 114n13, 155, 231–32, 233, 234, 299
1994 elections, ix, 95, 97, 98, 99, 104–7, 110, 112n3, 113n10, 114n13, 234, 251, 253, 260, 261, 298
1996 elections, 104, 108, 112n3, 114n13, 155, 233, 234, 253, 299
1998 elections, 108, 253
2000 elections, 66, 112n4, 141, 142, 234, 235, 253, 299
2002 elections, 109, 111, 150, 253
2004 elections, ix–x, 94, 111, 141, 142, 235, 236

Abernathy, Ralph, 152
abolitionist movement, 131
abortion, x, 144, 146, 148, 151, 152, 158, 191, 209, 251, 286
Abrahamson, Mark, 206
Abramowitz, Alan, 112n6
additive model of religious influence, 143
affirmative action policy, 107, 201, 203, 204
Ahern, David, 121
Aistrup, Joseph, 5, 21, 30, 49, 50, 92, 221, 228
Akins, Frances, 123
Albany Freedom Ride, 132
Aldrich, John H., 30, 252
Almanac of State Legislatures, 288
Althof, Phillip, 42
amateur activists, 42, 53
American Political Science Association's Committee on Political Parties, 14
American Review of Politics, 5
Anderson, R. Bruce, 283
anti-Semitism, 157
Appleton, Andrew M., 29
Arkansas Governor's Commission on the Status of Women, 128
Armey, Richard, 260, 301n1
Arseneau, Robert E., 18, 19
Atwater, Lee, xi, 230–31
authoritarianism, 190

Baker, Ella, 132
Baker, Tod A., 46, 47, 48, 124, 220, 232
Baker v. *Carr* (1962), 270

305

Baliles, Gerald, 286
Bankston, William B., 200
Barnett, Ross, 84
Barone, Michael, 99
Barth, Jay, 134, 152
Bartley, Numan V., 3, 4, 18, 79, 91, 221, 252
Bass, Jack, 3–4, 6, 84, 91, 221, 249–50
Beachler, Donald, 99, 103, 104, 106
Beck, Paul A., 18, 19
behavioral theories of Congress, 244
Berard, Stanley, 7, 8, 251, 298
Berger, Peter, 143
Berkman, Michael B., 144
Bernick, Lee E., 282–83
Beyle, Thad, 288
Bibby, John E., 50
biracial coalition, ix, 229, 250–51, 254, 261, 280, 286
birth control, 209
Black, Earl, 2, 4, 5, 20, 21, 91, 92, 146, 220, 221, 222, 230, 252, 254, 259–60, 269, 278–79, 279–80, 281, 283, 284, 286
Black, Hugo, 242
Black, Merle, 2, 4, 5, 20, 21, 91, 92, 146, 220, 221, 222, 230, 252, 254, 259–60, 269, 278, 279–80, 281, 283, 284, 286
black activism, 47, 284, 285
Black Belt, 242, 243
black belt thesis, 144
black congressional representation, 255–57, 271. See also congressional districting
black enfranchisement, 270, 273, 283
black feminism movement, 132
black Muslim, 153
black nationalism, 87
Black Panther movement, 65
Black Panther Party, 132
black political mobilization, 19, 234–35, 243, 277–78
black power, 87, 132
black separatism, 87
black women and southern politics, 130–31
Blank, Blanche, 42
blue dog congressional coalition, 255

Bobo, Lawrence, 200–204
Boggs, Lindy, 133
Bolling, Richard, 248
Bowman, R. Lewis, 3, 29, 42, 48, 126, 127
Boynton, G. Robert, 3, 42
Brady, David, 246, 247
Brady, Henry E., 152
Branch, Taylor, 74, 77, 78
Breaux, David A., 8, 53, 296–97
Breitman, George, 87
Brodsky, David, 5, 92
Brookings Institution, 172
Brooks, Thomas, 74
Brown, Thad, 180–81
Brown v. Board of Education (1954), 65, 67, 69, 84, 152, 225
Buchanan, Pat, 148, 154
Bullock, Charles S., III, 5, 21, 92, 103, 123, 135, 246, 247
Burnham, James, 245
Burns, James MacGregor, 245
Burrell, Barbara, 121
Bush, George H. W., ix, 231, 232, 233, 234, 299
Bush, George W., ix, x, xi, 141, 156, 234, 235, 295, 298
Byrd, Harry F., 243

Calhoun-Brown, Allison, 152
Cameron, Charles, 113n13
campaign activity, 56, 57
Campbell, Bruce A., 19
Campbell, Clarice T., 132
Canon, David, 256, 258, 259
capital punishment, 146, 155, 207, 233
Carmines, Edward, 198
Carp, Robert, 129
Carroll, Susan, 121
Carter, Dan T., 280
Carter, Jimmy, vii–viii, ix, 146, 148, 228, 229–30, 231, 233, 234, 236, 294–95
Carter, Valerie, 206
Carver, Joan, 127
Cash, Wilbur J., 192
Chafe, William, 79
Chafee, Lincoln, 52
children's campaign, 77
children's issues, 121

Christian Coalition, ix, 235
Christian Right. See religious right
Citadel Symposium on Southern
    Politics, The, xi, 4–5, 46, 48
Citizens Conference on State
    Legislatures, 271–272
civil liberties, 246
Civil Rights Act of 1964, xi, 219, 222,
    225, 227, 293
civil rights era, 219, 269
civil rights issues. See race relations
civil rights movement, 7, 18, 19, 25, 65–
    90, 119, 151, 152, 201, 203–4, 241,
    250, 276, 294, 298, 300; leadership,
    76–78; Marxist perspectives on,
    87–88; movement dynamics, 78–81;
    outcomes, 80–82, 288; and political
    consciousness, 70–73; and political
    mobilization, 73–78; reforms, 269;
    and urban black churches, 74–75;
    women in, 83–84, 131–33
Civil War, 65, 222, 296
Clark, Janet, 121, 124, 125
Clark, John A., 29, 49, 56
Clark, Septima, 132
Clarke, Harold, 125
Clausen, Aage, 244, 245, 246, 247
Clayton, Eva, 113n8
Cleaver, Eldridge, 70
Cleghorn, Reese, 78
Clinton, Bill, viii, 148, 232–34, 236,
    254, 295, 299
Cnudde, Charles, 3
coalition building, 183
Coates, Diane, 208
Cobb, Michael D., 204–5
Cochran, Augustus, 297
Colburn, David R., 77, 78, 79
cold war, 246
Coleman, Mary DeLorse, 276
Collier-Thomas, Bettye, 132
Collins, Mac, 259
Collins, Susan, 52
Committee on Civil Rights, 68
Community Food and Nutrition
    Program, xi
compassionate conservatism, 234–35
conditional party government theory,
    249, 250

Confederacy, 192, 193
Confederate flag, 236, 300
Confederate monuments, 111
Conger, Kimberly, 144
Congress and the South, 241–68;
    congressional leadership, 259–61;
    congressional transformations,
    249–53; party decline, 247; party
    leadership, 244, 247, 248–49
Congressional Black Caucus, 261
congressional districting, 8, 91–118,
    269, 270–71, 274, 276, 283, 285,
    298; and migration, 175; partisan
    effects, 99–102; post-1994, 107–9;
    race and, 92–95, 182–83, 254,
    255–57, 276; religion and, 150–51;
    voting and, 92–95
congressional voting patterns, 27
Congress of Racial Equality, 73, 75–76
conservative coalition, 242, 245–47, 252
Converse, Philip, 17, 19, 181
conversion, 19, 26
Conway, M. Margaret, 42, 121
Cooper, William J., Jr., 7
Cosman, Bernard, 2, 18, 220, 226
Cotter, Cornelius P., 30, 50
Cotter, Patrick R., 8, 296–297
countersocialization theory, 124–25
Cox, Gary, 248–49
Crawford, Vicki, 131
Crime, 207
Crotty, William J., Jr., 3, 43, 51
cultural issues, 207, 251, 253. See also
    social issues
Curry, Andrea E., 171
Curry, Constance, 132

Darcy, Robert, 121, 124, 125, 130–31
David, Paul, 24
David Index, 24
Davidson, Chandler, 5
Davidson, Roger, 244
Davis, Kenneth, 205–6
Day, Christine, 126
Deal, Nathan, 113n11
dealignment, 18, 149; among white
    moderates, 230
Dean, Howard, 236
death penalty. See capital punishment

decentralization of intergovernmental
    aid, 284
defense issues, 27, 233, 253
de la Cruz, G. Patricia, 171
DeLay, Tom, 260, 301n1
Democratic Leadership Council, 50
Desposato, Scott, 106
Devillers, Chester, 81–82
DeVries, Walter, vii, viii, 3–4, 91, 221,
    249–50
Dewey, Thomas, 223
divorce, 190, 209
Djupe, Paul A., 159
Dole, Robert, 233
Drescher, John, 280–81
dual-party system, 48
Du Bois, W. E. B., 71, 72
Dukakis, Michael, 231, 232, 236

Easley, Mike, x
Easley v. Cromartie (2001), 109
economic change, 292
economic issues, 25, 27, 121, 148, 251,
    253, 255, 271
Edds, Margaret, 167, 286
Edsall, Mary, 92
Edsall, Thomas, 92
education issues, 121, 200, 274
Egerton, John, 67, 69, 70
Eisenhower, Dwight D., 17, 223,
    228–29
Elazar, Daniel, 212
Eldersveld, Samuel J., 42, 57
electoral patterns, 23, 27–29
Ellender, Allen, 243
Ellison, Christopher, 206–7, 212–13
Emancipation Proclamation, 65
Emerson, Michael O., 149
English usage, 190
Engstrom, Richard L., 8, 294, 300
environmental issues, 200
Epstein, David, 113–14n13
Equal Rights Amendment, 128
Ewing, Cortez, 272

factionalism, 46
Fair Employment Practices
    Commission, 68
Farmer, James, 76

Faubus, Orval, viii
Feig, Douglas, 210–11, 212
Feigert, Frank B., 42, 56, 125
Fenno, Richard, 244, 250, 255, 256,
    259
Ferrell, Thomas, 133
Fields, Cleo, 113n12
Fifteenth Amendment, 65
Fiorina, Morris, 250
Firebaugh, Glenn, 205–6
Fisher, Sethard, 87
Fleer, Jack, 3
Flynt, Jack, 259
food stamps, xi
Ford, Gerald, 229, 230
foreign policy issues, 27, 148, 245, 246
Forman, James, 75
Fourteenth Amendment, 65, 108
Franklin, John Hope, 72
Franklin, V. P., 132
freedom schools, 132
Freedom Summer, 75, 132
Free Joan Little Movement, 132
Freeman, Donald M., 3
Freeman, Patricia K., 134, 282–83
Frey, William H., 172, 175, 177, 178, 179
Frist, Bill, 260
Fuller, Chet, 80–81, 82

Gallup Poll, 197
Garrow, David, 75, 77, 78
Gates, Henry Lewis, 87
Gatlin, Douglas S., 18
gay marriage issue, x, 141
gay rights, 66, 134–35, 146, 148, 151,
    152, 158, 209
gender gap, 126, 127, 134
gender roles, 122, 125, 191, 208–9; and
    migration, 209; racial and gender
    comparisons, 208–9
generational change, 19, 54
Gibson, James L., 50
Gilbert, Christopher P., 159
Gilens, Martin, 204–5
Gilmour, Terry L., 122
Gingrich, Newt, viii–ix, 260, 301n1
Giugni, Marco, 87
Glaeser, Edward L., 172
Glaser, James M., 5, 205, 255

Glass, Carter, 243
glass ceiling effect, 123, 124, 134
Glenn, Norval, 196–97
Goldwater, Barry M., x, 18, 222, 225–26, 227, 229
good old boy network, 122, 124, 134
Gore, Al, 141, 156, 231, 232–34, 236, 298
Gosnell, Harold F., 41, 51, 53
government management issues, 246
government spending issues, 200
governors in the South, 269–90, 294
Graham, Frank P., 69
Graham, Hugh D., 3, 4, 18, 79, 91, 221, 252
Gramm, Phil, 260
Grantham, Dewey, 296
Grau, Craig H., 275
Great Society Program, 145, 284
Greeley, Andrew, 205
Green, Daniel, 124
Greene, Kathanne, 135
Greene, Melissa Fay, 81, 82
Greensboro, 79
Gresham's Law, 143
Grofman, Bernard, 5, 105, 106, 107
Guinier, Lani, 83
gun control, 207

Hadley, Charles D., 29, 48, 124, 125, 126, 127, 130–31, 192–93, 199
Hall, Richard, 258
Hamer, Fannie Lou, 83, 132
Hamm, Keith, 276–77, 283
Handley, Lisa, 105, 106, 107
Harmel, Robert, 276–77
Havard, William C., 3, 91, 221, 252
Hawkey, Earl, 198
Hawks, Joanne, 123
Haydel, Judith, 133
Hayes, Jimmy, 111–12n3, 113n11
He, Wan, 171, 178
health care issues, 200, 234, 274
Heard, Alexander, 2, 17, 224, 225
Height, Dorothy, 132
Helms, Jesse, 260
Hero, Alfred O., 189
Hill, Kevin, 102, 103, 105–6, 107, 112n7

Hill, Lister, 242
Hill, Samuel, 74
Hirschfield, Robert, 42
Hispanics, 155–56, 235, 293; population growth effects, 183, 300
Hoffman, Laura Jane, 123
Holton, Linwood, 45
Hood, M. V., III, 149
hooks, bell, 87, 88
Hoover, Herbert, 145
Horton, Willie. See Willie Horton campaign ad
House reforms, 248
Hrebenar, Ronald, 284–85, 301n3
Huckaby, Elizabeth, 79
Huckshorn, Robert J., 50
Hulbary, William, 48, 126, 127
Humphrey, Hubert H., 227, 232, 236
Hunter-Gault, Charlayne, 132
Hurlbert, Jeanne S., 200, 208
Hyman, Herbert H., 205

ideology, 189–218; regional differences in, 197–211
immigration. See migration
interest group activity, 284, 300
interracial marriage, 202
Ippolito, Dennis S., 42, 51
issue orientations, 189–218; regional differences in, 197–211

Jackson, Jesse, 47, 55, 123, 231
Jacoway, Elizabeth, 78–79
Jeffries, Judson L., 286
Jelen, Ted G., 8, 206–7, 294, 298
Jewell, Malcolm, 48, 121, 270–71, 274–75
Jim Crow system, vii, 2, 67, 68, 71, 72, 73, 75, 77, 78, 79, 80, 82, 86, 111, 298
Johnson, Charles, 212
Johnson, Frank M., 84
Johnson, Lyndon B., 219, 222, 223, 225–26, 227, 229, 234
Johnson, Timothy R., 159
Johnston, Richard D., 21, 94

Kahn, Kim Fridkin, 121
Kapeluck, Branwell DuBose, 8, 294

Kelley, Anne, 48, 126
Kennedy, Edward, 231
Kennedy, John F., 17, 84, 144, 222, 223, 225, 232
Kennedy, Robert F., 84
Kerry, John, 141, 142, 236
Key, V. O., Jr., vii, x, xi, xii, 1, 2, 4, 6, 17, 24, 41, 42–43, 44, 71, 88, 91, 119, 144, 170–71, 182, 191–92, 193, 196, 212, 213, 224, 241–43, 245, 247, 270, 274, 275, 291, 292, 293, 294, 295, 297, 298, 300, 301
Kidd, Mae Street, 133
King, Martin Luther, Jr., 65, 66, 73, 75, 76, 77–78, 151
Kirkpatrick, Jeane, 301n2
Kluger, Richard, 78
Knuckey, Jonathan, 21, 106
Korean War, 69
Krehbiel, Keith, 249
Krysan, Maria, 200–204
Kuklinski, James H., 204–5
Kurtz, Michael J., 273–74

labor issues, 242, 246
Ladd, Everett Carll, 199
Lamis, Alexander P., xi, 4, 5, 20, 24, 91, 220, 221, 232, 254–55
Larsen, Amy, 199–200, 206, 208, 209
Laughlin, Greg, 113n11
Lawson, Steven F., 68
legislatures in the South, 269–90, 294
leisure time usage, 190
Lewis, John, 75
Lieberman, Joseph, 142, 156
Lincoln, Abraham, 222
Little Rock, 79
lobbyists, 134
Lockerbie, Brad, 56
logrolling, 248
Long, Earl, 273
Long, Huey, 243, 272
Long Dynasty, 272
Lott, Trent, 260
Lublin, David, 5, 92, 95, 99, 102, 103, 104, 107, 110, 112n4, 112–13n7, 113n9, 114n13, 221, 255, 275
MacManus, Susan A., 8, 123, 294
MacRae, Duncan, 244

Maggiotto, Michael, 123, 135
majority-minority districts. See congressional districting
malapportionment, 272, 274, 288
management activities, 57
Manley, John, 244
Marable, Manning, 87
Mars, Florence, 79
Martinez, J. Michael, 111
Martorano, Nancy, 283
Marxism, 151
material incentives, 53
Matthews, Donald R., 3, 244
Mayhew, David, 247
McAdam, Doug, 67, 69, 70, 86, 87, 88
McCubbins, Matthew, 248–49
McGlennon, John J., 7, 57, 294, 296
McGovern, George, 146, 229, 232, 236
McGovern-Fraser nominating reforms, 299
McKee, Seth, 103, 112n7
McKinnon, Jesse, 171
McLean, William, 199–200, 206, 208, 209
McNinch-Su, Ron, 111
McPherson, James M., 7
Medicaid, xi
Meier, August, 75
Mele, Christopher, 131
Mezey, Michael L., 211–12
Middleton, Russell, 205
migration, xi, 19, 26–27, 43, 46, 72, 128, 155, 159–50, 167–88, 274, 276, 292–93; and African Americans, 176–77, 182–83; defined, 185n2; foreign-born migrants, 174–76, 276; and ideology, 205–6; movers' backgrounds, 171–74; and party realignment, 180–81; retirees, 177–79; U.S. natives, 179; when and where, 173–74; who moves, 172–73; why, 173
military issues, 121
Miller, Penny M., 8, 122, 128
Miller, Zell, 52, 299
Miller v. Johnson ((1995), 110
Mississippi Freedom Democratic Party, 132
Mondale, Walter, 55, 230, 232, 236

Montgomery bus boycott, 77, 132
moral values issues, 209–10, 253. *See also* social issues
Moreland, Laurence W., 8, 46, 47, 48, 124, 220, 232, 294
Morgan, Ruth, 84
Morris, Aldon D., 67, 74, 86, 87
Morrison, Toni, 85, 87
mountain Republicans, 24, 27, 224, 229
Musick, Marc A., 206–7, 212–13
Muslims, 160
Myrdal, Gunnar, 68, 69

Nader, Ralph, 159
National Association for the Advancement of Colored People, 67–68, 73, 75–76, 111
National Black Election Study, 257
National Emergency Council, 71
National Journal, 52
National Opinion Research Center, 197, 205
National Organization of Women, 123
Navasky, Victor, 84
"Negro Republicans," 224
Newberger, Eric C., 171
Newby, I. A., 68
New Deal, 26, 199, 222, 223–24, 242–43, 246, 272
New Federalism, 282
Newmark, Adam, 123
New South, 81
Niemi, Richard, 112n6
Nixon, E. D., 77
Nixon, H. C., 270
Nixon, Richard M., 159, 223, 225, 226, 227–28, 229, 230, 234
Nobel Peace Prize, 76
Noelle-Neumann, Elisabeth, 143
Nownes, Anthony, 134
Nuwer, Deanne, 122

Obenshain, Richard, 45
O'Connor, Robert E., 144
Odum, Howard, 71, 192
O'Halloran, Sharyn, 113–14n13
Olson, David M., 282–83
Olson, Lynne, 131
one-party system, 122, 223, 242, 272, 294

open housing laws, 203
Overby, Marvin, 134

Parker, Mike, 113n11
Parks, Rosa, 70, 83
Parry, Janine, 128
party activists, 28, 41–64, 296; background differences, 41, 51; factionalism, 55–56; issue and ideological positions, 42, 51–52, 54; motivations, 42, 53; objectives, 42; organizational activism, 56–57; recruitment patterns, 42; regional conflicts, 56, 58; religious preferences, 51; urban-rural conflicts, 56, 58
party competition, 12–14, 22–24, 43, 48, 241, 283, 284, 285, 293
party decline, 12, 247
party development in the South, 11–40
party identification, 199
party machine, 41, 51, 53
party maintenance activities, 56
party organizational strength, 16–17, 29–31, 32, 293, 294
party realignment in the South, ix, 1, 6, 11–12, 16,17–32, 43–44, 48, 49, 52, 93–94, 142, 145–46, 190, 220–21, 224–25, 245, 251–52, 269, 271, 275–76, 277, 285, 288, 293, 294, 298; among white conservatives, 230, 280, 298; ideological, 254
party renewal, 12, 14–15
party switching, 46, 113n11
party system: basic concept, 11; cleavages, 14–16, 24–29
party transformation. *See* party realignment in the South
Patterson, Samuel C., 42
Peoples, Morgan D., 273–74
Pepper, Meredith L., 205, 209
Perot, Ross, 233
perverse partisan effects thesis, 97–99, 101–2, 105, 107, 110, 112n5, 112n6
Peters, Ronald M., 260–61
Peterson, David A. M., 159
Petrocik, John R., 106
Phil Burton Award, 99
Phillips, Kevin, 18, 221, 228, 234

Plessy v. *Ferguson* (1896), 65, 67–68, 152
pluralist hypothesis (model), 143–44,
    147, 155
policy dimension theory, 244
political opinions in the South, 189–
    218; methods of studying, 191–97
Polsby, Nelson, 301n2
Poole, Keith, 258
population movement. *See* migration
Population Studies Center, 171
pornography, 209
Powell, Jody, vii
Powers, Georgia Davis, 133
pragmatism, 54–55
Prather, Lenore, 129
Prescott, Frank, 272–73
presidential elections and southern
    politics, 219–39; after Reagan,
    232–35; before Goldwater, 222–25;
    nominating reforms, 231–32,
    298–99
presidential Republicanism, 220
professional activists, 42
Prothro, James W., 3
Prysby, Charles, 7, 21, 29, 49, 54, 294
public accommodations isues, 203
purism, 54–55, 146
purposive incentives, 53

race relations, x–xi, 2–3, 7, 25, 27,
    91–118, 148, 149, 151, 182, 191,
    197, 222–23, 225–26, 242, 243, 245,
    246, 247, 251, 252, 253, 255, 271,
    279, 281, 284, 294, 300; attitudes
    toward, 200–206
race riots, 65, 68
racial gerrymandering, 108, 109
Rae, Nicol, 5, 49, 50, 105–6, 107,
    220–21, 253, 260, 261
Raines, Howell, 74, 79
Ramirez, Roberta A., 171
Randolph, A. Philip, 71–72, 73
Ranney, Austin, 301n2
Ransone, Coleman B., 273
rational theories of Congress, 247–49
Reagan, Ronald, xi, 47, 146, 159, 226,
    230, 232, 234, 235, 248
realignment. *See* party realignment in
    the South

Reconstruction, 70–71, 145, 222
Reed, John Shelton, 4, 196, 197, 212,
    295
Reed, Ralph, 234
Reid, Traciel, 129, 134
religion: and African Americans
    in southern politics, 151–53;
    Catholicism,17, 154–56; Christian
    Coalition, ix, 235; evangelicals,
    ix, 142, 145–51, 148, 149, 156,
    235, 294; involvement levels,
    190; Jews, 156–57; mainline
    Protestants, 157–58; models
    of religious influence, 142–45;
    nonevangelicals, 153–60; non-
    Judeo-Christians, 159–60;
    Pentecostals, 235; and politics,
    25, 47, 141–66; seculars, 158–59;
    white fundamentalists, ix, 235
religious right, 51, 148, 149, 230,
    234, 235, 301. *See also* Christian
    Coalition
Remington, Lee R., 8
Reno v. *Bossier Parish School Board*
    (1997), 110
replacement of voters, 26
Republican Party: coalitional
    patterns, 142, 230; congressional
    representation, 257–59;
    organization in Georgia, ix;
    southern strategy, x, 4, 226–31, 234;
    top-down growth, 21, 276
responsible parties, 12, 32, 243–44
Rice, Tom W., 199–200, 205, 206, 207,
    209
Richardson, William D., 111
Ripon Society, 50
Robb, Charles, 286
Robertson, Pat, 148
Robinson, Jo Ann, 83
Rohde, David W., 249, 250, 252, 253
Roosevelt, Eleanor, 72
Roosevelt, Franklin D., 71, 72, 199,
    222, 223
Rosenthal, Richard, 258
Rouse, Jacqueline, 131
Rowland, C. K., 129
Rozell, Mark, 5, 21, 92
Rudwick, Elliott, 75

Rule, Wilma, 121
rule of biracial coalitions, 254–55
rule of black majorities, 254, 256
rule of white majorities, 254

Sabato, Larry, 282, 284
sacred canopy hypothesis, 143, 144–45, 147, 155, 157
Sanders, Randy, 281
Sanford, Terry, 280–81
Sapiro, Virginia, 121
Schachter, Jason P., 171, 178
Schaller, Thomas, 94
Scher, Richard K., 5, 8, 91, 92, 134, 274, 285–86, 294, 298, 300
Schiller, Wendy, 258–59
Schneider, Jerrold E., 246
Scholzman, Kay Lehman, 152
school desegregation, xi, 66, 201–3, 227, 298
school prayer, 151, 191, 210–11, 251
school tuition vouchers, 141
Schreiber, E. M., 18
Schultz, Debra, 132
Schuman, Howard, 200–204
Seagull, Louis, 221
security issues, 121
seniority system in Congress, 244–45, 249, 251
sex education, 209
sexual morality, 152
Shafer, Byron E., 21, 94, 301n2
Shaffer, Stephen D., 8, 53, 296–97
Shaffer, William R., 246–47
Shannon, W. Wayne, 245, 247
Shapiro, Jessie, 172
Shaw v. Reno (1993), 108, 109, 110
Sheatsley, Paul B., 204, 205
Shelley, Mack C., 247
Shuttlesworth, Fred, 76
Simmons, J. L., 196–97
Sinclair, Barbara, 245–46, 247, 248
Sitkoff, Harvard, 74
slave revolts, 65
Smeal, Eleanor, 123
Smith, Alfred E., 222
Smith, Christian, 149
Smith, Roger, 84–85
Smith v. Allwright (1944), 68

Snowe, Olympia, 52
social issues, 25, 27, 121, 150, 191, 254–55
social movements, 86–87
social-welfare issues, 25, 27, 199–200, 274
sociological theories of Congress, 244
sociology of religion, 142
solidary incentives, 53
Solid South, 17, 27, 43, 145, 222, 229, 242, 260, 297, 298
South and national politics, 292, 297–300
South Carolina primaries, 148, 299
Southern Christian Leadership Conference, 73, 75–76
southern distinctiveness, 189, 261, 274, 287, 288, 291, 292, 295–97, 299; causes, 211–13
Southern Grassroots Party Activists Project I, 28, 30–31, 48–49, 126–27
Southern Grassroots Party Activists Project II, 28, 30–31, 49, 54
Southern Legislative Council, 231
Southern Political Report, 5
Southern Political Science Association, 5
southern strategy, 226–31, 234
Specter, Arlen, 52
spiral of silence, 143
Stack, Carol, 81, 82
Stanley, Harold W., 4, 8, 20, 198, 298
Staton, Carolyn, 123
Steed, Robert P., 8, 46, 47, 48, 57, 124, 220, 232, 294
Steeh, Charlotte, 200–204
Stern, Mark, 79
Steuernagel, Gertrude, 121
Stevenson, Adlai, 223
Stewart, Marianne, 125
Stidham, Ronald, 129
Strong, Donald S., 2, 17, 220, 224–25
Student Nonviolent Coordinating Committee, 73, 75–76, 132
Students for a Democratic Society, 132
suffragist movement, 131
Super Tuesday, 231–32, 299
Survey of Income and Program Participation, 185n3
Swain, Carol, 102, 105, 107, 256

Swansbrough, Robert H., 5, 92
Swanson, Bert E., 42

Talmadge, Eugene, 272
Tarrow, Sidney, 70, 86, 87
Tate, Katherine, 257
Tauzin, Billy, 111–12n3, 113n11
Taylor, Elizabeth, 45
Thirteenth Amendment, 65
Thomas, Clive, 284–85, 301n3
Thomas, Sue, 121
Thompson, Robert, 276–77
Thurmond, Strom, xi, 84, 159, 223, 228
ticket-splitters, xi
Tindall, George Brown, 69, 70
Tocqueville, Alexis de, 143
Todd, John R., 56
tolerance, 206–7; and migration, 206
traditionalistic political culture, 122, 128, 212, 233, 269
Truman, Harry S, 68, 223
two-thirds rule, 299

Ujifusa, Grant, 99
urbanization, 292

van Assendelft, Laura, 287, 297
Vance, Rupert, 71
Verba, Sidney, 152
Vietnam, 246
Vigdor, Jacob L., 172
violence, 190
Voss, Stephen, 103, 104, 107, 255
Voting Rights Act of 1965, ix, 65, 95, 98, 111n2, 112n6, 114n13, 131, 175, 226, 250, 293
voting rights districts, 95–97

Wall, Diane, 129, 135
Wallace, George C., 159, 224, 226–28, 280, 281
Wallace, Lurleen, 280
Walsh, Bill, 94
Ward, Daniel S., 29
Warner, John, 45
Watergate, 228, 229
Watson, Thomas A.,
Wattenberg, Martin P., 20

Watters, Pat, 78
Welch, Susan, 121
welfare issues, 121, 200, 233, 234, 245, 246
Wells, H. G., 65
Whicker, Marcia Lynn, 121
Whitaker, Lois Duke, 121
White Citizens Council, 273, 300–301
white supremacy, 269
Wielhouwer, Peter, 56
Wiggins, Charles, 43
Wilder, L. Douglas, 286
Wilkins, Roy, 75
Williams, Hosea, 76
Willie Horton campaign ad, 232
Willow Creek Association, 144
Wilson, Bobby, 86, 87
Wilson, James Q., 42, 51, 53
Wilson, Thomas C., 205
Wolfenstein, Eugene, 87
Wolfinger, Raymond, 18, 19
women: and Arkansas politics, 128; and at-large elections, 123–24; in the civil rights movement, 131–33; and Florida politics, 127–28; in judicial politics, 129–30; and Kentucky politics, 122, 128–29; and majority-minority districting, 124; and office holding, 122–24, 294; and political ambition, 124–25, 130; and runoff elections, 123; in southern legislatures, 122–23; in southern politics, 119–39, 208; in southern state parties, 124–27; and Texas politics, 122
women's issues, 121
women's movement, 65, 131, 132
Woods, Barbara, 131
Workshop on Comparative State Party Activists, 46
World War I, 72
World War II, 68, 241
Wyman, Hastings, 5

Year of the Woman, 134
Yoder, Edwin M., 295
Young, Andrew, 151

Zinn, Howard, 75